Serge Gainsbourg

Serge Gainsbourg

An International Perspective

Edited by
Olivier Julien and Olivier Bourderionnet

BLOOMSBURY ACADEMIC
NEW YORK • LONDON • OXFORD • NEW DELHI • SYDNEY

BLOOMSBURY ACADEMIC
Bloomsbury Publishing Inc, 1385 Broadway, New York, NY 10018, USA
Bloomsbury Publishing Plc, 50 Bedford Square, London, WC1B 3DP, UK
Bloomsbury Publishing Ireland, 29 Earlsfort Terrace, Dublin 2, D02 AY28, Ireland

BLOOMSBURY, BLOOMSBURY ACADEMIC and the Diana logo
are trademarks of Bloomsbury Publishing Plc

First published in the United States of America 2024
This paperback edition published 2025

Copyright © Olivier Julien and Olivier Bourderionnet, 2024

Each chapter copyright by the contributor, 2024

For legal purposes the Acknowledgments on p. xv constitute
an extension of this copyright page.

Cover design: Louise Dugdale
Cover image: Self-Portrait by Serge Gainsbourg
(Courtesy of the estate of Serge Gainsbourg)

All rights reserved. No part of this publication may be: i) reproduced or transmitted in any form, electronic or mechanical, including photocopying, recording or by means of any information storage or retrieval system without prior permission in writing from the publishers; or ii) used or reproduced in any way for the training, development or operation of artificial intelligence (AI) technologies, including generative AI technologies. The rights holders expressly reserve this publication from the text and data mining exception as per Article 4(3) of the Digital Single Market Directive (EU) 2019/790.

Bloomsbury Publishing Inc does not have any control over, or responsibility for, any third-party websites referred to or in this book. All internet addresses given in this book were correct at the time of going to press. The author and publisher regret any inconvenience caused if addresses have changed or sites have ceased to exist, but can accept no responsibility for any such changes.

Whilst every effort has been made to locate copyright holders the publishers would be grateful to hear from any person(s) not here acknowledged.

Library of Congress Cataloging-in-Publication Data
Names: Julien, Olivier, 1969- editor. | Bourderionnet, Olivier, 1965- editor.
Title: Serge Gainsbourg: an international perspective/edited by Olivier
Julien and Olivier Bourderionnet.
Description: [1.] | New York: Bloomsbury Academic, 2024. | Includes bibliographical references and index. | Summary: "The first interdisciplinary, academic overview of Serge Gainsbourg – one of the most popular and reviled singers in France"– Provided by publisher.
Identifiers: LCCN 2023030672 (print) | LCCN 2023030673 (ebook) | ISBN 9781501365669 (hardback) | ISBN 9798765113172 (paperback) | ISBN 9781501365676 (epub) |
ISBN 9781501365683 (pdf) | ISBN 9781501365690
Subjects: LCSH: Gainsbourg, Serge–Criticism and interpretation. |
Popular music–France–History and criticism.
Classification: LCC ML420.G12 S45 2024 (print) | LCC ML420.G12 (ebook) |
DDC 782.42164092–dc23/eng/20230629
LC record available at https://lccn.loc.gov/2023030672
LC ebook record available at https://lccn.loc.gov/2023030673

ISBN: HB: 978-1-5013-6566-9
PB: 979-8-7651-1317-2
ePDF: 978-1-5013-6568-3
eBook: 978-1-5013-6567-6

Typeset by Integra Software Services Pvt. Ltd.

For product safety related questions contact productsafety@bloomsbury.com

To find out more about our authors and books visit www.bloomsbury.com
and sign up for our newsletters.

Contents

List of Musical Examples and Figures   viii
Notes on Contributors   ix
Acknowledgments   xv

Introduction: From Saint-Germain-des-Prés to the Sorbonne: The Emergence of Gainsbourg Studies   *Olivier Julien and Olivier Bourderionnet*   1

Part 1   Deconstructing the Gainsbourg Persona

"Docteur Jekyll et Monsieur Hyde": Gainsbourg in the Mirror

1. The Hidden Beauty of the Ugly   *Jeremy Allen*   11
2. Gainsbourg over Piaf: The Gendered Pantheon of *Chanson* Artists in French Music Biopics   *Isabelle Marc*   17

"Yellow Star": Gainsbourg & Jewishness

3. "Dieu Est Juif": Disappearing and Reappearing Jewishness in Serge Gainsbourg's Career   *Jonathyne Briggs and Nick Underwood*   29
4. "Le Sable et le Soldat": Serge Gainsbourg, Jewishness, Masculinity, and the Quest for Legitimacy   *France Grenaudier-Klijn*   35

"Vu de l'Extérieur": Gainsbourg's International Reputation

5. Contention and Consensus: Posthumous Press Coverage of Serge Gainsbourg in the UK   *Chris Tinker*   43
6. The Critical Song of Serge Gainsbourg   *Caroline Kennedy*   53

Part 2   Words and Music

"Du Jazz dans le Ravin": The Beginnings

7. Boris Vian's Visionary Criticism of the Early Work of Serge Gainsbourg   *Marianne Di Benedetto*   65

8   Fallen on Deaf Ears: *Confidentiel's* Visionary Blend of Jazz and
    Chanson *Olivier Bourderionnet*   71

"Là-Bas C'Est Naturel": Gainsbourg & World Music

9   "Latin" Gainsbourg and the Parisian Nightclub Scene *Sue Miller*   81
10 Gainsbourg and Musical Crossover: Issues in Sound Categorization and
    Stylistic Appropriation in the Study of *Gainsbourg Percussions*
    Danick Trottier   87
11 Gainsbourg in a Reggae Style: The Esthetics, Economics, and Politics of
    Aux Armes et Cætera *Marc Kaiser*   95
12 Gainsbourg and the Other: A Postcolonial Reading of *Gainsbourg
    Percussions* *Aurélien Djebbari and Elina Djebbari*   101

"L'Impression du Déjà-Vu": Local Inspiration & Francophone Legacy

13 Charles Trenet's Influence on Serge Gainsbourg: Swing, Irony, and
    Poetry *Claire Fraysse*   109
14 Singing Gainsbourg at the Time of the *Yé-Yé* (1962–6): The Perpetual
    Provocateur and His Muses *Andreas Bonnermeier*   117

"Qui Est 'In' Qui Est 'Out'": Gainsbourg & The British Invasion

15 "Extrêmement Pop": Gainsbourg and Swinging London *Kirk Anderson* 125
16 "Je T'Aime… Moi Non Plus": Jane Birkin and the English Preference of
    Serge Gainsbourg *Peter Hawkins*   131

Part 3 Beyond Songwriting

"Arts Majeurs"/"Arts Mineurs": Intertextual Perspectives

17 Cargo Cultist: How Serge Gainsbourg Pioneered Sampling
    Darran Anderson   141
18 "Un Amour Peut en Cacher un Autre": Serge Gainsbourg through the
    Prism of Transtextuality *Olivier Julien*   145
19 Serge Gainsbourg and the Romantic Piano *Nathalie Hérold*   157

"Les Dessous Chics": Gainsbourg & Musical Analysis

20 Evil Twin? The Poetics of Duality in Serge Gainsbourg *Catherine Rudent*   167
21 "Je T'Aime... Moi Non Plus": A *Songscape* Analysis *Thomas MacFarlane*   175

"En Relisant Ta Lettre": Gainsbourg & Literature

22 *Evguénie Sokolov*: Fake Genius, Genial Faker *Christophe Levaux*   183
23 Gainsbourg as a Dandy: Image and Literary Influences *Mickaël Savchenko*   191

"Des Flashes et des Eclairs": Gainsbourg & The Moving Image

24 *L'Eau à la Bouche*: Gainsbourg at the Forefront of the "Nouvelle Vague" *Jérôme Rossi*   199
25 "Cargo Culte": How Gainsbourg's *Melody* Film Invented a New Long-Form Audiovisual Language *Alex Jeffery*   207
26 Gainsbourg for Sale! Serge Gainsbourg and Advertising *Philippe Cathé*   215

References   224
Index   247

List of Musical Examples and Figures

Examples

9.1	The *son clave*	84
9.2	The *danzón baqueteo* pattern	84
9.3	Cuban flavors in "La Chanson de Prévert" (verse 2)	85
12.1	Excerpt from "Marabout"	104
18.1	"Jane B."'s lyrics as a hypertext of "Humbert Humbert's poem"	152
19.1	"Poupée de cire, poupée de son" (measures 1–4, x segment)	161
19.2	"Dépression au-dessus du jardin" (measures 1–2)	162
19.3	"Bébé gai" (measures 1–4, x_1 segment)	163
20.1	"Les P'tits Papiers"'s two melodic levels	168
20.2	Melodic and harmonic echoes in the first two measures of "Ford Mustang"	170
20.3	"Ford Mustang": melodic mirror on "Mus—*à gauche*, -tang—*à droite*"	170
20.4	"Ford Mustang": *"et à gauche à droite"*	171
20.5	"Elaeudanla téïtéïa"	171

Figures

18.1	*Les Classiques de Gainsbourg* (front cover)	150
18.2	A multifaceted network of relationships with high culture	154
19.1	Daguerreotype of Frédéric Chopin by Louis-Auguste Bisson (1849)	159
19.2	Gainsbourg's songs that refer to Romantic piano pieces	160
24.1	Symmetrical effect produced by the musical recurrences in *L'Eau à la bouche*	201

Notes on Contributors

Jeremy Allen is a Cornish freelance journalist, writing features for magazines like *Electronic Sound, Record Collector, Prog*, and *The Quietus*. His first book, *Relax Baby Be Cool: The Artistry and Audacity of Serge Gainsbourg*, published by Jawbone Press, received four-star reviews in *Mojo, Shindig!* and *Record Collector*.

Darran Anderson is the author of *33 1/3: Histoire de Melody Nelson* (Bloomsbury), *Imaginary Cities*, and *Tidewrack*. He is based in London where he writes for numerous publications on culture, technology, politics, and urbanism.

Kirk Anderson, Professor and Chairman of French Studies at Wheaton College (Massachusetts), United States, completed his BA in French at St Olaf College, USA, and his PhD in Romance Languages and Literatures at Princeton University, USA. At Wheaton, he teaches twentieth-century French literature and culture, Basic French, *chanson*, and French views of the United States. He has published on Louis-Ferdinand Céline and 1960s popular music in France. He is also the accordionist and guitarist for the Providence-based septet Consuelo's Revenge.

Andreas Bonnermeier earned a doctorate in Romance Literary Studies from the University of Bayreuth, Germany, with a dissertation titled "A genre and its interpreters—women's voices in French *chanson* and in Italian *canzone*." After working as a lecturer at the University of Bayreuth and at the West Saxon University of Applied Sciences in Zwickau, Germany, in 2006, he obtained a position at the Johannes Gutenberg University in Mainz, Germany, in the fields of language practice, literature, and cultural studies in French and Italian. Since 2002, he has published articles in *BAT* (*Bulletin des Archivs für Textmusik*) and *ATeM* (*Archives of Text and Music Studies*), with a specific focus on the relationship between words and music. Not only the topic of his research work, French *chanson* and Italian *canzone* also feature prominently in his teaching, with courses such as "Song and Society," "Non sono solo canzonette" ["They're not just songs"] or "L'Italia e la canzone: una nazione si racconta in musica" ["Italy and *canzone*: a nation told through song"].

Olivier Bourderionnet is Professor of French at the University of New Orleans, United States, where he teaches courses on contemporary French literature and culture, pop culture, and the cultural industries. His first book, *Swing Troubadour. Vian, Brassens, Gainsbourg: les Trente Glorieuses en 33 tours* (2011), examines the transformation of post-Second World War France through the prism of popular music and the impact of jazz on French *chanson*. He has contributed numerous book chapters to French and American volumes on the topics of French popular music and French cultural studies. His articles in academic journals—touching on a broad variety of topics such as music in the interwar period, music, and film, French Hip-hop culture, and more—have appeared in *Research in African Literatures, French Cultural Studies, Volume! La revue des musiques populaires, CFFS*, and *The World Journal of Popular Music*.

Jonathyne Briggs is Associate Professor of History at Indiana University Northwest, United States, and the author of several works on French popular music that have appeared in *History of the Journal of Sexuality, Modern and Contemporary France*, and *Volume! La revue des musiques populaires*, as well as the book *Sounds French: Globalization, Cultural Communities, and Pop Music, 1958–1980* (2015). In 2022, he served as guest editor for a special issue of *French Historical Studies* on music and French history. He is currently working on a monograph on the politics of autism in France since 1960 tentatively titled *Perpetual Children*.

Philippe Cathé is Professor of Musicology at Sorbonne Université (Paris), France. He also teaches at New York University-Paris. He is both a music theorist developing Nicolas Meeùs's theory of harmonic vectors and a musicologist specializing in French music from the end of the nineteenth century to the first half of the twentieth century. In addition, his research involves investigating the role of sound in film.

Marianne Di Benedetto is a PhD student at the University of Rennes 2, France. After gaining her *Agrégation de lettres modernes* qualification in 2016, she graduated from the Ecole Normale Supérieure de Lyon. She completed her master's thesis on the topic of Boris Vian's critical approaches to *chanson* in the 1950s. This research laid the foundations for her work on *chanson* musicographies in the 1950s and 1960s, two decades which saw a turning point for popular music in France, research she is now developing as a PhD student in Comparative Literature. Since 2016, she has also collaborated with Le Hall de la chanson (Centre national du patrimoine de la chanson, des variétés et des musiques actuelles), a theater located in the Parc de La Villette in Paris.

Aurélien Djebbari is a DJ specialized in psychedelic trance, crate-digging, and vinyl collecting. A former head of international varieties at Champs-Elysées Virgin Megastore and Fnac Forum in Paris, his expertise focuses on various musical genres, including Serge Gainsbourg's work.

Elina Djebbari is Associate Professor of Anthropology and Ethnomusicology at Paris Nanterre University, France. Her PhD dissertation focused on the National Ballet of Mali (EHESS) and her current research project explores transatlantic circulations, local processes of appropriation of Afro-Caribbean music, and dance creolized practices in West Africa.

Claire Fraysse is a Lecturer in Music and Musicology at Sorbonne Université, France, and a student of esthetics and musical analysis at the Conservatoire National Supérieur de Musique de Paris, France. A graduate from the Ecole Normale Supérieure (Paris-Ulm), France, she also held a one-year position as a Teaching Assistant of French at Yale University, United States (2019–20). She is currently completing a PhD thesis on rock cover versions.

France Grenaudier-Klijn is Senior Lecturer in French, and French Programme Coordinator at Massey University, New Zealand. Her research focuses largely on contemporary post-Shoah novelists in France, chief among them Patrick Modiano. The author of two books, including a 2017 monograph of Modiano's female figures, and several articles and book chapters, she is currently researching the figure of the *"ayant-été"* (Paul Ricœur) in the context of recent French post-Shoah fiction. In 2012, she contributed to a collective volume on the place of the body in relation to French *chanson*, examining the role of the cigarette in the public persona of Serge Gainsbourg.

Peter Hawkins is Senior Research Fellow in French at the School of Modern Languages of the University of Bristol, UK. In 2000 he published the first academic study of French popular music in English, *Chanson* (Ashgate). He has since published several articles on Léo Ferré and contributed a chapter on Ferré and the French poetic heritage to the volume *The Singer-Songwriter in Europe*, edited by Isabelle Marc and Stuart Green for Routledge (2016). In 2013 he recorded a double CD of the songs of Léo Ferré adapted into English (*Love and Anarchy*, Hoxa). He has reviewed books on French *chanson* for *French Studies, Volume! La revue des musiques populaires* and *Popular Music*, and regularly performs his own versions of songs by Jacques Brel, Georges Brassens, Barbara, Anne Sylvestre, and others.

Nathalie Hérold is Associate Professor of Music Analysis and Theory at Sorbonne Université, France, and a member of the Research Institute in Musicology (IReMus). She received her Doctorate in Musical Arts from the University of Strasbourg and holds a Diploma in Piano Instruction from the French National Music Conservatory. She serves as President of the French Society for Music Analysis (SFAM) and co-editor-in-chief of the academic journal *Musurgia*.

Alex Jeffery researches narrativity in popular music, with particular interest in long-form and multimedia works. Having completed a PhD on Gorillaz' 2010 transmedia project *Plastic Beach* at City, University of London, UK, he is currently writing a monograph entitled *Popular Music and Narrativity* for Bloomsbury. Parallel with this, he is also devising a practice-based project involving a science-fiction narrative about music and musicians, realized musically and audiovisually.

Olivier Julien is Associate Professor of Musicology at Sorbonne Université, France, where he graduated in 1999 with a PhD dissertation on the Beatles' sound. A member of *Volume! La revue des musiques populaires*' and *Vox Popular*'s editorial and advisory boards, he contributed to several publications in France and abroad—*Volume!, Analyse Musicale, Canadian University Music Review, The Bloomsbury Handbook of Rock*

Music Research, British Journal of Music Education, Popular Music, The Continuum Encyclopedia of Popular Music of the World, etc. He is also the editor of *Sgt. Pepper and the Beatles: It Was Forty Years Ago Today* (Ashgate, 2009 ARSC Award for Best Research in Recorded Rock and Popular Music) and *Over and Over: Exploring Repetition in Popular Music* (Bloomsbury, with Christophe Levaux). In April 2018, he organized the first international academic conference on Serge Gainsbourg, gathering thirty-five participants from a dozen countries.

Marc Kaiser is Associate Professor of Communication and Information Studies at Paris 8 University, France. His research focuses on the history of the French music industry and local music scenes in relation to public policies. He edited a special issue of *Volume! La revue des musiques populaires* on music video cultures (2018) and is currently studying cultural collaborative platforms in museum and patrimonial sectors (French National Research Agency project COLLAB).

Caroline Kennedy is an Australian visual artist, songwriter, educator, and practice researcher. She is currently a Senior Lecturer at Goldsmiths University London (School of Arts and Humanities), UK, where she teaches creative practice and songwriting.

Christophe Levaux is an FRS-FNRS researcher attached to the University of Liège, Belgium. His research, which focuses on twentieth-century experimental and popular music, is inspired by the Actor-Network Theory. His articles have been published in numerous music journals, including *Tacet*, *Rock Music Studies* and *Organised Sound*. He recently co-edited a book dedicated to repetition in popular music with Olivier Julien (Bloomsbury, 2018). His PhD dissertation, *We Have Always Been Minimalist*, was published in 2019 by the University of California Press.

Thomas MacFarlane has written various books and articles on popular music. His research explores connections between music composition, sound recording, and human culture. He has taught music composition and arts analysis courses at New York University, United States, and has given presentations at venues in Europe and the United States. Currently, he works as a writer, musician, and composer.

Isabelle Marc holds a PhD in French Literature from the Complutense University of Madrid, Spain, where she is now Associate Professor. Her research focuses on the relationship between esthetics, identity, and transcultural phenomena in the European context. She has published articles in journals such as *Modern & Contemporary France*, *French Cultural Studies*, *Belphégor*, and *Volume! La revue des musiques populaires*, and she co-edited *The Singer-Songwriter in Europe: Paradigms, Politics and Place* (2016), *Canon et écrits de femmes en France et en Espagne dans l'actualité (2011–2016)* (2020), and *Carmen revisitée/Revisiter Carmen* (2020).

Sue Miller is Professor of Music at Leeds Beckett University, UK. Her research interests include Cuban music (history, analysis, and performance), Latin music in the United

States, performance esthetics, improvisation studies, music and dance relationships in animation film, and French popular music. Her books *Cuban Flute Style: Interpretation and Improvisation* (2014) and *Improvising Sabor: Cuban Dance Music in New York* (2021) document and re-evaluate the history of *clave*-based Latin music in both Cuba and the United States. As a linguist with a degree in Languages (French, Hindi, and Linguistics) from the University of York, UK, and an MA in Applied Translation (with a specialism in French Popular Music and Culture) from the University of Leeds, UK, Professor Miller also has an interest in vernacular musics with a broad international reach and is currently researching Caribbean musicians' influence on twentieth-century French popular music.

Jérôme Rossi is Professor of Musicology at Université Lumière Lyon II. He is the author of numerous articles dedicated to post-Romantic music, as well as to the connections between music and cinema. He recently edited a collective volume for Symétrie : *La musique de film en France, courants, spécificités, évolutions*. He has also composed numerous scores for TV documentaries.

Catherine Rudent is Professor of Mediation and Geopolitics of Music at Université Sorbonne Nouvelle, France. She is the author of *L'album de chansons. Entre processus social et œuvre musicale* (Honoré Champion, 2011), and she co-edited *Made in France. Studies in Popular Music* with Gérôme Guibert (2018). She is also a founding member of the French-speaking branch of Europe of IASPM (The International Association for the Study of Popular Music). Her research focuses on the vocal styles of late twentieth- and twenty-first-century recorded popular music, on the stylistic hybridizations that characterize current French music, and on the role of social representations in the construction of musical practices and tastes.

Mickaël Savchenko received a PhD from the Paris 8 University, France, with a thesis on the poetics of the French *chanson*, which was largely devoted to Gainsbourg. He is also active as a poet and literary translator.

Chris Tinker is Professor of French at Heriot-Watt University, UK. His research interests are in media and popular music in France and Britain (1960s–) with particular focus on generation/aging, gender, celebrity, nostalgia, and charity. He is author of *Georges Brassens and Jacques Brel: Personal and Social Narratives in Post-War Chanson* (2005) and *Mixed Messages: Youth Magazine Discourse and Sociocultural Shifts in "Salut les copains" (1962–1976)* (2010), and is currently President of the Association for the Study of Modern and Contemporary France (ASMCF).

Danick Trottier is Professor of Musicology at the Université du Québec à Montréal (UQÀM), Canada, and a regular member of the Observatoire interdisciplinaire de création et de recherche en musique (OICRM) in the Université de Montréal, Canada. He has published articles in journals such as *Circuit*, *Dissonance*, *Filigrane*, *Intersections*, *Kinephanos*, *Les Cahiers Debussy*, *Les Cahiers de la SQRM*, *Perspectives of New Music*,

Speculum Musicæ, and *Volume! La revue des musiques populaires*. His research interests include music history, music sociology, and esthetics in twentieth-century classical and popular music.

Nick Underwood earned his PhD in modern Jewish and European history at the University of Colorado Boulder, United States, in 2016. His work has appeared in *Jewish Social Studies, Archives Juives, French Politics, Culture & Society, Urban History*, and *East European Jewish Affairs*. His last book, *Yiddish Paris: Nation and Community in Interwar France*, was published in 2022. He serves as managing editor for the journal *American Jewish history* as well as project manager for the Digital Yiddish Theatre Project. Currently, he is an assistant professor of history and the Berger/Neilsen Chair of Judaic Studies at the College of Idaho.

Acknowledgments

Outside of France and Francophone countries, Serge Gainsbourg is mostly remembered for his 1968 duet with Jane Birkin, "Je t'aime… moi non plus." Released in February 1969, the song hit number one in Britain, stalled at No. 58 in *Billboard*'s Hot 100 (*s.n.* 1970), and was a Top 10 hit in a dozen more countries, eventually achieving worldwide sales of six million copies (Crocq 1991). It was also denounced by the Vatican and banned from the radio in Spain, Italy, Brazil, Sweden, Portugal, Poland, and the UK,[1] becoming simultaneously the first foreign-language single and the first banned single to take the pole position on the other side of the Channel (Simmons 2001: 59). Indeed, Gainsbourg was "more than just a pop star," and he was even more than France's "pop superstar." To quote the words of James Truman in the October 1986 issue of *Spin* magazine, "For twenty years he … reign[ed] as [the country]'s leading drunkard, philanderer, beatnik, scandal-maker, and buffoon."

Despite "the overseas cult … that had been steadily swelling" when he died in March 1991 (Simmons 2001: 132), bringing together an array of scholars who might provide an international perspective on such a "Gallic symbol" (Maunsell 2001; Mottram 2010) was far from a foregone conclusion. For this reason, we are deeply indebted to the book's twenty-six contributors. Making that book available for a global readership was no matter of course either, which makes us all the more grateful to Leah Babb-Rosenfeld, Rachel Moore, and everyone at Bloomsbury. Finally, our thanks are due to Laura Dauzonne, Gerhild Fuchs, Lisou Gasquet, Pia Köstner, Barbara Lebrun, and Juliana Pimentel—who were, each in their own manner, instrumental in bringing this four-year project to fruition.

Olivier Julien and Olivier Bourderionnet

Note

1   See Anderson 2013: 44.

Introduction

From Saint-Germain-des-Prés to the Sorbonne: The Emergence of Gainsbourg Studies

Olivier Julien and Olivier Bourderionnet

Nabokov… I wanted to set this poem to music … a poem of superb modernism—the last quatrain is beautiful.
"My car is limping, Dolores Haze,
And the last long lap is the hardest,
And I shall be dumped where the weed decays,
And the rest is rust and stardust."
Some of the things I've done are not too shabby either, but compared to Rimbaud, neither Nabokov, nor I exist. Rimbaud was a visionary. Nabokov was not a visionary, and I'm a visionary in show business.

(Hubert-Robier 1990)

On November 14, 1990, Serge Gainsbourg received journalists François Hubert-Robier and Véronique Jacquinet at his home, Rue de Verneuil, for what was to be his last interview for French television. Emaciated, ill-looking, he took stock of his life and career, dwelling over their highlights, quoting Bernard Shaw, Nabokov, and Oscar Wilde, and interspersing references to Van Gogh, André Chénier, Brigitte Bardot, Schumann, and Delacroix with cryptic statements about his waiting for "the birds of prey that were out to get [him]."

— I've been waiting for them for thirty years, and I'm still here.
— Can you see those birds coming?
— Birds? I see ravens.

By then, he had already survived four heart attacks, undergone liver surgery, and begun suffering *delirium tremens*, vision loss, and respiratory problems (Verlant 2000: 436, 566, 659, 662, 664–5). In January of the previous year, "the doctors [had even] warned him that 'if he didn't stop drinking he would be blind in six months and dead in twelve'" (Simmons 2001: 118). At sixty-two, he was terribly worn.

"Are you tempted to call it quits? I mean, why another album, why … Do you feel like you still have something to prove to yourself—or to the public?" Given the crepuscular tone of the interview, Hubert-Robier's question came as no surprise. More surprising, though, was Gainsbourg's answer, who professed in an unusual burst of modesty:

> What I really care about are my children … because *they* will survive me, not my "work"—what do I care about my "work" … One must not survive oneself … I'm not second-rate, OK; I'm big time, but … it would be so vainglorious to say, "I'm going to leave something behind me!"
>
> (Hubert-Robier 1990)

A mere six years later, Lisou Gasquet and Karine Devauchelle defended the first theses in modern literature that proved him wrong—the former addressed "the lyrics of Serge Gainsbourg" over a thirty-year period (Gasquet 1996), the latter focused specifically on their metrics (Devauchelle 1996). In 1997, it was Cosima Cusson's turn to submit a dissertation entitled "Gainsbourg, des Amours perdues à L'herbe tendre, dix années d'écriture" ["Gainsbourg, from 'Les Amours perdues' to 'L'Herbe tendre', ten years of writing"]. By the time the book Gasquet drew from her master's research came out (2003), pioneering essays by Chris Tinker (2002) and Edwin Hill (2003) had made their way to academic journals, *Modern & Contemporary France* and *Volume! La revue des musiques populaires*. Along with "the palimpsest of paintings and graffiti" that kept proliferating on the walls of Gainsbourg's town house (Simmons 2001: ix), this nascent body of works continued to grow through the 2000s and 2010s. Extending to disciplines such as language studies (Luccioni 2011), history (Albert 2005; Frantz 2004), musicology (Castelbajac 2019; Jan-Muger 2016; Julien 2018), art history (Jaminais 2019), Romance philology (Lambrechts 2006; Lederer 2001; Roland 2001; Wéry 2002), comparative literature (Gassi 2017), psychology (Sablon 2009), and law (Valleteau de Moulliac 2010), it also began to spread beyond the borders of Francophone countries (Anderson 2013; Austin 2019; Burgoyne 2014; Friderichs 2015; Grenaudier-Klijn 2012; Grosse 2011; Holtmon 2021; Júlíusson 2010; Knuutinen 2016; Nováková 2017; Skibicki 2010; Sotonová 2015; 2019; Weiss 2003). Finally, in April 2018, the Sorbonne hosted the first academic conference on Serge Gainsbourg, "with more than 30 participants and a significant British and American contingent" (Lesprit 2018: 12). Bringing together a selection of twenty-six chapters by scholars originating from France, the UK, Spain, Belgium, Australia, Canada, Germany, the United States, and New Zealand, this book represents a further step toward his legitimation as a subject of research for academia.

Deconstructing the Gainsbourg Persona

The six chapters gathered in part I address the construction of Gainsbourg's public persona, both in his lifetime and posthumously. They begin with a contribution by Jeremy Allen, who discusses the songwriter's uneasy relationship with his own image.

Drawing a parallel with what Christopher Isherwood called Mick Jagger's "ugly beauty," he explains how his purported ugliness shaped his *beau-laid* persona, how it fed his work, and even his tastes in literature and painting (unless, of course, it was the other way round). Opting for a different approach, Isabelle Marc links the recent music biopic phenomenon to the elevation of *chanson* artists to a popular music pantheon. Comparing Johan Sfar's *Gainsbourg (vie héroïque)* with Olivier Dahan's *La Môme*, she points out a gendered bias in the way Piaf and Gainsbourg are shown overcoming their ugliness and childhood wounds—the former is pictured as a victim of romantic love, utterly destroyed by the accidental death of her one great love, while the latter emerges as a cynical and consummate seducer.

The following chapter deals with another key aspect of Gainsbourg's persona. Growing up in Paris during the Occupation, he was well aware that his Jewishness could mark him as distinct from his fellow citizens in a potentially dangerous way. Jonathyne Briggs and Nick Underwood examine how this (religious) affiliation surfaced at times in his lyrics, his music, and his public image from the 1960s through the 1980s, informing his esthetics and revealing a haphazard articulation of the French-Jewish identity. France Grenaudier-Klijn tackles that same issue from a narrower angle, focusing on one of Gainsbourg's most little-known songs. Written in 1967 at the request of the cultural attaché at the Israeli Embassy in Paris, "Le Sable et le Soldat" was intended to boost the morale of Tsahal, the Israeli armed forces. With its solemn tone, martial composition, and earnest lyricism, this song is a far cry from Gainsbourg's usual brand of provocation and nonconformity. Yet, at odds with both the playful irony permeating *Rock Around the Bunker* and the resigned bravado of "Juif et Dieu," it does have a place in his personal and artistic trajectory.

This part ends with a section on Gainsbourg's international reception and reputation. Based on a survey of his UK press coverage over the latter half of the 2010s, Chris Tinker's chapter looks into the development of his celebrity status in the British context. It reveals a recurring emphasis on his relationships with Jane Birkin and his daughter Charlotte, his winning Eurovision entry "Poupée de cire, poupée de son," and the controversies surrounding "Les Sucettes" or the song with which he boasted to have "toured around the world" (Hubert-Robier 1990), "Je t'aime… moi non plus." Highlighting his post-mortem influence on new generations of Anglophone popular musicians, it also draws comparisons and associations with other well-known cultural figures in France and beyond. As for Caroline Kennedy, she widens the scope by addressing Gainsbourg's reputation on the other side of the globe. Focusing on post-punk and indie-rock musicians in 1990s Melbourne, she looks into the influence of "Je t'aime… moi non plus" on subcultural Australian scenes and the likes of Mick Harvey, Ian Wadley, and Kim Salmon.

Words and Music

Part II's ten chapters consider Gainsbourg's output as a songwriter. Marianne Di Benedetto first takes on the reception of his 1958 album, *Du Chant à la une!*, through the eyes of French polymath Boris Vian. Two years earlier, the discovery of Vian performing his own material at the Milord l'Arsouille cabaret had been a revelation for a struggling Gainsbourg in search of career opportunities. Now it was Vian's turn to discover Gainsbourg and display an enthusiasm that set him apart from most critics of the time. Vian's influence resurfaces in the chapter Olivier Bourderionnet devotes to one of Gainsbourg's most adventurous early projects, the 1963 LP *Confidentiel*. Recorded in a trio configuration, it yielded a unique set of twelve percussion-free songs that met with a cool response from the French public—whose taste for these attempts at blending contemporary jazz with *chanson* had never fully developed.

The second section begins with Sue Miller's analysis of Gainsbourg's early Latin influences. Exploring his background as a performer and musical director within the Parisian nightclub scene of the 1950s, she provides insight into his use of Cuban *clave*-based rhythms up until the recording of *Gainsbourg Percussions*. Continuing the discussion, Danick Trottier outlines the significance of the latter LP in terms of its heralding the stylistic hybridization that would come to define "world music." Recorded during a period of transition in Gainsbourg's career, this shift toward musical "elsewhereness," he argues, was a symptom of the need for *chanson* to show its ability to modernize in a country faced with the Anglo-American invasion of its music market. Making a fifteen-year leap forward, Marc Kaiser's chapter concentrates on another groundbreaking LP, *Aux Armes et cætera*. Released in 1979, this album was not only Gainsbourg's first gold record: it was the album that gave rise to a new persona, made him a star at over fifty, and marked the beginning of a long-lasting reggae trend in French popular music. Conversely, the African musicians whose work had inspired *Gainsbourg Percussions* had to wait for twenty-two years before they received recognition for their "contribution" (Dicale 2009: 111–13; 2021: 238; Verlant 2000: 261–2). Looping the loop, Aurélien and Elina Djebbari reassess the latter album in light of the racial and gender issues associated with Gainsbourg's use of music genres arising from the "Black Atlantic."

Introducing the third section, Claire Fraysse offers another approach to Gainsbourg's formative years by addressing the influence of Charles Trenet on what he himself described as his "blue period" (Koechlin 2008: 8). This influence turns out to be apparent on three distinct levels: an innovative use of jazz in his arrangements, a sense of detachment and irony, and the will to create a unique and inventive blend of *chanson* and poetry. A songwriter for France Gall, Brigitte Bardot, and Petula Clark, Gainsbourg was also associated with the trend that signaled the end of so-called *chanson à texte* in the early 1960s. Andreas Bonnermeier analyzes his participation in the *yé-yé* movement as pointing to his ability to transcend the genre by adapting to these new performers' needs, all the while staying true to his trademark use of clever and provocative lyrics.

In the first chapter of the fourth (and closing) section, Kirk Anderson relates this shift in Gainsbourg's career to the EP he recorded at Fontana Studios in London, in 1963. Three years and a British Invasion later, he crossed the Channel again with the firm intention to return to France with a hit at a time when the *yé-yé* movement was losing steam. In so doing, he paved the way for a less derivative form of French pop to emerge. Pursuing the matter, Peter Hawkins presents a compelling piece on what he calls Gainsbourg's "English preference." As one might expect, he connects it with the songwriter's long-term relationship with Jane Birkin; yet he also makes a case for his enduring attraction to the artistry of British studio musicians.

Beyond Songwriting

Part III offers ten different takes on Serge Gainsbourg's output beyond songwriting. The first take is provided by Darran Anderson, who links Gainsbourg's inclination for borrowing classical melodies or entire sections from symphonies to his artistic background as a painter in the modernist era, and the tradition of Cubist collage and Pop Art appropriation. Interestingly, this practice appears to be integral to Gainsbourg's enduring legacy too, given that the proto-sampler has now himself been extensively sampled by the likes of Beck, MC Solaar, Massive Attack, De La Soul, and Die Antwoord. In the following chapter, Olivier Julien draws on literary theorist Gérard Genette's model of transtextuality to shed light on Gainsbourg's multifaceted network of relationships with high culture. Literature, poetry, art music: sweeping across the shades of "derivational practices," these relationships sketch the portrait of a self-proclaimed "minor artist" who spent his life priding himself on being "initiated" into "major art forms." Finally, Nathalie Hérold returns to Gainsbourg's inclination for the recycling or "reprocessing" of art music, examining the way some of his most popular songs reinvest the Romantic piano repertoire of Chopin, Liszt, and Beethoven. From a technical standpoint, such borrowings eventually reveal an attitude at once free and respectful toward the appropriation of the latter composers' work.

Continuing on the path opened by Hérold's chapter, Catherine Rudent and Thomas MacFarlane offer two readings of Gainsbourg's output through the prism of musical analysis. Starting from the poetics of the "evil twin," Rudent seeks to demonstrate how his songs engage musically, lyrically, and metaphorically with notions of reflection, echo, mirror image, and alter ego. Also grounded in musicology, MacFarlane's contribution relies on "*Songscape* analysis" to engage "Je t'aime… moi non plus" on its own terms—that is, as a recorded work. Over the course of the discussion, he pays attention to the ways in which the songwriter's artistry was extended through popular song, sound recording, and film, generating new insights into a unique and compelling creative practice.

Always eager to expand this practice, Gainsbourg published his first and last novel, *Evguénie Sokolov*, in 1980. Christophe Levaux exposes the book's many facets, exploring the different levels on which it can be read, and the ways it reflects on Gainsbourg's conceptions of art and music—in particular his own. Mickaël Savchenko then goes one step deeper into Gainsbourg's literary influences, presenting him as a dandy figure. In the last analysis, his attraction to the Decadent movement opens a window onto his esthetics, marked with ostentatious elegance, snobbery, misogynistic conduct, and cynical observation of society.

This part's last section opens with a chapter by Jérôme Rossi, who evaluates Gainsbourg's musical contribution to the French "Nouvelle Vague" movement. Taking the example of Jacques Doniol-Valcroze's *L'Eau à la bouche*, he explores the narrative-distancing effects created by the use of the eponymous song by Gainsbourg, a theme steeped in the intimate and sophisticated form of jazz which had just begun to invest French cinema after the release of *Sait-on jamais…* (1957). In a different register, Gainsbourg's 1971 album *Histoire de Melody Nelson* has been recognized and acclaimed as a key concept album of the 1970s. Alex Jeffery's chapter investigates how it inspired Jean-Christophe Averty with a television film that emerged from a solid tradition of French experimentation in music video throughout the 1960s. Using a variety of analytical techniques, he demonstrates the way the album's underlying themes and structures extend into its visual presentation to create a work of prescient multimodal coherence. Last but not least, Philippe Cathé examines the way Gainsbourg staged himself and his dubious reputation in the ads he directed for French television. Taking the reader back to the first part of the book, he argues that he managed to benefit from his relationship with the brands and companies who associated their corporate image with his own persona. All things considered, Gainsbourg was the true "item for sale" in these advertisements.

Part One

Deconstructing the Gainsbourg Persona

"Docteur Jekyll et Monsieur Hyde": Gainsbourg in the Mirror

1

The Hidden Beauty of the Ugly

Jeremy Allen

In 1983, the fêted French-Algerian actress Isabelle Adjani had a crack at a pop career like Brigitte Bardot, Catherine Deneuve, and Michèle Mercier before her. Adjani's master-puppeteer was Serge Gainsbourg, writer of such meta-masterpieces as "Poupée de cire, poupée de son," the 1965 Eurovision Song Contest winner that cast a Petrushka-like France Gall as a depressive starlet trapped in a nightmare of exposure: "My records are a mirror in which everyone can see me," she lamented. "I'm everywhere at once, my voice broken into a thousand pieces." Adjani had more control on her *Pull marine* album than Gall ever had, unusually writing the lyrics to five songs, with a co-write on the title track.

"Beau oui comme Bowie" was pure Gainsbourg though, with its tortured "franglais" pun on David Bowie's surname (beautiful, yes? Like Bowie?), it deliberately demarcated Adjani as the *belle* while he lurked in the shadows of his insecurities, *la bête à l'intérieur*. On the seven-inch single, Bowie is the subject of Adjani's fannish infatuation, with the layers becoming apparent as the song unfurls. Everybody would have known that these were Gainsbourg's words—he's the shady puppeteer behind the Bunraku figure who is expressing his man crush on Bowie through the guise of a beautiful, multi-talented, internationally famous, award-winning actress. Furthermore, when she sings: "A little bit of Oscar Wilde/A little bit of Dorian Gray," it's Gainsbourg singing too. He's the increasingly grotesque picture hiding in the attic as one of the world's most desired women does his bidding for him in public.

There's an old clip you can find on YouTube, where Adjani is performing the song dressed in a white suit with elegant black stripes, black gloves, and her shortish hair pulled back.[1] The lights gleam off a waterlogged runway and Adjani looks every inch the fashion model complete with ablated shoulder pads that were very much on trend in the 1980s. We then witness three or four costume changes, including a dark blazer pulled open to reveal a shiny necklace snaking down her thorax and abdomen, a black blazer with shimmering, diamante-encrusted ruff and collars, and finally a white wedding dress.

This TV appearance-cum-fashion show would have been in contrast to Gainsbourg, recognizable at that time as his alter ego Gainsbarre, who only really had one costume consisting of a striped suit top he'd acquired at a market, a shirt that looked as though it had been slept in, his blue jeans and Repetto shoes *sans chaussettes*, plus an optional pair of sunglasses if he was too hung over or was nursing a black eye. Add to that, the customary several days of stubble and an ever-present lit Gitane. Pop singer Etienne Daho used to go drinking with Gainsbourg in the 1980s and witnessed the duality for himself. When I interviewed him, he told me that he would enjoy his friend's company until

> the third person would come along, the person who appeared at the end of his life, Gainsbarre. It was a mask. And so he was very, very different. I didn't like Gainsbarre very much but I liked Gainsbourg. As Serge said himself: "When Gainsbarre drinks, Gainsbourg leaves."
>
> (Allen 2021: 243–4)

Gainsbourg was always most comfortable when he had something to hide behind, be it a persona or an actress. Born Lucien Ginsburg and nicknamed Lulu, he lived several lives: during his teens he'd been called Lucien Gimbaud in Saint-Léonard-de-Noblat—the young boy had had the name forced upon him when he'd been evacuated from Paris, his home city, to evade the German occupation, and one day he found himself hiding in the woods with an axe when Nazis called in at his school ("I'm the butcher's son," was to be his alibi).

In 1954, he'd submitted songs to the SACEM as Julien Grix, a brief identity without any real gusto. Serge Gainsbourg is a persona too, of course, with the drunk, disreputable Gainsbarre an extension of Gainsbourg—the darker twin in the shadows who he used to deflect blame and responsibility from himself, at a time in his life when his alcoholism had gotten out of control. The harder drinking had started in earnest in 1979, precipitated by his sudden rise to superstardom in France with *Aux Armes et cætera*. The partying every night until 4:00 am down at the Elysée Matignon, where a piano would come up through the floor for him to play led to a relationship breakdown with Jane Birkin as she became bored of the repetitive charade. Once free of true love, the shackles were off and he could unleash the ugliness with impunity. And he had the fallback: "It wasn't me, it was Gainsbarre."

Gainsbourg had always been a nervous performer, and only really settled those nerves with alcohol. "He had to drink a lot because otherwise he didn't have the courage to go on," Charlotte Gainsbourg told me for my book *Relax Baby Be Cool: The Artistry and Audacity of Serge Gainsbourg*, published by Jawbone Press in 2021. "It's funny when you imagine him being so provocative because he needed to be pushed, and he was really terrified" (67). He walked off a tour with Barbara in 1963 because he was being heckled, and hardly set foot on stage again for another fifteen years, other than to mime badly on chintzy TV shows. Barbara and Gainsbourg had much in common: both were forced to hide during the Second World War, and both had ancestral connections to Odessa, with antecedents who'd been forced to escape the pogroms and flee to France.

"We met at a gala the day after a journalist had said we were both very ugly, which was nice," said Barbara, sarcastically. "I thought he was very handsome, and we both suffered from similar anxieties: we're both skinny, we both love black ... I asked him to do a tour with me, which he very kindly accepted" (66). After Gainsbourg left the ten-date tour having only played three shows, she said: "His stage fright and his great shyness could make him sick before going onstage" (67).

It wasn't a new problem—you can see him visibly shaking performing "Le Poinçonneur des Lilas" on French TV back in 1959, his face etiolated with fear as he went through the motions, unsure of what to do with his body. As a thirty-year-old man who'd fallen back on the family trade when his dreams of becoming a famous painter had evaporated (his father was a pianist in bars), Serge had reluctantly started performing his own songs, but was more comfortable writing for *chanteuses*, which he did throughout his career: from Michèle Arnaud to Vanessa Paradis, via Birkin, Bardot, Anna Karina, Deneuve, Adjani, his daughter Charlotte, and so on. He might have been a failed film director, but he was adept at manipulating female actors and recasting them in his own image, a trick he repeated with over fifty *comédiennes*. Few declined the chance to become a Gainsbourg girl although Elodie Bouchez, who played the Lolitaesque fantasy figure of Stan's infatuation in the sad, occasionally stomach-churning *Stan the Flasher* (1990), demurred.

The music industry that he'd diffidently become a part of in the 1950s was in agreement that he wasn't likely to be a star performer. He was part of legendary music mogul Jacques Canetti's stable, and Canetti had him pegged as a writer-for-hire rather than a leading man. In his 1978 autobiography *On cherche jeune homme aimant la musique,* Canetti is effusive about many of his charges (Juliette Gréco, Marlene Dietrich, Edith Piaf, Charles Trenet, Maurice Chevalier, Jacques Brel), but finds little room for an artist who was signed by his right-hand man, Denis Bourgeois, the A&R who had the good sense to pair up Gainsbourg with France Gall, to great success.

Gainsbourg won the Académie Charles Cros Grand Prize for his debut album *Du Chant à la une!* in 1959, but he took time to establish himself as an artist in his own right. His international super hit "Je t'aime… moi non plus" with Birkin broke through a full ten years after he received his award, with little success on his own terms in between—a demonstration of patience that no major label would exhibit in today's cutthroat market. It was understandable that Gainsbourg was nervous about performing given the abuse—alluded to by Barbara—that he would receive largely because of his appearance. "We know his songs. He sings them himself with that reedy voice of his, without any gesturing. He gives the impression of being both melancholic and indifferent, with those dreamy eyes and ears like a flying elephant," wrote *Les Beaux-Arts Bruxelles* in an early review (quoted in Verlant 2000: 152), which built a descriptive caricature that fell back on racial stereotypes. It wouldn't be the first time he'd be insulted because of his appearance.

The young Lulu Ginsburg suffered at the hands of anti-Semitic teachers at school in Paris, and as a twelve-year-old, he was forced to wear the yellow Star of David badge and report every day to the police station. Nazi propaganda would have been pasted around the walls of Paris accentuating the features of "the enemy within," vile caricatures designed to vilify Jewry in their own city. He would have been faced with an occupying force taunting his physiognomy, and at such an impressionable age, knowing the way he looked could at any time result in him being loaded into a truck and disappeared. The humiliations he suffered came at him from many angles. It's little wonder he felt ugly.

"When I was growing up, we still had antisemitic writing on the wall that he'd erase," Charlotte Gainsbourg told me in an interview for *Relax Baby Be Cool*.

> There was a lot of graffiti, and there would be some nasty ones that he would get rid of. It's hard to remember what it was like—I mean, there's still a big antisemitism problem in France, but now he's looked at as kind of part of the French pantheon. He's part of the French culture, and he's very respected, but when I was growing up, he was still considered dirty and on drugs—even though he didn't do any drugs. He was this reviled man, and on top of it all he was Jewish. I really remember that as being very ruining.
>
> (230)

When Gainsbourg performed "La Marseillaise" with a Jamaican reggae band for the hit song "Aux Armes et cætera"—the National Anthem of France, no less—it raised the ire of many a right winger, including *Le Figaro* op-ed writer Michel Droit, a fervent Gaullist who later killed his safari guide in a shooting accident in Cameroon. Droit questioned Gainsbourg's loyalty to his country of birth and brought his nationality into question too, an anti-Semitic trope that can be traced through the centuries. Gainsbourg received hate mail as a result, some of which he kept in his attaché case, along with his daily supply of cigarettes and booze. He'd bring them out to amuse himself and his friends. One in particular, Jane Birkin told me, said he had "eyes like an electrocuted toad."

In many ways, Gainsbourg had the last laugh. For all his purported ugliness, he also had high-profile love affairs with beautiful women—Birkin was one, France's "sex kitten" Brigitte Bardot was another. "When people tell me that I'm ugly," he sings on "Des Laids des laids," "I laugh quietly, so as not to wake you up." Then he compares himself to Arthur Miller, who married Marilyn Monroe much to everyone's surprise. Beauty, of course, is subjective—so subjective in fact that it has its own aphorisms that are as commonly posted on Instagram as pictures of Serge and Jane at the time when their collective photogenicity was at its apotheosis: *beauty is in the eye of the beholder; beauty is power, a smile is its sword; everything has beauty, but not everyone sees it*, and so on...

On meeting Jane Birkin at her home in Paris's sixth arrondissement, I remember feeling awkward discussing Gainsbourg's animal magnetism, but it couldn't be avoided. I told her that I thought he looked handsome in his early forties. "Oh yes, I certainly thought so," she replied breathily, and then proceeded to tell me how attractive Petula Clark found him when they'd first met. One could say Gainsbourg was *beau-laid* like Mick Jagger. As Christopher Isherwood once wrote of Jagger (though he could have just as easily been writing about Gainsbourg): "[he is] very pale, quiet, good-tempered, full of fun, ugly-beautiful, a bit like Beatrix Lehmann; he has the air of a castaway, someone saved from a wreck, but not in the least dismayed by it" (2010: xxxv).

If Gainsbourg is ugly-beautiful, then that's a fair summation of his work too, with its contiguity of elements. The musician was a studied esthete who turned his home at 5 bis Rue de Verneuil into a cabinet of curiosities full of strange ornaments he'd collected: a man-sized écorché, l'Homme à tête de chou (the sculpture the album was named after), and a nineteenth-century tarantula globe-mounted on brass wire by Maison Deyrolle. His chair was reputedly as comfortable to sit in as a cilice was to wear, and the beauty of his black-daubed sarcophagus-cum-museum home was a hostile environment for his children. His need for order, and his sense of revulsion if anything were moved out of place, looks today like a form of obsessive, compulsive disorder.

Gainsbourg was also obsessed with Huysmans's novel *A Rebours*, a *fin-de-siècle* appreciation of beauty with some inspired comedy moments, which brought him plenty of inspiration where his interior decoration was concerned. Dalí was his other inspiration, having broken into the surrealist painter's apartment with his first wife Lise (Elisabeth) Levitsky in the early 1950s when they knew that the Spaniard and his wife Gala were away. The Ginsburgs were immediately taken by the juxtaposition of shiny objects set against a black mise-en-scene. That estheticism extended to a connoisseurship of art, and art history (he studied painting at the Ecole Supérieure des Beaux-Arts), and he brought some of the Cubist spirit of Juan Gris to his music, pasting sonic *papier collé* into his soundscapes to make everything very modernist, especially when he was looping rhythm tracks with Michel Colombier (the arranger's voice can be heard on "Bonnie and Clyde," repeating like a cuíca drum—Merlet 2019: 216). Juxtaposition is everywhere in Gainsbourg's work, whether it's the toilet innuendo of "Sensuelle et sans suite" set against pretty, piano-led decoration, or the thieving of Chopin's Preludes and Etudes to base "Jane B." or "Lemon Incest" around—fusing the Polish master with what he called *un art mineur*, such was his disparaging view of pop music.

He couldn't hide that disparagement once *Histoire de Melody Nelson* had bombed commercially. Ugliness came to the fore in the form of bitterness, largely because he felt he'd written his masterpiece and the world was largely ambivalent. Much of what came after appeared to be seeking attention or was unmitigatedly juvenile—the asses of *Vu de l'extérieur* or the flatulation fixation of his novelette *Evguénie Sokolov*, the song of the same name from *Mauvaises Nouvelles des étoiles* from 1981 which features a reggae accompaniment to the sound of breaking wind, and *Guerre et pets*, Jacques Dutronc's 1980 album which puns on *War and Peace* ["*Guerre et paix*"], but means *War and Farts*.

L'Homme à tête de chou was more focused lyrically, but again it was largely ignored at the time it came out. As self-referential as ever, Gainsbourg casts himself as the inverse Narcissus—a man with a cabbage head who is overwhelmed by his own ugliness—he beats a trainee hairdresser to death with a hotel fire extinguisher at the denouement. Musically, the arranger Alan Hawkshaw didn't quite reach the heights of Jean-Claude Vannier's *Melody Nelson*, but he rose to the operatic challenges nonetheless. For Gainsbourgians, *L'Homme à tête de chou* is a work that deserves to be mentioned in the same breath as *Histoire de Melody Nelson*, and yet it remains recondite, a failure then, and only a touchstone for the (cabbage) heads.

When Gainsbourg was finally successful in his own right, with *Aux Armes et cætera* in 1979, and then again with *Love on the Beat* five years later, he stepped fully into the limelight, a late-night chat show fixture who'd up the ante of bad behavior with each appearance in search of *audimat*. It's the word Jane Birkin uses, a French version of "ratings." The more shocking, the more people talked about him. In 1984, he famously set fire to a banknote, but this was only a prelude to an extraordinarily bellicose 1986 which involved verbally attacking singer-songwriter Guy Béart on the show *Apostrophes* and calling Rita Mitsouko's Catherine Ringer "a whore." And then there was the infamous propositioning of Whitney Houston, an awkward, indecent proposal that for many is all they know Serge Gainsbourg for. In fairness, three out of four of these incidents were laugh-out-loud funny, though the barb directed at Ringer was sad, exemplifying the tragic nature of the conflicted alcoholic.

Gainsbourg was attempting to take moral high ground he wasn't entitled to. Ringer had made several pornographic movies before her singing career took off, which somehow appalled a man who'd exhibited his partners in erotic and sometimes compromising poses in films and in high-minded men's magazines such as *Lui*. Gainsbourg no doubt saw what he was doing as art rather than pornography, though his pictures also elicited sexual response. The line between these is as wafer thin as a cigarette paper.

That moralism was evident again on one of the last singles he released before his death, "Aux Enfants de la chance" (1988), an anti-drugs song advising the children of France to stay clean and not shoot up. Sound salutary counsel, and Gainsbourg no doubt felt moved enough to write the song having first-hand experience of heroin addiction in the home and a two-year-old son to look out for, though coming from a man who'd spent most of his life drinking and smoking himself toward an early death, it had more than a ring of hypocrisy about it. "Aux Enfants de la chance" received large amounts of radio airplay in France, a viral hit before that term was coined. Something about its simplistic sanctimony chimed with audiences during the decade where rock stars became moral arbiters and the charity concert went global. Not so much viral, but very memeable, is the Gainsbourg quote: "Ugliness has more going for it than beauty does: it endures." (Simmons 2001: 30) Its cynicism seems to evade the guardians of the inspirational quote websites. In truth, Gainsbourg was a connoisseur of beauty, though if he went looking for "the hidden beauty of the ugly" in the song "Des Laids des laids," he could live with it only being skin-deep when it came to his sexual conquests.

Note

1 https://www.youtube.com/watch?v=ruO3wOUjBPU [accessed 12-12-2022].

2

Gainsbourg over Piaf: The Gendered Pantheon of *Chanson* Artists in French Music Biopics

Isabelle Marc

Along with a few other notable artists such as the "Brel-Brassens-Ferré trinity" (Looseley 2003: 68), the indisputable diva Edith Piaf and pioneer Charles Trenet, Serge Gainsbourg has come to epitomize French *chanson*. But *chanson* was always more than a solo act; in its earliest and "purest" form, it was actually viewed as an authentic and specifically French artistic expression opposed to commercial Anglo-American popular music (63–86). It is now a discursive trope for French popular music, sung in French, but no longer in sharp opposition to other types of music identified as foreign (Lebrun 2014; Rudent 2018). Despite the visible effects of globalization and internationalization, this metonymic relationship between *chanson*, the ACI ["*auteur-compositeur-interprète*," equivalent to the singer-songwriter], and French national identity is still operative nowadays (see Cordier 2014; Hawkins 2000; Looseley 2003; 2018). In recent years, it was even showcased in a number of music biopics such as Olivier Dahan's *La Môme*[1] (2007), Johan Sfar's *Gainsbourg (vie héroïque)* (2011), Florent Siri's *Cloclo* (2012), Lisa Azuelos's *Dalida* (2017), and Matthieu Amalric's *Barbara* (2017).

In the broad context of media convergence (Jenkins 2006), the resurgence of interest for such singers (and singer-songwriters) in France might be interpreted as a sign of a general need for comforting narratives carried by individual characters who came to represent collective values. By tracing exceptional individual trajectories, Dahan, Sfar, Siri, Azuelo, and Amalric revisit the nation's past resorting to a melodramatic, teleological vision of history. Their depictions of the lives and careers of Edith Piaf, Serge Gainsbourg, Claude François, Dalida, and Barbara present a coherent—albeit glorified—image of France's recent history to both a domestic and a global audience. In tune with the biographic boom characteristic of the postmodern era, they also portray the *chanson* star as an exceptional individual, evolving in a mass culture context, whose life is both glamorous and tragic. Finally, they reinforce what I believe to be a clear gender divide in French popular music—and, more broadly, in French culture. This chapter aims at showing how *La Môme* and *Gainsbourg (vie héroïque)* turned Piaf and Gainsbourg into heroic national figures, building on the myth of the modern artist and on the gender differences pervasive in the usual discourse on *chanson*. As I will argue, these two films contributed to expand and transform the figure of the *chanson* artist associated with the 1950s and 1960s into a contemporary transmedia character, mainly male, situated at the highest end of the esthetic assessment scale in contemporary French popular culture.

The *Chanson* Artists: "Poets" of Post-War France

Despite its being a model for the singer-songwriter as a genre (Marc & Green 2016: 11), the figure of the ACI is culturally specific due to its nearness with the French literary and poetic traditions as well as its opposition to foreign music. Throughout history, literature and poetry enjoyed a highly symbolic value in France. Born in the so-called era of Paris's *"cabarets rive gauche,"* the ACI transformed the archetype of the modern poet and placed it at the helm of the burgeoning French music industry while maintaining some "folk" values (craft vs industry, sincerity, etc.). As previous research has shown, the proximity between *chanson* and poetry goes back a long way and was enacted with the award of the National Poetry Prize to Georges Brassens in 1967 (Cantaloube-Ferrieu 1981; Marc 2017; Papanikolau 2007). From that moment on, the ACI became an avatar of the *"poète moderne,"* that is, a poet fully committed to his art, assuming Baudelaire's conception of the modern artist—"a singular man, whose originality is so powerful and clear-cut that it is self-sufficing" (1869b: 58). But it also drew on the myth of the *"poète maudit"*[2] who lives a tormented life, marked by an exceptional talent and excesses, misfortunes, and self-destruction. Each in their own manner, *La Môme* and *Gainsbourg* perpetuate this myth.

At a time when France was undergoing profound changes in the wake of Americanization and modernization, the Left-Bank singer-songwriter represented a compromise between high art (in the form of poetry) and the burgeoning mass culture. Artists such as Georges Brassens, Jacques Brel—and, to a lesser extent, early Serge Gainsbourg—were extremely popular while often perceived as "true" poets. These solo artists, who started their careers performing in small venues, crystallized the *chanson* genre. They underwent a process of progressive legitimization that included the publication of their lyrics in the "Poètes d'aujourd'hui" and "Poésie et chanson" book collections by Seghers (Bonnafé 1965; Clouzet 1974; Rioux 1969). In spite of (or thanks to) his provocative attitude, Gainsbourg's reputation as a major music artist and a poet was indeed well established at the moment of his death, when President François Mitterrand equated him with Baudelaire and Apollinaire (Simmons 2001: ix).

From the outset, the ACI model was overtly masculine. *Chanson* and the French music industry were as male-dominated as French society and culture were. Very few female ACIs emerged in the "classic era" (Barbara, Véronique Sanson, Anne Sylvestre). In turn, women were traditionally confined to the role of "mere" singers. Very often, they adopted a tragic, miserabilist persona, notably in the case of *chanteuses réalistes* such as Damia, Fréhel, and Edith Piaf (Dutheil-Pessin 2004). However, Piaf did not only epitomize this tradition: she also became one of the most prestigious *chanson* artists altogether, overcoming a number of odds—in addition to being a woman, she neither wrote nor composed her own material. As a result, the songs she performed were, like those written by her singer-songwriter counterparts, published by Seghers in 1974 (i.e., a decade after her death—Costaz 1974).

Nowadays, the great figures of *chanson* convey complex, sometimes ambivalent symbolism, including a taste for the "great" French poetic tradition, enhanced by the individual and collective nostalgic impulses specific to contemporary French culture, together with the pleasures associated with the accessibility of "good" popular music. In the first decades of the twenty-first century, their iconic status has increasingly been shaped by "celebrity culture," which became so pervasive in France (Dakhlia 2010). In addition, one may note a growing tendency to "feminize" *chanson*, not only in terms of an increased visibility and presence of women in music professions, but also of a questioning of heteropatriarchal representations in the *chanson* repertoire.

In this context, Piaf and Gainsbourg remain iconic figures of French *chanson*. Piaf became a national myth during her lifetime, an "invention" which would only grow stronger after her death (Looseley 2015: 83–132), and through which she would come to represent both France and *chanson*. A symbol of *chanson réaliste*, she went down in history as a tragic popular diva, a figure who "teaches us all, men and women, to recognize and assume the pathos we have in common" (120). In a different register, Gainsbourg was capable of combining the esthetics of *chanson poétique* and Anglo-American influences in a brilliant synthesis (Julien 2018), and he turned out to be an inescapable musical reference in France and abroad. As is usually the case with male ACIs, the way he is perceived is more multi-faceted, and often associated with artistic and intellectual innovation—even transgression. Again, the divide between emotion and reason seems to be very much at play. In their contemporary after-lives, music biopics *La Môme* and *Gainsbourg (vie héroïque)* contributed to consolidate Piaf's and Gainsbourg's status and their association with pathos and artistic genius, respectively. In order to better understand their cinematographic avatars, I will now linger over some of the general characteristics of music biopics.

The Solo Artist in Cinema

Over the past decade, French cinema's craze for portraying stars of *chanson* has been framed within the global "revival" of music biopics (Marshall & Kongsgaard 2012). These films also signal a new cinematographic trend which has recently aroused much critical interest (Brown & Vidal 2014; Cartmell & Polasek 2020; Custen 1992), fitting within the context of a global taste for the biographical mode in literature and culture in general. The main character is no longer a great man (a statesman, a scientist, a sportsman, etc.), but a singer-songwriter or the leader of a rock band who may not achieve progress for the community *per se*, but creates memorable, "great" popular music instead. Such films share with classical biopics a teleological vision of history, based on the "future perfect tense" (Brown & Vidal 2014: 6). Despite the influence of avant-garde esthetics, most of them resort to conventional—consensual—narratives and tend to favor a melodramatic mode.

According to Lee Marshall and Isabel Kongsgaard (2012), music biopics constitute a good example of the "rock ideology" (Keightley 2001), which combines the spectacular and "mass" character of popular music with elements of romantic and modernist esthetics in an individual figure—the aforementioned singer-songwriter or charismatic leader of a rock band. In this light, "good" popular music is the "authentic" expression of an author, an individual genius comparable to a *"poète moderne"* of *chanson*, capable of creating innovative, original, autonomous, self-referential, and ironic works. Moreover, most cinematographic biographies present what may be described as a "gender divide": few of them focus on exemplary women (Custen 1992), and when they do, they usually adopt a sentimental or erotic perspective (Binghman 2010). Music biopics do share this tendency. When addressing female artists, they cast them as victims, emphasizing aspects of their love lives and personal tragedies rather than focusing on their music.

In France, the global biopic phenomenon has often been met with expressions of contempt toward yet another symptom of Americanization. Raphaëlle Moine identifies three periods in the genre's history: the classical *film biographique* in the 1930s and 1940s, the "heritage" cinema in the 1980s and 1990s, and a third wave that originated with *La Môme* in 2007. This last successful trend is characterized by "the culmination of a gradual move away from the maxim *historia magistra vitae est* ['history is the teacher of life'], which affects both the type of person chosen and the way in which they are depicted" (2014: 57). This new type of French biopic's focus is no longer on an artist associated with high culture or politics, but rather a show-business celebrity, related to what she calls the *"peopolisation"* of French culture (2017: 127–8). Beginning with *La Môme*, and followed by other music biopics, I argue that this new protagonist is now epitomized by the popular music star, in line with a tendency to institutionalize French popular music. Following Dahan's internationally acclaimed film, the music biopic has now become the paradigm of the biopic in France—and, because of its commercial success, one of the paradigms of contemporary French cinema abroad.

To get back to Moine, she also addresses the gender divide in French biographic cinema, and analyzes how *La Môme* and *Gainsbourg (vie héroïque)* perpetuate gender stereotypes when it comes to represent artistic creation (105). In the following section, I will address these films as the epitomes of the French music biopic in terms of esthetic ideology and the construction of national and gender identities via what might be described as a process of "pantheonization" of popular music artists.[3]

Gainsbourg over Piaf? France's Favorite Song

La Môme and *Gainsbourg (vie héroïque)* were both critically and commercially successful films. They received several national and international awards, including an Oscar that went to Marion Cotillard for best female actress. In the process, they contributed to make Piaf and Gainsbourg emblematic figures of French popular music—and, by extension, of the entire French nation—to viewers in and outside France. Still, Piaf and Gainsbourg were not only two of the most renowned and beloved French popular singers: they were also the "least exemplary" if one considers their notorious history of substance abuse. Their biopics insist on their extraordinary talent while emphasizing their self-destructive behavior, which reinforces their tragic legends. In this respect, the films follow the narrative and esthetic structure of American mainstream biopics (Moine 2017: 100–5), that is, the intermingling of the personal with the professional, as well as artistic success with individual misery.

Using different narrative strategies, both films start with the central figures' marginal origins (Piaf is a street child, abandoned by her mother, forced into labor by her father, and Gainsbourg the son of Jewish Russian immigrants who was persecuted during Nazi occupation). From there, they eventually triumph over fate thanks to their extraordinary talent. In fact, their musical trajectories as well as their progress toward success and fame are secondary in comparison with the central plot focusing on their love life and addictions. This connection between suffering and "genius" clearly echoes the myth of the *"poète maudit"*—in Piaf's case, pain, whether physical or emotional, receives far more attention than her musical achievements.

Despite their relying on the generic (global) biopic formula, the way *La Môme* and *Gainsbourg (vie héroïque)* portray the musical artist is specifically framed within the French cultural context. Gainsbourg and Piaf are presented as visionary artists who came to embody the esthetics of modernity (originality and sophistication, sincerity, autonomy) within popular music. Several scenes show them in the process of creating musical masterpieces immediately identifiable by the French public (Piaf is seen rehearsing and performing, Gainsbourg composing and writing), and the focus is kept on the artist rather than the public's reaction—even though *La Môme* does show the audience's fascination with Piaf's live performances.

On the same train of thought, the differences between the Anglo-American rock star/singer-songwriter and *chanson*'s ACI are particularly salient. As hinted above, *chanson* defined itself in opposition to imported music. Along with the use of the French language, Frenchness is explicitly highlighted through locations and other referential elements, chosen over the most typically French images (Parisian streets and roofs, etc.).[4] What is more, "La Marseillaise" occupies a central place in both films. Piaf's musical "revelation" as an extraordinary singer takes place when the child Edith sings the national anthem in front of an improvised audience in the streets of Belleville. In *Gainsbourg (vie héroïque)*, the process of creating and recording "Aux Armes et cætera" (his reggae version of that same anthem), and the ensuing public controversy, are among the most detailed musical moments in the film.

The films also tend to deal with France's recent history from an unquestioning perspective, ignoring social and political circumstances altogether. Escaping Nazi persecution, for example, is presented as a dare game for young Gainsbourg. In Piaf's case, the war is simply not mentioned, although her activity during those years is well-documented.[5] This historical vagueness, though clearly rooted in the French context, plays with the audience's collective memory by including well-known characters in the French star system. This contributes to create a unifying, comforting narrative of the past based on individual stories rather than political and social facts and trends (Moine 2017: 122–6).

In her 2014 essay on the "contemporary French biopic," Raphaëlle Moine analyzes the adaptation of the genre to the French socio-cultural context as a sign of the primacy of the "culture of the individual," coupled with an increasing focus of the French media on the intimacy of ordinary people and celebrities (127–8). This break with the traditionally collective values of the *République* was pointed out by other critics who saw the contemporary biopic as a symbol of the triumph of liberal, individualistic, and capitalist ideology (Pigoullié 2011). Nevertheless, this ideology also shows through traditional French historical writing. For the nation's consensual and *popular* history is not primarily the story of social movements: it is rather a history based on the lives of great men [*"grands hommes"*] who embody France's values and pride. The list of such exemplary figures, mostly male, may change depending on the historical period and political spectrum (Amalvi 1998), but the country's hegemonic vision of its own history is not based on the acknowledgment of the role of collective actors and social groups. This brings to mind De Gaulle's plan to achieve unity through a shared vision of historical grandeur relying on exemplary characters belonging either to the Ancien Régime or the Republican period (Burguière & Revel 1993: 509). In a time of political and social crisis in France, the reinvented lives of Piaf and Gainsbourg as adapted to the screen bring comfort to and memorialize the nation (Pigouillé 2011).

The Emotional Performer and the "Total Artist"

Another striking characteristic of *La Môme* and *Gainsbourg (vie héroïque)* is their shared binary, even sexist vision of the musical artist. In this heavily gendered formula, the male artist is the creator (composer and lyricist), while the female artist, as a performer, assumes a reproductive role. This bias was pointed out by Moine too, who identifies a gender divide in biopics, where women are usually depicted as suffering, pathetic characters (2017: 101–6).

In essence, *La Môme* tells the story of an exceptionally talented woman marked by misfortune and tragedy. Life episodes are related to musical sequences (and vice versa), as the public follows the central character down her path to success and self-destruction. Underpinned by Marion Cotillard's convincing characterization, Dahan's account confirms and reinforces Piaf's tragic legend. Like a chronicle of a death foretold, it shows her progressing toward her tragic end, foreshadowed from the first scene in a New York setting—which simultaneously points to her Frenchness and international dimension. The story is then arranged in a more linear fashion, with a first part devoted to her miserable childhood and her discovery by Louis Leplée. This part is followed by her encounters with the two other men who will eventually help her become Piaf (the artist): Raymond Asso and Marcel Cerdan—the former helped her hone her performer's skills, the latter was her one great love. A second part then invites the audience to witness the rise of the star, along with a string of excesses and dependence, both on men and drugs. In short, Piaf is presented as a diamond in the rough polished by men (Leplée, Asso, Cerdan), a performer with portentous qualities, but dependent on the creative talent of others—a prodigious diva not only conducted, but fully modeled by her Pygmalions. Following the masculinist diva's tradition, stemming from Homer's Sirens, Piaf's characterization is closer to that of a monster than that of an actual woman (Leonardi & Pope 1996: 13). While she may not be presented as a menacing creature, the camera keeps her bathed in an expressionist, hyperbolic light, especially during her performances. Her white face, overly red lips, huge forehead, clumsiness, and excesses clash with traditional, heteronormative, and attractive femininity.

Piaf's voice—like that of a Siren—is indeed able to move her audience to the extreme, drawing endless applause and tears, as the shots of the public's reactions during the concert scenes reveal. Her talent lies in that voice, that is, in her emotional rather than intellectual power. And, however extraordinary she may be, the latter power does depend on others—she is a mere vessel for somebody else's vision. The interview she gives to a young American journalist on the beach, referring to love as the ultimate goal and purpose of life, confirms her fundamentally sentimental nature. The fact that she never attains love in the film places her alongside other unwomanly divas, whose talent was also their doom. And yet, the film omits the fact that the "real" Piaf was a sexually emancipated woman, who had many lovers, and that she herself acted as a Pygmalion for several young men who later became major *chanson* stars such as Yves Montand and Charles Aznavour. Put differently, Dahan's film refuses to acknowledge the empowered figure of Piaf.

Conversely, *Gainsbourg (vie héroïque)* is intended to be a "story"—not a realistic account, but a fiction based on the life of Serge Gainsbourg. The film emphasizes his moments of glory and, above all, his love affairs with female icons of French pop culture (Brigitte Bardot, Jane Birkin). The fictional nature of the film is achieved by the inclusion of animation elements corresponding to imaginary characters: the caricature of the Jew, who becomes the artist's alter ego ("La Gueule"), and also Sfar's graphic incursion in the plot, which introduces a distancing effect from the supposed fidelity of the portrait, especially in the first part of the film (before Gainsbourg meets Jane Birkin). The reference to a "heroic life" in the film's title is in line with the French tradition of distinguishing the country's heroes, honoring those exceptional beings who embody the homeland, being set up as role models for the national community.

Throughout the film, Gainsbourg is associated with two fundamental characteristics: he is a seducer, and a creator. Both make him an exceptional being whose extraordinary nature is highlighted from the start. As the international trailer puts it: "his lovers were legendary," "his music was visionary," and "his life was extraordinary." The narrative insists on two disadvantages that the young Serge Gainsbourg had to deal with: his ugliness, and his Jewishness. Overcoming both, he not only managed to escape the Nazi genocide, but went on to seduce extremely beautiful women, unattainable to most. The film also highlights his artistic talent from an early age, showing him as a painter, a poet, a pianist and, finally, a musical genius. Ample footage is dedicated to his creative process. Musical sequences show him composing alone, manipulating young singer France Gall, or writing "Je t'aime… moi non plus" for Brigitte Bardot—his muse of the moment. In other scenes, shot in a recording studio or at a concert, he is presented as the sole creator of a work that will go down in history. Visionary, transgressive, brilliant: Gainsbourg is a "total artist" whose innate creativity is stimulated by a succession of muses and breakups. It is also worth noting that the child Gainsbourg and "La Gueule" appear in several scenes portraying him as an adult, as a way to suggest the survival of the child genius and the rebel in the face of conventionalism. An interesting parallel could be made with "Le Peintre de la vie moderne," where Baudelaire defines genius as "childhood recovered at will, a childhood now equipped for self-expression, with mature faculties and an analytic spirit which permit him to set in order the mass of raw material he has involuntarily accumulated" (1869b: 62).

If one compares the two films, it appears that Piaf and Gainsbourg are both depicted as exceptionally talented personalities who reap the public's favor while being, at the same time, victims of their addictions. In the end, these films establish an artistic hierarchy between the performer and the creator, as well as regards to gender. Piaf does not write her songs: she performs what others write for her. Only twice in *La Môme* does she make decisions regarding her career and repertoire. Her creation is her performance, valued for its expressive and emotional dimension. As the film goes to great lengths to show her constant suffering, her unhappy life is presented as the source of the pathos found in her songs, and a reason for her success. As for Gainsbourg, he is portrayed as the absolute creator of his work, a work that does not rely on expressiveness and naturalness, but on the tongue-in-cheek quality of his lyrics, on musical and literary intertextuality, intelligence, and double entendre. In contrast to Piaf's esthetic simplicity and straightforwardness, he emerges as a complex, contradictory being, free from social conventions; he has no second thoughts about leaving his first wife and daughters, indulges in sex scandals and acts as a consummate seducer who overcomes all losses—unlike Piaf, who is the victim of romantic love, utterly destroyed, physically and emotionally, by the accidental death of Cerdan. He even has multiple personalities, goes through several transformations, and takes advantage of his failures to reinvent himself while fashioning female artists such as France Gall, Brigitte Bardot (at least, musically speaking), and Jane Birkin.

All things considered, *La Môme* and *Gainsbourg (vie héroïque)* reveal a gender divide that reproduces the patriarchal binary schemes in which the active subject is male, while the woman, even when exceptional, plays a secondary role, subordinated to the will of others, whether esthetically or sentimentally. The sexist bias, pointed out by Moine in these two films and other French biopics about women (2017: 100–6), reinforces the traditional hierarchy that still prevails in representations of mainstream artists in contemporary France. Originality, intelligence, transgression, and autonomy are shown as masculine virtues, while dependence, sentimentality, and pathos are all feminine attributes.

Conclusion

Focusing on two of the most successful and widely loved French singers, *La Môme* and *Gainsbourg (vie héroïque)* exemplify the way film and popular music feed off each other in their respective capacities for nostalgic evocation, and the re-creation of an individual and a collective past combined. As such, they flatter the national pride and satisfy the conservative impulse of the mainstream public, and the need to give coherence to the past, at least for the duration of a screening. In sum, they fit in and feed on the "retromaniac," nostalgic impulse that characterizes much of the popular music and cinema of recent decades (Marc 2014; Reynolds 2011: 385). As heritage cinema and classical biopics did in their heyday, music biopics now play a "commemorative function by revitalizing *lieux de mémoires* ['sites of memory'] in the course of revisiting them" (Moine 2014: 56). In France, a country which seems to have experienced a perpetual identity and cultural crisis since the post-war years, they are particularly suitable for cementing a patriotic, sentimental Hall of Fame. Built as victims and heroes, Piaf and Gainsbourg take on a national dimension that combines authenticity and stardom. Their posthumous biopics grant them the final reward of forgiveness for their excesses, and the ultimate, collective recognition of their genius, as if marking the last step before an official elevation by State decree to a popular music pantheon.

This popular music pantheon has the power to reconcile the public with national history through the re-creation of the lives of the country's great "popular" artists. The figures they honor are no longer the exemplary men celebrated in what Ozouf describes as the "cult of the Republic" (1984): they are stars of *chanson*, consensual figures who have now become transmedia *lieux de mémoire*, as pointed out by Looseley (2015: 189) and Sirinelli (2012). Born and raised in a mass-culture context, but direct heirs to the modern myth of the author, these artists have become epic heroes in the contemporary French collective imagination. Gainsbourg was certainly transgressive and provocative during his lifetime, but his biopic turned him into a romantic hero. Similarly, Piaf's character is glossed over at the expense of her tragic legend so as to create an all-emotional, pan-French, and global feminine figure. Both are thus deprived of any transgressive and questioning force. As in the *chanson de geste*, the exemplary lives of *chanson* stars—because successful in esthetic and commercial terms—bolster a vision of the past which reconciles tragedy and genius, the individual and the nation, the collective and the personal—a vision that appears to be coherent and reassuring in the face of post-modern fragmentation. In a context of political, socio-economic, racial, and cultural divide [*"archipélisation"*] (Fourquet 2019), these consensual figures come across an attempt to reunite France's mainstream public. In this sense, *La Môme* and *Gainsbourg (vie héroïque)* present a profoundly conservative vision that contributes to shaping a sentimental and uncritical national narrative, based on patriarchal esthetic mystifications, dressed up in melodramatic plots and memorable tunes.

Notes

1 *La Vie en rose* in its international version.
2 The expression *"poète maudit"* stems from Paul Verlaine's book, *Les Poètes maudits*. The original edition (1884b) contained notices of Tristan Corbière, Arthur Rimbaud, and Stéphane Mallarmé. The second edition (1888) included three more studies: "Marceline Desbordes-Valmore," "Villiers de l'Isle-Adam," and "Pauvre Lelian" (Verlaine himself).

3   For centuries, the French State has been distinguishing its most honorable citizens by housing their remains in the famous mausoleum named the Pantheon, a secular temple in Paris's fifth arrondissement.
4   In *La Môme*, the character of Marlene Dietrich goes so far as equating Piaf's voice with Paris.
5   As David Looseley observes, "she was certainly blacklisted by the national radio service for a short time after the Liberation" (2015: 68).

"Yellow Star": Gainsbourg & Jewishness

3

"Dieu Est Juif": Disappearing and Reappearing Jewishness in Serge Gainsbourg's Career

Jonathyne Briggs and Nick Underwood

Released in 1997, the second collection of the New York record label Tzadik's Great Jewish Music series highlighted the work of Serge Gainsbourg. Compiled by John Zorn, it contained covers of twenty-one of Gainsbourg's songs primarily drawn from the early part of his career. In the liner notes, Zorn suggested that the songwriter "downplayed his Jewish roots" and that Jewishness was not an active part of his public persona (1997). He also argued for a Jewish character to Gainsbourg's music, in his turns of phrase or his lyrics, although he understood how provocative it might be to redefine Jewishness in purely cultural terms. An active member of the Radical Jewish Culture movement in New York (Barzel 2014), Zorn advocated for the rediscovery of Jewish roots in myriad subgenres, and for him, Gainsbourg offered another example of how Jewishness might manifest in subtle ways.

Gainsbourg, however, was not always so subtle when it came to his Jewishness, whose public display took on varying forms and often came as a reaction to the hostility he experienced at one time or another in his career. He would outwardly embrace his Jewish roots after he had gained commercial and critical success in France. That this embrace occurred toward the end of his career and after his song "Aux Armes et cætera" was marked as "Jewish" by right-wing critics was important, as this public experience seemingly affected how he subsequently integrated his Jewish background into his music. Focusing on songs from the albums of his late period—*Mauvaises Nouvelles des étoiles, Love on the Beat, You're Under Arrest*—this chapter illustrates how Gainsbourg's Jewishness manifested itself in a more deliberate manner than Zorn asserts. Additionally, it contextualizes Gainsbourg's place as a Jewish pop music star in France, where Jewish artists made significant contributions despite the continued challenges of anti-Semitism from French society.

Lucien Ginsburg was born in Paris to a Jewish-Ukrainian family in 1928. His parents migrated to France following the 1917 Russian Revolution. Judaism was not explicitly practiced in his childhood household, but, as was the case with many Eastern European Jews in France, Jewish identity was not limited to religious practice—such was the tradition of "Franco-Judaism" (Berkovitz 1989). The Ginsburg family would have found in Paris a diaspora both nationalist and communist with roots in Eastern

Europe that eschewed Judaism as the primary means of defining Jewishness in favor of an overarching focus on Jewish culture, allowing for the rise of a secular Jewish identity across Europe (Underwood 2017). Lucien's early life was quite musical, due to his father's profession as a piano player and his own efforts to learn the instrument from a young age. Despite the draconian anti-Semitic laws and the threat of deportation to the camps, his family remained in the city during most of the Occupation—he would later reflect on his experiences of wearing a yellow star in the streets of Paris as an important early memory. And, as he moved into a career in popular music, he did not really emphasize his Jewishness, even though there was a visible presence of Jews in the post-war popular music scene.[1]

Studies of Jews and music in post-war France stabilize the ground from which we can understand Gainsbourg's output during his late period. Examining the links between Jews and music in late nineteenth- and early-twentieth-century Russian society, James Loeffler argues that music was "a gateway to European modernity" and that the story of Jews and music is about "the Jewish search for a modern identity not through politics or religion but through art" (2010: 2). In the post-war period, specifically in the Germanys, scholars have shown how Jews were bound to "German culture—in complex ways inextricably linked through experiences of the Holocaust and memories of Nazi atrocities" (Frühauf & Hirsch 2014: 1). European Jewish music was, therefore, a place to express modernity and articulate experiences. The scholarship on Jews in France in the post-war years does not explicitly make these connections between culture (here music), modernity, and memory, but they do demonstrate how Jews during those years attempted to rebuild their communities and gain "political and moral recognition" (Hand 2015: 21).[2] In the French case, rebuilding and memory of the Holocaust was an ongoing theme that Gainsbourg eventually embraced.

Gainsbourg's early work combined his lyrical flair for wordplay and quips with the style of jazz favored by the singer-songwriters who developed out of the Left-Bank cabaret scene during the 1950s. He lacked the theatricality of Jacques Brel or the earthiness of Georges Brassens, favoring instead the more classically informed approach of Léo Ferré (Briggs 2015: 74–5). Albums such as *Du Chant à la une!* (1958) point to his ability to emulate the popular styles of the moment, while still adding his own character to the music. Often his songs were character studies—for example "Le Poinçonneur des Lilas," one of his earliest successes. Gainsbourg soon proved himself a musical chameleon, not only in his embrace of different musical styles, but also in his ability to write successfully for other artists. His wordplay and humor, combined with his sense of melody, made him an in-demand songwriter in the burgeoning pop music market. By the end of the 1960s, he had found both commercial and critical success, even as he courted controversy with his breakthrough single "Je t'aime... moi non plus" in 1969.

His Jewish identity was not something he emphasized at this point, although, with his earnings from the single, he famously purchased a platinum Star of David from Cartier, which was also controversial given the rifts that the 1967 Six-Day-War in Israel caused among France's Jewish communities (Bensimon 1989; Isaacson 2017). As a provocateur, Gainsbourg was mining from his heritage to fashion his public identity now that more people were paying attention to him. Moreover, his timing coincided with a period of new interest in France about the experiences of the Jews during the Second World War and the role of the French in the Holocaust (see, for example, Klarsfeld 1978). The release of Marcel Ophuls's *The Sorrow and the Pity* in 1971 spurred a frank discussion of French actions during the so-called Dark Years, undermining the myths of resistance and origins of Jewish deportations during the war (Wolf 2004: 63–5). The confluence of scholarly, political, and cultural interest in all things about the Occupation and Vichy led Gainsbourg to dedicate an entire album to the subject of the Second World War in 1975.

Rock Around the Bunker is a concept album built upon the mockery of Nazi imagery and ideas while at the same time drawing on Gainsbourg's personal experiences from his youth. The LP is one of his genre experiments—a doo-wop and rock 'n' roll pastiche—coupled with songs presenting the seedy lives of Nazis as lustful caricatures that eventually escape justice for their crimes. While Gainsbourg often hid behind a persona in his songwriting, here he is voicing something direct: his memories of being labeled as Jewish in the song "Yellow Star." Evoking his childhood in Paris and having to wear the badge on his lapel beginning in 1942, he expressed a sense of pride and wonder, singing: "I won the Yellow Star." But alongside this sense of pride, he alludes to a Jewish "struggle for life" when he sings, *"J'ai gagné la Yellow Star/Je porte la Yellow Star/Difficile pour un juif/La loi du struggle for life"* ["I won the Yellow Star/I wear the Yellow Star/Difficult for a Jew/The law of the struggle for life"]. As the eighth track on the record, "Yellow Star" stands out on an album focused on the Nazis, as it is the only song to take the point of view of a Jew. It is also the song that precedes the album's title track and the last song on the record, "SS in Uruguay," which points toward the post-war flight of Nazis to South America and from justice. In a 1975 interview with magazine *Best*, Gainsbourg ascribed the record's lack of commercial success to the problem of honestly addressing the 1940s in France, going so far as to say: "if the French have such taboos and scruples towards Nazism, it's because so many of them were collaborators" (reprinted in Eudeline 2002: 418). The historical accuracy of Gainsbourg's quote notwithstanding—this is still a highly controversial claim to make—he pointed to the problematic topic of the role of the French during the war, perhaps overcompensating against the myth of the nation of *Résistants*. Indeed, it was not until 1994 that the French state would acknowledge its participation in the deportation of Jews in France to their deaths in Nazi extermination camps. On later reflection, Gainsbourg recognized the album as an exorcism, concerning both his Jewishness and the fetishization of Nazi iconography in the 1970s.

He would again strike up controversy at the end of the decade with his recording of "La Marseillaise" (the French national anthem), which he released as the lead and "title" single from his 1979 LP, *Aux Armes et cætera*. This would give him another commercial hit but draw the ire of French nationalists who noted Gainsbourg's Jewishness in their denunciation of his version. Their criticism was based on the musical style he chose to record the national anthem: reggae. Another genre experiment, the album was in fact the result of Gainsbourg's collaboration with Sly Dunbar and Robbie Shakespeare, the premier reggae rhythm section and producers in Jamaica. He would work again with the duo on the follow up, but it was *Aux Armes et cætera* that elicited a response that framed Gainsbourg in anti-Semitic terms. Michel Droit, perhaps his most ardent critic, wrote in *Le Figaro Magazine*:

> Many of us get alarmed, and with good cause, when anti-Semitism rears its ugly head in our modern world ... we all know that there are those who propagate anti-Semitism and those who provoke it. I say ... that Serge Gainsbourg ... has placed himself in that second category.
>
> (1979: 19)

In other words, Droit blamed Gainsbourg for provoking anti-Semitism while, at the same time, stoking it against him. Two weeks later, Gainsbourg published a response in the pages of *Le Matin Dimanche*: drawing a parallel with French nationalists' hostility toward Alfred Dreyfus at the turn of the century, he basically argued that Droit's reaction was rooted in his seeing "A Jew on their tricolored flag" (Verlant 2000: 513).

Aux Armes et cætera became Gainsbourg's biggest commercial success in France, but was also the cause a national scandal. As Edwin Hill explains, the album appeared at a time when "it became possible to acknowledge that France had entered the post-colonial era, that it was a medium-sized economy rather than a world power" (2003: 119), which exacerbated the reaction to the song in terms of sacrilege. On the subsequent tour, Gainsbourg faced death threats from right-wing groups at his concert in Strasbourg. The Alsace region, because of a long-established Jewish presence and its reputation as a stronghold of the French political right, has a long history of anti-Semitism (Wieviorka & Bataille 2007: 245–6). The National Union of Parachutists attempted to intimidate Gainsbourg and stop him from performing the anthem at that tour stop. Despite these threats, Gainsbourg sang the song, but without his backing band, to force the crowd to participate (Pascuito 2006: 132).

The centrality of Gainsbourg's Jewishness in Droit's critique spoke to the resurgence of anti-Semitism in France in the late 1970s, even as the French increasingly came to terms with their role in the Holocaust. In interviews, Gainsbourg dismissed all religious belief in general, but he made his Jewish identity an element of his lyrical and musical choices going forward as a reaction to the controversy (Bayon & Gainsbourg 1992: 29), even as his public behavior became more erratic during the 1980s. As an example, this identity resurfaced on his next record, 1981's *Mauvaises Nouvelles des étoiles*, which shared *Aux Armes et cætera*'s reggae style, but lacked the same controversy. Lyrically, Gainsbourg returned to a number of themes he had explored on previous records, but something new appeared: a meditation on religion that spoke to his fascination with his own Jewishness. On "Juif et Dieu," he invoked Jewish history and identity to consider the role of Jews in Western culture and history. Addressing the paranoid aspect of anti-Semitism, he began the song with the lines: *"Sais-tu que le Nazaréen/ N'avait rien d'un Aryen/Et s'il est fils de Dieu comme vous dites alors/Dieu est juif"* ["Did you know that the Nazarene/Was never an Aryan/And if he is as you say the Son of God, then/God is Jewish"]. He also highlighted the modern Jewish practice of name changing, singing, "Grigori Ievseïetch Apfelbaum called Zinoviev, Lev Borissovitch

Rosenfeld called Kamenev, Lev Davidovitch Bronstein called Trotsky" (all three were Bolshevik revolutionaries, anti-Stalinists, and born Jewish). In sum, he played around with tropes about Jews' relationship to the left, the Jewish history of name changing, and the overall idea of interconnectedness in Jewish culture and history that some, on both the left and right, buy into (Fermaglich 2018; Underwood 2017). Moreover, placing his Jewish identity alongside those of prior radical Jewish activists within the tradition of name changing allowed him to insert himself into a longer trajectory of provocation. In "Ecce Homo," Gainsbourg (né Ginsburg and enacting another name change by introducing his new persona Gainsbarre) sings of his own crucifixion, reinforcing the question of Jesus's (and God's) Jewishness.

The mixed reviews for *Mauvaises Nouvelles* did little to faze Gainsbourg's desire to continue to develop new musical ideas (Simmons 2001: 103). He continued to write for other artists in the early 1980s until he decided to record his next album, 1984's *Love on the Beat*, in New York. The album showed him working in a new genre: electro-funk. While he does not take a lyrical approach concerning Jewishness on this album, one could argue that he seems to have found the energy to explore the influence of anti-Semitism. The seminal track on the record, "Lemon Incest," was built around a musical motif from Frédéric Chopin's Etude for Piano No. 3 in E major, Op. 10. Gainsbourg had mined Chopin's works for previous compositions, but in the wake of the "Aux Armes et cætera" scandal, the appropriation takes on a potential new meaning. Chopin, the Polish-French composer, was critical of the role of Jews in music publishing in France during the nineteenth century, and his letters reveal his characterization of Jews as mercenary, parasitic, and alien (Halliman 2007: 272). Could we see a link here between Gainsbourg's new reappropriation of Chopin and a desire to raise awareness against anti-Semitism? If so, then the link between Chopin's work and Gainsbourg's final musical controversy—a duet between him and his then-thirteen-year-old daughter Charlotte suggesting sexual interaction—appears in a new light.

In a different register, his final original album, *You're Under Arrest* (1987), features a song by Rezső Seress, a Hungarian Jew who survived the labor camps during the Second World War. Working in funk and rap, *You're Under Arrest* is about drugs and loss. Possibly influenced by Gainsbourg's sense of his own end being near, the track listing actually includes two songs from his childhood, "Gloomy Sunday" and "Mon Légionnaire," the first of which was written by Seress when he lived in Paris in 1932. Of course, its presence here confirms Gainsbourg's ability to recontextualize older material with new sounds; but coupled with his late interest in Jewishness, it might also suggest how he found subtle ways of continuing that exploration as death was drawing near—in a way, "Gloomy Sunday" allowed him to connect several aspects of Jewish history and identity with roots that traversed the 1930s in Paris, Nazi Germany, the Holocaust, and the post-war years.

Before his untimely death in 1991, Gainsbourg increasingly grappled with Jewish identity, at times in response to critics and at other times as a resource for him to draw on to fuel his attempts at controversy. While he initially outwardly ignored his own Jewishness, he eventually found an artistic and cultural value in articulating it. The continued durability of his Jewishness is perhaps evident in the actions of some who travel to pay respects to him at his grave at Montparnasse by placing stones on his marker, a Jewish burial tradition. As others did before, fans continue to mark Gainsbourg's Jewishness, only now in his death.

Notes

1. In addition to singers of Jewish origin such as Barbara and Georges Moustaki, the post-war years in Paris also played host to Europe's premier Yiddish-language record label Elesdisc, which released records from 1948 to 1953. The Yiddish cabaret singer Dave Cash was one of its most well-known singers at the time, establishing France as a centerpiece of post-war Jewish musical production.
2. On the themes of rebuilding, politics, Holocaust memory, and French anti-Semitism, see Mandel 2003; Hyman 1998; Doron 2015; Weinberg 2015; Fogg 2017; Auslander 2005; Heuman 2015; Wolf 2004; Ouzan 2018; Schnapper 1983.

4

"Le Sable et le Soldat": Serge Gainsbourg, Jewishness, Masculinity, and the Quest for Legitimacy

France Grenaudier-Klijn

> *"The only messages that music can convey are patriotic anthems."*
> Serge Gainsbourg (2006: 111)

1967 proves a particularly productive year for Serge Gainsbourg, with his notoriety and media presence growing. He becomes a recurrent figure on television, appearing in close to thirty different programs (Verlant 2000: 319). He releases the EP *Mr Gainsbourg*, while creating music for numerous artists—Dominique Walter, Claude François, Régine, France Gall, Stone. He writes "Harley Davidson," "Contact," "Comic Strip," "Bonnie and Clyde," and "Je t'aime… moi non plus" for Brigitte Bardot, and composes for Minouche Barelli, representing Monaco that year at the Eurovision Song Contest. He also signs original scores for films and TV series: *Toutes folles de lui* (which includes an instrumental track intriguingly entitled "Goering connais pas!" ["Goering, no idea who that is!"]), *L'Horizon*, and *Vidocq*. He invites controversy with the musical *Anna* created for Anna Karina, with Jean-Claude Brialy, whose song "G.I. Jo," centered around the star ("How many stars on that flag"), is criticized for its anti-American and anti-militarist lyrics. But Gainsbourg's most unusual creation that year is without doubt "Le Sable et le Soldat," also known as "Le Sabre et le Soldat," "Le/s Sable/s d'Israël," or "Les Enfants d'Israël." This song—one of Gainsbourg's least familiar—is atypical in many ways from the artist's past and future repertoire. Yet, while puzzling, it also sheds light on several aspects of Serge Gainsbourg's kaleidoscopic persona(lity), namely his relationship to Jewishness and anti-Semitism, the military/police world, masculinity, and the quest for personal and esthetic legitimacy. After a brief outline of the song's characteristics and the context within which it originated, I will turn to these points in more details, prior to suggesting that this (Not So) incongruous track does in fact fully belong to the Gainsbourgian anthology.

The Curious Origins of an Unusual Song[1]

Early in 1967, Avraham Scherman, a cultural attaché at the Israeli embassy in Paris, is startled by the resemblance between "Le Poinçonneur des Lilas," heard on the radio, and a song often played in his homeland. "Le Poinçonneur," it turned out, was part of Les Frères Jacques's repertoire, who had toured Israel at the end of 1958. A hit then, it had been quickly translated into Hebrew. Once informed that the original composer was in fact a French musician of Russian and Jewish ancestry, Scherman, liking the song, requested an introduction. Keenly aware of the possibility of an imminent conflict between Israel and its Arab neighbors, the attaché sought to have a song composed specifically to galvanize Tsahal, the Israeli armed forces. Flattered by such—international—attention, Gainsbourg, who had not yet reached the height of his success, acquiesced to the commission, and wrote the song overnight. Quickly recorded by the songwriter himself, it was flown to Tel Aviv on June 4, to be translated in Hebrew and played on Kol Israel (The Voice of Israel), the Israeli public radio, the following day. Then, the Six-Day War erupted. Played only once on Kol Israel, the song laid dormant in its archives, only to be unearthed decades later. Since 2002, it is occasionally aired on RCJ (the Jewish community radio in France), but remains largely unfamiliar for the general public, including Gainsbourg fans; it is seldom mentioned by his biographers and is not included in the *Intégrale. Edition du 20e anniversaire* released by the Mercury label in 2011.

A Simple Tune[2]

"Le Sable et le Soldat" has a very simple song structure accompanied by electric organ, consisting of an eight-bar chorus alternating with a four-bar verse—ABABA'. It is written in common time; the melodic scale is natural minor, and the key G minor. The word "Israel" is repeated no less than twenty-one times, and references to the first person (*je*/I and *m'*/me) appear five times. There are also noticeable allusions to biblical history—the David vs Goliath episode—and to the geopolitical context of the time—the pyramids symbolizing the Egyptian foe. The lyrics are literal, devoid of puns, double entendre or irony, and insist on the resoluteness of the singer ready to die for Israel. A thematic crescendo is introduced through the succession of terms like "sand," "soil," "children," "cities," "land," which together paint the unified picture of a country complete with ancestral land (soil), inhabitants (children), and emerging modernity (cities). While neither overtly martial nor dramatic, Gainsbourg delivered exactly what he was commissioned to do: a military march, easy to memorize and perform. Let us now attempt to decipher the reasons that led him to create a song which he appears to have largely disavowed later and examine its links with the themes highlighted earlier.

An Anthem by "A Poor Uprooted Boy"[3]

Gainsbourg grew up in a secular environment. His parents did not practice religious Jewish rituals, nor did they eat kosher food, or celebrate traditional Jewish holidays (Verlant 2000: 18). If we believe Bernard Pascuito, Rabbi Zaoui, assistant of the great Sephardic Rabbi Sitruk (an intervention especially surprising given Gainsbourg's oft-mentioned Ashkenazi origins!), came to Rue de Verneuil to recite the Kaddish on March 2, 1991, at the request of the Gainsbourg family (his daughter Charlotte?), and the artist is indeed buried in Montparnasse's Jewish area (Pascuito 2006: 15). However, according to Ersin Leibowitch and Dominique Loriou, the artist was not interred in consonance with Jewish precepts, nor is he buried in the Jewish section of the Montparnasse cemetery (2011: 114).[4]

Conflicting accounts notwithstanding, Gainsbourg proudly assumed his identity as a Jew, as epitomized by his 1981 song "Juif et Dieu." He was also keenly aware of the nauseating reality of anti-Semitism. A child in Nazi-occupied France, he had been the target of anti-Semitic slurs at the hands of teachers (Verlant 2000: 23–4). He knew of the faith of two of his uncles struck down by the Shoah: his uncle Michel (Moshe) Besman, his mother's younger brother, assassinated at Auschwitz-Birkenau (Lelièvre 2008: 84), and his uncle Daniel, captured during a round-up, and sent to die in the Mauthausen concentration camp (Pascuito 2005: 25). He witnessed closely the aftermath of the Shoah on children, during his years as an art-teacher in the Champsfleur re-education institute in Maisons-Laffitte (Lelièvre 2008: 102). His political orientation—during the 1974 presidential elections, he lent his support to the conservative candidate Valéry Giscard-d'Estaing—would also be influenced by both the Soviet Union's inherent anti-Semitism, and the pro-Palestinian tendencies of members of the French Left (Verlant 2000: 445–6). Lastly, we recall his written response to rightwing journalist Michel Droit's diatribe following the release of "Aux Armes et cætera," which he notoriously signed "Lucien Ginsburg dit Serge Gainsbourg."

Beside the flattering recognition Gainsbourg would have felt at being asked to write such an anthem, we can therefore venture that it sat well with his clear sense of belonging to the Jewish people, even in the absence of any religious dimensions.[5] Writing a military march for the armed forces of Israel, at a time when the young nation was again under attack from its neighbors, and when, importantly, it benefitted from a largely positive image in France, would have had a quiet and unproblematic logic to it. While it would be misleading to suggest that Gainsbourg truly identified with Israelis—in a 1982 interview on France Culture, he stated to Noël Simsolo that, an Ashkenazi Jew himself, he was "not a guy from Israel"—we sense in the song a genuine solidarity. In particular, the use of the first-person pronoun and the resolute tone used throughout convey the sense of the singer-songwriter standing by the Israeli, not as one of them fully, but plainly as an ally, a friend, a comrade.

A Reluctant Patriot

In 1948–9, Gainsbourg was called to do his military service in Courbevoie, a period he would later blame for having introduced him to drinking (although we could argue that he was a particularly apt pupil), but also recall fondly for the ties he forged there: "It's in the army that I experienced my closest friendships, something I won't forget." (Pascuito 2006: 30) Indeed, throughout his life, he maintained ambivalent relationships with military and police institutions, as shown through the artifacts he collected, his choice of clothing, some of his songs, and other anecdotes. His *hôtel particulier* at 5 bis Rue de Verneuil enclosed a number of heirlooms and objects having to do with the police and the army. We find, among other things, a collection of police badges and shields, including a German "Polizei" insignia, a book on guns open on a display table, and a framed article by notorious anti-Semite Edouard Drumont entitled *"À bas les Juifs, vive l'armée"* ["Down with the Jews, three cheers for the army"] (Lelièvre 2008: 31), which he would have no doubt cherished with jubilant irony. In terms of clothing too, Gainsbourg showed a penchant for military-like dressing. Indeed, as I have argued elsewhere, the man wore a type of uniform (Grenaudier-Klijn 2012: 105). For the concert series he gave at the Palace in late 1979, he opted for a military jacket. On the picture initially considered for the sleeve of *Rock Around the Bunker*, taken by Tony Frank, Gainsbourg asked to be photographed wearing a Wehrmacht jacket, complete with eagle and swastika, in front of an enlarged black & white photograph of German soldiers parading.[6] Some of his songs—"Mon Légionnaire," "Kiss Me Hardy"—allude to the military world, most noticeably "La Nostalgie camarade" (1981), whose lyrics lose their ironic grip in the warmhearted conclusion, any incrimination being tempered by the generally understanding and affectionate tone in which Gainsbourg sings it. The songwriter also deliberately cultivated the legend around the alleged ties of his partner Bambou (a.k.a. Caroline von Paulus) to Nazi Fieldmarshal Friedrich von Paulus. Lastly, it is among police officers that Gainsbourg pursued some of his closest friendships—on his own confession, his friends in the police reminded him of his mates in the army (Verlant 2000: 90). Thus, he would drop by the police precinct of Paris's sixth arrondissement on a regular basis, and in the last two years of his life would become close to Michel Bouchet, head of the narcotics division in the French police.

Anecdotal as they may be, these small details are indicative of Gainsbourg's mixed feelings toward the masculine world of the police and the army. On the one hand, reflecting back on his military service, the artist denounced and criticized a brutish and inane environment, replete with latent anti-Semitism, violence, and idiocy. On the other, he seemed to have yearned for its orderly and Spartan esthetics, stable and noble values, and the male camaraderie, which, too shy, wary, or self-conscious, he rarely had the opportunity to experience. We could surmise, thereof, that writing "Le Sable et le Soldat" allowed him to put his musical talent to the service of a world seen through a partly distorting lens: the uncomplicated domain of the brave, manly, handsome, righteous, and patriotic *sabra*. Knowing how masterful Gainsbourg was at carving his own legend, his assertions to Patrick Bouchitey in 1984 that, had things taken a wrong turn in 1967, he would have gone to Israel not to fight, but to die for the "homeland" have to be taken with a very large grain of salt. Yet, if the song is imbued with the fervor befitting a military march, we also discern from its simple lyrics an earnest tenacity and slight melancholy denoting Gainsbourg's inherent isolation and quest for acceptance by (male) others in a clearly defined setting.

A Prelude to *Rock Around the Bunker*

Throughout his life, Gainsbourg was pulled between the dedication of the serious artist and the boisterous posturing of the media personality, conscientiously drip-fed by regular controversies. Moreover, as pointed out by Olivier Julien, he systematically, and ambiguously, denigrated the art form that contributed to his fame and success, qualifying it as an "*art mineur* [low art]" (Julien 2018: 49). Yet, there exists a moment in the singer-songwriter's career when the gap between these two poles lessened substantially. Rather, a moment when imagination and provocation, audacity and creativity, Anglo-American pop rock and ingenious alliterations in the French language walked hand in hand on uncharted territory: his 1975 LP *Rock Around the Bunker*.

If the recording of this album was completed in a week (Verlant 2000: 450), its conception lasted thirty years (Szpirglas 2011b: 41). Not surprising when we consider the album's ambitious scope, challenging theme, and visionary structure. *Rock Around the Bunker* tells the story of Nazism, from the emergence of the movement—the Night of the Long Knives—to the cozy retreat of remorseless Nazi criminals in Latin American havens. Crooning, rocking, whispering, Gainsbourg uses the first person, going as far as impersonating an SS and even Hitler himself, and blends burlesque humor and acid irony in a manner auguring of Pierre Desproges's infamous 1986 sketch on French anti-Semitism.[7] Like Desproges after him, the songwriter undermines an abject ideology by becoming the very character(s) he seeks to denounce. Succeeding at such ambivalence requires copious amount of self-belief and a hefty dose of legitimacy, hence the time required to mature, evolve, and refine his artistic intentions.

Returning now to "Le Sable et le Soldat," it is tempting to read the song as the seal of approval Gainsbourg needed to progress with *Rock Around the Bunker*. Let us remember that the song was never intended for a French audience; we can therefore discard reading it as a preparation of some sort, Gainsbourg's public token of anti-antisemitism. Rather, having written "Le Sable et le Soldat" at the request of an Israeli official enabled Gainsbourg to give *himself* the permission to proceed with an album, which, as he rightly anticipated, would be ill-received and largely misunderstood (Verlant 2000: 452). The phrase "Yellow Star," repeated twelve times through the eponymous song, which ends with a sardonic "Oh! Yeah," thus duplicates in a way the repeated "Israel" on "Le Sable." As if Gainsbourg was declaring: "Because I am a Jew, I give my support to Israel; because I am a Jew, who had to wear the yellow star during the Occupation, I can make puns on 'Smoke Gets in Your Eyes.' I have the legitimacy to do this. If not in your eyes, at least in mine."

In Conclusion: A Not So Incongruous Track

Suspicious of loudly proclaimed "good intentions," Serge Gainsbourg seldom endorsed public causes—he did not sing for the *Restos du cœur*, the food aid initiative launched by his friend Coluche—or signed petitions, even if he did issue generous checks for a range of causes, including the police orphanage. The singer-songwriter also had an uncanny ability to foretell the *zeitgeist* in French society, and we may wonder whether he would have acquiesced to Avraham Scherman's request in the 1970s and 1980s, when the government of Israel was being increasingly criticized in France. But the fact remains that in 1967, despite his stated rejection of any form of commitment to TV presenter Jean Paget that very year (Szpirglas 2011b: 41), he did write "Le Sable et le Soldat," at the request of the Israeli embassy, in full awareness of the song's intended purpose.

If the song displays none of the inventiveness and lyrical ambivalence that would soon become Serge Gainsbourg's trademark, and therefore sits somewhat at odds with the remainder of his repertoire, it does, however, have a place in the composer's personal and creative journey. Its simple lines stress the role played by Jewishness, anti-Semitism, masculinity, and "militariness" in the construction of the artist's persona(lity), questions and topics that would resurface time and time again throughout his career. The song also illustrates Gainsbourg's ongoing quest for (self-)legitimacy and (self-)acceptance, and the role an individual track may be playing in regard to an ulterior, more ambitious project, as is the case with *Rock Around the Bunker*. Lastly, "Le Sable et le Soldat" highlights the paradoxical underworld that characterizes the songwriter's motivations and richly kaleidoscopic creativity, and his ability to keep surprising us, even if only posthumously.

Notes

1 For this section, I am deeply indebted to Mourgues and Leprince (2018).
2 I am most grateful to my colleague Stephen Duffin for his illuminating comments on the song's musical structure.
3 *"Je n'ai pas de racines, je suis un pauvre garçon déraciné"* (Gainsbourg 2006: 36).
4 There are no longer denominational sectors in the Montparnasse cemetery. The Gainsbourg's family plot is located in the first division, first section.
5 According to Jérémie Szpirglas, Gainsbourg was photographed only once wearing a kippah (2011b: 50). However, in 1969, he bought a platinum Star of David pendant at Cartier, a gesture his daughter Charlotte emulated (Pascuito 2006: 167). See also Verlant 2000: 419.
6 Deemed overtly provocative, the picture was discarded (Szpirglas 2011b: 42).
7 Pierre Desproges created this sketch in 1986. It starts with the line *"On me dit que des Juifs se sont glissés dans la salle… Vous pouvez rester"* ["I am told Jews have made their way into the room… You can stay"].

"Vu de l'Extérieur": Gainsbourg's International Reputation

5

Contention and Consensus: Posthumous Press Coverage of Serge Gainsbourg in the UK

Chris Tinker

Media coverage of Serge Gainsbourg, whether in the French-speaking world or beyond, is of fundamental importance to our understanding of his significance. Moreover, posthumous coverage plays a distinct role in the ongoing construction of his celebrity. To use Cath Davies's terms, such media coverage "acts as an effective summation of the construction of [the] star persona when alive, whilst also signaling the development of [a] posthumous media image" (2012: 193). Posthumous celebrity also emphasizes the production of new meaning (184). Certain discourses of posthumous celebrity are, however, stronger than others, which are neglected, forgotten, or repressed (see Dyer 1979: 3; Palmer 2013: 384). As Joli Jensen observes: "Posthumous reputation is clearly a contested process, one that is continually being negotiated with and against mass mediation" (Jensen 2005: ix, xviii). This chapter will illustrate how posthumous press coverage of Gainsbourg in the UK context generates competing discourses concerning his musical, artistic, and creative contribution and his personal qualities, and develops a comparative UK/French dimension, which both reinforces and questions the originality of his contribution, the significance of the version of "Je t'aime… moi non plus" that he recorded with Jane Birkin, and his capacity to bridge a perceived cultural gap between the UK and France. At the same time, posthumous press coverage generates more fixed, consensual representations of Gainsbourg concerning his personal, family, and professional relationships. This study draws on an online (nexis.com) database search of the British press (2014–18, 964 articles) in a mix of national quality/tabloid and regional/local titles.

Competing Discourses

Personal Qualities

Coverage attributes to Gainsbourg and his work specific personal qualities, both desirable and otherwise, or a mixture of both. Positive assessments view him as a progressive figure—"multi-talented" (*s.n.* 2017e); a "stylish"/"style icon" (Robert

Johnston 2018; *s.n.* 2016f), identified, for example, with garments such as the pea coat (Davies 2015) and tennis shoes (Hills 2015); a "romantic icon" (Webb 2016), "charisma[tic]" (Wonfor 2015), and associated with the "spirit of '68" (*s.n.* 2017b), "unattainable cool" (Doig 2017), and the "avant-garde" (*s.n.* 2017d). In addition, his "italicized" handwriting is said to be "elegant" (Gibbons 2018). More negatively, Gainsbourg is regarded in base terms as "boorish" (Perrone 2015b), "ugly" as a young man (Holledge 2018),[1] "oversexed" (Kidd 2016); "sex-obsessed" (Leigh 2018); a "drunken sexpot" (Davis 2017); and a "dirty old man (naturally)" in André Cayette's 1969 film *Les Chemins de Katmandou* (Hodgkinson 2017). The use of dated terms such as "dirty old man" and "sexpot" in the UK context shows a reliance on clichéd journalese and traditional norms relating to male heterosexuality. For example, the term/catchphrase "you dirty old man" was not only the title of a 1973 Three Degrees song ("Dirty Ol' Man"): it was also famously used by Harry H. Corbett's character Harold Steptoe with reference to his father Albert in Ray Galton and Alan Simpson's 1960–70s BBC sitcom *Steptoe and Son*. Such terms also seem to be symptomatic of prevailing stereotypical British/Anglo-Saxon (in contrast with French) puritanical, self-consciously shameful attitudes toward sex in sections of the popular media. They are indeed reminiscent of bawdy/saucy vintage British seaside postcards and the *Carry On* comedy film series (1958–92), and resonate with popular stereotypes of "No sex please, we're British" (the title of the 1971 British farce by Alistair Foot and Anthony Marriot).

As well as including positively and negatively connoted terms, coverage also refers to ambivalent personal attributes, positive and/or negative according to the reader's personal value system. Gainsbourg and his sartorial style are said to be "rakish" (Cochrane 2014; Elan 2016b); he is referred to as "outrageous" (Willsher 2015), a "provocateur" (Chrisafis 2015; Lucas 2015), "elegant and scruffy" (McMullen 2016), "bohemian" (Cochrane 2014; Davies 2015; Myskow 2017; Warburton 2016), the alliterative "devastatingly disheveled" (Beddington 2016), "the subversive libertine" (Hoskyns 2015), "louche" (Foster, Ruby & Powell 2018; Selway 2017; Singer 2017), and a "maverick" (Bryan 2018a; 2018b).

Artistic Contribution

Gainsbourg's music is viewed for the most part positively, at times in sophisticated, complex terms: he is regarded as "a French cultural Titan" (McLean 2017), described following his death by the then President François Mitterrand as "our Baudelaire, our Apollinaire" (Day 2017); regarded as an exemplar in terms of versification/rhythm patterns, for example, where the song "Le Poinçonneur des Lilas" is concerned (Kimpton 2015). *Histoire de Melody Nelson* is reported to feature in a list of forty celebrated albums, and regarded by Chris Harvey as "sublime, an extraordinary collision of funk bass, spoken-word lyrics and Jean-Claude Vannier's heavenly string arrangements" (O'Connor, Harvey & Brown 2018). In interview, Johnny Nicholds of the Mustard and Blood musical collective describes Gainsbourg's "output" as "so eclectic it's practically impossible to define" (Rodger 2016). Verrico and Davis (2016) describe Gainsbourg's vinyl compilation album *Couleur café* (2016) as particularly "creative": "these collage-like recordings from early in his career are essential listening. Decades before 'world music' came into vogue, Gainsbourg was assimilating rhythms from Africa and the Caribbean." Moreover, such is the potential power of Gainsbourg as a positive symbol of European belonging that McColm (2016) effectively identifies him as a seemingly "trivial" but nonetheless "valid" reason for voting Remain in the 2016 UK Brexit Referendum.

Coverage also generates a positive view of Gainsbourg's status and influence both in French and wider international contexts. Press coverage locates Gainsbourg firmly within a broad French *chanson* tradition with references including Charles Aznavour, Jacques Brel, Michel Legrand, Edith Piaf, and Charles Trenet (Bremner 2018; Davis 2018; *s.n.* 2018c; *s.n.* 2018g). Reference is made to the UK-based Anglophone and Francophone popular music artists who cover his songs such as the Belgian singer Gabrielle Ducomble (*s.n.* 2014b; *s.n.* 2017a; *s.n.* 2016b) and Mustard and Blood (Rodger 2016), as well as to Gainsbourg's influence on and similarities with current/new generations of Anglophone artists and their own output including Arctic Monkeys (Hodgkinson 2018; Petridis 2018; Stolworthy 2018), Beck (Hodgkinson 2014a), Jarvis Cocker (Stanley 2014), the DJ duo Disco Smack (*s.n.* 2015a), Gaz Coombes (Cripps 2015), Gruff Rhys (Beech & Kaplan 2018; Bray 2018), and Texas's Sharleen Spiteri (Boyle 2015; Mugan 2016; Perrone 2015a; Rees 2017). The influence of Gainsbourg on Baxter Dury and the latter's recognition from French listeners—"beloved by the French as an English Serge Gainsbourg" (Male 2018) are also emphasized (*s.n.* 2014e; *s.n.* 2018h; *s.n.* 2018b).

On occasion, Gainsbourg's music is represented in negative terms. Chris Leadbeater (2017) associates Gainsbourg with the French "stereotype" that "their music is two-dimensional" and the "cliché" that "French music starts with Edith Piaf and ends with Serge Gainsbourg," and views Daft Punk, for example, as more representative of "the reality." Jay Rayner's 2014 review of the Blanchette restaurant in London's Soho also views Gainsbourg's musical output in negative terms: "Serge is still a whole dairy's worth of overripe cheese."

A range of views on Gainsbourg's musical contribution are mobilized in coverage that draws Franco-British comparisons. In a 2015 *Guardian* article by Michael Hann, critical of John Whittingdale—the then UK Culture Secretary—and his perceived "peculiarly reductive view of art, in which there have to be winners and losers, and winning is decided purely by commercial success," Gainsbourg is effectively viewed positively as an example of "dangerous iconoclasts, who kick against the establishment." Negative views of Gainsbourg's music are also generated via comparisons between the UK and France as well as other EU countries. Dominic Sandbrook (2015) emphasizes the success and reach of British popular culture on the world stage via a somewhat negative comparison incorporating Gainsbourg: "Perhaps, if Paris had beaten London for the right to host the [Olympic] Games in 2012, the world might have been treated to a retrospective of the works of Johnny Hallyday and Serge Gainsbourg." Allison Pearson's 2016 *Daily Telegraph* article "The idea that Britain's membership of the EU has led to our brilliance in the arts is beyond absurd," a response to an open letter

(May 19, 2016) published in the *Guardian* and the *Telegraph* by 282 actors, writers, artists, and musicians warning against the UK's cultural/artistic marginalization as a result of Brexit, also implies a rather negative view of European popular music culture—Gainsbourg included—particularly when compared with British output.

Finally, the question of Gainsbourg's originality and uniqueness as a musical artist is both reinforced and questioned in coverage. Gainsbourg's singularity is said to be without equivalent in the English-speaking world in an article citing the personal view of the British journalist Bernard Levin that "We do not have a Serge Gainsbourg" (*s.n.* 2018d). On the other hand, Jeremy Allen (2017) suggests that Kanye West is Gainsbourg's "modern-day equivalent": the former's mediatized 2018 meeting with US President Donald Trump is likened to the latter's burning of a 500 franc note on television in 1984; both musicians are said to rely heavily on specific influences (Gainsbourg on Chopin; West on Nina Simone); and the Kanye West-Kim Kardashian coupling is compared with that of Gainsbourg and Birkin.

"Je T'Aime… Moi Non Plus" and Its "Eroticism"

Unsurprisingly, "Je t'aime… moi non plus" (specifically the 1969 version featuring Gainsbourg and Birkin), including the controversy that surrounded its release, figures repeatedly in coverage. The song is often referred to in rather dated tabloid language which emphasizes the aforementioned long-held "cheeky" stereotypes of British/Anglo-Saxon embarrassment where the subject of sex is concerned: "saucy" (Clay 2015), "salacious" (Khaleeli 2015a), "steamy" (Hall 2018; Stuckert 2017; *s.n.* 2016e), "steamily cheesy" (*s.n.* 2018f), and the "classic ode to le rumpy pumpy" (Elan 2016a). At times the terms used are emphatically alliterative: "orgasm ode" (Selway 2017), "sexy song" (Buckley & Creighton 2015; Harris 2016), and "scandalously steamy song" (Dirvanauskas 2016). The moaning, sighing, "panting" (Hassell 2017) and "heavy breathing" on the track is the subject of speculation (Kidd 2016; *s.n.* 2016d) as well as scientific explanation (Chisholm 2016). Interviews with Birkin scotched rumors that the couple were being recorded having sex (Myskow 2017; *s.n.* 2016d). Although the original and lesser known 1967 Gainsbourg/Bardot version of the song receives little coverage, Bardot's letter to the record company asking for the song not to be released due to its "steamy" content following the objection of her then husband Gunter Sachs is cited (*s.n.* 2014d).

The ability of the song to generate strong reactions, if not embarrassment, in the UK context, is also referenced in reviews of an edition of the student television quiz show University Challenge, during which the contestant Oscar Powell from Peterhouse College, Cambridge displays a particularly expressive reaction, screwing up his face.[2] In certain examples of British coverage, the song is not to be taken seriously and is identified as a suitable subject for "parody." A comedy version of the song "Je t'aime ('Allo 'Allo)" (1986) by the characters René and Yvette (Gordon Kaye and Vicki Michelle) from the BBC comedy, *'Allo 'Allo!* (Legge 2017), along with a further "spoof version" (1971) by the comic actors June Whitfield and Frankie Howerd, are mentioned repeatedly.[3]

In addition, certain accounts challenge the supposed eroticism of the song. Shari Low fails to "find anything remotely sexy about a rasping ditty that sounds like an advert for a dodgy chat line" (2015), while a 2015 *Scottish Daily Mail* article asks,

> Isn't it time we admitted "Je t'aime" is about as sexy as the Pope? The combination of a wheezy French walrus and peeping English sparrow is so unerotic it could be part of an EU initiative to persuade people to save themselves for marriage, or indeed, forever.
>
> (s.n. 2015c)

In contrast, Craig McLean (2018) recognizes the subjective and varied response to the song: "[Gainsbourg] wrote the sexiest—or, sleaziest, depending on your view—song ever, 'Je t'aime… moi non plus.'" Stefan Kyriazis (2015) notes the capacity of the song to produce individual, contrasting responses within listeners: "Almost 50 years later the iconic opening organ still manages to be stirringly seductive AND raise a smile." Catherine Gee *et al.* (2014) associate the song with a stereotypical British schoolboy sexual fantasy ("the masturbatory promise of its unmistakable organ sound thrilling British schoolboys well into the mid-1970s") while explaining the actual, denotative meaning of the song: "The untranslatable title (literally, 'I love you, me neither') celebrates the sublimation of the self through erotic bliss." In interview, the singer-songwriter Charli XCX both valorizes and problematizes the erotic qualities of the song: "This song makes me feel sexy—it makes me want to have sex. But there's also an uncomfortable element to it—it's very on the line" (s.n. 2014c).

Beyond "Je t'aime… moi non plus" and its affirmation of heterosexual identities, press coverage on occasion articulates gay or queer alternatives within Gainsbourg's musical repertoire. Claire Sawers describes how "Piaf's hit 'Mon Légionnaire' went on to be a gay disco anthem in the Eighties, after Serge Gainsbourg recorded it and added new connotations" (s.n. 2016a). In interview, Héloïse Letissier (also known as Christine and the Queens, Chris and Redcar) associates the queering in his own work with that of Gainsbourg in his song "Love on the Beat":

> It's a record that complicates the narrative of Serge Gainsbourg, because it's really queer. It's about back rooms and sex with men, and French people don't listen to that record. Serge Gainsbourg remains the dude who had shitloads of girlfriends.
>
> (Pollard 2018)

Cultural Link between France and the UK

A final area of discord in UK press coverage concerns Gainsbourg's supposed status as cultural link between France and the UK. On the one hand, Gainsbourg is credited with bridging a perceived division between the two countries. For Roisin O'Connor (2017), Gainsbourg is an exception to the rule that "British and US audiences still take some convincing before they connect to a non-English language song." Darin Hutson (2015) also identifies him as one of the few "odd exceptions" to the rule that French music does not travel well and is not generally successful in the UK. "Je t'aime… moi non plus" is singled out as a song forming part of an eleven-minute "soundtrack" that "rang in the New Year" (2019) in London, "celebrat[ing] Europe's finest musical artists," and emphasizing the capital's relationship with Europe despite the prospect of Brexit (*s.n.* 2018o). Gainsbourg is also viewed as a way of bridging the cultural gap between France and the UK in coverage of Jane Birkin's 2017 symphonic Gainsbourg tribute concert at the Barbican Centre in London: "All those young couples at Jane Birkin's Barbican homage to Serge Gainsbourg last month were a sign that there's still a chance to narrow the cross-Channel divide" (Cairns *et al.* 2017). Indeed, Clive Davis's review (2017a) of the concert points toward a "mainstream[ing]" of Gainsbourg in the UK, given its sponsorship by the quintessentially British quality brand Marks and Spencer. In one particular article, however, the Franco-British divide is viewed as too great a challenge for Gainsbourg. For Davis (2018), Gainsbourg would have effectively enjoyed greater popularity in the English-speaking world if he had performed songs in English, given a perceived resistance on the part of English-speaking audiences to non-Anglophone songs.

Toward Consensus: Gainsbourg's Relationships

As a whole, coverage generally builds a shared understanding around Gainsbourg's personal, familial, and professional relationships focusing on Birkin, two of his children Charlotte and Lucien ("Lulu"), as well as the singer France Gall, particularly following her death.

Life, Death, and Beyond: Jane Birkin

Press coverage repeatedly reinforces the dynamics of Gainsbourg's relationship with his long-term partner Jane Birkin from their initial meeting and reportedly difficult start on the set of Pierre Grimblat's 1969 film *Slogan* (Holledge 2018; *s.n.* 2018d), to their relationship (coverage of photographic exhibitions of their life together with their family—Cook 2018; Kennedy 2018b) and to Gainsbourg's death and beyond, particularly Birkin's practice of paying tribute, keeping his memory alive, and effectively valorizing their relationship and his legacy.

Press accounts of the relationship emphasize a meeting of two radically distinct characters. In interview, Birkin's brother Andrew refers to "the attraction of opposites," while William Cook comments, "They could scarcely have been less alike. She was young and lovely, health and innocence personified. He was seedy and dishevelled, yet he oozed Gallic élan" (2018), and Birkin herself describes their differences in comparative terms, limiting her view of herself to her physical attributes: "He was a great man—I was just pretty" (Enoch 2018).

The professional/artistic relationship of Gainsbourg and Birkin is represented in varied and complex terms. For example, Gainsbourg is viewed as a relatively neutral/equal "artistic collaborator" (*s.n.* 2017d) and a more paternalistic "mentor,"[4] while

Birkin is identified as his "muse,"[5] describes the pleasure of performing the songs that he wrote for her following their separation, views herself as a conduit for a distinct, feminine ("fragile, girl") side of his personality (McLean 2017), and describes how Gainsbourg wrote poems following their split in order for her to "feel his hurt and live his pain" (Rice 2017).

Coverage also represents Birkin maintaining a relationship with Gainsbourg in death. In interview, she describes "not wanting to let Gainsbourg go" (Bennion *et al.* 2017), and recounts how she placed a "felt monkey, given to her by her uncle when she was five" (Helliker 2017a; 2017b) in Gainsbourg's casket, which she carried around with her and hated the thought of losing (also pictured with her on the 1971 *Histoire de Melody Nelson* album cover photo by Tony Frank). In a review of her 2017 symphonic Gainsbourg tribute concert at the Barbican, Clive Davis recognizes that "It was [Birkin's] intimate connection with Gainsbourg's spirit ... that gave the evening an otherworldly dimension" (2017). Jennifer Selway (2017) also situates Birkin, who "sings Serge's songs more than a quarter of a century after he died," alongside other famous female personalities who "transform their lives into an act of remembrance" following the deaths of their "famous or powerful" male partners—an account which suggests the maintenance of traditional female-male gender roles.

Gainsbourg and Birkin's association is also emphasized in fashion coverage, for example, relating to a commercial-charitable collaboration between her brother Andrew Birkin and the French brand Claudie Pierlot involving the production of T-shirts featuring images of the couple in aid of Anno's Africa (in memory of Andrew's son Anno), which "allows underprivileged children to access education and self-expression in both visual and performance arts" (Sowray 2015). Gainsbourg and Birkin's association is also credited as an influence on the model Alexa Chung's fashion range—her "grey sweater" featuring the words *"J'ai du vague à l'âme,"* is "a nod to Alexa's obsession with Parisian chic and the relationship between Serge Gainsbourg and Jane Birkin" (as well as a reference to Gainsbourg and Franck Langolff's song for Vanessa Paradis, "La Vague à lames") (Freeth, McGuire & Lankston 2015).

Gratitude and Understanding: Charlotte Gainsbourg and Lulu Gainsbourg

Press coverage also represents Gainsbourg's relationship with two of his children Charlotte and Lulu (Lucien), particularly the former given her international career as a film actor. Charlotte is associated with a challenging "unusual bohemian upbringing which involved being looked after by nannies, while her parents partied until the early hours of the morning" (Corner 2017), as well as the "lofty reputations" of her parents "to live up to, or at least be compared to" (Hall 2018), particularly given their musical output. More positively, however, in an interview, she emphasizes the "modesty" they instilled within her and "just being able to watch the way they worked. Neither of them ever took themselves seriously, they were always aware that everything can go away very quickly—an excellent lesson to learn so early" (McMahon 2018). While Gainsbourg's musician son Lulu is less known to British audiences, he similarly expresses a positive image of Gainsbourg in interview: "definitely a great dad ... So sweet. Loving" (Potton 2015).

While coverage recounts the controversy in France surrounding the release of Charlotte Gainsbourg's duet with her father, "Lemon Incest," she explains to Anglophone readers that the lyrics are "a provocative statement" but ultimately "innocent," although it might seem "weird" to say so (McLean 2018). Both Charlotte and Lucien emphasize Gainsbourg's "playful" approach in the song, which, for Lulu, is possibly indicative of Franco-British cultural differences: "Serge was more playful about things like that than the average Brit" (Potton 2015). However, Charlotte suggests that a similar controversy would be far "worse" given today's moral climate, even if, for her and her father, "it was so pure. It was just a love declaration" (Day 2017).

From Eurovision to Lolita: France Gall

Press coverage focuses on Gainsbourg's relationship with France Gall and her winning Eurovision performance of "Poupée de cire, poupée de son" (1965), viewed as innovative where Eurovision entries of the time are concerned[6] and in simple yet complex terms: "a superficially frothy slice of French bubblegum pop with layers of irony and double meaning hidden in the lyrics, which seems to be a critique of the very genre of music it represents" (Lucas 2015).

Coverage also includes reference to the controversy surrounding the song "Les Sucettes" (France Gall, 1966), described as a "sexually suggestive song about lollipops" (Stow 2018), which led to the "abrupt end in 1966" of her partnership with Gainsbourg (Kennedy 2018a; Midgley 2018), who is said to have "referred to her as his first Lolita" (*s.n.* 2018a). On occasion, British press coverage questions the significance of the controversy surrounding "Les Sucettes" in terms of the negative effects on Gall and within the context of current public debates regarding the #MeToo movement against sexual harassment and assault (Groskop 2018), and growing awareness around child sexual abuse in the aftermath of the Jimmy Savile case in the UK. For example, a *Sunday Times* review of an album of Gainsbourg's songs performed by female artists *Vamps et Vampire: The Songs of Serge Gainsbourg* describes the "faux-innocent" song as "more unsettling to our post-Jimmy Savile ears than any of the conventional shockers" (*s.n.* 2014a).

Conclusion

As the foregoing discussion shows, recent UK press coverage of Gainsbourg combines competing and more consensual discourses. Competing discourses relate to his work and personal characteristics, develop a comparative UK/French dimension, highlight a perceived cultural gap between the UK and France, and maintain stereotypical views of British puritanical attitudes to sexuality. More consensual discourses focus on Gainsbourg's personal, family, and professional relationships. At his "best," Gainsbourg is represented as an original progressive, sophisticated, influential, and inspirational figure, potentially accessible to Anglophone audiences. At times, however, opposing views are mobilized, or Gainsbourg is represented in ambivalent terms. Gainsbourg's relationship with Jane Birkin is effectively promoted as part of the ongoing maintenance of his legacy. Coverage of his relationship with his daughter Charlotte and son Lulu seeks to understand the—at times—sexually transgressive qualities of the song "Lemon Incest." While the painful experiences of France Gall in relation to "Les Sucettes" are recognized and recounted, there is the suggestion that this episode might be reinterpreted in light of current developing social and sexual mores. British press accounts of Gainsbourg serve then not only to provide Anglophone readers with insights into and views on the man, his life and his work, but also contribute toward generating social, cultural, and sexual debates of domestic relevance. While this chapter has underlined the value of Anglophone and non-French/non-Francophone media representations to our understanding of Gainsbourg's significance, focusing on written press coverage, future research could usefully consider the importance of other mass and social media forms as well as the roles of individual media producers.

Notes

1   However, in a 2015 article problematizing "ugliness," Stephen Bayley cites Gainsbourg's own positive view of the term: "Ugliness is superior to beauty because it lasts longer."
2   Aftab 2015; Cockroft 2015; Alice Johnston 2016; Khaleeli 2015b; Levy & Brooke 2015; Proto 2015; Sanderson 2016.
3   *s.n.* 2018i; *s.n.* 2018j; *s.n.* 2018k; *s.n.* 2018l; *s.n.* 2018m; *s.n.* 2018n; *s.n.* 2018p; Hardcastle 2014.
4   Townsend 2015; Helliker 2017a; *s.n.* 2017d; *s.n.* 2017c.
5   *s.n.* 2015b; Hoskyns 2015; Davis 2017; Myskow 2017.
6   Lucas 2015; Hodgkinson 2014b; *s.n.* 2018e.

6

The Critical Song of Serge Gainsbourg

Caroline Kennedy

Serge Gainsbourg's songs can be considered a quintessentially French collection. Yet corralling Gainsbourg's output within conceptions of *chanson française* is to limit our understanding of his work. As Chris Tinker puts it,

> One of the most striking features of many of Serge Gainsbourg's songs is their frequent reference to contemporary American mass culture such as film, comic strip and popular music. In addition, Gainsbourg's musical arrangements often draw on jazz and rock 'n' roll styles exported from the USA, and his lyrics reveal a distinct penchant for *franglais*. Gainsbourg is thus responsible for creating a distinctly Americanized form of *la chanson française* in terms of its linguistic and musical representation.
>
> (2002: 187)

In addition, Gainsbourg's songs represent an ongoing material interlocution with song form itself, as it unfolds culturally. This chapter considers the international impact of his work through two prisms: its influence on Australian songwriters and musicians from the 1990s to the 2000s; and the contextual setting for his song, "Je t'aime... moi non plus." It is important to note that these ways of addressing Gainsbourg can be described as being written from within the wheelhouse of songwriting as intellectual labor.

"Je T'Aime... Moi Non Plus" and the Australian Music Scene

Gainsbourg's work often constituted a critical extension of what was possible for song. This is evidenced in the excited reception many of his recordings prompted, from the banning of "Je t'aime... moi non plus" in Spain, Britain, Italy, Brazil, Sweden, Portugal, and Poland, to the "commercial failure" of *Histoire de Melody Nelson* before the album's subsequent success as his "masterpiece" (Anderson 2013: 24, 44, 100). His famously outrageous propositions regularly shocked audiences, and his songwriting reveals an approach that took in conventional song form as a space in which to play and confront—a form that could be broken down, reformed, abstracted, and, at times, perverted. In this mode of making, plays with form and content fuse with social, theoretical, and interpersonal revelation, expanding the potential of song to become a critical expressive art form. While Gainsbourg was always interested in what would work in terms of the latest popular music trends (Woodbury 2016), his songwriting also manifestly contravened any presuppositions that may have been made regarding song's role as merely "popular music," a fodder for teen consumption, or purely commercial composition.

It was this potential that Gainsbourg saw in song and that he assertively materialized in his work, arguably making it attractive to young artists in Australia from the 1980s and 1990s (and beyond). For them, Gainsbourg's songs were sometimes heard popping up on the radio as missives from France. During the 1990s, his music was to be found on cassettes and vinyl in op shops (both in major cities and small towns), although not as readily as they were desired.[1] Hence they were copied, compiled, and shared, passed round in social and artistic groups on cassette tapes. I first listened to a Gainsbourg tape that had been compiled from original recordings in a share house in the early 1990s. Not much later I heard Kim Salmon—of seminal punk band the Scientists and experimental art rock band the Surrealists—cover "Je t'aime… moi non plus" in a live set in Melbourne. Gainsbourg's work had become internationally influential at that stage, his songs being part of the fabric of independent rock and pop scenes in Australia, a sometime influence and touchstone.

Having regularly covered "Je t'aime… moi non plus" in his live solo sets during the 1990s, Salmon still intermittently plays the song today. He says of his discovery of Gainsbourg:

"Je t'aime… moi non plus" met my ears at a very formative stage of my musical development. Prior to age thirteen I had a cursory interest in the music of the 1960s but it was now 1970 and post-psychedelic weirdness was finding its way onto the radio. The Hammond organ loomed large in the soundscape, the way it could evoke the spiritual and erotic at the same time, and never so convincingly as in "Je t'aime… moi non plus." Add to this its insistent throbbing bass and the fact that the lyrical content appeared to be the moans and mutterings (in French to boot) of a man and a woman having sex! It's a miracle it found its way onto radio but it did, and it was a smash hit! This certainly informed my concept of what defined a "song" at this still innocent age for me. It's a far cry from a narrative sung in verses and choruses over some chords strummed on an acoustic guitar. The 1970s were definitely a new era and I was suddenly interested in its apparently new kind of music. This song in particular "fucked" with my idea of what music was at the start of my musical journey. If anything, I had to "find my way back" to things resembling narratives in verses and choruses.[2]

Salmon grew up in Perth, one of the most remote cities in the world, but his engagement with Gainsbourg became part of his psychic creative imaginary. Gainsbourg may have been for him—as he was for others—an example of an artist who considered the question of what a song is as part of the composing process. Indeed, Salmon answered this ongoing question in various experimental and expressive engagements with song form as his years of practice evolved. From "I'm Keeping You Alive" (a philosophical rant that drives towards psychopathy) to "Swampland" (an expression of emotion devised through the literal mapping of blues terrains), his use of lyrics evokes Gainsbourg's modus of the double and triple reference. His plays with expectation and contravention of "ordinary" narrative arcs are expressive of Gainsbourg's influence too.

By 1982, Mick Harvey of the Bad Seeds had also heard Gainsbourg's music while living in Berlin, and he was affected by it to the extent that over time, from 1996 onwards, he translated into English and then performed four albums of Gainsbourg's songs—by any standard a major undertaking of respect. As he noted in an interview for *Flood Magazine* in 2016:

> he wasn't particularly worried about style or the genre these songs were going to be presented in. He was just interested in being as successful as possible. He kept opting for the fashionable production style that was happening at the time, and he hired producers and arrangers who would put his songs into that form. He was concerned with writing the songs—that's what he was interested in.
>
> (Woodbury 2016)

This interest in the song *per se* is an important gift of Gainsbourg to songwriters and something of a conceptual platform for those who were eager to learn from the way he engaged with song form. Even as he pursued commercial success, it seemed that what he wanted to say was something that could be controlled in composition, through the structure of the song. He composed as if song were the vehicle for a key concept, and wrote so that even when his songs were covered or re-produced, they inevitably delivered what he intended in terms of content. To put it differently, Gainsbourg's lyrics were characteristically loaded up with meanings that could fold out to those who were aware of their conceptual layers, as exemplified by "Les Sucettes"—whose crass double entendre in the lyrics was understood by some of the audience, yet not by all.

As for him, multi-instrumentalist and composer Ian Wadley discovered Gainsbourg in a car during a road trip from Brisbane, Australia, after he found a cassette of his songs in the op shop of a country-town where his touring band had stopped.

> We covered "Je t'aime" in Minimum Chips. I thought it was significant at the time that within a year of us doing so, Mick Harvey and Nick Cave were also covering it. It felt like something was in the air. Gainsbourg continued to be an influence for us. He was a kind of mystery figure and we were trying to figure out who he was and why he was big in France. The music appeared to be ahead of its time, borrowing from what was happening in American and UK rock and pop, but poking fun at that as well.[3]

Like Wadley, many artists in independent song-based music scenes in Australia did not study music in formal settings—the sharing of information and music contributed to autodidactic creative cultures. In this context, Gainsbourg was instructive of a certain approach to songwriting and recognition of critical practice. His work was emblematic of a particular type of contextually aware, reflexive process; when hearing it, it seemed a blueprint for experimental songwriting, as opposed to oft-traveled paths in experimental music that posited song as a form one should move away from. Gainsbourg showed what it was to be truly experimental within the boundaries of this conventional form. Playing with ideas of song convention, he referenced multiple contexts—French culture, American culture, historical folk, pop song forms— and drew in a range of strategies to introduce double entendre, burlesque, cynical romanticism, tender awkwardness, confrontation, and presentations of heightened and unaddressed elements of sexuality. These strategies defined a space for songwriters to consider songcraft, performance, and identity as elements that could come alive and converge as through-lines in bodies of song-based work. This, in turn, created space for an enhancement of songwriting's potential as multi-disciplinary, trans-disciplinary, and artful. In this world of making, song structures were foundations that held the keys to whole worlds proposed by songwriters as artists. Gainsbourg's expression as a performer of his own songs was certainly revealing of this if we consider his investing the song, his embodied way of working through the intersection of voice, body, memory, performance, melody, and structure. He traveled as the active progenitor of his songs into television stations and film clips, but always raising song as a form of play and critique. To quote the words of Kim Harrison: his songs were "simultaneously 'throw-away' pop numbers and intelligent, distanced commentary on 'throw-away' pop numbers, and, as such, [they] subvert[ed] the genre in which they [were] working" (2005: 136).

Songwriting Strategies

As mentioned above, Gainsbourg's lyrics are studded with his signature double entendres, so much so that one should really speak French to understand the effect of his wordplays as they unfold in his songs. And yet, the use of double (or triple) entendre seemed to be something Salmon adopted at least in part because of this influence. Thanks to it, themes could now shift and be in flux within one song, subjects could move to and from sexual romance and vistas of darkly threatening underworlds, as they actually do in songs like "Anemone" or "Feel." These tactics can be mapped back to a "Gainsbourgian" strategy in songwriting.

Chris Tinker proposed that Gainsbourg's sense of "playing" with the American form of popular song was a way of engaging with a song form embedded in the *société de consommation* (2002). In doing so, Tinker suggests Gainsbourg contributed to a sense of an opening out of *chanson française* to broader international influence(r)s. Conversely, Barbara Lebrun examines the tendency of contemporary French songcraft to become swamped by values that are Anglophonic ("sensual rather than intellectual"), naming Gainsbourg as a 1960s progenitor of this type of deviation from arguably more critical or intellectual song form typical of French song or *chanson française* (2014: 160). These two distinct ways of situating Gainsbourg within a national sense of French *chanson* see him on the one hand as a progressive craftsperson, absorbing and repurposing American-style popular song approaches in the pursuit of updating contemporary French songcraft; on the other hand, he may be seen as a populist swayed by American cultural imperialism.

This question of Gainsbourg's songwriting values can be answered in the way his work functions and engages with the broader, contested, remit of songwriting craft. His was a critical approach to the form. This idea of criticality that inheres in the art form is described well by Australian artist Helen Johnson when she asserts painting as a critical form. She describes painting as a "site for the production of meaning … a rich field of loadings, neuroses and suggestiveness that can be drawn out alongside esthetic qualities to complicate the making of meaning, and in turn the possibilities for its reception" (2015: 56). If we consider those principles to be transferable to an understanding of song form, critical song might be understood as something that reflects upon the conditions of its own production from within its own form, possessing within its structure the accretion of contextually connected "loadings, neuroses, and suggestiveness." Critical song might be seen to hold to light certain elements of culture, expanding the potential of song form itself, extending the possibilities of what is admissible both musically and culturally. Gainsbourg certainly understood this potential of song form and undertook these procedures in as knowing and significant a way as any other seminal international songwriter. We know he understood these matters, because Gainsbourg clearly denotes questions and assertions directed toward scenes and communities of songwriters and their audiences. Issues raised in song may be socio-cultural and articulated through word play or directness in the lyrics—as in "Je t'aime… moi non plus." Or they may be intersections into heretofore inviolate conventions of the form itself, plays with duration, style, theme, or instrumentation—as, for example, in "Lemon Incest." The use of such strategies and tactics in song affects the sensibility of musical communities and cultures which in turn redirects song's agency and purpose. What is raised in this modus, for Gainsbourg and the Australian songwriters who were influenced by him, is the idea of the critical song as a conceptual space. Of course, this is arguably true of all songs on some level, but a Gainsbourgian style of songcraft carries meaning that continues to fold out. It is a songcraft emblematically under question, where both suggestion and perplexity accrue through time, and where strategic influence gains traction and momentum in a diversity of practices. It is the cut-through that keeps cutting, as opposed to the temporary influence that wanes as culture moves on.

Through Gainsbourg's effect upon Australian songwriters and musicians we can see his achievement of imbuing song with a loaded-up criticality. "Je t'aime… moi non plus"—the song that most influenced Salmon in the 1970s—reveals this unfolding panoply of affect, meaning, and influence. Known the world over as the song that put its author into mainstream consciousness, it is often misunderstood and crassly interpreted. The most famous version of the song—with Jane Birkin—was released in 1969: that year, it charted in the UK and had significant impact elsewhere. The charting world it entered in 1969 included American Top 40 songs like "Aquarius"/"Let the Sun Shine In" from *Hair*, "Sugar Sugar" by the constructed band the Archies and "Honky Tonk Women" by the Rolling Stones. The terrain of this chart music reveals much in light of Gainsbourg's release of the same year.

"Sugar Sugar" was a number one American hit in a year when American cultural colonizing was really gathering pace. Carefully crafted, catchy fluff created by professional songwriters, its subject is ostensibly falling in love (the lyrics "pour your sweetness over me" draw on the classic theme of girl as candy). These absolutely standard things to say in pop song may also be read as statements about sex and the carnal. The happy tunefulness, the harmonic sounds and the agreement of the audience to understand the song as entirely innocent helped that it caused no outrage. "Honky Tonk Women," sitting at number four on the *Billboard* Pop charts that same year, presented slightly more overt sexual themes in a more radical and realistic way. A song that many understood to be about a dalliance with a sex worker was never considered to be too outrageous to be heard by the public and was played widely across most American and international radio stations. It was an advancement upon "Sugar Sugar" in terms of its openness about sex, yet there was a reliance upon a certain level of wanton ingenuousness from the audience that meant the song qualified for worldwide airplay—possibly with just enough outrage to ensure interest, but not enough to create undue difficulties such as the song being banned from radio.

Into this context came "Je t'aime… moi non plus." Comparatively, its incontrovertible presence in terms of conceptions of the explicit or erotic must have been astoundingly direct when heard for the first time. It still sounds direct. As Salmon notes, for a young boy in Australia it was staggering to even hear it on the radio, especially since the climax of the song might also be perceived as the recording of a woman's sexual climax, the perfect hilarious self-reflexive joke for those "in on it." This was a romantic song, but it also played with the idea of popular song form as something that builds musically to its "payoff." Gainsbourg's joke was to work with the twin concepts of musical and sexual climax, the two mirroring each other in mainstream conceptions of popular song. Gainsbourg used the declarative love song as the conceptual frame, much like early-century visual artists turned everyday objects into art. As a songwriter, he engaged directly with themes that were also at play in "Sugar Sugar" and "Honky Tonk Women"—carnal desire, intimacy, and the impact and very feel of intimate contact—but he did so in a direct way with the shades open, as it were. The character-players in "Je t'aime… moi non plus" are equals, for whom desire recedes and re-awakens in waves for both parties; love is declared and undeclared in rounds that, like musical forms, become music. The woman is not made an object in the way that females desired in these other songs of that year were. Rather, the duet proposes the woman as an equal player in the narrative of love, capable of the sexual pleasure she overtly expresses in the song, advancing toward and also dismissing her lover. Ultimately, in our experience of listening, the song itself becomes the object of our scrutiny and question.

Conclusion

In these moves within song form, Gainsbourg turned up the volume on central yet conventionally muted themes of American popular song culture—transgressive desire, sexual immediacy and rebellion, disruptions of mainstream convention, and questions about admissibility. Gainsbourg's themes of romance, sexuality, and desire held a mirror to the unspoken, fraught world held within our everyday attachment to what we think of as contemporary popular song. Yet Gainsbourg took popular song-form to its natural edge—he gave audiences precisely what they had come to desire in popular song, a space of disruption, surprise, questioning, and pleasure. If he pushed this to the limit of what people could accept, as he seems to have done for example with "Lemon Incest," it was nonetheless because the logic of the form demanded this edge be discovered.

The gift of Gainsbourg's work for songwriters through time has been this proffering of song form as an experimental and experiential space. In the song as proposition, material elements of the literary, sonic, musical, stylistic, personal, autobiographical, and embodied coalesce in a way that is responsive to, and critically engaged with, the broader world. These tactics and strategies expand our prospects for the function of song in our worlds, extending its critical and artistic potential. Perhaps this is why so many of his peers still think of Gainsbourg as a key international songwriter: like all seminal artists, he was engaged with both the broader world of context and the form of song itself. It is precisely this questioning (and repurposing) of song from within its very conventions that allows us the opportunity to inhabit new worlds of perception.

Notes

1   Op shops are the Australian version of the UK's charity stores. Often church connected, they are second-hand stores run on donations of clothes and bric-à-brac. They were much frequented by 1980s and 1990s Australian underground musicians seeking to buy clothes and music cheaply.
2   Interview with Kim Salmon, September 2022.
3   Interview with Ian Wadley, September 2022.

Part Two

Words and Music

"Du Jazz dans le Ravin": The Beginnings

7

Boris Vian's Visionary Criticism of the Early Work of Serge Gainsbourg

Marianne Di Benedetto

From the time of his very first musical performances, Serge Gainsbourg was seen as one of French *chanson*'s most controversial artists. Thirty years after his death, it is possible to look back with a wider perspective on his prolific work. This chapter focuses on the beginning of his career as a singer-songwriter, and on the reception of his first Philips album, *Du Chant à la une!*, through the eyes of music critic and writer Boris Vian, then a prominent A&R man in the French record industry.

The artistic kinship between Vian and Gainsbourg have already been commented on (Bourderionnet 2011; Verlant 2000): it is therefore interesting to pay particular attention to the former's vision of the latter. Gainsbourg first heard Vian perform his own songs at the Milord l'Arsouille cabaret in 1956. From then on, Vian would always remain a role model (Simsolo 1984: 61). In 1958, it was Vian's turn to discover Gainsbourg. The few texts he wrote at the time are illuminating for anyone interested in Gainsbourg's early work. Now gathered in *Variétés*, they consist of two reviews published in *Le Canard enchaîné* (November 12, 1958) and *Bonjour Philippine* (February 1959), respectively, and two presentation texts for a show at Les Trois Baudets theater in November 1958. In these texts, Vian captures a sense of a singer-songwriter in the making and his very first audiences. He displays an enthusiasm for the new "Canetti artist," with an affection toward Gainsbourg that sets him apart from most critics of the time. Moreover, he cannot be accused of retrospective illusion, considering he died prematurely on June 23, 1959, before Gainsbourg even released his second album—*Serge Gainsbourg No. 2*.

How do these texts represent Gainsbourg, his nascent work, and their public reception? In defending him so eloquently, long before he was widely accepted by the general public, Vian develops a sharp and holistic esthetic analysis of the songwriter's art—lyrics, music, and performance, on stage and on record. Finally, his writing, in particular his rhetorical and lexical choices, appears to be inspired by Gainsbourg's first songs; every line is a powerful tribute, which is also worth analyzing.

Vian and Gainsbourg: Cross Paths and Admiration

"One evening, at Milord, I spy Boris Vian, all pale under the spotlight, spewing forth a series of ultra-aggressive texts before a dumbfounded crowd. That night, I really got an earful from him" (Serge Gainsbourg, quoted in Verlant 2000: 154). According to Sylvie Rivet, who initiated their one-on-one meeting in 1959, Gainsbourg always claimed Boris Vian as "his master" (227). To him, Vian made *chanson* a worthy art form. Even though he had put an end to his own singing career two years before writing about Gainsbourg, Vian remained a leading figure in the French music industry: working for two record companies (Philips and Barclay), he was a prolific lyricist, an occasional composer, and a recognized jazz and *chanson* specialist. In other words, he was quite familiar with the musical landscape of the time.

Some of his texts allow today's reader, as they allowed the public of the time, to meet a thirty-year-old singer-songwriter named Serge Gainsbourg who caught his attention from the earliest days of his career. Jacques Canetti knew of his interest in the up-and-coming singer, which is why he invited him to introduce Gainsbourg to the public for his first show at his theater, Les Trois Baudets. "Who is he? Where does he come from? These are the questions everybody asks" (Vian 2001: 231). In the show's program notes, Vian aroused the spectator's interest in the manner of Diderot at the beginning of *James the Fatalist* (1797: 25). Yet unlike the French novelist, who wanted to confuse and frustrate the reader, he did answer these questions, providing a complete information sheet on Gainsbourg. He presented his Russian origins, his educational and musical background, the beginning of his musical career as a pianist, and his first songs, with both casualness and precision: "expelled from Condorcet high school, he then studies architecture, which he drops for painting, which he drops for the electric guitar" (Vian 2001: 232).

The article published in *Bonjour Philippine* provides additional information. Vian returns to Gainsbourg's beginnings and mentions the persons "responsible for [his] existence," ranging from Michèle Arnaud (who first encouraged him to go on stage) to his own parents, not forgetting Denis Bourgeois and Jacques Canetti (who produced his first album), and finally his arranger Alain Goraguer. Showing his intimate knowledge of the environment, Vian ironically adds: "people are sensitive in this business, so you have to think of everyone" (239). The rest of the text describes Gainsbourg as a "strange character … difficult to define" or a "funny individual," echoing an impression that was apparently shared by many critics of the time—André Halimi, for example, portrays Gainsbourg as a "disturbing and misty" man, and equates him with "an anxiety we enjoy bearing" (1959: 175). Thus, as early as November 1958, Vian picks up on his ambiguous personality, a trait that Gainsbourg himself always tried to put to good use to avoid categorization—as he confessed to Lucien Rioux in 1969, "I am an odd one … Extremely difficult to define" (16).

A Highly Mixed Reception: Vian against the General Public

While Gainsbourg captivated Vian and a handful of critics (he was to receive the Académie Charles Cros Grand Prize on March 14, 1959), his first album was met with cold reception. The press found it "too dark, too negative, too cynical" (76).

Furthermore, it only sold about 300 copies on its first release, for which Vian bluntly admonishes the public:

> Oh, I can already see a specimen listener with a brain covered in lard and a big belly full of optimism protesting that everything is fine and that this modern youth hates what is beautiful ... A big belly blocks your view, or ready-made sentences, or a restful conformism.
>
> (2001: 239)

Obviously sarcastic about the commercial failure of *Du Chant à la une!*, Vian emphasizes how unfair he thinks it is. Six months after the album's release, he prefers to focus on the controversies raised by Serge Gainsbourg "the artist," in which he sees some sort of a consecration—"he already gives the public rumor a lot of work [and] shines brightly in the promotion of Philips discoveries" (239). Among these contrasting opinions, Vian's is particularly enthusiastic; he wishes that Gainsbourg's record "will not be the last" (220) and begins his review for *Le Canard Enchaîné* specifying: "Unpaid publicity. I no longer work at Philips and even if I did, it would be exactly the same"[1] (229). But Vian does not only stand by his claim: he opposes Gainsbourg's detractors with precise arguments and tries to raise public awareness. True to his conception and practice of music criticism, he offers a detailed analysis of Gainsbourg's record, commenting it with pedagogy.

The musical quality of the album is first put forward, starting with Goraguer's arrangements in order to "honor those who are always forgotten." Demonstrating his technical expertise, Vian marks these arrangements (they are all given a note "between 17 and 19 out of 20"), explains that if the piano sometimes sounds off-key, it's because it should have been tuned to the vibraphone, and he calls "Le Poinçonneur des Lilas," "Douze Belles dans la peau," and "La Femme des uns sous le corps des autres" "complete successes (form, style, endings, etc.)" (221). He also defends the way Gainsbourg performs his songs ("listen to the author!"), conceding that his voice may be "a little dull," and his "nasals a little too nasal." But "he doesn't sing opera," he adds; "if you want opera, buy Depraz." It should be noted here that Vian himself is the first in a line of singers with what Catherine Rudent has called "ugly voices"—that is, singers who assume a "technical clumsiness" that can make the audience uncomfortable (Rudent 2010: 71–3).

Above all, Vian insists that Gainsbourg deserves attention because he is breathing new life into the way French songs are made. He appreciates his "strange and real universe" (231) and the fact that he is also musically innovative. In his opinion, Gainsbourg clearly stands out from the stars of the moment: "Le Poinçonneur des Lilas," for example, is "the powerful song prototype that is missing from Yves Montand's current show" (221). With his characteristic corrosive irony, he describes "Ronsard 58" as a "song whose musical style is *not old-fashioned*," unlike "so many of the songs written in France today, that still keep in style with jazz music of 1935 (which was perfect for 1935)" (221). In short, Vian honors a new singer-songwriter who dares to do things differently. An extravagant architectural metaphor sums it up well: "We may, in 1958 and beyond, try to build something other than a stone pavilion with blue-green ceramic inlays and earthenware cats on the roof" (222). As in his other writings on *chanson*, Vian doesn't just express an opinion with his well-known verve: he seeks to analyze the songs as complex esthetic entities. In so doing, he can be seen as an important precursor to Popular Music Studies as they have developed on an international scale since the turn of the 1980s, and also to what Stéphane Hirschi calls "cantologie," that is, a French academic discipline that aims to study *chanson* from every angle, without prioritizing text, music, or performance (2008).

Creative Criticism: A Tribute through Writing

Another point of interest is that Vian seems to pay tribute to Gainsbourg in the very way he writes about him. Through his pen, he shows that he shares more than a way of singing and making songs with this promising artist: he and Gainsbourg share a style, and a way of thinking. As he usually does when he writes about *chanson*, Vian chooses a middle way between criticism and creation, doing what Valérie Dufour calls "creative criticism" (2015). This leads him to cultivate a remarkable stylistic inventiveness, but always in the service of explaining the songs and the artist. For instance, he introduces Gainsbourg, whom he sees as an heir to André Breton (222), with a poetic text with surrealist inspirations, addressed to the audience of Les Trois Baudets:

> He writes and sings songs to give a dark laugher.
> He likes chachlik, Edgar Poe and speed.
> He needs thirty years of life
> He punches the end of his verses.
> He evolves in a strange and real universe.
>
> (231)

Here, Vian distorts the set expression "sour laughter"—playing on colors in French: *rire jaune/rire noir*—to allude to Gainsbourg's cynicism, while the second line is kind of a Dadaist enumeration that juxtaposes a Middle Eastern marinated meat (the chachlik), a famous writer, and a concept; he thus defies logic to say between the lines the hope he places in this very creative and original singer-songwriter. This short poem also allows Vian to sublimate the usual criticism addressed to Gainsbourg at the time—"too dark," "too negative"—and to celebrate his audacity.

An even more striking example may be found in the presentation text Vian wrote in order to introduce Gainsbourg on stage for the same show at Les Trois Baudets: he makes an eloquent pastiche of the song "La Recette de l'amour fou" ["The Mad Love Recipe"], which is already a pastiche itself from magazine recipes (Bourderionnet 2011: 100). Entitled "La Recette du Gainsbourg fou" ["The Mad Gainsbourg Recipe"], this text deliberately rewrites the song: it takes up its structure, its imperative verbs, and its vocabulary.

> Take a twenty-five-year-old boy
> Good at painting, music, song

> Good at life, you know!
> Put him in a room with a piano and a pen
> Let him roam, let him search,
> Let him do as he pleases.
>
> (233–4)

One may also note a reference to the haunting "hole" of the now cult song "Le Poinçonneur des Lilas"—"*des p'tits trous, des p'tits trous, encore des p'tits trous…*"—to announce Gainsbourg's future success in a prophetic way, paying tribute once again to the artist's talent through imitation (234). The strong intertextuality between Gainsbourg's songs and these texts strikingly shows how much Vian already admires the newcomer, at a time when the majority of critics and the public are still skeptical, if not clearly hostile.

Finally, one last element that speaks to Vian's eloquent and visionary tribute to the young Gainsbourg is the way in which he repeatedly stages his words, as if he were literally advocating on behalf of Gainsbourg. In these various texts, Vian shows great rhetorical mastery and follows the principles of the "judicial genre" as presented in the manuals of ancient rhetoric, that is, a type of discourse aimed at accusing or defending someone in the most relevant way possible. Indeed, he respects the rules of argument layout. First of all, he rephrases the accusations made against Gainsbourg so as to better refute them: "You will come and tell me that this young man is a skeptic, that he is wrong to see doom and gloom, that it is not 'constructive' … (Yes, you do say things like that)" (222). Then he applies to prove the listeners wrong and invites them to review their judgment by provoking them. He goes further in *Bonjour Philippine*, transforming the press column into a courtroom, narrating a fictitious pleading: "Serge Gainsbourg, stand up. You are accused of writing fierce songs. You're accused of having a sharp tongue, looking at life through dark-tinted glasses, etc." Like a good lawyer, Vian answers in his place and then offers a defense and illustration of the music critic's role who loves an artist. But, as is most often the case with Vian, comedy soon takes over; the plea goes off the rails and it turns into a vaudeville in which the brilliant speaker ends cuckolded:

> You blame Serge for this song called: "La Femme des uns sous le corps des autres." May I ask you a question: was Gainsbourg the one who invented adultery, and didn't the word exist before him? … Do you feel hurt, sir?/On that note, he gets up and leaves. And I recognize the person who was with him. She's my wife!
>
> (239–40)

In sum, Vian shares with Gainsbourg a worldview and a vision of art, both very demanding and provocative, a kinship that he demonstrates, as Gainsbourg did from the outset, in the very way he expresses himself.

Conclusion

In contrast to the general public and most of the critics, Vian was one of the first writers of his time to claim his admiration for Gainsbourg and to publicly defend the quality of his songs. In so doing, he offers today's reader a valuable insight into the mythical beginnings of an icon. Moreover, these critical articles and program notes written by Vian seem to offer a complete overview of Gainsbourg's first steps as a singer-songwriter and of his now legendary debut album. According to Lucien Rioux, he was, in this respect, truly visionary: "[Gainsbourg] was cursed, here he is popular. Marginal, he is surrounded by the brightness of the spotlights. Denied, he was applauded. Rejected, he became a thought leader, a model, an example" (1969: 8).

Note

1   Wishing Gainsbourg that *Du Chant à la une!* will not be his last record is clearly reminiscent of Marcel Aymé's notes for the album's back cover, save that these notes are more ambiguous and not so sales-oriented—Aymé describes Gainsbourg's lyrics as "bitter" and "melancholic," his music as "a little stingy," and he merely wishes him good luck for the future (1958).

8

Fallen on Deaf Ears: *Confidentiel*'s Visionary Blend of Jazz and *Chanson*

Olivier Bourderionnet

Similarly to world-famous musician Miles Davis (1926–91), Serge Gainsbourg had a long career through which he constantly attempted to reinvent himself and refused to be bound to one style or musical idiom in his quest for commercial success and artistic longevity. A celebrated jazz trumpeter as early as the late 1940s, Davis progressively cast aside bebop in 1959 to explore modal music and eventually went on to adopt electric instruments and elements of rock music in his sound by the end of the 1960s (Carr 2009: 217–18; Davis with Troupe 1990: 297; Myers 2015: 113–14; Santoro 2004: 72–8). Like many others, both Davis and Gainsbourg became aware, during that same decade, that jazz music—their idiom of choice—was not to maintain its leading position as a popular art form. Audiences and the music industry had already shifted their attention toward newer styles and sounds. In the case of Serge Gainsbourg (who, unlike Davis, never had a career as a jazz performer), a clear departure from acoustic jazz orchestrations in search of a pop or rock sound emerged earlier in the decade and constitutes a milestone (no pun intended).

Gainsbourg's trajectory can be broken into a number of periods: the jazz-infused first period, followed by the "pop" Gainsbourg of 1965 that consequently gave way to British-rock-flavored albums, a Jamaican period, etc. (Briggs 2015: 74–7; Hawkins 2000: 163; Looseley 2003: 33). Interestingly, when looking at his work as a singer-songwriter, *Gainsbourg Percussions* (1964) seems to be the first and obvious breaking point, when he supposedly shifted from the tradition of *chanson* he had so far identified with, in an attempt to break free from formal conventions. "*Chanson* is outdated, it's stale" he lamented at the time (Verlant 2000: 116–17). The quality of his lyrics changed on *Percussions*, where the dominant register is that of the farce. If one excepts the lyrics of "Ces Petits Riens" (perhaps stylistically more in tune with his earlier writing), the LP reveals a rather schoolboyish humor that was to resurface in his subsequent work. From a strictly musical standpoint, it represents a stylistic shift from his first four albums where jazzy arrangements dominated a patchwork of songs, some flavored with sounds of early rock 'n' roll, twist, and Latin music. Gainsbourg's collaboration with Boris Vian's former arranger, the late pianist and composer Alain Goraguer, had begun on his first release, *Du Chant à la une!* (1958). It continued on until *Percussions* and beyond. Yet, while the team stuck to a formula that seemed bent on including a variety of styles, the clear intention on *Percussions* was to prominently feature African rhythms, a number of which turned out to have been blatantly plagiarized from Miriam Makeba and Babatunde Olatunji (Simmons 2001: 40; Verlant 2000: 261–2). Today, the idea has become widely circulated that *Percussions* represents an early venture into what was not yet called "world music" (Picaud & Verlant 2011: 135–6). The album looms large in the first decade of Gainsbourg's production and its critical reception tends to overshadow the much less talked-about—and strictly percussionless—*Confidentiel* that preceded it in 1963. Despite the fact that it represents a much more radical artistic departure from the early works, it appears as a historic, albeit failed encounter between Gainsbourg and *chanson*'s most selective audience. Obtaining very modest sales with only 1,500 copies sold of the first release (116), and tucked between *Gainsbourg N° 4* and *Gainsbourg Percussions*, *Confidentiel*'s symbolic dimension is often overlooked, even though it could be argued that it sums up essential elements of Gainsbourg's artistic vision.[1]

In this chapter, I examine the *Confidentiel* moment in Gainsbourg's career, highlighting both the adventurous blend of jazz and *chanson* it created and the modernity of its esthetic project. I also attempt to present it as an important turning point in Gainsbourg's musical trajectory since its commercial failure marks the artist's decision to gradually move away from the jazz idiom. In doing so, I propose a few additional remarks on *Percussions* having to do with the jazz arrangements on this album.

A Minimalist and Self-Reflexive Album

On *Confidentiel*, Gainsbourg seems to brush aside many of his earlier preconceptions toward assembling a successful collection of individually arranged songs for an album. With the help of *"directeur artistique"* ["producer"] Claude Dejacques, the record's minimalist approach turns the raw material of his songwriting into a powerful formal statement. The very title seems to disclose the singer's intention to reveal more of himself in an instrumental configuration reminiscent of Georges Brassens's set up. Throughout the record, he is backed only by guitarist Elek Bacsik, who plays an electric/acoustic jazz guitar, and Michel Gaudry on double bass. Both seasoned bebop musicians, Bacsik and Gaudry contribute a modern-jazz sound to the set of songs. Some of the arrangements sprouted from the trio's collaboration during the rehearsal sessions for a series of shows that preceded the recording.[2] According to Michel Gaudry, a number of them were created on the spot, in the studio, after Gainsbourg demonstrated the songs on the piano for his two backing musicians (Merlet 2019: 130). Rhythmic patterns played on the guitar and distinct bass riffs bring Gainsbourg's music a new vocabulary and a drastically different flavor from the sound of Goraguer's orchestra. In the studio, Bacsik overdubbed a second guitar part to "La Saison des pluies" (a track he actually cosigned with Gainsbourg—Picaud & Verlant 2011: 110) as well as on two other tracks. Except for the fact that the songs on *Confidentiel* leave no room for any individual improvisation from either musician, the recorded trio does boast the sound and mood of a jazz album. With its distinct, syncopated jazz-guitar accompaniment, the rhythmic approach is influenced by American music of the 1950s rather than by that of Grappelli and Reinhardt's Hot Club de France—who can be heard on early recordings by Charles Trenet and whose influence sometimes surface in Brassens's music. *Confidentiel* indeed borrows from many forms of African-American music: blues, spirituals, rhythm and blues, jazz. Its percussion-free, minimalist orchestration offers a selection of vocal melodies backed by a walking bass line and a sparse, be-bop-inspired guitar "comping" that leaves much space for the vocalist. Very few direct equivalents in the vocal jazz album category produced in the United States come to mind, with the exception of Julie London's *Her Name Is Julie* (1955), a collection of jazz songs recorded in the exact same configuration as *Confidentiel*. It is probably no coincidence that in 1954, Elek Bacsik had met and performed with Barney Kessel, the guitarist who, a year later, backed London on her *Her Name Is Julie* (Merlet 2019: 129). Also drumless, the Nat King Cole trio (guitar, piano, and bass) included two harmonic instruments. In 1957, the trio Jimmy Giuffre 3 was one of the first, post-bebop groups to offer a drumless instrumental jazz album.

Alas, to the public of *chanson* whom Gainsbourg was still trying to reach in late 1963 and early 1964, the musical sophistication of the *Confidentiel* project probably came across as too radical. Reviewing one of the October shows of the trio's performance at the Théâtre des Capucines for *Combat*, critic Michel Pérez noted the quality of the songs and Gainsbourg's marked effort to appear somewhat detached from his audience (Dicale 2009: 104–5). Grasping the originality of Gainsbourg's attempt to merge nonmainstream jazz with *chanson* required an ear sufficiently trained to this style to embrace the absence of drums and enjoy the minimalist character of the music. In short, it is possible that a large segment of the French public Gainsbourg was hoping to reach might not have been sufficiently sophisticated to become attached to his new form of *chanson*. In an interview given soon after the release of *Confidentiel*, Gainsbourg lamented: "Jazz has no impact. The low circulation of jazz releases is telling. The French are anti-jazz. That is why my approach is risky. In jazz, I like the avant-garde, Jackie McLean or innovators like Art Tatum" (Merlet 2019: 129).

Confidentiel as the Ultimate Post-Modern *Chanson* Work

In a way, the commercial failure of *Confidentiel* sums up the uncomfortable position of *chanson d'auteur* often lamented by Gainsbourg (Verlant 2000: 117). Acting upon the need for *chanson* to become musically progressive if it were to remain relevant, Gainsbourg refused to compromise with what he perceived as the infantilization of pop. In "Le Temps des yoyos," a line such as "J'ai mis mon banjo au temps des yé-yé" [*"I tuned my banjo to the yé-yé sound"*] suggests his desire to modernize and adapt. At the same time, "Chez les yé-yé"—the album's opening track—stresses the singer/character's obsession over winning back his lover/muse from the *yé-yé*'s, determined as he is to not be ignored by the younger generation.

Throughout *Confidentiel*, it becomes obvious that many aspects of the lyrics match the experimental character of the music to transcend the genre of *chanson*. The self-reflexive dimension present here goes far beyond the ambiguity commonly at play between the artist's life and the artist's persona, where "the musical work and its execution serve the musician's performance of a persona" (Auslander 2006: 102). Without a doubt, the lines do become blurred in "Chez les yé-yé" or "Le Temps des yoyos," where the singing voice using the first person comes across as being the artist's, singing about his yearning for success. Yet in both songs the radical and dominant aspect is that of the actual work becoming the subject of the work rather than the artist turning into the subject of his own songs. When Fréhel sings *"je prends de la coco"* ["I do coke"], the subject matter of the lyrics (substance abuse) remains an external topic to the song itself. Performatively, Fréhel's own damaged body and the biographical resonance of the lyrics create the effect of reflexivity, merging the singer's persona and the artist into one individual (Conway 2004: 93; Frith 1998: 187–97). Alternatively, with "Chez les yé-yé" and "Le Temps des yoyos," the song itself becomes the topic of its own creation as a work of art. One might object that this device is as old as songwriting itself.

Gainsbourg had already showed his taste for self-reflexive devices with "Du Jazz dans le ravin" or "La Chanson de Prévert." Around the same time, Brassens had produced similar self-aware songs such as "Le Pornographe du phonographe" ["The Phonograph's Pornographer"] and "Trompettes de la renommée" ["Trumpets of fame"]. However, this self-reflexive dimension takes a more extreme, postmodern turn in "Chez les yé-yé" and "Le Temps des yoyos." While Brassens's songs questioned the star-system, show business, and the strain associated with making a living by performing and projecting a public persona, the subject matter of Gainsbourg's songs questions the creative process of songwriting itself. Gainsbourg opens a window into the work while it is being written and his lyrics echo the musical statement that the minimal, yet adventurous arrangement makes. By introducing a mirror game between the lyrics and the formal experimentation of the music, he finally transcends the self-reflexive dimension of *chanson*, bringing it to a new level.[3]

A Performative Modern *Chanson* for the 1960s

Modernity spreads over the entire *Confidentiel* album. It affects the architecture of the songs, their rhythmic and strophic layout, as well as the combined materials used—the sounds of the instruments, the quality of the voice recording, the musical idiom and the language. Gainsbourg had already made use of the English language in "La Femme des uns sous le corps des autres" (1958), "Black Trombone" and "Intoxicated Man" (1962), filling the latter songs' lyrics with catchy borrowings such as "pick-ups," "pin-ups," "smoking," and "living room." As early as in his first release, the depressed ticket-puncher of "Le Poinçonneur des Lilas" carried a copy of *Reader's Digest* in his coat pocket. The evocative power of these few words (likely lost on English native speakers) conveyed an exotic character to Gainsbourg's writing at the time.

At the turn of the century, Anglomania and the use of English words in everyday conversation had been a phenomenon that Marcel Proust gently mocked (Karlin 2005: 206–14); Gainsbourg, for his part, found much inspiration in the trend and understood its catchiness in the rapidly changing world of 1960s France. All things considered, *Confidentiel* marks the beginning of a systematic use of English words as props in his lyrics. The language of advertising, magazines, cinema, commerce, expands the scale of English language words already in circulation. Clearly interested in their euphonic quality, Gainsbourg draws from this pool of new words such as *Kleenex*, *Remington*, *Talkie-Walkie* (a mysterious French transformation of the word "Walkie-Talkie") and he also fills his lyrics with references to fashionable consumer products—the Rolleiflex camera (previously featured in the 1959 bossa nova "Desafinado"), nylon stockings, electric razors, etc. As Denise Glaser pointed out during a 1965 interview with Gainsbourg, it seems to have been the artist's preoccupation from the start to produce a form of *chanson* that spoke of its time in the language of its time.[4] Staging a subtle dialogue between content and form, the *Confidentiel* project appears to be built on this very principle and makes Gainsbourg's first twelve-inch album a conscious *mise en abyme* of his artistic vision.

Gainsbourg's Long Farewell to Jazz

In October of 1964, only ten months after *Confidentiel*, the release of *Percussions* marked Alain Goraguer's return for one last full-album collaboration with Gainsbourg. Looking for success and still in search of a form of *chanson* that could match the modern esthetics of the 1960s, this time Gainsbourg opted, with Goraguer's help, to give percussion instruments center stage, after banning them entirely from *Confidentiel*. This second project under Claude Dejacques's wing reinforces the impression already present on *Confidentiel* that the artist enjoys more leeway.[5] On *Percussions*, Goraguer's musical orchestrations can be divided into two categories: on the one hand the dominant, African-inspired orientation, marked by the use of many percussion instruments and background female vocalists; on the other, contemporary jazz arrangements that mark a departure from those he wrote for Gainsbourg's first records. As mentioned earlier, these jazz tracks, which constitute my focus here, also mark the end of Gainsbourg's adventure in that particular musical idiom. On two of them ("Quand mon 6.35 me fait les yeux doux" and "Coco and Co") the orchestra provides a high-energy accompaniment where the percussion elements compete with the singer's voice. The drummer's performance is no longer restricted to the use of brushes as in "Le Poinçonneur des Lilas," for example. Drummer Christian Garros uses sticks, a driving ride cymbal and is given ample space for drum breaks. On these tracks, the approach in Michel Portal's alto saxophone playing presents similarities with that of American saxophonist Jackie McLean. Gainsbourg had discovered McLean's sound a few years earlier through the Living Theater production *The Connections,* as he recalled during his lengthy interview with Noël Simsolo (1982).[6] With "Machins choses" however, the musical ambiance becomes much more hushed. The high-energy, Charlie-Mingus-orchestra-like sound of "Quand mon 6.35 me fait les yeux doux" is replaced by a softer sound one might more readily associate with cocktail-lounge music. Over Eddy Louiss's harmonies played on the Hammond organ, Portal's saxophone now evokes Paul Desmond from the Dave Brubeck quartet. With the exception of earlier efforts such as "Du Jazz dans le ravin" and "Intoxicated Man," Goraguer's arrangements for Gainsbourg had included relatively few parts where the session musicians were asked to solo, until *Percussions.* On "Machins choses," "Quand mon 6.35 me fait les yeux doux," and "Coco and Co" they are given free rein. These three tracks, along with the entire *Confidentiel* album, represent the symbolic end of a creative encounter between chanson and jazz that had begun in the 1930s with Mireille, Pills et Tabet, and Charles [Trenet] et Johnny [Hess].

Boris Vian in the 1950s had vowed to continue that tradition and modernize it. In his view, too many of the jazz arrangements written for *chanson* in post-Second World War France still relied on a style of jazz dating back to the 1930s (1966: 170–1). With the help of Alain Goraguer and Jimmy Walter, he managed to pair the sounds of modern jazz with chanson. His recordings made a very strong impression on Gainsbourg (Simsolo 1984: 61–3) who, in turn, chose to further explore that direction obtaining outstanding results on a purely artistic level, but failing on the commercial level. By the following year, Gainsbourg had come to the conclusion that the new musical landscape of the 1960s had little use for jazz and that he now needed to compose rock music to finally reach celebrity. Echoing Boris Vian's review of *Du Chant à la une!* (1958), he even told Lucien Rioux that "Today's jazz, all of those trying to adapt it are stuck in the style of 1955 or so" (1969: 72).[7] Abandoning his attachment to jazz esthetics as well as to some of the *auteur* values of *chanson* associated with the Canetti brand, he gave up live performances around the same period.

If it is true that Gainsbourg's trajectory can be characterized by a succession of brutal break-ups (with painting, with jazz, or music partners), his production nevertheless shows that throughout different periods he continued to refer to the esthetics of his formative years. I have explored elsewhere the ongoing influence of jazz music on Gainsbourg's prosodic approach, his use of quotes, borrowings, and rewriting of existing material (Bourderionnet 2011: 66–7). Jazz remained a reference throughout his explorations of other genres. After *Rock Around the Bunker* (1975) had featured a rock version of "Smoke Gets in Your Eyes," he recorded a cover of "Gloomy Sunday" for his final release, *You're Under Arrest,* attesting to his lasting attachment to the jazz repertoire—this album's title itself was likely inspired by Miles Davis's own *You're Under Arrest* album, released two years earlier. Recording sessions for an upcoming album scheduled to take place in New Orleans in 1991 even suggest that he was, by the end of his life, on the cusp of reconnecting with his old muse by returning to the roots of jazz music. Unfortunately, he passed away before he could make the trip to Louisiana.

Notes

1. The LP soon became a much sought-after rarity among collectors, until its re-release in 1983.
2. In October that year, Gainsbourg appeared every Thursday at the Théâtre des Capucines in a trio. The first of these shows was attended by many Parisian celebrities including Juliette Gréco and Georges Brassens. The studio album *Confidentiel* was recorded two weeks later, in mid-November, and a selection of live recordings from the Théâtre des Capucines in October 1963 was eventually released as bonus tracks on a 2001 re-release of *Confidentiel*, then as a live album titled *1963—Théâtre des Capucines* in 2009.
3. A couple of years later, the lyrics to "Poupée de cire, poupée de son"—the song he wrote for France Gall—further explored the realm of self-reflexivity in songwriting and performance. A line in the song translates as follows: "My records are a mirror/In which everyone can see me" [*"Mes disques sont un miroir/Dans lequel chacun peut me voir"*].
4. https://www.ina.fr/ina-eclaire-actu/video/i05063703/interview-de-serge-gainsbourg-par-denise-glaser [accessed 05-05-2023].
5. Claude Dejacques (1928–98) had been recommended to Jacques Canetti at Philips by Boris Vian. He is credited as producer on *Confidentiel*. Gainsbourg's earlier albums had been recorded at studio Blanqui but *Confidentiel* (only a three-piece band) was recorded at studio DMS. Dejacques also began a collaboration with singer Barbara in late 1963 and became her artistic director in 1964. *Barbara chante Barbara*, her first album for Philips singing her own material, was also recorded at studio DMS. The record presents a number of similarities with *Confidentiel* in terms of its minimalist jazz orchestration. Guitarist Elek Bacsik is featured on one of the songs, Pierre Nicolas (Brassens's bassist) appears on several tracks, and other jazz musicians such as Michel Portal (who played saxophone on *Gainsbourg Percussions*) are also featured.
6. Jackie McLean appeared in a production by the Living Theater staged in Paris in the early 1960s. A film adaptation by Shirley Clark was released in Cannes in 1961. The influence of McLean's sound is traceable in some of the songs on *Percussions*. Drugs—the theme of the play—are also the subject of "Coco and Co."
7. In his review, Vian had written: "You will hear 'Ronsard 58,' ... a jazz song whose musical style is *not old-fashioned*, for once, unlike so many of the songs written in France today, that still keep in style with jazz music of 1935 (which was perfect for 1935)" (1958: 6).

"Là-Bas C'Est Naturel": Gainsbourg & World Music

9

"Latin" Gainsbourg and the Parisian Nightclub Scene

Sue Miller

That Serge Gainsbourg made use of Cuban music on recordings such as "Mambo miam miam" (*mambo/chachachá*), "Couleur café" (Cuban *son*), "L'Eau à la bouche," and "Cha cha cha du loup" (*chachachá*) is well known. Perhaps less explored, at least in terms of musical influence, is his background as a performer and musical director within the 1950s Paris nightclub scene and the important role his father Joseph Ginsburg had on his musical development. Both Joseph and Serge (Lucien) Ginsburg worked in Parisian cabarets, and the history of live music in Paris therefore holds a key to understanding Gainsbourg's eclectic artistic output. This chapter, specifically, is a musical investigation into the influence of both transnational Cuban music and the pan-Caribbean popular music-making context of the French capital on his early work. Musical analyses of Gainsbourg's Cuban-influenced recordings not only reveal his overt use of Afro-Cuban elements: they also uncover subtle lines of influence rooted in the more *típico* legacy of the grassroots culture of Cuban music performance.[1]

Cuban music was well established in Paris by the 1930s and was a feature in many clubs. At 42 Rue Fontaine, La Cabane cubaine, for example, featured a house band—the Orchestre Typique Castellanos—which lasted up until the early years of the Second World War. In 1941–2, Joseph Ginsburg was the regular pianist there before the dangers of occupation forced him to move to the free/southern zone to be able to work and earn money to send to his family (Verlant 2000: 43). Before and after the war, Melody's Bar housed another influential Caribbean band, the Barreto brothers led by Cuban guitarist Don Emilio Barreto, which included another Jewish pianist, Raymond Gottlieb (Dalmace 2017: 14). Gottlieb went into exile during the war, returning to the band in 1946. Cuban flautist and saxophonist Hériberto ("Filiberto") Rico was in the Barreto band too before he created his own group, Rico's Creole Band—which performed an eclectic mix of Cuban and French Caribbean styles at La Coupole in Montparnasse for over thirty years, and was a firm fixture of Parisian musical life.

John Cowley, a discographer of French Caribbean recordings, mentions that Rico's Creole Band managed to record French HMV (His Master's Voice) sessions in January 1940, then again in February–March 1941, after the beginning of the German occupation of Paris.² Emilio Barreto's band also managed to perform and tour up until 1941, but then he and most of his musicians were interned at the German concentration camp at Compiègne. According to Alain Boulanger, Emilio Barreto remained interned for the duration of the war before returning to the capital in 1946 to recommence his performance career (2018: 59). Jewish musicians such as Ginsburg and Gottlieb may have been more integral to the Cuban and Caribbean music-making scene than is revealed through the band publicity of the time, and there remains more research to be done on this area of hidden history.

The Parisian Nightclub Cultures of Joseph and Serge Ginsburg

Joseph Ginsburg was a pianist and bandleader with the Tortorella's Jazz Band and Les Blue Star Boys, who performed regularly at Maxim's, Les Enfants de la chance, and La Cabane cubaine (1940–1). He also directed the house band at the Madame Arthur cabaret (75 Rue des Martyrs) before Serge Gainsbourg took over from 1954 to 1956, composing or adapting repertoire to fit the acts there using a variety of musical styles.

For many years, both Joseph and Serge (Lucien) Ginsburg were musical directors for the cross-dresser/transgender acts at Madame Arthur's, where the Cuban *chachachá* style was undoubtedly used for the striptease acts, as exemplified by Serge Gainsbourg's tongue in cheek composition "Cha-cha-cha intellectuel" (Bouvier & Vincendet 2009: 66).³ In fact, what was considered exotic and tropical in 1950s France is illustrated well in the CD collection *Chansons exotiques pour cabarets et music-halls, rythmes orientaux et tropicaux*. Here, music from Cuba, the Mediterranean, Italy, Spain, and Turkey played out with an emphasis on the Right-Bank Paris nightclub scene. Featured on the CD alongside *mambo* big bands (such as those led by Jean Constantin, Dario Moreno, Bob Azzam, Don Barreto y su Cuban Boys, and Marino Marini) were Sophia Loren, Harold Nicholas (singing in Italian!), and Parisian transgender singer Coccinelle. Born Jacques Dufresnoy in 1931, Coccinelle started her career at Madame Arthur's in 1952, accompanied on piano by Joseph Ginsburg (Comoy 2017: 16).

Serge Gainsbourg, in addition to directing the band at Madame Arthur's, performed at the Milord l'Arsouille cabaret at 5 Rue de Beaujolais, and was resident pianist for the summer season for many years at the Club de la Forêt at Le Touquet (Verlant 2000: 110, 123–4). He always claimed that he owed his musicianship to his father—not just for playing and teaching him the piano at home, but for introducing him into the world of musical entertainment. Verlant reports that Gainsbourg's father would play, for his own pleasure, "Scarlatti, Bach, Vivaldi, Chopin, or Cole Porter. He would interpret Manuel de Falla's *La Danse du Feu* or South American tunes. He was a complete pianist" (19). Gainsbourg's penchant for jazz, the American songbook, "world" music, and for the mixing of styles undoubtedly grew from his father's piano playing, his cabaret work in Paris, and from his musical experiences on the summer season circuit. As for his Latin influences, they can be traced, via musical analysis, to these grassroots connections, related as they are to the transnational influence of Cuban music from the 1920s and 1930s through to the mid-1960s. In order to demonstrate his understanding of *clave*-based "Latin" music, I will examine briefly here his Cuban-influenced recordings.

Gainsbourg's Cuban-Styled Repertoire

Gainsbourg drew upon the Cuban styles of *bolero* ("Les Amours perdues"), *mambo* ("Mambo miam miam"), *chachachá* ("Cha cha cha du loup"), Cuban *son* ("Couleur café"), and, more subtly, *danzón/habanera* ("La Chanson de Prévert"), often combining them with other stylistic elements—"Laissez-moi tranquille," for example, is a *chachachá*-rock hybrid. His album *Gainsbourg Percussions* has the most overt use of Cuban rhythmic elements and among the uncredited percussionists on this recording were the French studio percussionists André Arpino, Michel Delaporte, and Jean-Pierre Drouet, who worked regularly with one of Gainsbourg's long-term arrangers, Alain Goraguer (Merlet 2019: 146–7). The assumption that these were Cuban players attests to the well-executed rhythm section playing. One could, however, ask why eminent Cuban musicians in the Barreto, Castellanos, and Rico bands were not engaged for Gainsbourg's Cuban-styled studio recordings. The actual session players may have learnt the styles directly from these Cuban musicians or perhaps via Goraguer himself, who possibly studied with them or listened to them play in the clubs of Rue Fontaine—a.k.a. "Calle Cubana" (Boulanger 2018: 22). Certainly, many musicians from Guadeloupe and Martinique assimilated Cuban styles (e.g., saxophonist and bandleader Félix Valvert), and a few French musicians may also have done so. French Jewish musicians Raymond Gottlieb and Joseph Ginsburg performed in Cuban bands in the city, but were perhaps not promoted much in the publicity posters of the day as promoters wanted to engage authentic (and exotic) Caribbean performers. As with New York, there appears to have been a mix of Cuban, French West Indians, and Jewish musicians in these Cuban bands, and Raymond Gottlieb was indeed an integral part of this Latin Paris scene.[4]

Whether or not Serge Gainsbourg went to hear these bands in Paris is not clear, and his experiences may have been mainly through his father's piano playing at home and through his use of the aforementioned styles in the cabaret bars. His Cuban-styled work mostly belongs to his 1950s and early 1960s repertoire, when Cuban big band *mambo* and *chachachá* were popular internationally. In "Mambo miam miam" (recorded in 1959), those styles are less typical in that the *timbales cha* bell pattern is played on the triangle (and possibly with a lightly played high cymbal), with variations against the one-bar *clave* neutral conga *tumbao* pattern.[5] Christian Garros is credited as playing drum kit on the recording, so he may well have adapted the drum set to play some of these rhythmic textures. Less frantic than the big band *mambos* of Pérez Prado or Tito

Puente, the *mambo* elements in this song reside in the swing band orchestration, the call and response between the vocals and the horn section lines, and the foregrounding of the bongo *martillo* pattern and fills.

The flute enters at 01:27 behind the vocal line with a violin *guajeo*-styled short solo in 2–3 *clave* referencing the *charanga típica* tradition, and thus the origins of the *chachachá*. Use of the *quijada* (jawbone) instead of the *güiro* on beat one is less common in *chachachá* but not unheard of, particularly in Cuban *son*. Alain Goraguer arranged this piece around Gainsbourg's melody and the vocal line is phrased in 2–3 *clave* with the arrangement also following 2–3 *clave* direction. Even without these percussive elements, Gainsbourg's melodies and his vocal phrasing demonstrate some understanding of Cuban music as the next example demonstrates further.

Créativité "Parfumée de Rumba"

What Gilles Verlant describes as a "rumba seasoning" (2000: 191) was more than a flavoring in Gainsbourg's songs. As a matter of fact, a Cuban feel runs through a large segment of his earlier work. Alain Goraguer, who worked on the orchestration and arrangements for the film tracks "L'Eau à la bouche" and "Cha cha cha du loup," contributed to the Cuban and jazz elements on these recordings in the main. However, Gainsbourg's melodic lines and vocal delivery together with his stylistic rhythmic inflections demonstrate his affinity with jazz and Latin phrasing. As producer Claude Dejaques intimates, "His swing was better than everyone else. I think his Slavic origins have something to do with this: via jazz and his pianist father he inherited a sense of phrasing and a distinctive sense of rhythm" (178). In "La Chanson de Prévert," for example, his vocal phrasing follows a Cuban *clave* (Example 9.1) and *baqueteo* two-bar rhythmic organization (Example 9.2), as demonstrated in the following analysis.

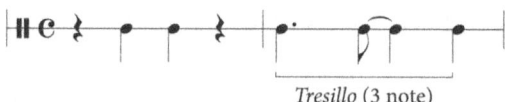

Tresillo (3 note)

Example 9.1 The *son clave*.

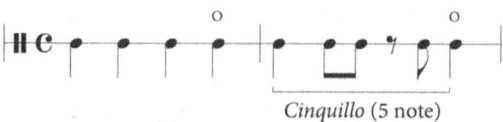

Cinquillo (5 note)

Example 9.2 The *danzón baqueteo* pattern.

"La Chanson de Prévert" and "La Canción de Prévert"

Luca Cerchiari traces the history of "Les Feuilles mortes" as a jazz standard with French origins. Originally an instrumental piece by Joseph Kosma for a 1945 ballet by Roland Petit (*Le Rendez-vous*), it first appeared as a song, with words by Jacques Prévert, in Marcel Carné's film adaptation of Petit's ballet (*Les Portes de la nuit*, 1946) and was popularized in France by Yves Montand's version, followed by Juliette Gréco's. Further recordings of the song in English translation by Johnny Mercer ("Autumn Leaves") resulted in subsequent interpretations as a jazz standard (2012: 110–17). Gainsbourg's "reinterpretation" of the song in "La Chanson de Prévert" adds further layers to its history, and beyond these textual references lie musical ones, which link to the history of transnational popular music making in Paris. Listening to the recording, there is a sense of Cuban *clave* with touches of the *cinquillo* rhythm, emblematic of the twentieth-century Parisian Cuban music scene, underlying the rhythmic movement.

The emphasis on beat four in the bass line and the guitar accompaniment (missing beat one by entering on the "and" of beat one or beat two) provide a backdrop that suggests Cuban *son* and earlier twentieth-century *típico* styles. As shown in example 9.3, Gainsbourg uses touches of rubato, anacrusis, and an emphasis on the three-side of the *clave* (linked to the *tresillo* and *cinquillo* rhythms) on "don-ne," and he has a tendency to start phrases on beat four or the "and" of four coinciding with the bass. While not written deliberately in a Cuban popular style, the phrasing draws on *clave* feel from Cuban dance styles that were played in Paris for over thirty years before the recording was made. The *cinquillo* pattern with the *danzón* two-bar pattern alongside the *son clave* two-bar timeline under verse 2 demonstrates these correlations between Gainsbourg's vocal phrasing and the *contradanza* (*danzón baqueteo* and *son tresillo*), reflecting Filiberto Rico's Orquesta *Típica* Cubana influence, the *danzón* background of Les Frères Castellanos, and Emilio Barreto's roots in the charanga of Tata Pereira (Boulanger 2018: 43, 73).

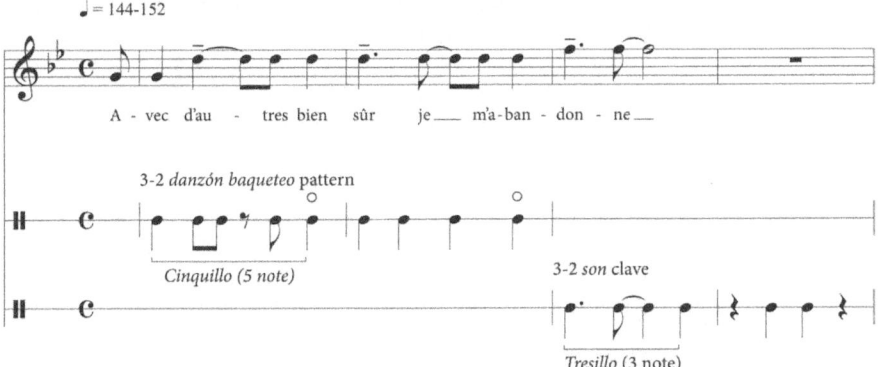

Example 9.3 Cuban flavors in "La Chanson de Prévert" (verse 2).

As the son of Russian Jewish immigrants, Gainsbourg was part of an entertainment industry that tapped not only into record industry demands but into more grassroots scenes, many of which diverged from those experienced by Left-Bank *chanson* artists such as Brel and Brassens. For all the talk of cultural appropriation surrounding his use of Cuban, Brazilian, and African sources, Gainsbourg was actually drawing on the musical world he grew up in. As Louis Laibe, the artistic director at Madame Arthur's, recalls, "We wrote songs in all styles: blues, waltzes, javas, African mood pieces, South American *mambos* and pure music hall" (quoted in Verlant 2000: 108–9). Performing in multicultural and subcultural environments, Serge Gainsbourg was indeed different from the ACI trinity (*"Auteur-Compositeur-Interprète"*) of Brel, Brassens, and Ferré (Lebrun 2014; Looseley 2003). His Latin feel in his vocal phrasing certainly demonstrates that a natural absorption of Cuban styles has taken place. In sum, as I have argued throughout this chapter, his participation in the French music industry was more multi-layered and ambivalent than that of the other great figures of 1950s and 1960s French *chanson*.

Notes

1. Many of the Paris-based Cuban musicians were from the orquesta *típica* and charanga traditions, and also classically trained (Miller 2014: 1–7, 184–5).
2. John Cowley, email message to author in 2008. For more information on French Caribbean early recordings, see Cowley 2014: 201–358.
3. "Cha-cha-cha intellectuel" (1957) was not recorded, but performed for a number (possibly acted?) by Laura Lor (Bouvir & Vincendet 2009: 66).
4. See Miller 2021 for more on the Jewish contribution to Cuban music performance in New York.
5. The two-bar *clave* pattern acts as a timeline or organizing principle of Cuban music. One bar is more syncopated, the other bar more "on-beat," and the pattern runs in either 2–3 or 3–2 direction. The *clave* pattern is often not stated, but implied by the patterns of the other instruments and suggested by the phrasing of the vocal lines and improvised phrases of the soloists. See Miller 2014 and 2021 for more on *clave* feel.

10

Gainsbourg and Musical Crossover: Issues in Sound Categorization and Stylistic Appropriation in the Study of *Gainsbourg Percussions*

Danick Trottier

For effective contextualization of the heuristic and musicological issues raised by the study of the album *Gainsbourg Percussions*, an interview given to *L'Union*—a regional newspaper headquartered in Reims—on December 31, 1964, is a good place to start. When asked "do you consider yourself avant-garde, as do your admirers?" Gainsbourg replies in the affirmative, saying he has "assimilated modern jazz." In response to the question, "what do you aim for in your songwriting?," he adds: "modern parlance… 'Franglais,' layered over ultra-modern jazz" (quoted in Verlant & Salmon 1994: 46). Any jazz connoisseur would be dumbfounded at such a claim, as the album's songs share so few similarities with jazz idioms, except for "Coco and Co" (the last of the twelve tracks) with its cool jazz inflections, most notably in the interactions between the piano, saxophone, double bass, and the drum kit. Yet the album's title is clear when it comes to naming its leading instrumental component: percussion as a central element of the accompaniment, featuring mainly congas, djembes (or drums), timpani, and shakers.

We now know that this artistic endeavor stems more from stylistic appropriation, if not a by-the-book cultural pillaging in which the authorial status of the source material is not identified. Gainsbourg appears here less as a composer than as the architect of a phonographic project reworking pre-existing musical material. In fact, musical structures for many of its songs borrow—without attribution—from Babatunde Olatunji's *Drums of Passion* (1959) and from the 1962 album *The Many Voices of Miriam Makeba* (Picaud & Verlant 2011: 135–42). A sense of this can be gotten by listening to "Akiwowo (Chant to the Trainman)," the first song on Olatunji's album: in both its percussive texture and melodic inflections, one can easily recognize "New York USA," the seventh track on *Gainsbourg Percussions,* so much so that originality is limited to the French lyrics and the vocals.

The author wishes to thank Stacey Brown for her work in translating the current chapter from French into English.

From this perspective, the way the album must be approached hinges on a simple equation, but with complex and troubling consequences as to the album's value and posterity, from a musical standpoint as much as from cultural and political ones. This equation may be summarized as follows: Gainsbourg + the Other, meaning everything he appropriated both stylistically, starting with the percussion, and musically, starting with the original songs that remain unattributed, thus bypassing copyright legislation's intended recognition of the work of others. In this context, it's a matter of understanding how a musical product could have been conceived of in this way and how it could have garnered such praise at the time.

Issues of Sonority in the Album's Reception

This LP released in late October 1964 was Gainsbourg's sixth album, and once again brought together the musicians with whom he was accustomed to working at the time: Claude Dejacques as producer, Alain Goraguer as musical director, arranger, and pianist, as well as seasoned musicians Christian Garros and André Arpino (drums), Michel Gaudry and Pierre Michelot (double bass), and Michel Portal (saxophone), the latter being responsible for the jazz colorings in a song like "Coco and Co" (Merlet 2019: 143–52). Today it is known that Goraguer's work was decisive for Gainsbourg's music in the first half of his career. This is especially true when it comes to arrangements and stylistic exploration (Picaud & Verlant 2011), so much so that Goraguer appears to be an exceptionally familiar figure in the history of French *chanson*: the arranger as master of stylistic coherence across various tracks (Rudent 2011: 92–102).

Gainsbourg Percussions emerged in the context of a transition in the musician's career between the image of a singer of *chanson* where lyrics and singer-songwriter status dominate, to the image of a rebel-rocker backed by his association with Jane Birkin, his "talk-over" vocal style, as well as his more rock-like sound. Yet the album has remained a major milestone in his career, particularly due to the pair of hits responsible for its reception: "Couleur café" and "New York USA." In fact, to explain the resulting sound, the term "avant-garde" recurs frequently in the language of the period, as attested by Gainsbourg's January 3, 1965, interview with Denise Glaser on the program *Discorama*. This interview, which can be viewed on YouTube, is significant for several reasons as to the value placed on the record.[1] Glaser begins by quoting from the song "Machins choses" ["Thingies"], thereby toying with a familiar, even uncouth language register that is characteristic of some of Gainsbourg's lyrics. That the literary dimension is introduced at the outset is meaningful in more ways than one and demonstrates the fact that Gainsbourg, as a singer-songwriter, is judged primarily for his lyric-writing.[2] Added to this is the fact that Glaser heaps praise on the album, calling it "very good," and going so far as to state "it occupies a special place in the history of *chanson*," in part due to his "way of playing with words!" She emphasizes, among other things, the success of the songs and the fact that the LP is a cohesive project, which makes Gainsbourg uncomfortable.

While the lyrics may be perceived as innovative for the originality of their language and their use of a banality associated with the everyday, combined with strong imagery like that of New York skyscrapers, the music poses an altogether different challenge, because it is perceived through an exogenous trait. In that same interview, Gainsbourg's reticence becomes palpable when Glaser mentions the music. The prevailing catchword is "marriage," reflecting the idea of musical fusion in the form of attraction, such that, for the interviewer, innovation means the union of two elements. On the one hand are Gainsbourg's lyrics, on the other are what Glaser calls "African music," then "Afro-Cuban music," and finally "jazz music." It is both this notion of "marriage" and the reluctance to define the musical Other by passing through three vastly different musical universes—Africa, the Caribbean, and the United States—that provide context for the network of signification in which this album's reception took place. The value placed on Gainsbourg rests specifically on the way he brought musical innovation drawn from elsewhere into the sphere of the French music scene associated with *chanson*. His innovative featuring of percussion—instruments primarily associated with jazz—became part of a groundbreaking gesture in the eyes of his contemporaries. This favorable opinion supporting the notion of musical advancement has persisted over time; for example, more than thirty years after the release of the album, the *Encyclopédie de la chanson française* still uses the term "avant-garde" to situate and qualify *Gainsbourg Percussions* (Verlant 1997: 53).

The idea of an avant-garde album must therefore be framed in the context of music in France of the 1960s, a scene characterized by "a great divide" (Guibert 2018: 7): French *variété* carried by *chanson* with its poetic leanings and singer-songwriters (Barbara, Brassens, Ferré, etc.), and *yé-yé* music focused on Anglo-American music with its rockers (Hallyday, Mitchell, Vartan, etc.). Still a long way off were the stylistic innovations that would be Gainsbourg's calling card, such as sonic and moral provocation ("Je t'aime... moi non plus," "Lemon Incest") or "talk-over," *franglais*, and concept albums *à la française* (*Histoire de Melody Nelson*, *L'Homme à tête de chou*). However, it is clear that in 1964, making percussion the central component of an album, using everyday language, and evoking cultural elements from elsewhere were regarded as groundbreaking. Gainsbourg's innovation was thus very real to people of that era, so much so that the appropriation of the musical content at the heart of many songs went unnoticed. Taking the approach of presenting *Gainsbourg Percussions* as an album in which he was appropriating and adapting the music of Olatunji and Makeba would have been highly problematic; the process may have been considered interesting, but the modifier "avant-garde" would have caused complications. It is thus the relationship to the musical Other that must be studied in greater depth to understand the artistic project at the core of the album.

The Musical Other and the Issue of Stylistic Innovation

When listening to Gainsbourg with contemporary ears, it is quite difficult to put things in perspective, because our way of listening has been formatted by several decades of musical fusions and world music in a context of globalization. Studying this album therefore requires contextualization, so that, without necessarily minimizing its forms of appropriation, the album's nature can be understood through its relation to the musical Other. In this case, nothing is simple and nothing should be presented unequivocally. The 1960s are certainly a period marked by strong winds of change in the West, demonstrated by exceptionally well-known political movements as much as the transformation of Anglo-American popular music and French *chanson*. All the more so that Gainsbourg already showed interest in musical "elsewhereness," demonstrated as much by the two pillaged musicians as by the references to the United States, which later led him to produce "Anglo-American songs with original French-speaking lyrics" (Julien 2018: 53). To some extent, this openness to the musical Other, identified here as anything outside France, constitutes his musical signature, and in this there is a real contribution as well as an openness that benefits Francophone *chanson* as a whole.

These strong winds of change sweeping through the West came amid improvements in relation to Africa, since the context of the *Trente Glorieuses* (the post-Second World War thirty-year boom period) was as synonymous with political demands as it was with decolonization. One outcome of this context was an openness to the Other, as much to the marginalized Other of the West as to the Other of the non-Western world known then as the Third World, meaning many countries with colonial pasts. The fact that Gainsbourg and his acolytes drew from two albums of non-Western music produced in the West attests to the shift in the circulation of this music. For example, Olatunji's *Drums of Passion* is the work of a Nigerian percussionist and was released by CBS in 1959 (and then Columbia in 1960), which points to an openness toward African music. Yet the situation is not that simple. The period in which Gainsbourg's album was released was also one when the crossover was at a turning point on the American charts. *Billboard* withdrew R&B in 1963, just to reinstate it the following year. As shown by David Brackett (1994), the American tracks that managed a crossover in this period were those that made the most concessions to the conventions of the American ballad and the tunes of Tin Pan Alley; the songs that stayed truest to the idioms of soul, gospel, and the blues struggled to achieve crossover, such that the music of the Other received unequal treatment. Nonetheless, the context was undergoing change, seeing the exploration of newer music realities. Based on Gainsbourg's interest in the United States and Anglophone music (Tinker 2002), it is important to situate this 1964 album in a broader context.

In conceiving and working on a new album like the one *Gainsbourg Percussions* would become, the appropriative gaze was turned toward Anglo-American pop insomuch as Olatunji's and Makeba's albums were produced in a phonographic context specific to Western recording studios. This fact can be seen in the track breakdown on the two albums, with songs adopting a more Western verse-chorus form. Gainsbourg and his musicians thus benefitted doubly from this appropriation they were undertaking: a musical "elsewhereness" so long as it was legitimized by a typically Western phonographic transformation. It is all the more important to clarify this fact since the term "world music" had yet to be coined at the time when Gainsbourg's album was released. Rather, the world music category emerged in the

1970s to encompass the production of traditional music originating in non-Western countries. Still, commonalities shared by Gainsbourg's approach and the world music that would come later reside in the representation of the Other, a point that deserves special attention.

The two most sought-after continents for world music are South America and Africa, both reduced to a power of attraction with a view of the Other fueled by cultural stereotypes: the Other is not Western, the Other is exotic, the Other is sensual, the Other is mystical (Guilbault 2001). These stereotypes have enabled the circulation of these continents' music by giving it an exotic aura, meaning a vague elsewhereness to be mined for materials for an artistic project. *Gainsbourg Percussions* is no exception to this observation, as the album came about at a time when France's relationship to many African countries was shifting from decolonization to neocolonialism. In this way, the development of a world music category reveals a situation in which the representation of the Other is fed into by values and stereotypes that end up reducing the musical diversity of the latter two continents to a few general characteristics: percussion, choir, and call and response on the production side of things, with dance, pleasure, and sensuality on the side of reception to name only those found on the 1964 album.

Representation of the cultural and musical Other thus relies on these general characteristics that function like so many cultural stereotypes, for the album prominently depicts the stereotypes of the period. "Couleur café" ["Coffee color"] can be used as a synecdoche for the LP: "how I love your coffee color," as the song says, could not be more overt in evoking the "exotic skin" of the Other hailing from the south, particularly in the lyrics depicting a sexual tension leading to the idea of a sleepless night.[3] The use of the verb "to excite" in this song opens the door to focusing as much on rhythmic components associated with the African Other as on values in which dance, pleasure, and sensuality legitimize the artistic process, one of equating skin color with carnal pleasure.

The musical appropriation at the core of the album thus seems motivated as much by the musical innovation of percussive accompaniment as by the new themes that this representation of the Other legitimized, in this case the showcasing of carnal pleasure. So then, Gainsbourg and his acolytes were fully aware of the all-musical lifeblood they could draw from models like those of Olatunji and Makeba, while evoking foreign images and cultural stereotypes both Western with New York and Louisiana, and non-Western with the presence of a women's choir and the call-and-response form found in a song like "Tatoué Jérémie." However, these stereotypes are used innocently in terms of the relationship to the Other, that is through the image one can conjure up of a country in which one has never set foot. For example, "Là-bas c'est naturel" ["Over There It's Natural"] references Kenya through jungle cries and childlike descending vocal inflections. In this song, it is more exoticism of the Other in the form of fantasy that is depicted than true nature. While this nuance cannot excuse the appropriative gesture and the consequences that followed in the representation of the Other, it does at least clarify the imaginary world that fueled *Gainsbourg Percussions*.

Conclusion

The equation evoked previously shows France's relationship to the outside world, in this case the cultural and musical Other. Although in France *Gainsbourg Percussions* was considered groundbreaking and labeled avant-garde, this situation can be attributed to the fact that world music as a concept didn't yet exist, and foreign influences, including Anglo-American pop, were channeled through *yé-yé*'s stylistic traits and musical values. It can certainly be said that within the borders of Mainland France, the album did in fact break new ground as to the manner in which a crossover was achieved, by pillaging the musical Other not only for their music, but also for the stereotypes that restricted their representation in the Western imagination and their circulation in the recording industry. It is quite likely that the album would have encountered roadblocks had it been released in the Anglo-American world; pale copies of a few songs by Olatunji and Makeba could have been judged severely. In some ways, Gainsbourg and his acolytes' endeavor was perfectly suited to the circumstances surrounding *chanson*; there were gains to be made in moving toward foreign music that could be passed off as innovation.

Rhetoric about Gainsbourg often focuses on two factors for assessing his legacy: permanent provocation as an artistic stance (Salgues 1989), and cheating as a way of positioning oneself in the music scene (Hawkins 2000: 158–66), which is the case for *Gainsbourg Percussions*. The 1965 interview with Glaser can once again be a point of reference: in the latter, Gainsbourg's attitude is masking an irony that creates an awkward situation with the laudatory adjectives used by the interviewer to describe the album. One gets the sense that he is well aware that he cheated by appropriating the music of the Other without making explicit mention. As for provocation, it lies in the staging of the Other through the previously mentioned stereotypes, especially the body in a sexualized state that enables resorting to exoticism. Gainsbourg's ironic tone and his uncomfortable, ill-concealed smile during the interview encourage a more nuanced reading of the era's judgment of *Gainsbourg Percussions*. In addition to that it should be pointed out that while some tracks such as "Couleur café" and "New York USA" result in a transcription done in due form, others seem less finished and show signs of being incomplete in their form. "Joanna," "Là-bas c'est naturel," and "Les Sambassadeurs," for example, seem to exist more in a rhythm-infused dance-like atmosphere than one of a finished *chanson*. Yet as Gainsbourg had anticipated, the French music scene obsessed with the evolution of its own *chanson* didn't suspect a thing.

Notes

1   https://www.youtube.com/watch?v=IOKdl__icpg [accessed 08-18-2022].
2   Many studies have highlighted the particular attention devoted to the lyrics in the reception of French *chanson* regarding its relationship with literature and, most of

all, poetry, the status of the author being at the core of that attention (Hawkins 1993; Julien 2018). The value judgment based on the literary dimension of songwriting is present across the board, and particularly in this 1965 interview with Glaser. The poetic quality of *chanson* will become a major stake as Anglo-American popular music, dominated by everyday language, will start to reshape French production.

3 The original song lyrics—*"Ce soir la nuit sera blanche"* (literally, "this evening the night will be white")—contain a double meaning characteristic of Gainsbourg, with the word play around "white" in the expression *nuit blanche* ["a sleepless night"].

11

Gainsbourg in a Reggae Style: The Esthetics, Economics, and Politics of *Aux Armes et Cætera*

Marc Kaiser

In 1977, the word "reggae" entered one of France's most prestigious dictionaries, *Le Grand Robert de la langue française*. It was exactly at this time that reggae was experiencing a global media and commercial craze. In line with the practices of the French music industry (Kaiser 2018), international stars like Bob Marley and the Wailers staged shows with local singers who would sing French-language versions of English and sometimes Jamaican hits.[1] As one may judge from "Marilou Reggae" (1976) and "Zanzibar" (1977), Serge Gainsbourg too found inspiration in these sounds. Yet, in an interview he gave following the release of his first reggae album, *Aux Armes et cætera*, he associated this turn with a musical adventure rather than mere opportunism (Inandiak 1979).

Before Gainsbourg took to reggae, Caribbean versions of "Je t'aime… moi non plus" had already been recorded by the Tropical Islanders (1970) and Judge Dread (1974).[2] History has it that he knew nothing of it (which seems quite unlikely). Nevertheless, these versions were part of a musical tradition linked to lascivious calypso songs and a route linking France to England through the Caribbean. Although in spite of himself, Gainsbourg was also part of it thanks to this song, which also played a key role in his meeting with the musicians of *Aux Armes et cætera*, as recalled by his collaborators at the time (Dicale 2009; Mikaïloff 2016), or drummer Sly Dunbar (Blum 2015). Gainsbourg was in fact the first white musician to record in Kingston. This led Peter Tosh's manager to say to him, "it may be good for you to come here to do reggae, but it is better for us, because with your credibility you will take reggae to France" (Inandiak 1979).

As had already been the case with any popular music trend since the beginning of the twentieth century, the emergence of French-language reggae resulted from transnational dynamics and local appropriation (Kaiser 2014). Due to his position in the music industry, Gainsbourg was truly instrumental in these dynamics. Bands such as Milestone or Les Gamacks certainly played a role too—these bands came from Dominica, officially an English-speaking territory, but situated among the French islands, where most people speak a French-based Creole. However, Gainsbourg's first reggae album marked a turning point in several ways: esthetically, it "established

Francophone reggae's pedigree," as suggested by Bruno Blum (West Indian 2008); economically, it provided Gainsbourg with his first real commercial success and gave rise to a new persona; lastly, from both a political and cultural standpoint, it legitimated the participation of a white artist in "black diasporic culture" (Hill 2003: 122) and the emergence of a new French scene. The following pages will address the album from these three angles.

Dub Poetry *à la Française*

It was through Island Records' founder Chris Blackwell that Gainsbourg and his team organized recording sessions in one of Jamaica's renowned studios, Bryon Lee's Dynamic Sound,[3] with reggae legends Lowell "Sly" Dunbar, Robert "Robbie" Shakespeare, the I Threes, Radcliffe "Dougie" Ryan, Michael "Mao" Chung, and Uzziah "Sticky" Thompson. True to habit, he arrived on the island with mere song titles and vague chord sequences (Mikaïloff 2016). The album was recorded in record speed— six days from start to finish, including a couple of days spent with the backing band. Gainsbourg wrote the lyrics in one night in his hotel room after hearing the musicians play. The legend has it that the musicians first started to "take the mickey out" of him, but that the atmosphere became warmer as soon as they realized it was he who wrote the only French song they knew: "Je t'aime... moi non plus" (Simmons 2001: 87).

According to Edwin Hill, *Aux Armes et cætera* took French *chanson* "where it had never geographically or musically gone before" (2003: 116). In fact, Gainsbourg was primarily in search of a genuine, "dirty," or "roots" sound which in no way resembled the second-hand, sanitized, and "Frenchified" reggae that was already heard at the time on French radios. As Sly Dunbar recalls,

> The only time he said something was when we said we'll overdub some other instruments and he said "No, no, no, no, no, it's okay, it's what I want—I want it real, raw, no overdubs, just simple."
>
> (quoted in Simmons 2001: 88)

In other words, Gainsbourg knew exactly what he was looking for. In contrast to the deejays who toasted on top of a backing track, his spoken voice provided a rhythmic lead that inspired the musicians throughout the recording sessions. As his artistic approach of the time repeatedly shows, the placing of the voice seem less important to him than the words (Julien 2018). *Aux Armes et cætera* follows dub poetry directly, adding an original touch *à la française*, with Gainsbourg acting more like a poet than a singer, performing "talk over" on reggae rhythms while invoking political, social, and sexual issues.

Another distinguishing feature of the album is that it includes two covers, which was quite unusual for Gainsbourg. In addition to his well-known and very personal adaptation of the French national anthem ("La Marseillaise"), he cut a French-language version of "You Rascal You" (1932) written by Jacques Plante: "Vieille Canaille." Apart from being a possible veiled reference to Jane Birkin's future partner, Jacques Doillon (Simmons 2001: 96), he opens up here to the Jamaican tradition of reinterpretation and riddims (Manuel & Marshall 2017).

In his youth, Gainsbourg said he wanted to be "Courbet or nothing" (Maubert 2005: 23). Years later, he still thought of his work as related to art, as attested by his associating "Aux Armes et cætera" with a Caribbean version of Liberty Leading the People.

> "Aux Armes et cætera," it's in a way Delacroix's painting in which the woman with the flag, perched on a pile of corpses of Rastas, would be none other than a Jamaican with her breasts overflowing in the sun, in revolt with an amazing heroic, erotic chorus ... a throbbing reggae!
>
> (quoted in Verlant 2006b: 64)

This original and controversial cover echoes the words of Jane Birkin, for whom Gainsbourg was in his Cubist period at that time (Perrin 2013), breaking with the realism and romanticism of his early years. Finally, like a painter in action creating a unique work, he was himself a source of inspiration for the musicians' improvisations during the recording sessions:

> we were inspired by his rhythm and his image. We watched him work. It was a bit like when Miles Davis improvised the music for *Elevator to the Gallows* by watching the film. It's the rhythm, but also the pictures which had inspired it.
>
> (Sly Dunbar, quoted in Blum 2015)

Aux Armes et cætera ultimately provided various sound illustrations which overturned the canons of French chanson (Hill 2003; Julien 2018), setting what Blum describes as a "language for Francophone *chanson* that worked with reggae" (West Indian 2008).

From Gainsbourg to Gainsbarre and Generational Success

Until *Aux Armes et cætera*, Gainsbourg's fans had been small in numbers, though faithful (Dicale 2009). With this album—recorded in September 1978 and released in March 1979—he got through to a mass audience and earned his first gold record. Having been a celebrity, he became a star at over fifty, exploding "brutally from twelve thousand to one million records sold" (Picaud & Verlant 2011: 5). As Peter Tosh's manager had predicted, reggae was becoming popular in France to such an extent that Gainsbourg boasted that it was he, not Bob Marley, who introduced the French to this musical genre (Simmons 2001: 86).

Among other things, his reggae version of "La Marseillaise" was about sex, marijuana, and fascism. The song's title was reportedly suggested by the twelve-volume *Grand Larousse* (another French reference dictionary), where the transcription of the second refrain simply states "Aux Armes, etc." (Inandiak 1979). As expected, it led to a series of scandals, which had no small part in its success.[4] Michel Droit, a future member of the French Academy, gave voice to conservative and anti-Semitic opinion by condemning the desecration of France's national anthem while, at the same time, attacking the singer's physique. A couple of weeks later, Gainsbourg retorted that his adaptation was "heroic in its pulsating rhythms and the dynamics of its harmonies," and "just as revolutionary" as Rouget de Lisle had intended it (Inandiak 1979).

Death threats, bomb alerts, and intimidation at his concerts followed. On January 4, 1980, a famous incident occurred in Strasbourg. Having unsuccessfully called for the cancelation of the concert, veteran paratroopers occupied the front rows of the venue to warn him that they would not tolerate his desecrating the anthem again. Although the show had been cancelled—the Jamaican musicians were already gone—Gainsbourg came on stage and began to sing the anthem *a cappella*, forcing the paratroopers to stand to attention and sing along with him. In Sylvie Simmons's words, "Playing the tough guy took a lot of alcohol for a shy man to pull off." For Birkin, this was precisely the moment Gainsbarre—Gainsbourg's "dissipated, alcoholic alter ego"—was born (Perrin 2013; Simmons 2001: 97; 2015).

To some, the album's success was generational. Dicale argues that it allowed Gainsbourg to put forward another image of him, especially with young people:

> The kids who bought *Aux Armes et cætera* identified with a singer who annoyed their parents. With this album, Serge Gainsbourg was both a new artist and a familiar star … For ten years, he had outraged, shocked, annoyed, by repeating provocations and deviant behaviors with perhaps more consistency in town than on stage. At a time when young people were quick to follow stars posing as a brother, a father or a lover, he offered the image of an old punk-rocker uncle who filled teenagers with glee. And he embodied a paradoxical consensus: with *Aux Armes et cætera*, he was compatible with punk rock, with the nascent new wave and even with the new mainstream French pop of variety *chanson* of Daniel Balavoine or Michel Berger, two big suppliers of radiophonic hits that were laced with indignation against the state of the world.
>
> (2011: 225)

While right-wing newspapers "called the record 'repugnant' … the kids in their turn called it 'cool'" (Simmons 2001: 89), elevating Gainsbourg to the same level as the Sex Pistols or Jimi Hendrix in diverting national anthems. Indeed, he was aware of this new image, announcing in a TV interview that "it's not going to make people's teeth, but their dentures grind" (Holtz 1979). A tour followed that same year: judging by the live recording at the Palace nightclub in Paris, it was a real success.

Despite this success, Gainsbourg was deeply affected by the Strasbourg episode and the anti-Semitic backlash that followed (Hill 2003: 119). Released in 1981 on his second reggae album, "Juif et Dieu" ["Jew and God"] stands out as just retribution for this affair. That same year, he retaliated by buying Rouget de Lisle's original manuscript, and by having a platinum Star of David made for him by Cartier. For Dicale (2011), the political impact of his work was henceforth affected by the new media figure represented by Gainsbarre, mirroring the image of *Mauvaises Nouvelles des étoiles*, which was a semi-failure without much artistic and political influence.

The Politics of *Aux Armes et cætera*

Prosody *à la Gainsbourg* was characterized by a desire "to weld French words to the English language's rhythm and melody" (Julien 2018: 53). More broadly, Blum analyzes that Black music came to be at the heart of the musician's creative process:

> it's jazz, it's African music and Cuba, it's Rhythm 'n' Blues, it's English rock which is a substitute for black music, it's blues, funk with Billy Rush and of course reggae. And where he really pulled it off was with reggae. The high point of this dimension to his work was this reggae period.
>
> (GDB 2015)

Gainsbourg took part in the Gilroyan Black Atlantic and played a role as a smuggler by re-appropriating reggae and its oppositional dimension in particular: his words were tinged with afro-centrism, echoing Rasta ideology and "Back to Africa" movements. In an interview with French newspaper, *Libération*, he went so far as to claim, "logic would have me go to Africa next time ... because I am moving away from America and England" (Inandiak 1979).

Aux Armes et cætera became associated with a political statement when Gainsbourg pointed out on television: "reggae is a revolutionary music. 'La Marseillaise' is a revolutionary song. People danced to the Carmagnole ... We will dance to 'La Marseillaise'" (Holtz 1979). The album also allowed the encounter between a protesting musical genre and a French youth in the midst of questioning.

> For the first time, Gainsbourg was being listened to by teenagers who recognized themselves in his postures, perhaps even more than in his career and in his songs. They were on the same wavelength with his certain sluggishness, a certain subversion, a certain disgust. Punks in squats, vaguely nihilist *petits-bourgeois*, students whose political interest in reggae anticipated alter-globalization, young music lovers who not only dreamt in English, but who wanted songs from the present time ... The rebellious power and all the turbulence and new values that reggae bore in 1979 added to the blasphemous appropriation of "La Marseillaise." Gainsbourg piled up signs and messages that reinforced each other.
>
> (Dicale 2011: 226)

His first reggae opus thus opposed the subordinate racial categories of the French Republic he had himself faced since childhood. It also unified all racialized minorities under the French tricolor. As a musician, Gainsbourg sought to be part of a disruptive esthetics, while at the same time bringing together diverse traditions in the political and cultural context of 1970s France (Francfort 2007). His interpretation of "La Marseillaise" made it possible to listen to the message of the national anthem differently, and to reclaim Republican symbols and meanings (Francfort 2007; Hill 2003).

All things considered, *Aux Armes et cætera* brought together the two main factors that explain the importance of reggae in French pop culture as defined by Jérémie Kroubo Dagnigni (2010): the album is part of both an old French tradition of rebellious thought, and a musical genre that denounces slavery, colonialism, exclusion, and oppression. Since its release, French reggae actually developed around these two dimensions. First, the 1980s and early 1990s saw the emergence of a Parisian raggamuffin scene with its own sound systems (Youthman Academy, High Fight, Jah Wisdom), its specialized stores (Blue Heaven, Blue Moon), its radio shows on Radio Ivre or Radio Nova, and its groups and artists (Ragga Dub Band, Ras Negus, Azikmen, etc.). Like Princess Erika, Daddy Yod, General Murphy, Daddy Nuttea, or Tonton David, most participants were of Caribbean and African origin and their music challenged modes of cultural assignment. The latter half of the 1990s was then marked by the assertion of French reggae properly speaking, with groups mostly composed of white musicians (Sinsemilia, Tryo, K2R Riddim, etc.). Common denominators included partying, hanging out, and smoking marijuana (Lavige & Bernardi 2003), in a way that remained oppositional. Subsequently, French-speaking reggae/dancehall artists of the twenty-first century have mostly been Caribbean and, in the footsteps of Lord Kossity or Raggasonic, have clearly claimed postcolonial positions. Remarkably, the performers of the latest generation, as embodied by Biga Ranx, are mostly white, from small towns, and sing in English. According to Sonjah Stanley Niaah (2010), these various forms of production and consumption have now made France the second most important nation in the global reggae market. And, as the organization of a "Gainsbourg Reggae Festival" suggested in 2010,[5] *Aux Armes et cætera* surely had something to do with it.

Notes

1 For example, adaptations by Philippe Villiers (Jimmy Cliff's "You Can Get It if You Really Want"), or even Doudou (Max Romeo's "One Step Forward").
2 Tropical Islanders, The. 1970. *Do It Your Way*. WIRL MMS-013 [33 rpm]; Dread, Judge. 1974. *Working Class 'Ero*. Trojan Records TRLS 100 [33 rpm].
3 A couple of years later, *Mauvaises Nouvelles des étoiles* featured the same musicians, but was recorded at the Compass Point Studios in Nassau, Bahamas.
4 Although he wasn't the first to reinterpret it: in 1792, "Le Retour du soldat" was already an early parody of "La Marseillaise," and among other versions were Django Reinhardt and Le Hot Club du Quintette de France's "Echoes of France" in 1946.
5 https://www.sortiraparis.com/scenes/concert-musique/articles/34959-un-hommage-reggae-a-serge-gainsbourg-a-la-java [accessed 03-20-2019].

12

Gainsbourg and the Other: A Postcolonial Reading of *Gainsbourg Percussions*

Aurélien Djebbari and Elina Djebbari

To the memory of our father Alain Djebbari.

From classical music to reggae, from jazz to rock, the eclecticism and diversity of Serge Gainsbourg's musical inspirations are widely perceivable through his record production. Among these inspirations, African-derived elements arising from Paul Gilroy's Black Atlantic (1993) have been merely analyzed through the lens of plagiarism and musical theft (Verlant 2000: 261–3). Rather than dwelling on such "borrowings," this chapter offers a postcolonial reading of *Gainsbourg Percussions* by analyzing its use of musical traits pertaining to a potentially "black sound" (Waksman 1999), not forgetting the many references to Africa and the Caribbean that run through the lyrics of some of Gainsbourg's best-known songs. Our hypothesis is that the visions of Africa and the Caribbean conveyed in the album play with stereotypes related to racial and gender issues that were debated within the context of decolonization in 1960s France. By looking at the record as the starting point of Gainsbourg's African turn, we will first address issues of copyright and imitation process regarding the use of African musical features. Then we will try to show how these "African" elements serve as a basis for the creation of esthetic musical codes that were to become enduring musical prescriptions. Finally, a close analysis of some of the songs' lyrics will bring to light the critical questioning of the artist in relation to the apprehension of otherness.

Artistic Appropriation and Copyright Issues

In the early 1960s, Gainsbourg was already a sought-after songwriter. Yet his career as a solo artist had not yet taken off. Following the commercial failure of *Gainsbourg Confidentiel* (1963), he thus decided to rethink the way he conceived music by reconciling artistic and marketing strategies (Dicale 2021: 217). Ahead of his contemporaries in the field of French "variétés," he considered the 33-rpm record as a unitary work rather than a gathering of scattered singles (which was still the most common practice in those days). More exactly, he conceptualized the writing of an album according to the precept of classical tragedy: unity of place, time, and action. Inspired by his passion for painting, he also expressed the idea of ending the reign of harmony in the same way abstract art had moved beyond the reign of realistic representation. "In music, when form explodes, all that remains is percussion. Harmony disappears" (Verlant 2000: 262).

A few years before (1959), *Drums of Passion* by Nigerian percussionist Babatunde Olatunji had been released in the United States. The recording had met with great success and made a strong impression on a small circle of Parisian producers and songwriters. Although the term was not in use back then, it may be regarded as an early example of a "world music" album marketed across the Atlantic.[1] At the same time, the "taste for otherness" (L'Estoile 2007) that soared in France during the interwar period was eventually giving way to American rock 'n' roll and *yé-yé*. Despite the decolonization processes and independence struggles that often put Africa on the front pages of newspapers, the continent was still considered as being on the margins of the globalizing recording industry. In this particular context, *Drums of Passion* was a revelation for Gainsbourg. Always eager to stand out from his contemporaries, he found in the record the inspiration for a new and original way to create music, by incorporating African percussions to his own production. Accordingly, *Gainsbourg Percussions* was recorded in October 1964 at Studio Blanqui in Paris.

Under the guidance of arranger Alain Goraguer, the record featured several musicians including five percussionists, twelve backing vocalists, and jazz musicians such as Georges Grenu and Michel Portal on saxophone, Eddy Louiss on organ, Christian Garros and André Arpino on drums, and Pierre Michelot and Michel Gaudry on double bass (Merlet 2019: 143–52). Among the album's twelve tracks, three heavily drew on *Drums of Passion*: "Jin Go Lo Ba" (which became "Marabout"), "Kiyakiya" ("Joanna"), and "Akiwoko" ("New York USA"). The process extended to "Là-bas c'est naturel" and "Pauvre Lola," both inspired by South African singer Miriam Makeba's "Umqokozo."[2] This was not the first time Gainsbourg appropriated somebody else's work. In 1959, he had already pulled a promotional trick by falsifying the credits on the cover of *L'Eau à la bouche*'s soundtrack—while Alain Goraguer had actually written most of the music, the mention read: "Serge Gainsbourg—words and music." And even though the SACEM[3] work declaration form established a fair sharing of royalties, Gainsbourg initiated a practice he would pursue throughout his career: claiming to be the main, if not the sole credit owner on record sleeves. This practice resulted in the successive disaffection of his appointed arrangers—Alain Goraguer, Michel Colombier, Jean-Claude Vannier, and Jean-Pierre Sabar (Lerouge 2001: 5–6).

From African Inspiration to Gainsbourg's Originality

Be it on the record sleeve or the "work declaration form," the borrowings from Olatunji and Makeba remain unspecified on *Gainsbourg Percussions*. Even the percussionists who play on the recording are uncredited. However, Gainsbourg did not try to hide these "borrowings," which were well known to his close collaborators. He ironically confessed: "to the Africans I nicked two [or] three things, cynically, off the books ['*au noir*']…" (Verlant 2000: 262). In an interview conducted by TV presenter Denise Glaser, he went further, conceding he had been inspired by "Nigerian folklore."[4]

— You have managed to marry two very different elements: a kind of African, or Afro-Cuban music or jazz music, with your own lyrics. I believe that the rhythms are not new, it is their marriage that is new.
— Yes, that's for sure. The rhythms are not new. They come from Nigerian folklore. The French language adapted to these rhythms, that is new.
— Why African rhythms?
— Because we are in the twentieth century, and after, at least next to electric guitars, we must impose something violent upon ourselves.[5]

Here, Gainsbourg acknowledges the re-use of existing musical material as one of the resources his artistic creativity relies on. Indeed, if his idea was to offer something "new" by appropriating rhythms from "Nigerian folklore," the latter rhythms were anything but "new." Still, the interview does not address the actual existence and identity of the artists whose music had been "nicked." This clearly illustrates the widespread idea that traditional music is "without author" (Guillebaud, Stoichita & Mallet 2010), and free to use in disregard for copyright laws.

Beyond musical appropriation,[6] *Gainsbourg Percussions* introduces musical features that would subsequently become staples in Gainsbourg's work. In addition to the omnipresent percussion, the call and response patterns between the lead singer and the female backing vocalists echo traits that are usually (and quite stereotypically) attributed to African music genres (Tagg 1989). At the forefront of such traits, the responsorial form and the high-pitched female voices found on songs such as "New York USA" are sought for as vocal techniques signaling African musical and sonic esthetics. On this matter, Alain Goraguer explains: "I keep wonderful memories, we had fun like crazy, especially when we showed the French backup singers how to take high-pitched Negro women voices" (Verlant 2000: 263).

The attention paid to the materiality of sound is not only apparent in the choice of musical instruments and vocal timbres: it also shows through the peculiar use of words and scansion. By all measures, *Gainsbourg Percussions* initiates a change in Gainsbourg's writing process (Dicale 2021: 218). The usual narrative gives way to a frenzy of words, jigsaws of sounds, and thoughts used like projectiles. For instance, the repetition of syllables in "Marabout" is used to deconstruct the words and sentences over the percussions copied from Olatunji's record. The emphasis on the very term "marabout" allows for alluding to an imaginary Africa, not only through the literal meaning of the word, but also through its iteration at a fast tempo (Example 12.1). This play on repetition over various rhythmical patterns creates a haunting and hypnotic impression, giving a trance-like feeling to the song despite its brevity (it is about two minutes long).

The minimal lyrics otherwise refer to a twisted version of "Trois Petits Chats," a children's nursery rhyme based on the reduplication of syllables. This situates the song in a more familiar context for audiences likely to understand the reference, and makes it possible to create a "surprise effect" or feeling of disorientation—such

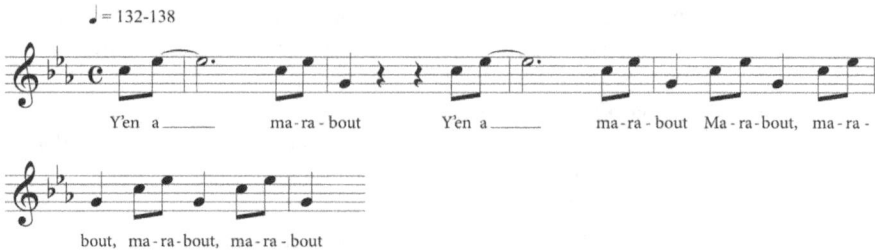

Example 12.1 Excerpt from "Marabout."

disjuncture between words and music actually pervades the whole album. On the one hand, the process may suggest a paternalist condescension toward African music and musicians—used without being credited, deemed as being reproducible at will or reworked in a play with a children's song. On the other hand, some lyrics do complicate such a reductive interpretation by questioning racial and gender stereotypes, which were highly sensitive in the context of postcolonial France.

Gainsbourg's Critical "Practice of Stereotypes"

Gainsbourg's lyrics are usually praised for their quality and ubiquitous puns, their sophisticated use of double entendre, and their intertextual erudition. In this respect, their pertaining to the depiction of an exotic elsewhere presents a critical "practice of stereotypes" (Herzfeld 1992) that should be analyzed with regard to the context of the 1960s at large. Among others, "Joanna"'s lyrics feature problematic verses such as "Joanna is from Louisiana/When she's on a diet/It's a hand of bananas" [*"Joanna est bien de La Louisiane/Quand elle suit un régime/C'est un régime de bananes"*]. Beyond their apparent ribaldry (the backing vocalists keep on singing *"léger, léger"*), they combine highly connoted images. "Diet," for example, points to the required regulation of the female creole body (here, "from Louisiana"), otherwise described as being able to dance lightly despite being overweight. The association of "banana" with "Louisiana" also refers to the colonial plantation system and global economy of tropical products, while allusions to Josephine Baker's banana dance and to the pervasive analogy banana/phallus surface. Accordingly, the description of Joanna's banana diet is tinged with discrimination and the exploitation of the Black female body marked by the history of the slave trade and colonialism.

Similarly, "Là-bas c'est naturel" is filled with bird, monkey, and other animal cries to suggest an African savannah atmosphere. The lyrics go: "Over there it's natural/Over there in Kenya/For all the Naturals/It's OK/Each one is in two-piece [swimsuit] minus one/Each one in this black paradise/In monokini" [*"Là-bas c'est naturel/Là-bas au Kenya/Pour tous les Naturels/C'est OK/Chacune est en deux pièces moins une/Chacun dans ce noir paradis/En monokini"*]. The reference to "monokini" introduces a humorous shift in the depiction of an idealized

"Black paradise" located in Kenya. Moreover, the allusion to the debates over the monokini and related "naturalness" issues in the French context of the 1960s mirrors the supposed absence of modesty and fantasized primitiveness of the "Naturals" in Kenya. It also echoes a 1968 interview for Swiss television during which Gainsbourg confessed his own dislike of the mini-skirt [*"minijupe"*] worn by contemporary young women, pointing out their "lack of modesty" compared to previous times.[7] The provocative aspect of the song is directly related to body politics, whether through the lens of colonial morality regarding "natural" bodily practices or through that of contemporary feminist struggles. Here, the images of women with long hair and monokini depart from the common representations of Kenya, associated with safaris and Masai. The lyrics tellingly disrupt enduring colonial stereotypes about African "naturalness," confronting these images to contemporary debates in postcolonial France.

Finally, "Couleur café"'s lyrics convey the image of the lascivious and sensual mixed-race young woman (*"métisse"*), who sways and rolls her hips so as to appeal to the narrator's desires. The term "coffee," used to describe the skin color of the creole woman, is associated with the virtues of the drink ("to upset," "to excite") and the sexual arousal triggered by the Caribbean *mulata* offering herself. These combined tropes, again, reflect upon the role of colonial powers in the development of plantation economy and creole societies through slavery in the New World. According to this reading, the woman depicted as a sensual object is—like coffee—a product of Western imperialism. In the end, though, the potential light-heartedness of such romantic encounters ("love without philosophizing"), metaphorically compared to coffee that quickly filters, turns out to be non-satisfactory. Only a long period of time might allow to "forget everything" and overcome the traumas of slavery and colonialism, or at least to get rid of the symptoms of "postcolonial melancholia" and guilt (Gilroy 2004). As attested by "Black and White" (recorded a mere four years later), this play on skin colors will continue to appear in later songs, along with intertextual references,[8] resonating with the violence of racial relations and imperialism that will shake the world throughout the 1960s (Civil Rights Movement in the United States, Vietnam War, etc.).

Conclusion

Despite the moral controversy regarding copyright issues, *Gainsbourg Percussions* appears to be a pioneering album in the realm of musical encounters between French *chanson* and African-derived musical features. As such, it should be regarded as a landmark album in the process that would lead to "world music" in the 1980s. Among the other records heralding this trend was the *Getz-Gilberto* album featuring American saxophonist Stan Getz and Brazilian vocalists João and Astrud Gilberto, which also came out in 1964. Two years later, George Harrison took up the sitar under the guidance of Ravi Shankar, and in 1969, jazz saxophonist Archie Shepp performed live with Tuareg musicians at the Algiers Pan-African Youth Festival. The latter artists are often seen as precursors in the history of late twentieth-century world beat, from which Serge Gainsbourg is generally excluded. And yet, *Gainsbourg Percussions* does testify to the emergence of the world music market in postcolonial France.

From a more general point of view, this essay also aimed at reassessing Gainsbourg's musical contribution to the making of an "esthetics of global imagination" (Erlmann 1996). Our postcolonial perspective on *Gainsbourg Percussions*'s lyrics seems to point to a political awareness in the face of colonial imperialism and the correlative gender and racial issues characteristic of 1960s France, while contradicting the common view of Gainsbourg as individualistic and politically uninterested—he himself denied delivering any kind of political messages in his songs. Scholars have analyzed the notion of "cover" as a key constituent of the creative process in popular music (Plasketes 2010). Gainsbourg used it and abused it, and he was in turn subject to it. Since the 1990s, some of his musical motifs have been sampled by the likes of Beck, the Kills, Texas, Blonde Redhead, Portishead, Kylie Minogue, Goldfrapp, Dimitri from Paris, Bob Sinclar, De La Soul, MC Solaar, IAM, or Brad Mehldau. But his music inspired artists of African origins too. Cameroonian singer Odile Obélé cut a jazz cover of "La Javanaise"; Cap Verdian artist Jesers recorded a rap version of that same song; Beninese singer Angélique Kidjo recorded "Ces Petits Riens," while Congolese singer Jean-Paul Wabotaï took over ten tracks in his album *AmourS Gainsbourg* (2010) before creating the show, "Gainsbourg l'Africain" (2018). In sum, Gainsbourg's African-inspired work is part of a continuous process of borrowings, appropriation, and re-use that make some of his signature landmarks a contemporary shared heritage. As a striking *mise en abyme*, the process mirrors the enduring legacy of the musical innovations arisen from a Black Atlantic that never ceased to inspire popular musicians all over the world.

Notes

1 This label started to spread at the initiative of British producers (including Peter Gabriel) in 1987 (Brennan 2001).
2 From *The Many Voices of Miriam Makeba* (1960).
3 French Society of Authors, Composers and Music Publishers.
4 Gainsbourg actually made a mistake when saying *"Nigérien"* (from Niger) instead of *"Nigérian."*
5 https://www.ina.fr/ina-eclaire-actu/video/i05063703/interview-de-serge-gainsbourg-par-denise-glaser [accessed 07-02-2022].
6 Unlike Makeba, Olatunji eventually obtained compensation (Dicale 2021: 238; Picaud & Verlant 2011: 136).
7 https://www.rts.ch/play/tv/edition-archives/video/serge-gainsbourg?urn=urn:rts:video:13887336 [accessed 03-20-2023].
8 Interestingly, this theme was later reworked in the lyrics of the song performed by Guadeloupean singer Joëlle Ursull (ex-Zouk Machine) at the Eurovision Song Contest in 1990, "White and Black Blues."

"L'Impression du Déjà-Vu": Local Inspiration & Francophone Legacy

13

Charles Trenet's Influence on Serge Gainsbourg: Swing, Irony, and Poetry

Claire Fraysse

"When I was ten years old, my favorite singer was Charles Trenet" (Verlant 2000: 38). Making this confession to his biographer Gilles Verlant, Serge Gainsbourg not only shared an anecdote about his childhood: he also revealed the name of one of his early influences. Regarded as the pioneer of "modern *chanson*" (Rioux 1966: 42), Trenet marked a turning point in the history French songwriting: in 1938, his unprecedented success on the stage of the Parisian music-hall ABC signed the fusion between popular *chanson* and poetry (Cantaloube-Ferrieu 1981: 14). Often labeled "the first popular *auteur-compositeur-interprète*" ["singer-songwriter"], he was behind the "post-war renaissance of poetic popular songs" (Hawkins 2000: 92), redefining the characteristics of *chanson*, namely "a melding of music and poetry capable of expressing the most complex aspects of individual perception, sensibility and ideas which, at the same time, remains accessible to popular audiences" (Nettelbeck 2003: 281). As envisioned by Paul Valéry in 1937 when he wondered whether "a purely oral and auditory literature [would] not replace, in a rather short time, the written literature" (Cantaloube-Ferrieu 1981: 11), this new conception of *chanson,* both popular and artistic, ushered in the modern era. Indeed, "some of its best-known names have confirmed it: Léo Ferré, Georges Brassens, Jacques Brel, Serge Gainsbourg, and … Alain Souchon all see Trenet as a precursor" (Hawkins 2000: 85).

While the connection between Serge Gainsbourg and Boris Vian is well established, the relationship between Gainsbourg and Trenet might seem less obvious at first. This chapter does not propose to explore the full extent of the latter's influence on the former, but seeks to shed light on this filiation by focusing on three major areas: first, their shared love for jazz music that brought them to adapt this musical form to *chanson* in an innovative way; second, Gainsbourg and Trenet were both masters of irony; finally, Trenet opened the path to a new way of putting French poetry into song, a path which Gainsbourg further explored.

"Swing Troubadour": Jazz Influence in Trenet's and Gainsbourg's Songs

Jazz in *Chanson*

One of Trenet's major innovations was to import swing into chanson: by enriching it with new rhythms and sounds, he opened it to a "transcultural identity" (Bourderionnet 2011: 6). To Boris Vian, "this new pulsation ... was born from the conjunction of a remarkable poetic gift and the vitality of jazz fully assimilated by a fine sensitivity" (1996: 169). During the Second World War, swing music was deemed morally decadent by French collaborationists. In 1941, Trenet pushed the provocation further by adapting Verlaine's famous poem "Chanson d'automne" to a swing song, orchestrated for a jazz band. If Trenet's most used musical ensemble was the 1930s big band, Alain Goraguer's musical arrangements for Gainsbourg's first three albums modernized the jazz trend in *chanson* by drawing inspiration from 1950s cool jazz and adding classical instruments such as the flute or the vibraphone to the standard jazz combo ("Ce Mortel Ennui," "Du Jazz dans le ravin"). Goraguer crossed this jazz vocabulary with Caribbean inspirations like *mambo* or *chachachá* in a pre-Latin jazz vein, using bongos, congas, claves, and Afro-Caribbean dance rhythms ("L'Alcool," "Mambo miam miam," "Cha cha cha du loup"). His creativity and virtuosity as an arranger raised *chanson* to an unprecedented level of sophistication.

The witty state of mind and the hedonist esthetic associated with swing radically transformed *chanson*, both in its performance and composition. Twenty years after Trenet's first success, Gainsbourg got to grips with the art of quotation, the freedom of improvisation, and the principles of variations on a theme, applying them to his writing process like a jazz musician (Bourderionnet 2011: 6). Indeed, jazz music is a characteristic element of Trenet's and Gainsbourg's lyrics. Under the influence of swing music, they paired the French language with a new style of prosody, influenced by the English language. In his first success "Y'a d'la joie," Trenet accentuates the penultimate syllable of every three-syllable verse ("Y'a d'*la* joie") in a syncopated way, contrary to the traditional French prosody that accentuates the last syllable of a sentence. In this way, the French lyrics are sung with what sounds like English accentuation (70). Olivier Bourderionnet also noted a swing prosody in "Le Poinçonneur des Lilas," attributable to a combination of cadence and movement within the metric structure, coupled with a violence of tone in the poetic associations and in the semantic fields of death, boredom, and depression: "the elasticity of the meter, reminiscent of La Fontaine's '*vers mêlés,*' confers to [his] poetry a rhythmic specificity that strikes us as the metaphorical expression of jazz phrasing" (50).

French Adaptation of Scat

Opening *chanson* to new poetic perspectives, Trenet and Gainsbourg both excelled at combining words not only for their meaning, but also for their sound. Highlighted by a perfectly intelligible diction, Trenet's use of alliteration and onomatopoeia brings

Lucienne Cantaloube-Ferrieu to liken it to an adaptation of American scat (1981: 75). This pleasure of sound was indeed a major characteristic of Trenet's singing style, one through which he greatly enriched the rhythmicity of the French language. In "Débit de l'eau, débit de lait," Trenet turns the entire song into a giant tongue twister where the alliterations in *d*, *b* and *l* create the impression of a French scat performance. In "Il pleut dans ma chambre," the noise of the rain is symbolized by the strings' pizzicato and the singer's joyful "tipititap" scat. In "Le Soleil et la lune," assonances (*"de ces chats, de ces chats qui s'ennuient"*), obsessive repetitions (*"la lune est là, la lune est là, la lune est là"*), and talk-over technique give the French language a swinging freedom. In his turn, Gainsbourg made these tools his own, so much so that some critics noted that "sound mattered more than meaning" in his songs (Clayson 1998: 63). The pleasure of sound does sometimes appear to dominate, for example in Trenet's "Annie, Anna" or Gainsbourg's "Elaeudanla Téïtéïa." Annie and Anna are sisters: their names give rise to a rocky comparison, guided more by a game of sound associations than by meaning (*"lessive/lascive," "poitrine/vitrine," "apparat/à Paris"*). As for Gainsbourg's enigmatic title, it stems from the phonetic transcription of the name "Laetitia," spelled out and obsessively repeated throughout the song.

French Irony

The Art of Detachment

Along with the swing appropriation, irony is another main component of modern *chanson*. Trenet's irony is most often perceptible in the surprising outcomes of his songs: while the narrative seems joyful and light, its ending may be much darker, as in "Je chante" ["I sing"]: in the key of C major, the narrator praises his vagabond life until the last verses, when he is arrested and hangs himself. The disjunction between the text and the light-hearted music enhances the element of surprise, and Trenet's dramatic detachment creates a strong sense of irony. Gainsbourg made similar use of a gap between light music and dark narration in "La Femme des uns sous le corps des autres" ["Some Men's Wives beneath Other Men's Bodies"], where a catchy riff based on parallel thirds in A♭ major travels between the different instruments (flute, saxophone, guitar, vibraphone, etc.) and accompanies a complaint about adultery and marital homicide. At times, the second half of the riff is indeed played a half-step down, as if the sarcasm of the lyrics contaminated the music and made the main key more confused.

On another level, in Trenet's "L'Héritage infernal" ["The Infernal Inheritance"], humor strikes right from the opening with a squeaky brass chord and continues through with the first humorous rhymes in *"age,"* accentuated by the singer's enunciation (*"héritage," "mage," "fromage"*). The lyrics tell of a complicated inheritance and list the heterogeneous bequeathed objects ("his father's table, his mother's armchair, a cuckoo clock, an old pair of suspenders, a bottle of Vittel, a lace headdress"), which surely inspired Boris Vian in his "Complainte du progrès"—where he draws a list of extraordinary domestic objects at a frenzied tempo. In "L'Héritage infernal," the grotesque enumeration eventually becomes out of control, bringing Trenet to mix the listed objects in a confusing gibberish—"a lace clock, a headdress with Vittel water, an armchair with suspenders, a cuckoo table"—before he begins to imitate the sounds of gossip coming from the neighborhood, gradually turning it into the cackling of chickens. The light orchestration, the strings pizzicato, the piccolo answering the bass clarinet, the chromatic ascents and descents and the frenetic rhythm section all participate in the comical aspect of the narrative. This frenzied and disparate enumeration device is also noticeable in Gainsbourg's "Marabout," a caustic reference to a French nursery rhyme based on a *dorica castra* ("Trois Petits Chats"), where expressions are linked according to the sound of their last syllable and the first syllable of the following word (*"Mara*bout, bout *d'f*icelle, c'est la vie, vie *de chien"*). Here, the severely twisted nursery rhyme is accompanied by African drums that were plagiarized from Babatunde Olatunji's album, *Drums of Passion*.

Parodies and Rewritings

Several of Trenet's songs such as "Landru"[1] or "L'Hôtel borgne" tend to be steeped in dark humor and murder stories, a genre inherited from the 1890s *chanson réaliste*, but the joyful swing orchestration always compensates for the cynical scenarios and puns. As for Gainsbourg, his first album *Du Chant à la une!* (1958) draws inspiration from American "noir" novels to depict suicidal thoughts ("Le Poinçonneur des Lilas"), gloomy relationships ("Ce Mortel Ennui"), or car accidents ("Du Jazz dans le ravin"). In Bourderionnet's words,

> it is through the influence of the "noir" genre from America that crime resurfaces in *chanson*. Gainsbourg not only appropriates the musical element of the 1950s thriller, namely jazz, but he transforms *chanson* into a new category of the noir genre.
>
> (2011: 90–1)

In doing so, the songwriter conjugates multicultural influences to modernize a long-standing tradition of murder stories in French *chansons*, as Trenet did before him.

From another perspective, Gainsbourg's song "Sois belle et tais-toi" is an example of his penchant for parody: on a *chachachá* rhythm, the singer enumerates a list of animals and their cries (*"Le ramier roucoule/Le moineau pépie/Caquette la poule/Jacasse la pie"*[2]) before concluding with the order to his lover, *"sois belle et tais-toi"* ["be beautiful and keep quiet"]. The misogynistic association of a woman with a noisy bestiary is compounded by this double imperative. The mockery is also perceptible in the flute's voluble counterpoint, which punctuates the singer's speech. This list of animal cries is also reminiscent of Trenet's song "Boum!," in which the singer lists objects and animals with their corresponding onomatopoeia—*"La pendule fait tic-tac-tic-tic/Les oiseaux du lac pic-pac-pic-pic/Glou-glou-glou font tous les dindons/Et la jolie cloche ding-ding-dong"* ["The clock ticks/The birds of the lake peep/All turkeys gobble/

The bell rings"]. This list leads to the joyful explosion of a loving heart. The syntactic construction of the verses is similar in both songs: the verb/complement inversion in the second part of the stanza in Trenet's song is taken up by Gainsbourg, who, in turn, inverts the verb/subject position. Finally, in Gainsbourg's song, love is no longer the pulse of the world: the lover is reduced to silence. All these elements prompt the listener to identify in "Sois belle et tais-toi" a cynic re-writing of Trenet's "Boum!," in which a disenchanted and misogynic tone dominates.

The "swing irony" Trenet and Gainsbourg excelled in manifests itself in different ways: Trenet's dramatic distance is less self-deprecating than Gainsbourg's and his irony often relies on the gap between the lively rhythms and melodies and the darker elements hidden in the bend of a line. On the other hand, Gainsbourg's cynicism, inherited from the *fou chantant*'s distant casualness, is more frontal. His use of the "self-depreciating irony of the double take, which the French call *deuxième degré*, is probably one of Gainsbourg's major contributions to the range of techniques available to the *chanson* artist" (Hawkins 2000: 159).

Poetry and Modern *Chanson*

Poetry in *Chanson*

In 1941, Trenet's adaptation of Verlaine's "Chanson d'automne" into a swing song heralded a new era in the history of French *chanson*:

> Charles Trenet ... is to be credited with pioneering the process of taking texts that belong to the canon of poetry in print and turning them into songs that are not only recorded, but often mixed with a jazz rhythm and widely broadcast on the radio.
>
> (Bourderionnet 2011: 27–8)

Even though performers such as Yvette Guibert had already set poems to (popular) music before the First World War (Hawkins 2000: 174), with "Verlaine," Trenet operated a fusion between a new style of music and the French literary canon. Similarly, Gainsbourg set numerous French poets to music: in "La Nuit d'octobre," Afro-Caribbean rhythms and elaborated arrangements give Musset's poem a new twist. As for "Baudelaire," it is a bossa nova version of Baudelaire's "Le Serpent qui danse" (1861: 64–6), half-recited, half-sang, where the singer plays with the pleasure "of phonation with the control of breath and breathing" (Bourderionnet 2011: 35). Naming this adaptation after the poet is reminiscent of Trenet's choice to simply call "Verlaine" his swing version of "Chanson d'automne." In addition to Musset and Baudelaire, Gainsbourg adapted poets such as Nerval ("Le Rock de Nerval"), Hugo ("Chanson de Maglia"), and Arvers ("Le Sonnet d'Arvers"), using rock 'n' roll rhythms or jazzy orchestrations with variable creativity and success. But perhaps Gainsbourg's greatest achievement lies in the intertextuality woven with famous works of poetry, as in "La Chanson de Prévert" or "Je suis venu te dire que je m'en vais," where his "practice of palimpsest reveals the importance of an oral re-appropriation ... of a heritage until now confined to the school space" (Bourderionnet 2011: 65). Gainsbourg's postmodern collage in these two songs introduces a new approach in setting poetry to popular music.

Chanson and Poetry

What Cantaloube-Ferrieu calls Trenet's "undeniable poetic character" (1981: 14) was recognized as early as the 1930s: his friendship with intellectuals such as Max Jacob or Jean Cocteau brought him closer to Surrealism. Thanks to his literary sensibility, Trenet "opened up the possibility of using popular song as a form of poetic expression capable of accommodating a wide variety of feelings and subjects" (Hawkins 2000: 87). His lyrics pay tribute to poets he admired. Among other examples, the song "Il pleut dans ma chambre" hides a discreet nod to Verlaine—*"il pleut dans ma chambre/il pleut dans mon cœur"* ["It's raining in my room /It's raining in my heart"] recalls "Il pleure dans mon cœur"'s opening lines: *"Il pleure dans mon cœur/Comme il pleut sur la ville"* ["It's raining in my heart/As it rains on the town"] (1874: 9). In "Y'a d'la joie,"

> The Eiffel Tower which *"part en ballade"* ["goes for a stroll"] and *"Comme une folle ... saute la Seine à pieds joints"* ["Like a crazy fool ... jumps over the Seine with her feet together"] ... is [also] echoing a motif common to much of pre-surrealist literary and artistic output, from the opening lines of Apollinaire's poem "Zone" through Chagall's paintings to the early film of René Clair, *Paris qui dort*.
> (Hawkins 2000: 89)

This game of literary references was taken up by Gainsbourg, who oriented his esthetic mainly toward the romantic poets and writers of the nineteenth century—Baudelaire, Musset, Constant, Poe—putting himself in the character of a *"poète maudit* born too late" (Anderson 2013: 86). The first lines of "Initials B.B." are strongly reminiscent of the incipit of "The Raven" by Poe and, as already mentioned, "Je suis venu te dire que je m'en vais" is based on the re-writing of Verlaine's most famous lines from "Chanson d'automne." Eventually, Gainsbourg came to consider talk-over as the most adequate device when it came to setting to music the complex prosody of his lyrics (Julien 2018: 53). However, despite sound engineer Dominique Blanc-Francard's claim that this technique "was completely new in France" (Simmons 2001: 137), one could argue that Trenet had also used it long before Gainsbourg, not to better serve the prosody of his lyrics, but rather for theatrical purposes ("Le Soleil et la lune," "Que reste-t-il de nos amours?").

Trenet's decisive influence on Gainsbourg manifests itself through an ensemble of features encompassing both a poetic vision of *chanson* and the fusion of artistic and popular esthetics. Although Gainsbourg stressed, on several occasions, his total disregard for *chanson*, which he considered "a minor art, [intended] for minors" (Simmons 2001: 82), his taste for words, the attention he paid to their sounds, and their setting to music betray an undeniable respect for the genre, as well as an awareness of its rich heritage. Indeed, Trenet and Gainsbourg's ability to capture sensations through the reminiscence of an instant made them both guarantors of "a tradition in which singer-songwriters made the genre into a popular vehicle of self-expression of a poetic and even literary kind" (Hawkins 2000: 85). To put it differently: their inventiveness opened French *chanson* to a transcultural and transnational dimension, while maintaining the essential features of the genre.

Notes

1 Henri Désiré Landru was a serial killer who murdered several women and was arrested in April 1919. His public trial excited the crowds and made him an infamous figure of the interwar period. In his song, Trenet refers to how Landru burned these women's bodies after killing them.
2 "The woodpigeon coos/The sparrow peeps/The chicken cackles/The magpie chatters."

14

Singing Gainsbourg at the Time of the *Yé-Yé* (1962–6): The Perpetual Provocateur and His Muses

Andreas Bonnermeier

When thinking of the *yé-yé* movement in France, one does not necessarily associate it with the name of Serge Gainsbourg. And yet, if one considers the many songs he wrote for female performers such as France Gall or Brigitte Bardot, *yé-yé* did mark a turning point in his career. Between 1962 and 1966, other female singers—for example, Petula Clark and Régine—included some of his songs in their repertoire, thereby contributing to his popularity. This chapter examines Gainsbourg's and his female performers' role during the *yé-yé* era while taking a close look at the body of songs they produced together.

Gainsbourg's Female Performers: The Pygmalion and His Muses

Serge Gainsbourg's difficult beginnings as a singer have been widely documented. Although he began performing in Parisian cabarets and releasing records in the late 1950s, success remained elusive, prompting him to write for other artists. These performers were all the more important considering some of them became muses and sources of inspiration for him. In addition to Michèle Arnaud, who ran the Parisian cabaret Milord l'Arsouille and who was the first to perform songs by Gainsbourg in 1958 ("La Recette de l'amour fou," "Ronsard 58"), Catherine Sauvage ("Les Goémons") and Juliette Gréco ("Les Amours perdues," "L'Amour à la papa") need to be mentioned here. It was above all Gréco's renditions of "Accordéon" (1962) and "La Javanaise" (1963) that boosted Gainsbourg's reputation as a songwriter. Gréco turned these songs into classics, and they remained a part of her stage repertoire until the end of her career. In the 1960s, Gainsbourg's songs were recorded by other established performers such as Isabelle Aubret ("La Chanson de Prévert") or Françoise Hardy ("Comment te dire adieu," "L'Anamour"). It is worth noting that long before Jane Birkin came into

Translated from the German by Pia Köstner.

his life, British singer Petula Clark included some of Gainsbourg's compositions in her repertoire with considerable success. Finally, he played the role of a Pygmalion for some of these female performers, giving their budding careers the necessary push. As Louis-Jean Calvet observes,

> Throughout his life, Serge Gainsbourg made women sing. He knew how to prepare tailor-made texts for them, adapted to their personality, to their image or to the image he had of them, what he wanted to show of them (and, in the case of Birkin, to her accent); he knew how to compose melodies that were made for their voices, their vocal range, their capabilities.
>
> (2013: 31)

Gainsbourg's role as a Pygmalion is particularly evident when one considers France Gall, whose career only took off through his compositions. Another notable artist who performed songs Gainsbourg wrote for her was Régine, a nightclub owner who began her singing career in the mid-1960s, and celebrated her first success with "Les P'tits Papiers." Finally, it is essential to mention Brigitte Bardot and Jane Birkin: while Bardot recorded several of his songs during the decade ("L'Appareil à sous," "Bubble gum"), British singer Jane Birkin became Serge Gainsbourg's true muse after they released the duet "Je t'aime... moi non plus" (1969), which caused both scandals and polemical discussions (Verlant 2000: 384). Birkin, who also lived with Gainsbourg, even became his performer *par excellence* (Calvet 2013: 31), and continued releasing albums exclusively made up of his compositions until his death.

Gainsbourg and *Yé-Yé*

In the early 1960s, French *chanson* was facing a major upheaval. If the previous decade had been the heyday of *Chanson d'auteur* (embodied by such figures as Georges Brassens, Jacques Brel, or Charles Aznavour), the new musical styles that originated in the Anglo-American cultural arena began to influence French singers and songwriters. Beginning in 1961, *yé-yé* became a musical trend in France and was hugely popular among young people. Melodies with fast beats and raucous arrangements dominated, while the lyrics receded into the background. Suddenly, they became "commensurate: naïve and soft, sometimes silly, peppered with onomatopoeia" (Fontana 2007: 100). The *yé-yé* sound soon established itself as the ideal backdrop for youth dance halls such as the Golf Drouot in Paris, while rhythmic—and sometimes frenzied—dance styles such as the twist influenced the musical production. It was the time of the *idoles* and the *copains*, whose representatives—Johnny Hallyday and Claude François, but also Sheila, Sylvie Vartan, and Françoise Hardy—enjoyed tremendous success. This new generation of artists became the objects of a veritable star cult. *Chanson* turned into a commodity as its distribution was being accelerated by the portable turntable. Record companies did not want to lose out on this trend, especially since record sales in those years reached dimensions that contemporary artists could only dream of. But promoting this new musical style had an immediate consequence: the "classic" French *chanson* of the 1950s, mainly performed in the cabarets of the "Rive Gauche," suddenly seemed out of date. To adapt to the spirit of the times, mainstream artists such as Dalida tried to reinvent themselves, recording songs in the new style (e.g., "La Leçon de twist"). Although a sought-after songwriter, Gainsbourg had begun his career too late to be regarded as a popular *chanson* artist (Verlant 2006a: 66–7). While his early albums no doubt included sophisticated songs, sales were disappointing, and even hits such as "Le Poinçonneur des Lilas" (1958) now sounded old-fashioned. Unsurprisingly, he was initially very skeptical of the *yé-yé* phenomenon; yet he soon had a change of heart and started writing for *yé-yé* idols "in order not to croak" (221). He commented on these *"exercices de style"* ["exercises in style"] (260), as he called them, as follows: "I turned my coat when I discovered it was lined with mink" (Rioux 1994: 287). It is also worth pointing out, especially with regard to Gainsbourg's female performers, that his music productions in those years fell into two camps: on the one hand, he wrote songs that fit perfectly into the *yé-yé* zeitgeist thanks to their modern, innovative character; on the other hand, he produced songs whose essential originality turned them into timeless classics. The following sections will explore some of these songs in more detail.

Sucettes, Appareils à Sous and Advice on Love: Brigitte Bardot, France Gall, Michèle Torr

One of Gainsbourg's first songs in the *yé-yé* style was "L'Appareil à sous," released in 1962, and performed by none other than Brigitte Bardot. Bardot, who had been one of the most famous actors in France since the 1950s, had not yet made her debut as a singer. Until 1967, Gainsbourg wrote a series of tailor-made songs for her. "L'Appareil à sous" appropriated typical elements of the immensely popular twist in terms of melody and rhythm, a popularity which was also observable in television broadcasts of the time. On the textual level, however, "L'Appareil à sous" already featured plays on words and double entendre, a trademark that Gainsbourg would develop further during those years. The tune begins with: *"Tu n'es qu'un appareil à sou-/Pirs/Un appareil à sou-/Rire/À ce jeu/Je/Ne joue pas…"* Here, Brigitte Bardot's character appears as an emancipated and progressive woman who seems altogether unimpressed by men's mechanical overtures. The message of the song, however, is only discernible on closer listening, as the playful character of the text in combination with the rhythm of the twist suggests a certain lightness. The same lightness is also noticeable in "Les Omnibus" from 1965, another of Gainsbourg's songs for Bardot. Once again, the lyrics use puns to describe the relationship between women and men, whereby the text's originality consists of the fact that different interpersonal relations are associated with different modes of transportation: *"Y a les maîtresses/Des hommes express/Il y a les femmes/Des hommes pullman/Celles qui aiment la compagnie/Des Wagons-lit/Quant à moi ce que j'aime le plus/C'est de loin tous les omnibus."* On a musical level, it is striking that melody and rhythm still convey a certain lightness, but no longer adhere to the *yé-yé* style as clearly as was the case in "L'Appareil à sous." "Bubble gum," which Brigitte Bardot also released in 1965, is similar in that it focuses on the female protagonist's relationship with a man. In this song, Gainsbourg once again showcases his unique visual language, combining a catchy melody with lyrics that reveal all their subtleties only upon closer listening. Here, waning passion is compared to a piece of chewing gum that one would like to just spit out: *"Entre mes bras tu étais comme/Tu étais tendre et sucré comme/Tu as perdu ta saveur comme/Mon bubble bubble-gum/Si je pouvais t'balancer comme/Mais tu me colles aux semelles comme…"*

Besides Bardot, it was above all France Gall who popularized Serge Gainsbourg's songs in the years of *yé-yé*, thus guaranteeing the songwriter's financial stability. Four songs in particular deserve a closer look: "Laisse tomber les filles" and "N'écoute pas les idoles," from 1964, "Poupée de cire, poupée de son" from 1965, and "Les Sucettes" from 1966. The first two are typical of the *yé-yé* sound, where the rhythm section, with its dominant beats, is foregrounded. While the female character in the first song offers advice on love (*"Laisse tomber les filles/Un jour c'est toi qu'on laissera/Laisse tomber les filles/ … /Un jour c'est toi qui pleureras"*), the second addresses the cult around youth idols, a theme typical of *yé-yé* and its time: *"Ces chansons que tu fredonnes/Comment veux-tu que je les aime? Personne/N'a jamais pu/Me faire croire que l'on se donne/A cœur perdu/Pour se quitter à l'automne/Bien entendu."*

In 1965, Gainsbourg and France Gall became famous beyond France's borders when the latter won the Eurovision Song Contest for Luxembourg with "Poupée de cire, poupée de son." The fast *yé-yé* style rhythm, which is also evident in France Gall's rather harsh-sounding and staccato-like interpretation, almost hides the fact that Gainsbourg embedded deeper levels of meaning in this text as well: *"L'amour n'est pas que dans les chansons/Poupée de cire, poupée de son/Mes disques sont un miroir/Dans lequel chacun peut me voir/Je suis partout à la fois/Brisée en mille éclats de voix."* In "Poupée de cire, poupée de son," Gainsbourg dissects the myth of the idol (Rioux 1994: 171), echoing a statement by France Gall where she compared her work as a performer in those years with working in a factory (Fontana 2007: 109). This song already suggests an erotic-amorous undertone, which Gainsbourg would further develop a year later in the song "Les Sucettes"—on the surface, its text seeks to entertain with witty plays on words about a supposedly harmless subject set to a typical *yé-yé* melody. Between the lines, however, a clear erotic component becomes palpable: *"Les sucettes à l'anis d'Annie/Donnent à ses baisers/Un goût ani-/sé lorsqu'elle n'a sur la langue/Que le petit bâton."* Much has been speculated and written about the extent to which France Gall, who was still very young at the time, was aware of this erotic dimension (Borowice 2010: 96). What is certain, however, is that this was one more song in which Gainsbourg skillfully and subtly undermined the *yé-yé* style and its often-simplistic texts.

Occasionally, Gainsbourg also wrote for other *yé-yé* performers, such as Michèle Torr. Like France Gall, Torr began her career in the mid-1960s,[1] but she was less successful than her contemporaries. In search for new songwriters to work with, she recorded Gainsbourg's "Non à tous les garçons" in 1965. At first glance, this is yet another song that gives young girls advice on love: *"C'ui-ci est bien trop beau/Pour être malin/C'ui-là n'est pas idiot/Il est vilain/Et tu dis non/Toujours non/Non/Non à tous les garçons."* The melody is in keeping with the lyrics, in tune with the zeitgeist, and the arrangement is accordingly catchy. Still, the words also include an ambiguous twist at the end, no doubt surprising for a tune supposedly primarily aimed at teenagers: *"Fais comme moi/Moi je dis oui/Toujours oui/Oui/Oui à tous les garçons."* As was the case with "Les Sucettes," it is unlikely that the young Michèle Torr was aware of this ambiguity. In any event, it remained Gainsbourg's only title in the performer's repertoire. The following section is a discussion of more mature female performers interested in Gainsbourg's songs.

P'tits Papiers, Sheriffs and the Beatles: Isabelle Aubret, Petula Clark, Dalida, Régine

A number of performers who had enjoyed popularity before the *yé-yé* period emerged also turned to Gainsbourg for new material during those years. For example, he wrote the lyrics to "Il n'y a plus d'abonné au numéro que vous avez demandé" for Isabelle Aubret in 1963 (the music was by Henri Salvador). Moreover, he penned for her "Arc-en-ciel" (1964) and "Pour aimer il faut être trois" (1965), the latter going in the opposite direction of the songs written for France Gall, because contrary to what the title suggests, it does not involve a true *ménage à trois*. Rather, the third element is love itself: *"Oui pour aimer il faut être trois/L'amour et moi sommes deux sans toi/Sans lui ne reste que toi et moi."* The songs he wrote for Isabelle Aubret also stood out musically. Rather than following the typical *yé-yé* style, they were based on the *chansons* of the 1950s, or on classical works of composers such as Brahms.

Another performer who featured several of Gainsbourg's songs in her repertoire with great success was Petula Clark. In 1962, she released "Vilaine Fille, mauvais garçon," a song in which Gainsbourg once again plays with ambiguities: *"Viens avec moi par les sentiers interdits/A ceux-là qui nous appellent à tort ou à raison/Vilaines filles, mauvais garçons..."* Although the melody and arrangement seem whimsical, they are not characteristic of *yé-yé*, unlike "Ô ô Sheriff" from 1964, which, from a musical standpoint, offers a typical example of this style. The subject matter of the song, however, is less typical, as it portrays a cowboy who is a clumsy and awkward lover. Probably the best-known tune that Gainsbourg composed for Petula Clark is "La Gadoue" from 1965, in which he playfully takes up a quintessentially "English" theme, the bad weather, which is especially, though by no means exclusively, unpleasant on holiday: *"Du mois de septembre au mois d'août/Faudrait des bottes de caoutchouc/Pour patauger dans la gadoue."* Finally, "Les Incorruptibles" from 1966 situates the protagonist in Al Capone's Chicago of the 1920s, also a rather unusual subject for *yé-yé*.

Dalida, who started her career in France with songs that sounded exotic and Italian, was also looking for new songwriters and ideas in the 1960s. She only recorded one song by Gainsbourg: "Je préfère naturellement" (1966). It too takes up an "English" subject matter and may be regarded as a tribute to the Beatles, thus bridging the gap to *yé-yé*. This song is yet another example of Gainsbourg's passion for playing with language. In this particular case it applies to everything that denotes the English language and culture. The word "anglais" appears no less than twenty times in the lyrics, and thus functions as a hook: *"Les quatre garçons de ce groupe* anglais/*Ne s'habillent que de tissus* anglais/*Ils vont chez le même tailleur* anglais…"

Finally, one cannot fail to mention Régine, another female artist who started singing in her thirties and to whose career Gainsbourg contributed considerably. During the heyday of *yé-yé*, Régine—who was up to this point better known as an entrepreneur of Parisian nightlife—enjoyed notable success with "Les P'tits Papiers" (1965). Gainsbourg saw her as a "modern Fréhel" (Borowice 2010: 208), and he wrote several more tailor-made songs for her. In the lyrics of "Les P'tits Papiers," he artfully plays with different types of paper, creating kaleidoscopic associations between images and verbal expressions, while Régine performs this song, whose melody is atypical of the time and has a rather classical character, just as masterfully, making it her trademark: *"Laissez parler/Les p'tits papiers/A l'occasion/Papier chiffon/Puissent-ils un soir/Papier buvard/Vous consoler."* Two more songs—"Il s'appelle reviens," "Si t'attends qu'les diamants t'sautent au cou"—which Gainsbourg wrote for Régine in the same year also became classics in her repertoire, and had a lasting influence on her style as a performer. In 1967, after the *yé-yé* trend had faded, Gainsbourg kept on writing songs for her, including "Pourquoi un pyjama," and "Capone et sa p'tite Philis." Here too, he remained true to himself as provocation and ambiguities pervaded the songs' lyrics.

From Provocation to Classics of *Chanson*

What then remains of Serge Gainsbourg, his female performers, and *yé-yé*? It is, for one, the realization that this was a particularly productive period in Gainsbourg's life and that he had succeeded with a wider and younger audience for the first time (Verlant 2000: 301). As an author and composer, he became a permanent fixture, using his talents in manifold ways—while writing contemporary songs that superficially corresponded to the *yé-yé* trend, such as the ones written for France Gall and Michèle Torr, he also gave free rein to his passion for puns and ambiguities, earning a reputation as a provocateur. Moreover, he was also active as an author and composer for established female performers looking for new material during the *yé-yé* years. Gainsbourg still incorporated more classical forms of *chanson*, but gave them their own, typical form. Finally, it is in the period from 1961 to 1966 that he took on his role as a Pygmalion for female performers of note, as was the case with Brigitte Bardot and Régine. And it was largely thanks to their renditions that many of Gainsbourg's compositions from those years became classics as their provocative dimension faded into the background.

Note

1   Her greatest successes include "C'est dur d'avoir 16 ans" and "Dans tes bras (j'oublie ma peine)" in 1964.

"Qui Est 'In' Qui Est 'Out'": Gainsbourg & The British Invasion

15

"Extrêmement Pop": Gainsbourg and Swinging London

Kirk Anderson

Introducing a chapter on French pop from 1968 onward, David Looseley observes:

> [F]rom the early 1970s one may detect—in *chanson* and in popular music generally—a drive to experiment by appropriating rather than imitating Anglo-American styles and rooting them in French experience, to restore authenticity by expressing oneself in a language (metaphorically and literally) of one's own but *reinventing* that language in the process.
>
> (2003: 39)

This is a particularly felicitous description of a capital shift in French pop music practice. However, I want to argue that Looseley situates it too late, overlooking straws in the wind well before the "events" of May 1968. Two years previous, a "furious wind of change and innovation" (Verlant 2000: 406) blew through the French charts, scattering most of *yé-yé*'s survivors, particularly those who specialized in imported British and American hits.[1] That wind carried in Michel Polnareff, Jacques Dutronc, and Antoine, who enjoyed their first radio success at nearly the same time, and who, writing their own songs or collaborating with others, preferred appropriation to imitation. By then, Serge Gainsbourg had behind him six poorly selling albums and seven years of obscure toil, followed by the fame and royalties of "Poupée de cire, poupée de son," a Eurovision Song Contest winner and international best-seller sung by France Gall. It was however in early 1966 that a significant number of radio listeners heard his voice for the first time, via "Docteur Jekyll et Monsieur Hyde," and then "Qui est 'in' qui est 'out,'" whose titles aptly evoke their author's deep ambivalence about success as defined by airplay and record sales.

Interviews at mid-decade reveal a Gainsbourg thirsty for commercial success, ready to become a "turncoat" if the coat was "lined with mink," according to his oft-cited quip (Verlant 2000: 376). Meanwhile, his ears had been open to new sounds and exotic rhythms since the *Gainsbourg Percussions* album (1964), if not earlier. Market shifts in 1965-6 would allow him for the first time to kill the commercial and exotic birds with one stone, and this time without the intermediary of a Petula Clark, Juliette Gréco, or France Gall.

French singers felt the temptation to record across the Channel well before London was "swinging." First, the English studios had a technological lead. In 1963, Eddy Mitchell marveled at an early four-track recorder: "Frankly, we wondered how we would fill all four," he recalls, "two tracks seemed like a lot to us" (1979: 69). Second, the English studio musicians and engineers set a standard that left the French frustrated with their own. Françoise Hardy, unhappy with her first two albums, got permission to record the next two at Pye Studios in London, and didn't return to the Paris studios for years (2008: 71). In early 1966, Michel Polnareff agreed to sing his first single, "La Poupée qui fait non," in French, but only on the condition that he could record it in London (Paquotte & Diterzi). Two future members of Led Zeppelin accompanied him, and the scarf he wears on the sleeve, red and white stripes on a blue background, looks less like a French tricolor than a Union Jack.

Gainsbourg too made a record in England, as early as 1963, though he didn't have to cajole anyone at Philips—apparently it was their decision. Label mate Johnny Hallyday had recently recorded songs for half an album at Fontana Studios, under the musical direction of Harry Robinson. Among them, "Elle est terrible" (Eddie Cochran's "Somethin' Else") became Hallyday's biggest seller that year. Small wonder then that Philips chose the same studio and the same producer for Gainsbourg a few months later so that he might finally have a hit.

But—and here's that ambivalence again—Gainsbourg's sharpest attacks on the pop music industry appear in his most commercial records. France Gall's recordings of "N'écoute pas les idoles" and "Poupée de cire, poupée de son" may serve as well-known examples. Gainsbourg's first London tracks include "L'Appareil à sous" and "Vilaine Fille, mauvais garçon," in which the money machine makes a separate appearance, as a *machine* instead of an *appareil*:

> Kids these days are all a little crazy
> But the clattering of the money machine
> Will cover up the voice that says, right or wrong,
> Nasty girl, bad boy.[2]

Either short on inspiration or wanting to hedge his bets, Gainsbourg chose for this EP, save for the country-flavored curiosity "Un Violon, un jambon" ["A Fiddle, a Ham"], songs that had already been recorded by Bardot, Gréco, and Petula Clark. If the goal was to reproduce the sound of the Hallyday tracks, the record succeeded. The electric guitar and drums of "Vilaine Fille, mauvais garçon," for example, capture the same English "beat" sound that launched the Beatles that year. Alas, the experiment still failed to produce the hit Philips executives had hoped for. One can only speculate as to why. Critics haven't been kind to this disc, but the performances are as good as the compositions, among them one of Gainsbourg's best-loved songs, "La Javanaise."

Biographer Gilles Verlant reports that the whole episode "deeply displeased" Gainsbourg (2000: 319), but then so did the poor sales of his previous records. The money machine didn't yet clatter loudly enough to cover up the anti-*yé-yé* voice, which was at this point still his own. For a time, he abandoned beat music and the London scene. But the next two albums, *Gainsbourg Confidentiel* and *Gainsbourg Percusssions*, sold no better. So, in 1964 and 1965, he decided to "turn his coat" for good, and this time with no pressure from the record company. A change in attitude comes through in remarks to friends and interviewers. On the one hand, "I ply a different trade. That stuff [the *yé-yé*'s], that's American pop. American songs with subtitles" (quoted in Verlant 2000: 329). Then several months later, "I'm going into the rock business, real rock. I'll write twelve of them this year. I've waited six years, and that's enough" (379). The contradiction is merely superficial, though, because Gainsbourg meant to create "rock" music that would transcend *yé-yé*. Already, his compositions for France Gall, if not "rock," amounted to more than subtitled American songs.

Things had changed since "Vilaine Fille, mauvais garçon," not only for him but even more for English music. The British Invasion was by now in full swing. Meanwhile, the commercial disappointment of his last two albums, as well as several disastrous live appearances, shifted his priorities: "I've decided to pay the bills ... That's the last record I'll make before buying myself a Rolls" (342). And so, this time by choice, he returned to Fontana Studios to prove that imitation isn't the only way to bring English pop to a French audience. Gainsbourg's A&R director, Claude Dejacques, wrote a liner note for the resulting EP:

> Getting off the airplane in London, Serge carried a briefcase of ideas and the possible versions of those ideas. One night in the little clubs of Soho was enough for the rhythms of British pop to inspire the melodies for these four songs and the very structure of the verses.
>
> (1966)

The anecdote challenges us to take Dejacques literally, and to identify something English in the structure of the verses, or rather something Anglo-American, since the British pop he refers to owed so much to American soul, R&B, and rock.

Granted, the music of "swinging London" wasn't swing music; the term denotes much less a jazz rhythm than a way of life, and both appealed to Gainsbourg at different points of his itinerary. But Olivier Bourderionnet's metrical analysis of Brassens, Vian, and Gainsbourg in *Swing Troubadours* nevertheless offers one approach. Without claiming to identify the recipe of a perfect fusion of French *chanson* and mid-1960s English pop, I hope just the same to indicate a few of its ingredients by looking at the four tracks of the *Marilu* EP, recorded in the first days of 1966 under the direction of Arthur Greenslade.

It should go without saying that the objects of focus here conflate *language* and *music*. The language, with its auditory and semantic dimensions, also brings together elements of both French and English: nothing new for Gainsbourg. As for the music, this brief study will focus on rhythm and instrumentation, where the "pop" character of these songs is most salient. When rock and roll first arrived in France, would-be defenders of *chanson* complained that rock rhythms simply didn't suit the French tongue. That argument was taken up again more recently by French artists explaining why they don't sing in French.[3] If they are right, then Gainsbourg's project was bound to fail, all the more so as, despite his stylistic departures, he remained faithful to the *chanson à texte* tradition and hadn't yet abandoned singing for "talk-over." Could this foreign music accommodate authentic French lyrics?

The claim about rock's incompatibility with French speech patterns merits deeper examination than it will get here. Two particularities of the language make this claim debatable nonetheless. First, the option of omitting, or not, the unaccented *e* offers lyricists and singers remarkable metrical variability (Bourderionnet 2011: 19–20). Piaf for example stretches *"la vie en rose"* to five syllables, while Brassens needs only that many for *"je m'suis fait tout p'tit."* Second, French lacks the fixed stress accents of English, a lack which according to Darius Milhaud "opens the door to freedom for the composer" (quoted in Bernac 1970: 35). Admittedly, it is a relative freedom. Bob Dylan's first French apostle Hugues Aufray released *Aufray chante Dylan* in 1965 and later recalled how he wanted to perform the sentence

> "Comme j'avais beaucoup marché, j'étais très, très fatigué." I accented the first syllable of <u>mar</u>-ché, and [lyricist Pierre Delanoë] told me: "In French, we say mar-<u>ché</u> with an accent on the last syllable ... I had to fight to have it my way.
>
> (Aufray 2007: 86)

A younger Dylan admirer, Francis Cabrel, frequently stresses the penultimate syllable. In both cases, the lexicon stays entirely French, but the diction betrays an American accent. As for Aufray's contemporary, Serge Gainsbourg, the traditionalist Delanoë would have wanted him to sing something like this: "Docteur Je<u>kyll</u>, il a<u>vait</u> en <u>lui</u>/Un m'<u>sieur</u> <u>Hyde</u> qu'é<u>tait</u> son mau<u>vais</u> génie." Instead, he repeats, while singing, the same stress accents used in his spoken introduction: "Non, je n'suis <u>pas</u> le <u>Doc</u>tor <u>Je</u>kyll... Mon nom est <u>Hyde</u>, <u>Mis</u>ter <u>Hyde</u>." Moreover, the words *Mister* and *Monsieur* cohabit in the sung text, with a stress on the first syllable in either case.

This shift of stress away from the conventional final syllable isn't systematic, but it goes well beyond proper nouns and anglicisms. The lead song of the EP, "Marilu," reveals the same tendency. In fact, the first verse translates almost spontaneously into English with the stresses intact:

<u>Dis</u>-moi Ma<u>ri-lu</u>	<u>Tell</u> me, Mari-<u>lu</u>
<u>Veux</u>-tu Ma<u>ri-lu</u>	<u>Would</u> you, Mari-<u>lu</u>
Ré<u>pondre</u> à <u>cette</u> <u>question</u>	<u>An</u>swer for <u>me</u> this <u>question</u>
Si tu n'veux <u>pas</u>, tu <u>dis</u> non	<u>If</u> you don't <u>want</u> to, <u>say</u> <u>no</u>
Je ne t'en <u>vou</u>drais <u>pas</u>	<u>I</u> wouldn't <u>hold</u> a <u>grudge</u>

The somewhat obscure "Shu ba du ba loo ba" flaunts its retro status in its title, which recalls not English pop but American doo-wop music. The female chorus sings *"<u>Shu</u> ba <u>du</u> ba <u>loo</u> ba"* with an American accent and trochaic stress pattern. That aside, the stress accents here remain fairly conventional, excepting *"un <u>gad</u>get"* and *"il lui <u>ré</u>pond."* This is the only lyric on the record to contain any *vers féminins*, that is, lines ending with an unaccented *e*: <u>ti</u>re, fi<u>celle</u>, <u>di</u>re, l'<u>aime</u>. Those allow the singer to more naturally emphasize the penultimate syllable. The theme, on the other hand, defies convention: for the favors of his beloved, a man finds himself in competition with a mechanical stuffed animal. The lyricist who dismissed *yé-yé* as "Tino Rossi music with electric guitars" (Georges Bratschi, quoted in Verlant 2000: 359) has now resolved to "pay the bills," but nevertheless refuses to turn his back on modernity.

Still, television host Denise Glaser has something else in mind when she tells Gainsbourg "Now you're singing like a one-man Beatles."[4] Clearly, the instrumentation on the *Marilu* EP has a lot to do with it: the "nasty guitars," the "caffeinated backup vocalists," the "sour organ" have never appeared on a Gainsbourg record before (Jarno 2008). But Claude Dejacques's sleeve notes invite us to dig deeper. When Gainsbourg, with his "briefcase of ideas," arrives in London in December 1965, the Beatles' *Rubber Soul* has just begun its forty-two-week ride on the UK album charts. If in fact "one night in the little clubs of Soho" sufficed to turn Gainsbourg's ideas into songs, what are the chances that this brand-new Beatles masterpiece played no part?

"Shu ba du ba loo ba" features a standard rock harmonic structure: each verse begins like a familiar twelve-bar blues, and then repeats bars 9–12 to make an even sixteen measures. But note the particular dialogue between the piano and the rhythm guitar: the piano chords fall on the first and fourth eighth notes of each measure (the downbeat and the afterbeat of two), while the guitar accentuates the third and sixth (beat two and the afterbeat of three). On *Rubber Soul*, "The Word" begins with the same piano/guitar interplay over the same chord changes. Gainsbourg's penchant for musical borrowing is amply documented; here, he has covered his tracks somewhat by setting "Shu ba du ba loo ba" at a faster tempo than "The Word," and by displacing the voice parts in a pattern that alternates with the Beatles' vocal track, so that their juxtaposition sets up a call and response. The appropriation stops short of expropriation.

"Qui est 'in' qui est 'out'" was the first Gainsbourg track to reach the French Top 20; his niece and nephew remember their excitement upon hearing it on Europe 1 radio (Verlant 2000: 405). Its scansion, anapests throughout, matches in regularity the relentless four-to-the-bar beat of the rhythm section. Having rhymed *"ma veste"* with "Reader's Digest" earlier in his career ("Le Poinçonneur des Lilas," 1958), Gainsbourg doesn't stop here at *"foule"* and "Liverpool," but even brings together the two languages on a purely orthographic level. The backup singers shout "in!" while he sings *"gin," "nitroglycérine,"* and *"bottines."* Against their "out!," he sings the purely visual rhymes *"toute," "mazout,"* and *"écoute."* This lyric is both the most meticulous and the most contemporary of the four, celebrating transitory pop culture and by so doing becoming a part of it. Certainly the "little lads from Liverpool" [*"les p'tits gars de Liverpool"*] need no footnote, but "Barbarella," the "Gemini" spacecraft, and the "Bus Palladium" now belong to 1960s trivia. The phrase *"Cash-Box"* refers to a periodical: it's safe to suppose that Gainsbourg, who had evoked the *"machine à sous"* and the *"appareil à sous"* on his previous London disc, savored the candor of its title, since the publication was devoted to the American record business. Lexically, Gainsbourg does here for popular song what Apollinaire, the apostle of modernism, did for poetry in 1913, with his *"sténo-dactylographes"* and *"hangars de Port-Aviation"* (7–8).

Musically, "Qui est 'in' qui est 'out'" asserts itself from the very first notes. Picaud and Verlant call it "uninhibited rock in French" and note its debt to American garage bands (2011: 170). More immediately, one can trace the opening fuzz guitar to the Yardbirds' "Heart Full of Soul" and of course the Rolling Stones' "Satisfaction." The drummer, as in "Marilu," sets down an implacable four-beat also borrowed from "Satisfaction," which in turn came from American soul music. The rhythm and the fuzz guitar give this track a ferocity that, for the first time in a Gainsbourg composition, exceeds the truculence of the lyrics.

At mid-decade, the *yé-yé* phenomenon had run its course, clearing the way for Polnareff, Dutronc, Nino Ferrer, Antoine, and even Serge Gainsbourg as a singer-songwriter. Writing original lyrics that reflect contemporary French life instead of eternal romance or an imported experience, while setting them to music that appeals to a young, massive, and increasingly cosmopolitan audience, became possible when that audience, approaching adulthood but too young perhaps for Brel or Brassens, no longer settled for "subtitled songs." For Gainsbourg, the British Invasion could not have arrived at a more opportune moment. It not only provided a way out of the art/commerce impasse that had defined his career thus far, but also inaugurated one of the richest phases of that career: in London's newly opened Chappell Studios, he would create the pop symphony "Initials B.B." and "69 année érotique," again with Arthur Greenslade. "Je t'aime... moi non plus" and the album many consider his apogee, *Histoire de Melody Nelson*, would soon follow.

Notes

1   Johnny Hallyday, Richard Anthony, and Claude François enjoyed a fan base massive enough to continue recording successful adaptations into the 1970s. Ronnie Bird, despite enthusiastic support from the nascent rock press, was not so lucky.
2   *"Les enfants du siècle sont tous un peu fous/Mais le cliquetis de la machine à sous/Couvrira cette voix qui dit à tort à raison/Vilaine fille, mauvais garçon."*
3   See, for example, HushPuppies guitarist Olivier Jourdan in Davet 2008: "Rock only suits the rhythm of the English language. I could never listen to rock in French" [*"Le rock ne peut convenir qu'à la rythmique de la langue anglaise. Je n'ai jamais pu écouter de rock en français"*].
4   https://www.ina.fr/ina-eclaire-actu/video/i04230110/longue-interview-de-serge-gainsbourg-par-denise-glaser [accessed 04-23-2022].

16

"Je T'Aime... Moi Non Plus": Jane Birkin and the English Preference of Serge Gainsbourg

Peter Hawkins

The meeting of Serge Gainsbourg and Jane Birkin on the set of the film *Slogan* in 1968 marked a turning point in the careers of both of them. It was still the early days of Birkin's career as a film actress, and the point at which Gainsbourg's fame reached a new level of public awareness. Both were on the rebound from major crises in their personal relationships—Gainsbourg had recently separated from Brigitte Bardot, Birkin had seen the end of her brief marriage to composer John Barry—and their meeting was the opposite of love at first sight: Birkin first thought Gainsbourg condescending and unpleasant, and Gainsbourg had no time for the little English girl (Dicale 2021: 375). However, with some help from the director Pierre Grimblat, the initial hostility was rapidly converted into a relationship of durable complicity (Verlant 2000: 172–3). What was it about the young and seductive Birkin that attracted the cynical forty-year-old? She no doubt represented for him the open and indulgent spirit of "Swinging London," then at the peak of its influence. English pop music had taken over the American youth market: the fashion for "flower power" and the bohemian, alternative values of the "hippy" and "beatnik" generations were at the height of their popularity—"Free love" was being openly practiced in festivals such as Woodstock and the Isle of Wight. Birkin came from a liberal upper middle-class family who very quickly adopted Gainsbourg. In spite of his sexual cynicism, he appreciated the warmth of Birkin's family background and maintained a friendly relation with her brother Andrew (376–7).

For her singing debut, Birkin seems to have had few inhibitions when she was asked to take over Brigitte Bardot's part in "Je t'aime... moi non plus." Fueled by its daring content, the new version, recorded in London with an orchestration by Arthur Greenslade, became an international hit record and made the Birkin-Gainsbourg couple famous overnight. The arrangements were reminiscent of the church-inspired, organ-based style popular in Anglo-American hit records of the time, such as "When a Man Loves a Woman" by Percy Sledge and "A Whiter Shade of Pale" by Procol Harum. The suggestive sighing of Birkin and the explicit erotic references of Gainsbourg's lyrics pushed back the frontiers of censorship in the representation of sexual relations, and the song's title provided a manifesto of the disenchanted lucidity about sexuality that had been Gainsbourg's attitude since his earliest songs—for example, "La Femme des uns sous le corps des autres" ["Some Men's Wives Beneath Other Men's Bodies"]. Eventually, the banning of the record by the guardians of public morality, such as the Catholic Church and the BBC, magnified its success and gave a measure of its public impact as an expression of the liberalization of sexual attitudes. As for the song's title ("I Love You... Me Neither"), it perfectly summed up the ambivalent nature of Gainsbourg's English preference. He then began to compose songs for his new favorite singer—"Jane B." (whose melody was borrowed from Chopin), "69 année érotique" ["69 Erotic Year"]—and went on to involve her in his major concept album of 1971, *Histoire de Melody Nelson*, asking her to interpret the voice of the English adolescent Melody, and using her image on the record's cover.

In fact, Gainsbourg had been a regular patron of English recording studios long before he met Birkin. His early albums had been orchestrated by Alain Goraguer in a *chanson* style with jazz influences. In this respect, his crossing the Channel to cut his own version of "La Javanaise" in 1963 was a real breakthrough—orchestrated by Harry Robinson in a truly "pop" style, the recording contrasted with his first live radio performances of the song as a waltz with a piano accompaniment. Very French in its style and content, this song alluded both to an obscure form of slang called "Javanese" [*"javanais"*] and to the popular French dance known as "Java." It had originally been written for the "Muse of Saint-Germain-des-Prés," Juliette Gréco, who incorporated it into her repertoire and made it famous (Dicale 2021: 160–1). In contrast to Gréco's version, Gainsbourg's recording suggests a syncopated Anglo-American style with a female chorus that is reminiscent of Roy Orbison's records.[1] As the 1960s went on, Gainsbourg made more and more use of the English recording studios and session musicians, moving on with "Docteur Jekyll et Monsieur Hyde," "Qui est 'in' qui est 'out,'" "Comic Strip," and "Chatterton." What was he looking for? In all likelihood, a British "pop" sound and a rock beat, which was then very much in fashion. What seems even more striking is his increasingly frequent allusions to English culture—the title of "Docteur Jekyll et Monsieur Hyde" is borrowed from Robert Louis Stevenson, "Qui est 'in' qui est 'out'" refers to English fashion trends, "Comic Strip" alludes to English Pop Art, and "Chatterton" is an even clearer allusion to English literature. It thus comes as no surprise that the heroine of his first concept album, *Histoire de Melody Nelson*, was an English adolescent knocked down by a highly symbolic English car, the Rolls Royce.[2]

All this provides a contrast with Gainsbourg's songs of some ten years earlier, in which the references were rather more to the French literary and poetic tradition, with musical settings of poems by Alfred de Musset ("La Nuit d'octobre"), or Gérard de Nerval ("Le Rock de Nerval"). But what is significant is that his first London recordings feature a crude rock backing that seems to be deliberately ironic. Yes, it was also the period of the beginnings of what became known as French *yé-yé*, and his intention seems to have been to make fun of both a probably ephemeral musical style, and the tradition of "Left Bank" songs with literary pretentions. For him, popular songs were, in a famous quotation from this time, "a minor art, [intended] for minors" (Simmons 2001: 82). One can guess, from his numerous quotations and references to literature, art, and classical music, that his own tastes were oriented toward "high culture" and that in comparison popular music was lightweight and superficial. But it will be this popular music that will bring him his first commercial success, with songs written for the teenage star France Gall, such as "Poupée de cire, poupée de son" ["Wax Doll, Sawdust Doll," 1964], and many more. In sum, this was when he "turned his coat after he discovered it was lined with mink," in his famous quip (Gainsbourg 1991: II, 303).

Gainsbourg's preference for English popular musical culture will continue through the 1970s: his albums *Rock Around the Bunker* (1975) and *L'Homme à tête de chou* ["The Man with the Cabbage Head," 1976] were entirely recorded in London, but only the backing tracks for *Vu de l'extérieur* ["Viewed from Outside," 1973]. The orchestrations for all three were provided by Alan Hawkshaw and his session musicians (Dicale 2021: 492). Gainsbourg moves toward the "talk over" technique, progressively abandoning the melodic component of the songs, which provokes an ironic distancing, especially in *Rock Around the Bunker*, where he undertakes a merciless satire of the Nazi ideology that poisoned his youth in occupied France. The wild and exaggerated rock music ridicules the pretensions of Hitler's ideology by reducing it to an ephemeral and superficial fashion. It was perhaps only in Britain that he could have completed such a project without creating a scandal, such were the French sensitivities about references to the German occupation.[3] The inspiration for *L'Homme à tête de chou*, on the other hand, was drawn from American pulp fiction, in which he perfected his "talk over" technique against the rather mechanical backing tracks recorded by British session musicians—from this period onwards, he only very rarely drew on French musicians, preferring the style of Anglo-American musicians and arrangers.

It is possible that even the "reggae turn" in Gainsbourg's recorded output was suggested by the British musical fashion of the period—in the 1970s, Bob Marley's records were very much in vogue in the UK. In the previous decade, he had already tried to renovate his musical inspiration by borrowing exotic musical styles—see, for instance, *Gainsbourg Percussions* (1964). He had also practiced a form of musical irony in juxtaposing a classical literary style with an unexpected musical genre, as in the aforementioned "Rock de Nerval." And the idea of setting the French national anthem to a musical style drawn from British postcolonial culture was perhaps suggested by the punk version of "God Save the Queen" by the Sex Pistols two years earlier. "Aux Armes et cætera" (1979), his reggae treatment of "La Marseillaise," was of course a subversive gesture, in spite of his protests that it was in keeping with the revolutionary spirit of the original song by Rouget de Lisle. But if that were the case, why choose an anglophone musical style rather than one inspired by Francophone Africa or the Caribbean, as Bernard Lavilliers did later? Would it be wrong to see in this choice a certain reservation about the national(ist) culture of France? Juxtaposed with the provocation of *Rock Around the Bunker*, could it imply a disenchanted commentary on the experiences of his youth under the German occupation, as in the song "Yellow Star"? Having been obliged to wear the sign as a Jew, he made it a source of pride, in spite of the desperate efforts of his parents to hide him and protect him from the anti-Semitic purges (Salgues 1989: 99–106). He probably remained skeptical about the republican values symbolized by the national anthem, whilst proudly proclaiming at the same time his

French citizenship, as in his confrontation with an extreme right-wing audience in Strasbourg in 1980, when he sang the "Marseillaise" *a cappella* and without a reggae accompaniment (Verlant 2000: 523–5).

The album *Mauvaises Nouvelles des étoiles* ["Bad News from the Stars," 1981] marks the end of the reggae experiment, and Gainsbourg now turns to the electronic funk of New York for the album *Love on the Beat* (1984). The choice of this musical style alludes to the urban realism of the songs of Bruce Springsteen, and perhaps also to the minimalist rock of Lou Reed and the Velvet Underground. All the songs on this new album are given titles in English, as the album's name suggests, but the texts recited in "talk over" are in a sophisticated, almost literary French style. This leads us to reflect on the relations between the two linguistic forms of expression. Here is an example from the lead track on the album, with an erotic text in elegant and polished octosyllabic verse:

> *Brûlants sont tous tes orifices*
> *Des trois que les dieux t'ont donnés*
> *Je décide dans le moins lisse*
> *D'achever de m'abandonner*[4]

The juxtaposition with the chorus repeating "Love on the beat" demystifies the Francophone literary eroticism with the punning slang of "beat,"[5] emphasized by the slight syncopation, which draws attention to the brutally phallic character of the description. The use of violent female cries in the background, behind the fairly aggressive funk rhythm, makes this piece a sort of "hard porn" version of "Je t'aime... moi non plus." There are similar linguistic juxtapositions in other tracks, such as "No Comment." The quotation of the last words of the British Admiral Lord Nelson, the hero of the battle of Trafalgar, "Kiss me, Hardy" is subverted by making it a celebration of homosexual promiscuity, including a reference to the uncompromising canvases of the English homosexual painter Francis Bacon. The track "Sorry Angel" tells the story of a suicide, as a veiled allusion to his separation from Jane Birkin in 1980, and is reminiscent of tracks from Lou Reed's album *Berlin*, celebrating the victims of the bohemian lifestyle. Probably the most controversial track on the album, his duet with his teenage daughter Charlotte, plays in similar fashion on an anglophone irony. While the chorus repeats the phrase "Lemon Incest" in English, over a rhythm track appropriate for a children's discothèque, the lyric celebrates *"l'inceste de citron,"* the ambiguous relations between Gainsbourg and his daughter, as if it were a lemon-zest flavored aperitif or a cocktail. We aren't far from a more provocative version of his famous double-entendre song "Les Sucettes" ["Lollipops," 1966], written for France Gall.

Gainsbourg's second American-inspired album, *You're Under Arrest*, has fewer tracks with English titles, but the word play between anglophone titles and slang references works in a similar fashion to the previous album. Thus "Five Easy Pisseuses" alludes to Bob Rafaelson's *Five Easy Pieces*, starring Jack Nicholson, and shows his contempt for fleeting sexual relationships. In a similar fashion, "Baille baille Samantha"

["Yawn, Yawn, Samantha"] expresses his disillusion with the behavior of his drug-addict girlfriend. Other titles are even more explicit on the sexual front, such as "Suck Baby Suck" with "the CD of Chuck Berry, Chuck." The name of the pioneer rocker is probably only quoted for the rhyme, but perhaps also as an allusion to his well-known suggestive song "My Ding-a-Ling."

While the decadent "Gainsbarre" represented himself hanging on the arm of "Samantha" in the seedier parts of New York, Jane Birkin was long gone—they had separated a few years earlier, in 1980. But throughout the 1980s Gainsbourg continued to write songs for her and produced, along with his own recording manager Philippe Lerichomme, three significant, tailor-made albums: *Baby Alone in Babylone* (1982), *Lost Song* (1987), and *Amours des feintes* (1990). As in the past he used Alan Hawkshaw and his British musicians, and the backing tracks were recorded in studios in London or elsewhere in the UK. As one might expect, many of the titles played on the English/French duality of Birkin's public image: "Baby Alone in Babylone," "Overseas Telegram," "Lost Song," "32 Fahrenheit," "Love Fifteen." What is striking is the way the songs on these albums seem to transpose the sentiments of Gainsbourg himself so as to have them interpreted by his former partner. In "Une Chose entre autres" ["One Thing Among Others"], he declares "More than anyone else you have had the best of me" [*"Tu as eu plus qu'un autre le meilleur de moi"*] and it appears, according to several of his closest friends, that he was still very attached to her (Verlant 2000: 539–41, 592). The sentiments expressed in the songs are of great delicacy, with an ambiguity that provides a striking contrast with the crude language of his solo albums. One thinks of tracks like "Fuir le bonheur de peur qu'il ne se sauve" ["Fleeing Happiness for Fear It Might Run Away"], or "En rire de peur d'être obligée d'en pleurer" ["Laughing About It for Fear of Being Obliged to Cry"]. What is even more striking is the return of melodies, some of them rather sophisticated and not necessarily borrowed from classical composers, as had often been the case in the past. The ambiguity of the sentiments is blatant, as in the song "Rupture au miroir" ["Break-Up at the Mirror"].

Sur le miroir au rouge à lèvres
Elle m'a laissé un mot d'adieu
"Pardonne-moi petite Jane
Je m'en vais, j'veux refaire ma vie"[6]

But who exactly is leaving whom? Often these sentiments are veiled by a certain reserve, masked by a clever metaphor, as in "Les Dessous chics" ["Chic Underwear"], or the subtle "Amours des feintes" ["Loves of Pretense"], whose title plays on the famous *Pavane pour une infante défunte* [*"Pavane for a Dead Princess"*] by Maurice Ravel. A 2012 video of the latter song draws attention to the nostalgic images of the "lost loves" of Birkin and Gainsbourg, but also to the "pretense" and the "appearances" of these familiar images very widely known by the French public through the mass media.

These late songs are probably among the best Gainsbourg ever wrote, as much for their "lyrics" (the word he himself preferred to use) as for their melodies. Many of them were chosen by Birkin for her tribute album to Gainsbourg, *Le Symphonique*

(2017), in which they were showcased with classical orchestrations worlds away from the English-inspired electric guitar arrangements of Hawkshaw and Alan Parker. The promotional concert for the album was followed by a world tour, for which Birkin recruited the symphony orchestras of many countries—among others, Quebec and Japan. Of course, the "symphonic turn" had often been taken by singers toward the end of their careers, from Julien Clerc to Peter Gabriel—it's a rather predictable move. But, in this case, it did represent an international tribute to the music of Gainsbourg and an allusion to his many borrowings from classical music.

May one conclude that this kind of international recognition was always part of Gainsbourg's career plan? Nothing is less certain. The ironic resonances of his juxtapositions of English and French, of familiar and exotic musical styles, can only really be interpreted in the context of French culture. His borrowings from diverse musical sources have given him a "cult" reputation in the English-speaking world, but in the end his only major international commercial success was with "Je t'aime… moi non plus." The robust cynicism of his last years will probably have protected him from the sirens of posterity. But the very existence of this collection of essays is perhaps a sign of a growing recognition of the subtlety of his creative talent. His flirtation with English culture and music inaugurates his openness to foreign and exotic influences, and yet these are anchored in his work by his constant cultivation of an elegant French style in his lyrics. The tension between these two forces gives a particular savor to his recorded output and provides the source of many ironic effects. The richness of his collaboration with Jane Birkin is probably the most lasting result of his assimilation of English culture and the inspiration for many of his most memorable songs.

Notes

1. For example, "Blue Bayou."
2. It was precisely at this period that Gainsbourg acquired a vintage Rolls that, so the story goes, he never drove. The symbolic statuette from the bonnet of the car, called "The Spirit of Ecstasy," became one of his most treasured possessions (Clayson 1998: 130).
3. A couple of years earlier, the publication of Robert Paxton's book *La France de Vichy* created a passionate debate among historians and in the national press. See Temkin 2003.
4. "Burning are all your orifices/Of all the three the gods have given you/I decide in the least smooth one/To finally release myself."
5. *Bite* in French slang means "prick."
6. "On the mirror with her lipstick/She left a farewell message/'Forgive me little Jane/I'm leaving, I want to rebuild my life.'"

Part Three

Beyond Songwriting

"Arts Majeurs"/"Arts Mineurs":
Intertextual Perspectives

17

Cargo Cultist: How Serge Gainsbourg Pioneered Sampling

Darran Anderson

In 1812, the army of Napoleon entered the scorched and eerily-depleted city of Moscow. It should have been a jubilant moment for the French leader. Instead, ruin lay ahead. Rather than endure a siege, the defenders simply melted away, leaving the invaders to conquer a city of ghosts. The Russians knew Napoleon's forces were in far too deep. And the Russians knew that the harshest depths of winter were coming. When re-enacting this tale of triumph and defeat in his *1812 Overture*, Tchaikovsky famously made use of cannons as a musical instrument, adding shock and bombast to his rousing anthem. More subtly, but just as profoundly, the composer incorporated snatches of earlier music into his score; stories of emotion, history, and identity are told melodically. The traditional Russian folk song "At the Gate, the Gate" appears. So too does the Russian Orthodox hymn "O Lord, Save Thy People." And there, battling glorious and beleaguered against the Russian songs, is "La Marseillaise"—the French National Anthem, born during the revolutionary climate when the French Republic was under attack, becoming for Tchaikovsky the sound of a proud, dying army.[1]

In the 1950s, another French revolutionary, one of Russian extraction, was propping up a piano in a Paris bar. Serge Gainsbourg played *chanson*, jazz, and dance numbers for the patrons, throwing in flourishes of classical music. In a few years, he would begin to write his own songs as well as hits for others, especially *chanteuses*. Yet for all his originality, Gainsbourg will never lose the practice of utilizing the classics for his own ends. Indeed, it was part of his originality. For Gainsbourg's re-imaginings of earlier songs, the way he synthesized segments of the old to make startling new creations, pre-empted the world of musical sampling decades in advance—not only in the innovations it would bring, but also the problems it would face.

Performing straightforward cover versions never suited Gainsbourg. He lacked the prerequisite generic handsomeness and silken voice. Though he possessed no shortage of charisma and cool, even in his endearingly gawky youth, Gainsbourg's alternating acerbic and absurdist sense of humor meant his cover versions would always have a subversive, even acerbic, note. He was a natural provocateur and with the *chanson* scene being outflanked with the delinquent arrival of rock 'n' roll, Gainsbourg was quick to adapt, incorporating musical signatures from the United States to enliven Gallic popular song, but also using the disposable instant-gratification of the American pop model as a Trojan Horse for more sophisticated ideas and irony. Most significant of all was the influence of the contemporary US/UK Pop Art movement that accompanied rock 'n' roll, which prompted Gainsbourg to write songs simultaneously celebrating and satirizing the excesses of the consumer age ("Harley Davidson," "Ford Mustang," etc.) and the idea of fashion itself in "Qui est 'in' qui est 'out.'" He also learned to recontextualize its ephemera the way Roy Lichtenstein had with comic books, and Andy Warhol had with supermarket products. This technique of visual sampling (and thefts), Gainsbourg applied to music.

It is tempting to see two distinct strands emerge in the early decades of recorded sampling, dividing purveyors of high art, that is, experimental composers like Pierre Schaeffer and the Groupe de Recherches de Musicales, and much more commercial and populist innovators like Joe Meek, George Martin, and the BBC Radiophonic Workshop, who used the emerging techniques of sampling, loops, tape-splicing, and electronics to make novelty records, radio jingles and television theme tunes (Brend 2012). The reality was that most of those working with samples had elements of both (these were the days when the neo-Dadaism of Fluxus was proving that art was whatever you could get away with). This was perhaps best exemplified in the Beatles' sound-collage "Revolution 9," the attic filled with dreams and nightmares in the doll's house that was the White Album.

Though a painter by background, Gainsbourg was too much, or perhaps not enough, of a cynic to abandon the life of writing popular music and venture into the avant-garde. Instead, forgoing dissonant tape loops with pretentious titles, Gainsbourg would simply sample works from his classical past on his piano. Then he would sample with a band, strings, and recording studios. Long before commercial samplers were available, Gainsbourg was already doing so only using actual orchestras, as demonstrated in his inspired use of a portion of the "New World" Symphony by Antonín Dvořák for the explosive chorus of his single "Initials B.B." In one sense, Gainsbourg was using the past as a scrapyard to build marvelous new things, but in another he revitalized music that had been canonized and then buried in the classical canon, making them seem as vibrant as the first time they'd been performed. He would do this again and again throughout his career, to varying degrees of success, transformation and interpolation; from Beethoven's Piano Sonata No. 23 in F minor, Op. 57 ("Appassionata"), for instance, Gainsbourg fashioned "Ma Lou Marilou." Often, it was as a starting point from which he would radically depart, the spirit of a piece, or a brief refrain to which he would return. From Beethoven's Piano Sonata No. 1 in F minor, Op. 2 No. 1 came—loosely it must be said—the Eurovision-winning "Poupée de cire, poupée de son." "Some Small Chance" was modeled on Adagio in G minor by Tomaso Albinoni. Gainsbourg raided Offenbach, Brahms, Grieg. "My Lady Héroïne" was inspired by *In a Persian Market* by Albert W. Ketèlbey, while "Charlotte Forever" referenced the Andantino ("Ivan Sings") from Aram Khachaturian's *Album for Chidren*, Book 1. It went beyond melody—the lyrics of "Bonnie and Clyde," for example, were based upon the poems Bonnie Parker would send, extolling her legendary exploits with Clyde Barrow, to newspapers, something Gainsbourg the enthusiastic self-publicist evidently admired.

Above all, he returned to, and reinvented, the composer he admired most of all, for his virtuosity and lovelorn melancholy: Frédéric Chopin—an admiration inherited from his father. From beyond the grave, the Polish composer provided melodies for "Jane B." (Prelude for Piano No. 4 in E minor, Op. 28) and "Lemon Incest" (Etude for Piano No. 3 in E major, Op. 10), while "Dépression au-dessus du jardin" was inspired in its ascendant melancholy by Etude for Piano No. 9 in F minor, Op. 10. It was something Chopin himself practiced—his Fantaisie-Impromptu in C♯ minor, Op. 66, for instance, borrowed from Beethoven's "Moonlight" Sonata (Oster 1947).

The problem arose for Gainsbourg, and prophetically for the music industry, when he sampled living artists, without due diligence. His 1964 album *Gainsbourg Percussions* was a sudden radical diversion into Afro-Caribbean chants and polyrhythms. While his openness to explore and expand was commendable, it was also too good to be true. The album drew far too heavily from Babatunde Olatunji's album *Drums of Passion*. The controversy places Gainsbourg among painters and sculptors before him (the Orientalists, Post-Impressionists, Cubists, etc.) who were embroiled in accusations of appropriation and theft from other cultures, especially formerly colonized ones. It also places him as a forerunner of the sampling controversies to follow.

As commercial samplers became gradually available and affordable, recording artists used them to deconstruct and reconstruct existing music. This process had impish avant-garde qualities, more magpie-ish than the earlier forms of *musique concrète*. Controversies of other kinds however were not far in its wake. Brian Eno and David Byrnes's *My Life in the Bush of Ghosts* offered a multi-channel view of the rapidly globalizing world, but it also foretold the fragmentations and resistances this would bring, particularly in the song "Qu'ran"—which they respectfully dropped from reissues of the record for fear the sampled Islamic chanting would be deemed offensive, or even heretical. This coincided with the early use of turntables in hip-hop, where people would dance to instrumental loops and breaks, culled from old funk and soul records, while MCs rapped over the top. If early hits like the Sugarhill Gang's "Rapper's Delight" were almost note for note interpolations of earlier songs (Chic's "Good Times"), by the time Public Enemy exploded onto the scene, it was clear that samplers could offer dynamic, condensed, and complex worlds of sound, constructed from the treasures and the wreckage of what had come before.

The Golden Age of hip-hop, as it is now seen, partly collapsed because copyright caught up with the guerrilla techniques that were fueling the innovation (McLeod & DiCola 2011: 19–35). As hip-hop artists started selling platinum records and gaining increasing visibility on the formerly reluctant MTV, lawyers started coming after them for the samples they'd used. At the basis of this was an issue of fairness and justice. Many of the original artists who'd written and performed the sampled tracks were getting older, had fallen on hard times or were eking out a living still touring. If a song propelled up the charts thanks to a hook, a riff, or a beat they'd created, who would deny they should be rewarded? Clyde Stubblefield's drum break from James Brown's "Funky Drummer" graced countless records and yet he remained largely uncompensated. Gregory C. Coleman, the drummer behind the "Amen break" (from "Amen, Brother" by the Winstons), which permeates great swathes of hip-hop and dance music, died penniless and homeless. The problem was it was often the middlemen in the legal, financial, and record industries that profited most from the process. It had also a brutally chilling effect on hip-hop's kaleidoscopic phase creatively, especially when the

Turtles sued De La Soul and Gilbert O'Sullivan sued Biz Markie for unlicensed samples (Vaidhyanathan 2001: 141). Artists turned to making their own music leading to the rise of visionary producers like Dr Dre, Timbaland, J Dilla, and so on. Sampling never died in hip-hop. It remains in existence in its aristocracy. And it exists as samizdat in the underground, through mixtapes. Yet the risks are great, especially from record companies and artists estates seeking any revenue they can get these days with the diminishing of record sales, as well as the rise of third-party companies who will buy up rights and pursue violations mercilessly.

It was, however, during a boom in sampling in the 1990s that the posthumous reputation of Serge Gainsbourg began to soar. His later years, when he'd become a public caricature of himself to some extent, had faded from memory or existed outside France only in fleeting glimpses of TV notoriety. This was neither a rehabilitation nor a reinvention so much as the re-emergence of the musical visionary he'd once been. Though his persona and sound were imitated by the likes of Jarvis Cocker, Beck, Stereolab, and Air (Simmons 2001: x, 132–3), a parallel rise in acclaim came from hip-hop artists who began to sample his work including the aforementioned De La Soul, MC Solaar, and Massive Attack, to name but a few. This prompted a reassessment of his work; not just the brooding atmospheric classics like *Histoire de Melody Nelson*, but the startling soundtrack work he created with Michel Colombier and Jean-Claude Vannier—the drum loops of "Requiem pour un con" and "Evelyne," the cop show funk of "La Horse" and "Danger," or the psychedelic raga of "Psychasténie" and "New Delire."

Perhaps Gainsbourg would have enjoyed his continuing relevance, being sampled by some who were not even born when he was alive. Perhaps he'd have been flattered to see himself in the position that Chopin occupied for him. Perhaps Gainsbourg would have been a contrarian and rejected the compliments, acknowledging that in all art there is some degree of theft and so he should be paid handsomely for the privilege. It is worth remembering however that the source of Gainsbourg's greatest controversy was in appropriating lyrics from "La Marseillaise" in his reggae song "Aux Armes et cætera," an act that was taken as much as an insult as an innovation. We might also reflect on that piece of music and all the places it has been associated with since its inception, from revolution to defeat to glory, from Rouget de Lille's Strasbourg where it was penned, to Napoleon's derelict Moscow to Tchaikovsky's, where his *1812 Overture* was performed, to a Jamaican recording studio where Gainsbourg recorded his partial cover and then back to Strasbourg, where he sang it onstage in defiance of death threats (Verlant 2000: 523–5). Its journey is not done. Indeed, all music is passing through time and through lives, changing contexts as it does, complete on pages of musical notation but unfinished to us, its listeners, performers, and interpolators. This is precisely what continues to give it life.

Note

1 Napoleon's forces had, in fact, "Veillons au salut de l'Empire" as an anthem.

"Un Amour Peut en Cacher un Autre": Serge Gainsbourg through the Prism of Transtextuality

Olivier Julien

> Every object can be transformed, every manner imitated, and no art can by nature escape those ... modes of derivation that define hypertextuality in literature and more generally define all second-degree artistic practices, or hyperartistic practices.
>
> (Genette 1997a: 384)

Parody ("in the classical sense, or the alteration of only the verbal register of a melody"), paraphrase, transcription ("or the purely instrumental type of transformation"), arrangement, variation, transposition ("a change of key or a change of mode within the same key"): in the last pages of *Palimpsests*, Gérard Genette touches on "the mind-boggling transformational capacity [that] is the very soul of musical composition, and not only in its 'classical' state, since the same principles are known to operate in jazz, for instance, or classical music" (387–8). Not forgetting recorded popular music, where the practices of "borrowing, transformation, adaptation, remixing, quotation, pastiche ... or cover recording" (Lacasse 2010: 31) are so widely spread that they inspired musicologist Serge Lacasse to develop a concept derived from the literary model of transtextuality: transphonography (2000; 2008; 2018). Less ambitious in its use of Genette's typology, the present chapter draws on its categories to shed light on the way Serge Gainsbourg managed to suggest a special relationship with "high culture," making him a perfect example of this "creature-creator who has," in the words of Pierre Bourdieu, "to be produced as a legitimate creator ... in order to legitimate his product" (1996: 245).

Five Types of Transtextual Relationships

Genette approached what he eventually came to call "transtextuality" in several books from the late 1970s onward, beginning with *Introduction à l'architexte* (1979), whose English translation was published by the University of California Press as

The Architext in 1992; *Seuils* (which deals, as indicated in its English title, with *Paratexts*—1997b); and the more hypertextuality-focused *Palimpsestes* (1982), whose English translation also dates from 1997. As for the way these concepts articulate, they fit into what he describes as "the textual transcendence of the text ... all that sets the text in a relationship, whether obvious or concealed, with other texts" (1997a: 1).

On that basis, one may distinguish up to five types of transtextual relationships. The first is what Genette calls "intertextuality"—a concept that was originally explored by Julia Kristeva (1969), but which he defines, "no doubt in a more restrictive sense, as a relationship of copresence between two texts or among several texts: that is to say, eidetically and typically as the actual presence of one text within another" (1-2). The second of Genette's five types of transtextual relationships is "paratextuality," i.e.,

> the generally less explicit and more distant relationship that binds the text properly speaking, taken within the totality of the literary work, to what can be called its *paratext*: a title, a subtitle, intertitles; prefaces, postfaces, notices, forewords, etc.; marginal, infra-paginal, terminal notes; epigraphs; illustrations; blurbs, book covers, dust jackets, and many other kinds of secondary signals, whether allographic or autographic.
>
> (3)

In short, paratexts are "those liminal devices and conventions, both within the book (*peritext*) and outside it (*epitext*), that mediate the book to the reader" (Macksey 1997: xviii).

Metatextuality—Genette's third type of transtextual relationship—deals with the relationship that is most often labeled "commentary" in the sense that "it unites a given text to another, of which it speaks without necessarily citing it (without summoning it, in fact sometimes even without naming it). Put differently, it is the *critical* relationship par excellence" (Genette 1997a: 4). As for "hypertextuality," it is concerned with "any relationship uniting a text B (... the *hypertext*) to an earlier text A (... the *hypotext*), upon which it is grafted in a manner that is not that of commentary" (5). Consequently, the "hypertext" may be defined as "any text derived from a previous text either through simple transformation"—which Genette calls *transformation*—or "through indirect transformation"—in which case he labels it *imitation* (7). Finally, "architextuality" refers to

> a relationship that is completely silent, articulated at most only by a paratextual mention, which can be titular (as in *Poems, Essays*, The Romance of the Rose, etc.) or most often subtitular (as when the indication *A Novel*, or *A Story*, or *Poems* is appended to the title on the cover), but which remains in any case of a purely taxonomic nature ... the fact that this relationship should be implicit and open to discussion ... or subject to historical fluctuations ... in no way diminishes its significance; generic perception is known to guide and determine to a considerable degree the readers' expectations, and thus their reception of the work.
>
> (4)

Following this presentation "in the order of increasing abstraction, implication, and comprehensiveness" (1), Genette brings two important clarifications. "First of all, one must not view the five types of transtextuality as separate and absolute categories without reciprocal contact or overlapping. On the contrary, their relationships to one another are numerous and often crucial." Second,

> If one views transtextuality in general not as a classification of texts ... but rather as an aspect of textuality, ... then one should also consider its diverse components (intertextuality, paratextuality, etc.) not as categories of texts but rather as aspects of texts.
>
> (8)

In the same line of thought, I will now rely on these categories to address the aspects of a complex and sophisticated web of relationships between what Serge Gainsbourg himself described as an *"art mineur"* ["minor art"] and "major art forms" (Simmons 2001: 98; Verlant 2000: 608).

Metatexts and Architextual Relationships

Aside from the growing body of academic research on Gainsbourg's work and persona,[1] an obvious place to look for instances of his establishing metatextual relationships with high culture would be the critical reaction to the novel he published in 1980 with Gallimard, *Evguénie Sokolov*. Unfortunately, this track doesn't prove to be very conclusive. Despite its author emphasizing the fact that entering France's most prestigious publishing company was like "entering into good company" (Ribowski 1980), the book received rather mixed reviews. The worst came from *Le Journal du dimanche*'s literary chronicler, Annette Colin-Simard, who wrote: "It is Gainsbourg's first novel and, let's hope, the last one he will write. The grossness of its subject is beyond the imagination" (quoted in Simmons 2001: 100). Concurrently, other critics found

> a synthesis of [Gainsbourg's] main literary influences in this little tableau so harshly rendered. Through Sokolov, we see the silhouette of Des Esseintes, the alter-ego of Huysmans in *A Rebours*. The clinical horror of the descriptions evokes Lautréamont's *Chants de Maldoror* and Defoe's *A Journal of the Plague Year*. The profound disgust for humanity brings to mind Rimbaud and Léon Bloy.
>
> (Verlant 2000: 534)

More examples of such relationships may be found in Gainsbourg's being dubbed, as early as 1958, by such literary figures as Boris Vian—who published a laudatory review of *Du Chant à la une!* in *Le Canard enchaîné* (1958)—or Marcel Aymé, who wrote the liner notes to that same album.

Serge Gainsbourg is a twenty-five-year-old piano player who became a songwriter, lyricist and singer. He sings about alcohol, girls, adultery, fast cars, poverty, miserable jobs. His songs—inspired by the experiences of a youth which life did not favor—have an accent of melancholy, bitterness and, above all, the directness of a police report. They are set to spare music in which, in contemporary fashion, the concern for rhythm eclipses the melody. My wish for Gainsbourg is that fate might shine on him, especially since he deserves it, and that it brings some splashes of sunlight into his songs.

(1958)

One could hardly think of a less committed statement than wishing for Gainsbourg "that fate might shine on him." However, this statement's significance lies not so much in its content as in the fact that Marcel Aymé had been described, three years earlier, as "one of the best and most successful French writers of today … known on two continents" (Bowen 1955).

If one identifies architextuality with the "generic perception … known to guide and determine to a considerable degree the readers' [or listeners'] expectations" (Genette 1997a: 5), instances of architextual relationships with high culture are even more absent from Gainsbourg's output. An interesting comparison could be made with these late-1960s and 1970s progressive rock musicians who were "eager to 'dignify' their work … by freighting it with trappings of classical music" (Rockwell 1992: 493). As Jean-Eric Perrin observes,

> The bridges between "classical" music and twentieth-century popular music are often narrow, tottering, and leading to dead ends. At the close of the century, looking back over the shoulder, one can only note the incompatibility of temperament and character between "light" and "serious" music. Attempts at merging them all turned out unnatural, shotgun weddings, arranged marriages that were broken up as soon as they were contracted.

(1994)

As we will see, Gainsbourg did share these musicians' need to affect "a cultured sensibility" (Rockwell 1992: 493). But his avoiding to throw ostentatious architextual bridges between art music, literature, and his own work probably contributed to his being perceived as "the only [popular] artist" whose attempts at merging light and serious art turned out love matches.

Paratextuality

In *Paratexts*, Genette argues that

> A paratextual element, at least if it consists of a message that has taken on material form, necessarily has a *location* that can be situated in relation to the location of

the text itself: around the text and either within the same volume or at a more respectful (or more careful) distance.

(1997b: 4)

The first spatial category is what he calls the "peritext," that is, "Within the same volume ... such elements as the title or the preface and sometimes elements inserted into the interstices of the text, such as chapter titles or certain notes" (4–5). Conversely, the "distanced elements" are "all those messages that, at least originally, are located outside the book, generally with the help of the media (interviews, conversations) or under cover of private communications (letters, diaries, and others)." This second category is what Genette calls the "epitext." And, naturally, both categories "completely and entirely share the spatial field of the paratext. In other words, for those who are keen on formulae, *paratext = peritext + epitext*" (5).

To get back to progressive rock musicians, their "need to parody [classical music] to the point of ludicrousness" (Rockwell 1992: 493) shows through every inch of their record sleeves and labels—one only has to think of their using song titles such as "Prelude," "Fugue," or "Rondo," their naming an entire album *Concerto for Group and Orchestra* (Deep Purple) or their presenting LP track listings as "multimovement suites" (Macan 1997: 40–6). Gainsbourg's sleeves as peritext also engage in a dialog with high culture, apart from two major differences: first, they exemplify David Looseley's observation that "Artistic legitimacy in France ... was ... identified with a national *literary* tradition; so it was natural for singer-songwriters to build their reputation and self-image by identifying themselves with a high-cultural form, namely poetry" (2003: 38); second, and more importantly, they convey the image of a songwriter asserting a special relationship with high culture rather than actually trying to identify himself with the poets whose work he set to music.

For example, on the back cover of *Serge Gainsbourg No. 2* (1959), one may read:

Of the "Claqueur de doigts," I would say he hangs around juke-boxes here and there; of "L'Amour à la papa," that "I'm not interested"; of "Indifférente," that it is about a bad loser, and of "Adieu créature," that it is about a "cheater."

As for "La Nuit d'octobre," I will answer for it to Musset only, and I know he will forgive me.[2]

Similarly, the back cover of *L'Etonnant Serge Gainsbourg* (1961) features a quotation that makes him appear as a connoisseur of seventeenth-century French poetry:

You will recognize, I hope, that I am a little less cruel in my words than I was yesterday. And if I still have some bitterness left, I will quote this madrigal by Jean de Lingendes to apologize:
Nay, all the blame on heaven lies
That gave her charms so rare,
And not upon my eyes.[3]

In a less literary vein, one might also mention the way Gainsbourg is represented on the picture that was used on the cover of a 1996 compilation by Decca Records entitled *Les Classiques de Gainsbourg* ["Gainsbourg's Classics"] (Figure 18.1). The picture's setting is clearly reminiscent of the way classical musicians such as Maurice Ravel or Igor Stravinsky have been photographed when composing at the piano. And yet, considered within the broader context of the epitext, Gainsbourg's pose on that picture is not that of a songwriter in line with progressive rock musicians' "claim to artistic seriousness" (Rockwell 1992: 493). As hinted in a 1967 TV special during which he could be heard commenting on the daguerreotype of Chopin on his piano's music desk, it is in fact the pose of a songwriter who claims, in a more subtle way, to be on familiar (and deferential) terms with such composers.

> I've put Chopin here because ... He looks like he's judging me. Very harshly. When I'm searching for a tune, I look at him, and he's telling me—one could almost add a balloon... He's telling me: "it's crap." And then, when the tune is nice, he says: "at a pinch"... He's my conscience.
>
> (Joyeux 1967)

To paraphrase the aforementioned notes on *Serge Gainsbourg No. 2*'s back cover: "As for 'Jane B.,' I will answer for it to Chopin only, and I know he will forgive me"—I'll come back to it.

Figure 18.1 *Les Classiques de Gainsbourg* (front cover).

Intertextuality

Broadly speaking, Genette identifies three types of intertextual practices: quoting, plagiarism, and allusion. Aside from his early settings to music of poems by Alfred de Musset ("La Nuit d'octobre"), Gérard de Nerval ("Le Rock de Nerval"), Charles Baudelaire ("Baudelaire"), Victor Hugo ("Chanson de Maglia"), and Félix Arvers ("Le Sonnet d'Arvers"), Gainsbourg's discography provides two clear examples of the first practice (i.e., "quoting ... with quotation marks, with or without reference"—1997a: 2). The first one appears in "Un Poison violent, c'est ça l'amour," a duet from the TV musical *Anna* (1967) whose lyrics begin with an excerpt from a 1662 sermon by Bossuet: "Sur l'amour des plaisirs" ["Love of pleasure"].

> What is that other characteristic of a life of the senses, that alternate movement of appetite and disgust, of disgust and appetite ... the soul floating ever uncertain between ardor which abates and ardor which is renewed?[4]

Furthermore, Gainsbourg makes sure the listener won't miss the reference when he continues, asking Jean-Claude Brialy:

— You know who wrote this?
— No.
— Bossuet.

By the same token, "Glass Securit" (1987) ends with the last stanza from Stéphane Mallarmé's "Une Négresse par le démon secouée" (1887: 14–15). Here again, the poem is cited word for word; and here too, Gainsbourg makes sure the listener will not miss the quotation marks, nor the reference—he introduces the quote with the words, "I open my lexicon. Mallarmé dixit (I quote)."

When referring to "plagiarism" (his second type of intertextual relationship), Genette mentions Lautréamont, who notoriously described it as "necessary. Progress implies it. It holds tight an author's phrase, uses his expressions, eliminates a false idea, and replaces it with just the right idea" (Ducasse 1973: 283). On a more basic level, this "less explicit and less canonical form" (Genette 1997a: 2) consists in quoting *without* quotation marks, as illustrated by "Chatterton"'s uncanny resemblance with the introduction of a conference on theater by Alphonse Allais—in each verse, Gainsbourg lists historical figures who died tragic deaths before concluding: "As for me, I don't feel too well" (Achard 1962: 3).

In a different but related register, Genette's third type of intertextual practice is "allusion," which he defines as "an enunciation whose full meaning presupposes the perception of a relationship between it and another text, to which it necessarily refers in some inflections that would otherwise remain unintelligible" (Genette 1997a: 2). Of course, Gainsbourg's deconstructing and rearranging the most famous verses from Verlaine's "Chanson d'automne" (1866: 57–8) in "Je suis venu te dire que je m'en vais" fits this definition to the letter. *Anna* provides another example with a song whose title refers to Stendhal's *De l'amour* and concept of "crystallized desire" (1822): "C'est la cristallisation comme dit Stendhal." And other examples again may be found in songs Gainsbourg wrote for other singers—typically, Jane Birkin's "Exercice en forme de Z," whose title makes an even less veiled reference to Raymond Queneau's *Exercices de style* (1947).[5]

Hypertextuality

As mentioned earlier, Genette distinguishes two types of hypertextual relationships that work as "a pair of symmetrical and inverse transformations"—the schematic opposition being "saying the same thing differently" (transformation), and "saying another thing similarly" (imitation) (1997a: 6). For obvious reasons, examples of the latter type may be difficult to identify at first glance (or first hearing). Considering particular songs and albums in connection with their epitext nonetheless provides interesting clues, as one may judge from *Histoire de Melody Nelson*'s final track, "Cargo Culte," whose lyrics are structured as two genuine sonnets (Gainsbourg 1991: I, 231–2). Moreover, these sonnets' rhyming scheme and structure were, by Gainsbourg's own admission, inspired by José Maria de Heredia's "Les Conquérants" (Szpirglas 2011a: 16), which makes them a perfect example of what Genette calls, within the relational category of "imitation," "pastiche-as-homage" (1997a: 102).

For equally obvious reasons, examples of "transformation" are much more common in Gainsbourg's lyrics. In most cases, they fall under the subheading of "transposition," as exemplified by "La Noyée" (which basically consists of a "transtylization"[6] of Rimbaud's "Ophélie"—1891: 27–9), "Ronsard 58" (one of the few songs whose lyrics he didn't write), or "Initials B.B."—a "heterodiegetic transposition"[7] of Edgar Poe's "The Raven" (1845: 1–5) adorned with echoes of Charles Baudelaire's "Poem XXXI" from *Spleen et idéal* (1857: 75–6). On the dividing line between "imitation" and "transformation," an even more eloquent example would be "Jane B.," whose lyrics were admittedly inspired by a poem found in a book that was to have a profound influence on Gainsbourg: Nabokov's *Lolita* (Szpirglas 2011a: 20; Example 18.1).

Lyrics and epitextual elements aside, "Jane B."'s peritext brings out another dimension of Gainsbourg's relationship with high culture: as indicated on the single's label, the music itself is based on a "transtylization" (to be specific, a "stylish

"Humbert Humbert's poem"	"Jane B."
Wanted, wanted: Dolores Haze.	Description: blue eyes, light brown hair,
Hair: brown. Lips: scarlet.	Jane B., English woman.
Age: five thousand three hundred days.	Age: between twenty and twenty-one.
Profession: none, or "starlet."[8]	Studies drawing.[9]

Example 18.1 "Jane B."'s lyrics as a hypertext of "Humbert Humbert's poem."

orchestration"—Genette 1997a: 388) of Chopin's Prelude for Piano No. 4 in E minor. Given the song's fidelity to its hypotext, "After a prelude by Chopin"[10] is anything but an empty phrase—even the original key has been kept. The same applies to those phrases found on the labels of four more singles from the 1970s and 1980s: "My Lady Héroïne" ("Serge Gainsbourg after a theme by Kaetelbey [sic]/Serge Gainsbourg"[11]), "Baby Alone in Babylone" ("After the 3rd Movement of Brahms's 3rd Symphony Arrgts Gainsbourg/Gainsbourg"[12]), "Lemon Incest" ("After Chopin's Etude No. 3 in E major op 10 Arrgts Gainsbourg/Gainsbourg"[13]), and "Lost Song" ("After Grieg–Peer Gynt Suite No. 2 op. 55 Arr. Gainsbourg/Gainsbourg"[14]).

In a similar vein, "Pour aimer il faut être trois" and "Charlotte for Ever" bear more than a striking resemblance with Brahms's Hungarian Dance No. 1 and the Andantino from Khachaturian's *Album for Children*, Book 1, respectively. Except that, this time, the composer and writer credits merely read "[S.] Gainsbourg."[15] And so do those of "Ma Lou Marilou"[16] (despite the song originating in an eight-bar passage from the first movement of Beethoven's "Appassionata" Sonata), "Initials B.B."[17] (where a "brief vivacious snippet" of the first movement of Dvořák's "New World" Symphony may be heard during the chorus—Anderson 2013: 29), not to mention "Machins choses," "Dépression au-dessus du jardin,"[18] "Bébé gai,"[19] "Poupée de cire, poupée de son"[20] and "Dépressive"[21]—whose family likeness with Brahms's Hungarian Dance No. 4, Chopin's Etude for Piano No. 9 in F minor, Op. 10, Liszt's *Liebesträum* No. 3, the fourth movement of Beethoven's Piano Sonata No. 1 in F minor, Op. 2 No. 1 and the second movement of the "Pathétique" Sonata have been outlined in several books over the years (Allen 2021: 88, 91; Bouvier & Vincendet 2009: 502, 619; Dicale 2021: 19, 224, 233, 467, 593, 684; Merlet 2019: 150, 158, 301, 370; Picaud 2019: 80, 236, 344; Picaud & Verlant 2011: 152, 336, 393, 434; Raykoff 2021: 89; Trottier 2021: 159).

"A Sense of Refinement"

Of all the relational categories addressed in the previous pages, hypertextuality turns out to be the most relevant when examining the links between Gainsbourg's output and art music. On the verge of peritextuality, "plagiarism" ("Charlotte for Ever"), "allusion" ("Poupée de cire, poupée de son"), or "quoting" ("Initials B.B."), they sweep across the shades of "derivational practices" (Genette 1997a: 391) while confirming the permeability of Genette's five types of transtextuality. In sum, they act as the keystone of a multifaceted network of relationships between "a commercial songwriter in search of '… legitimacy'" (Julien 2018: 50) and the antagonistic world of high culture (Figure 18.2).

That being said, a closer look at the musical hypotexts involved in such relationships reveals an intriguing detail: they do not suggest the same erudition as the literary corpus drawn from the textual transcendence of Gainsbourg's lyrics—most of them might be described as "classical favorites." As surprising as it may be, this corroborates Alain Goraguer's recollection that

Serge had no musical culture—at least, classically speaking. He was more a musician … of instinct. Thanks to his father, Brahms and Chopin pervaded his childhood. Nevertheless, he wasn't very skilled in harmony. He was not necessarily a good pianist either, but he had one quality: taste; a sense of refinement, and a real flair for melody too.

(Lerouge 2001: 6)

Beyond their ability to dazzle the average pop music listener, Gainsbourg's connections with nineteenth- and early twentieth-century art music finally provide a twofold insight into his connections with high culture as a whole. Encompassing the spectrum of transtextuality, but carefully holding apart from its most ostentatious category, they sketch the portrait of a self-proclaimed "minor artist" who spent his life boasting that he was "initiated" into "major art forms"—"architecture, painting, and classical music" (Léridon 1986). At the same time, they emphasize his being rooted in a tradition of popular music that was always eager to affirm its "literary [rather than musical] credentials" (Hawkins 2000: 10). As he half-heartedly confessed in a 1989 interview with French television (this will be my last epitextual example), this commercial songwriter in search of legitimacy was, first and foremost, a commercial songwriter in search of "*auteurist* legitimacy" (Harrison 2005: 54).

Figure 18.2 A multifaceted network of relationships with high culture.

— Would you like to leave a trace?
— It's already done, but I'm still working on it.
— How would you like people to remember you in 2010, 2040, 2050?
— They'll probably say what they said of Baudelaire: sometimes shady, sometimes violent; quite inclined towards eroticism, but with an accurate language, and a style.

(Grumbach 1989)

Notes

1   See, for example: Albert 2005; Austin 2019; Brunet 2023; Burgoyne 2014; Castelbajac 2019; Cusson 1997; Francfort 2007; Frantz 2004; Gasquet 2003; Gassi 2017; Grenaudier-Klijn 2012; Hill 2003; Holtmon 2021; Julien 2018; Natta 2022; Pulkrabová 2022; Rossi & Guilloux 2021; Sablon 2009; Sotonová 2015; Tinker 2002; Vannieuwenhuyze 2023.
2   "Du 'Claqueur de doigts,' je dirai qu'il sévit devant les juke-boxes d'ici et d'ailleurs, de 'L'Amour à la papa,' que 'ça ne m'intéresse pas,' d'"Indifférente,' qu'il s'agit d'un mauvais joueur et d'"Adieu créature,' d'un 'tricheur.' Quant à 'La Nuit d'octobre,' je n'en rendrai compte qu'à Musset, et je sais qu'il me pardonnera" (Gainsbourg 1959).
3   "Vous reconnaîtrez, je l'espère, que je suis un peu moins cruel dans mes propos que je ne l'étais hier et s'il me reste un peu d'amertume, je citerai pour m'excuser ce madrigal de Jean de Lingendes: La faute en est aux dieux/Qui la firent si belle/Et non pas à mes yeux" (Gainsbourg 1961).
4   "Qu'est-ce autre chose que la vie des sens, qu'un mouvement alternatif de l'appétit au dégoût, et du dégoût à l'appétit ... l'âme flottant toujours incertaine entre raideur qui se ralentit et l'ardeur qui se renouvelle" (Bossuet 1862: 206).
5   The allusion is all the more obvious as the lyrics also mention Raymond Queneau's most famous character, Zazie (1959).
6   As the term itself suggests, "transtylization" may be defined as "a stylistic rewriting, a transposition whose sole function is a change of style" (Genette 1997a: 226).
7   Within the subcategory of "diegetic transposition" (the transposition "from one period to another, or from one location to another, or both"), Genette distinguishes between "homodiegetic transposition" and "heterodiegetic transposition," where "the setting of the action changes, and so does the identity of the characters involved" (1997a: 296–7, 310).
8   Nabokov 1955: 257.
9   "Signalement: yeux bleus, cheveux châtains/Jane B., Anglaise de sexe féminin/Âge: entre vingt et vingt-et-un/Apprend le dessin."
10 Birkin, Jane avec Serge Gainsbourg. 1969. "Je t'aime… moi non plus"/"Jane B." Fontana 260 196 MF [45 rpm].
11 Gainsbourg, Serge. 1977. "My Lady Héroïne"/"Trois millions de Joconde." Philips 6172 026 [45 rpm]. The theme in question is actually borrowed from *In a Persian Market* by Albert Ketèlbey.
12 Birkin, Jane. 1983. "Baby Alone in Babylone"/"Con c'est con ces conséquences." Philips 814 599-7 [45 rpm]. The LP's label features another misprint—it reads "After

the 3rd Movement of Brahms's 2nd Symphony." Birkin, Jane. 1983. *Baby Alone in Babylone*. Philips 814 524–1 [33 rpm].

13 Charlotte & Gainsbourg. 1985. "Lemon Incest"/"Hmm Hmm Hmm." Philips 884 129–7 [45 rpm].
14 Birkin, Jane. 1987. "Lost Song"/"Leur Plaisir sans moi." Philips 888 342–7 [45 rpm].
15 Aubret, Isabelle. 1965. "Les Amants de Vérone"; "Rue de la Gaîté"/"Pour aimer il faut être trois"; "No Man's Land." Polydor 27 172 [45 rpm]; Charlotte & Gainsbourg. 1986. "Charlotte for Ever"/"Pour ce que tu n'étais pas." Philips 888 165–7 [45 rpm].
16 Gainsbourg, Serge. 1976. "Marilou sous la neige"/"Ma Lou Marilou." Philips 6042 272 [45 rpm].
17 Gainsbourg, Serge. 1968. "Initials B.B."; "Bloody Jack"/"Ford Mustang"; "Black and White." Philips 437 431 [45 rpm].
18 Deneuve, Catherine. 1981. "Dépression au-dessus du jardin." *Souviens-toi de m'oublier*. Philips 6313 172 [33 rpm].
19 Birkin, Jane. 1974. "My Chérie Jane"/"Bébé gai." Fontana 6010 102 [45 rpm].
20 Gall, France. 1965. "Poupée de cire, poupée de son"/"Le Cœur qui jazze." Philips B373 524F [45 rpm].
21 Birkin, Jane. 1978. "Dépressive." *Ex Fan des Sixties*. Fontana 6325 353 [33 rpm].

19

Serge Gainsbourg and the Romantic Piano

Nathalie Hérold

The recycling or "reprocessing" of musical material across epochs, genres, and styles is a key feature of Western art music as well as popular music, and Serge Gainsbourg's output is particularly worth considering from this intertextual perspective.[1] Many studies focusing on his music draw attention to the interconnection of some of his songs with other musical—as well as literary—sources, with specific attention given to the Romantic piano repertoire. However, beyond the mere identification of the musical works that inspired him, little has been said about the technical aspects of such "borrowings." What exactly inspired Gainsbourg in these pieces? How was this material reinvested in the elaboration of new musical compositions? These are the questions I intend to answer in the following pages.

Some Contextual Considerations

Gainsbourg was generally perceived as an avid admirer and connoisseur of high culture. Interested in art music, painting, and literature since his childhood (Verlant 2000: 74), he attended such iconic institutions as the Académie Montmartre, the Académie de la Grande Chaumière, the National School of Fine Arts, and the Ecole Normale de Musique (36, 71, 75, 83, 84). He also admired famous painters like Dalí, was very enthusiastic about poetry (Baudelaire, Musset, Rimbaud, Verlaine), and cultivated a keen interest in art music and the great pianists of his time. According to his father Joseph, he had "'an impressive collection of piano LPs': Scarlatti's sonatas by Horowitz, all the Brahms stuff by Julius Katchen, Chopin's complete works by Cortot (except for the Polonaises by Rubinstein), Rachmaninoff's concertos by Richter, and so on" (332).

Gainsbourg's imagination and creative practice were obviously stimulated by his early exposure to the "classics" of literature and music. The presence of material borrowed from such sources in his own output—Brahms's Symphony No. 3 in F major, Op. 90 in "Baby Alone in Babylone," the first movement of Dvořák's Symphony No. 9, Op. 95 in "Initals B.B."—contributed to his being perceived by Denise Glaser as a "master forger."[2] As the couple of copyrights issues he faced over the years attest (Dicale 2021: 238, 813), his appropriation of other musicians' works was indeed inherent to his creative practice, which resulted in a large network of intertextual—and, more generally, intermedial—relationships.

Moreover, the dialectic between "high art" and "low art" remained a motif in his discourse over the years. In a television program hosted by Bernard Pivot in 1986 (that is, a mere four years before his death), he still supported the idea that all his songs should be considered as "minor things,"

> Except for some, which ... came close to Rimbaud...
> *Some?*
> Some, lately.
> *Which ones?*
> "Mélodie au-dessus du jardin," [*sic*] "Melody Nelson," "Sorry Angel" ... my last songs for Charlotte [Gainsbourg], my last songs for Isabelle Adjani ... and those for Jane Birkin.
>
> (quoted in Julien 2018: 51)

Gainsbourg and the Piano

Gainsbourg's piano practice began with formal lessons in classical music with his father, soon followed by a job as a bar pianist. When he spoke about his piano playing, he often mentioned Chopin's Etudes, the latter's "Valse de l'adieu," and Rachmaninoff's Preludes (Gainsbourg 2001). As his first wife Elisabeth Levitsky recalls,

> When we lived [rue Labiche], there was a newspaper music critic ... That guy, who lived downstairs, used to send us registered letters: "Stop butchering Bach and Chopin!" For me it was Bach, for Lulu it was Chopin. And both of us were convinced that we were the best players in the world, of course!
>
> (quoted in Verlant 2000: 122)

Beyond his musical practice, the piano also constituted an essential composition tool for Gainsbourg, as he explained in a 1984 interview with Belgian television.

> I compose on the Steinway, very classical ... You know, there's a new generation of little rascals out there who have these top of the range, ultra-sophisticated instruments, and who make demos recorded on eight tracks, or whatever, with reverb, delays, echoes, and at the end of the day the album is not as good. I compose with my two hands, and so I've got the rhythmic, harmonic, and melodic structure. "That's all," on the Steinway.

In other words, composing on the piano allowed him to keep a direct link with the musical material itself while keeping away from new technologies. Yet he also used the instrument for experimental purposes, in order to generate the creative moment itself:

> For [*Love on the Beat*], I played the piano for twelve hours—twelve hours non-stop, my fingers were bleeding. But, the tunes which ... I decided to work on ... were composed ... in two, three minutes, sometimes thirty seconds.[3]

Finally, the piano—of which he owned several models throughout his life—played a central role in the construction of Gainsbourg's identity as a creative artist through its presence in many photographic representations (Marchand-Kiss 2015: 130, 146–8), in his lyrics (e.g., "Charleston des déménageurs de piano"), and even in the films he directed (for example, *Charlotte for Ever*).

Gainsbourg and Romantic Piano Music

As far as Gainsbourg's relationship with Romantic music is concerned, the figure of Chopin appears to be a reference point. Among other examples, a copy of the well-known daguerreotype by Louis-Auguste Bisson sat on his piano (Verlant 2000: 295; Figure 19.1). Likewise, arriving at a recording session in Belmar, New Jersey, he reportedly exclaimed: "What am I doing here? My music, it's Chopin…" (Dicale 2021: 766)

Figure 19.1 Daguerreotype of Frédéric Chopin by Louis-Auguste Bisson (1849).

"Poupée de cire, poupée de son" *France Gall (1965)*	Piano Sonata No. 1 in F minor, Op. 2 No. 1 (Ludwig van Beethoven)
"Jane B." *Jane Birkin (1969)*	Prelude for Piano No. 4 in E minor, Op. 28 (Frédéric Chopin)
"Bébé gai" *Jane Birkin (1974)*	*Liebestraüm*, S. 541 No. 3 (Franz Liszt)
"Ma Lou Marilou" *Serge Gainsbourg (1976)*	Piano Sonata No. 23 in F minor, Op. 57 (Ludwig van Beethoven)
"Dépressive" *Jane Birkin (1978)*	Piano Sonata No. 8 in C minor, Op. 13 (Ludwig van Beethoven)
"Dépression au-dessus du jardin" *Catherine Deneuve (1981)*	Etude for Piano No. 9 in F minor, Op. 10 (Frédéric Chopin)
"Lemon Incest" *Charlotte & Gainsbourg (1984)*	Etude for Piano No. 3 in E major, Op. 10 (Frédéric Chopin)

Figure 19.2 Gainsbourg's songs that refer to Romantic piano pieces.

Beyond the composer himself, Chopin's image conveys a certain idea of sensitivity and sentimentalism. "Play Chopin/With disdain" [*"Jouez Chopin/Avec dédain"*], he sang in "La Recette de l'amour fou" (1958). Besides, wasn't it Gainsbourg's female conquests who said, "he behave[d] 'like a man from the nineteenth century?'" (Verlant 2000: 295) It comes therefore as no surprise that a number of his songs reinvest the pianistic repertoire of Chopin and other Romantic composers such as Beethoven and Liszt. All things considered, it is possible to identify no fewer than seven songs explicitly referring to Romantic piano pieces, which constitute the corpus of songs analyzed in the remainder of this chapter (Figure 19.2). These songs cover a large part of Gainsbourg's creative period, from the 1960s through the 1980s, and they all refer to rather popular pieces—a Prelude and two Etudes by Chopin, Liszt's "Dreams of Love," and three sonatas by Beethoven. It should also be noted that these songs are all closely related to female figures, be it as performers (France Gall, Jane Birkin, Catherine Deneuve, Charlotte Gainsbourg), or as the subject of the song itself (Marilou).

Some Analytical Insights

Gainsbourg-Beethoven

In "Poupée de cire, poupée de son," the first three measures of the verses are clearly reminiscent of the second theme of Beethoven's Piano Sonata No. 1 in F minor, Op. 2 No. 1, last movement, in the tonality of its recapitulation (F minor) (Example 19.1).

Example 19.1 "Poupée de cire, poupée de son" (measures 1–4, x segment).

Broadly speaking, the xyxy' phrase structure echoes the symmetrical structure of Beethoven's theme, the y segment (by Gainsbourg) ending on the dominant, whereas Beethoven's "version" ends on a tonic—which only appears at the end of y' in "Poupée de cire, poupée de son." Regarding harmony, the i–bVI–bIII progression resonates with Beethoven's movement too, and so does the secondary dominant G (third measure of the y and y' segments). On the other hand, the lowered second scale degree (G♭, first measure of y and y') is specific to Gainsbourg's song. One may also note a metrical shift of half a measure, which eliminates the upbeats (anacruses). The song's bridge is devoid of such references, but another allusion to Beethoven may be found in the song's introduction with a flute part reminiscent of the passage in broken octaves and thirds preceding the statement of the sonata theme.

Similarly, a more than substantial part of "Ma Lou Marilou"'s melody comes from the second theme of Beethoven's Piano Sonata No. 23 in F minor, Op. 57, first movement, in the tonality of its recapitulation (F major). The song's phrase structure (xyxy' again) is even more "classical" than its Beethovenian model, which bifurcates immediately after the repetition of the x segment. By contrast, the timbral alternation between the female chorus and the singer's voice subtly deconstructs the structure of Beethoven's theme. Regarding durations, the general metrical framework is unchanged, but Beethoven's compound meter is transformed into a simple meter played with a shuffle feel. The verses' harmonic pattern certainly comes close to Beethoven's harmonization, except that the color of A♭ major, in the introduction and the coda, is specific to Gainsbourg's song—even though it subtly recalls the tonality of the sonata's second theme by a juxtaposition with the key of F major, which provides some chromatic tension.

Another example is provided by "Dépressive," whose first four measures refer, in a less explicit manner, to Beethoven's Piano Sonata No. 8 in C minor, Op. 13, second movement. Here, the melodic material—transposed from A♭ major to G major, and embedded within a new rhythmic context—is revealed progressively, until it becomes apparent in the third and fourth measures of the verse. In addition to the slow tempo and omnipresence of the piano timbre, the varied repetition of this section in the formal context of a vocal-instrumental series of variations contrasts with the rondo form of Beethoven's movement. Interestingly, the lyrics closely correspond to the title given by Beethoven to this sonata: "Pathétique"—a "psychological content" that might have been related by Beethoven himself to those of the Piano Sonatas No. 1 in F minor, Op. 2 No. 1 and No. 23 in F minor, Op. 57 (Massin & Massin 1967: 598, 610).

Gainsbourg-Chopin

When it comes to Chopin, Gainsbourg's relationship with Romantic music leads to rich and complex songs with deep emotional content. From a musical standpoint, "Jane B." closely follows the first twelve measures of his Prelude for Piano No. 4 in E minor, Op. 28, with an unchanged structure and minimally modified melody. As with "Dépressive," limiting the borrowed material to the Prelude's first section allows to embed it within a strophic form, which includes a central instrumental verse, as well as a final truncated section that fades out. The rhythmically flexible bass guitar part carefully follows Chopin's chromatic bass; nevertheless, the complex Chopin-like pianistic counterpoint is not accurately reproduced, especially since it would have been difficult to arrange it for the rhythm section of Gainsbourg's track. This track's main innovation lies in the addition of a countermelody played by the violin section in the second and third verses, the first measures of which reproduce the chromatic descent of the upper left-hand passage in the Prelude. Finally, the gloomy character of Chopin's Prelude, which Alfred Cortot retitled *"Sur une tombe"* ["Above a grave"] (Gavoty 1974: 499), is mirrored in the song's lyrics, in particular through the end of the final verse ("You sleep by the side of the road/A flower of blood in your hand"[4]).

In "Dépression au-dessus du jardin," the first two measures of the verse are loosely based on the first four measures of Chopin's Etude for Piano No. 9 in F minor, Op. 10 (Example 19.2). The arrangement is freely integrated into a binary meter, and the internal ternary structure of the verse deviates from Chopin's binary structure, integrating two central "prolongation measures" and two concluding ones—which progressively bifurcate from the first two measures. Based on a guitar solo, the bridge develops several patterns deriving from the verse. In comparison with Chopin's Etude, the harmonic progression consists of an entirely new development—it modulates, through the parallel major key, a half-step up. Due to its formal structure (based on the alternation of a verse and a bridge), the song's overall tonal plan is thus G minor–G♯ minor–A minor. Another salient feature is the pervasive sound of the piano, which probably serves as an allusion to Chopin's left-hand formula in the introductory measures.

Conversely, most of "Lemon Incest"'s melodic material comes from the first twenty measures of Chopin's Etude for Piano No. 3 in E major, Op. 10 transposed to C major. Embedded within a common time frame (as opposed to Chopin's duple meter), the song is widely based on syncopated rhythms. The xyxy' phrase structure

Example 19.2 "Dépression au-dessus du jardin" (measures 1–2).

is reminiscent of Chopin's, which also consists of irregular segments whose lengths extend over odd numbers of measures. The contrasting vocal timbres (Charlotte Gainsbourg, Serge Gainsbourg, and backing vocals) do not systematically coincide with this phrase structure, while Gainsbourg extends the y' segment by two measures in order to prepare the return to the first x segment. Furthermore, the song introduces a few harmonic differences, especially at the song's melodic climax—where Chopin's fourth and sixth chord is replaced with a tonic chord in root position—and at the end of the y' segment—where the two "additional measures" introduce a minor chord on the fourth degree. The choice of this piece—also known as "Tristesse" ["Sadness"]—for setting lyrics as controversial as "Lemon Incest" allows the song to integrate a complex network of meanings.[5]

Gainsbourg-Liszt

As regards the one and only reference to Liszt, the light character of "Bébé gai" is not far removed from a certain image associated with this composer's music. The song's melodic material refers to the last statement of the theme from *Liebestraum*, S. 541 No. 3 (Example 19.3). The small melodic variant in the third segment (x_3) of the $x_1 x_2 x_3$-$x_1 x_2' x_2'' x_4$ phrase structure refers to a previous statement of the theme in that same piece. Gainsbourg's song—in E♭ major—adds several features, such as the integration within a simple time context and a number of rhythmic diminutions suggesting stuttering.[6] The xx' structure of Liszt's theme is almost unchanged, with an arrangement of the x' section, reduced by two measures, which preserves Liszt's melodic sequence ($x_2' x_2''$), but provides a new conclusion pattern (x_4). As for Liszt's harmonic structure, its broad lines give rise to a harmonic scheme within which the instruments develop several harmonic variations.

This brief analytical path through Romantic-piano-inspired compositions by Gainsbourg was meant to help identify the recycled musical material—be it melodic, harmonic, rhythmic, metric, instrumental, and/or structural—at the root of some of his most popular songs. It also provides a perspective on the diversity of techniques used to develop such intertextual relationships, and highlights the creativity and imagination involved in the transformation of the original musical material. This rather free attitude toward the appropriation of the Romantic piano repertoire—generally regarded as "serious," even sacred—appears in line with Gainsbourg's relationship with high culture. Whether playing with words or playing with music, he paid homage while flirting with transgression.

Example 19.3 "Bébé gai" (measures 1–4, x_1 segment).

Notes

1. In this chapter, which focuses on the analysis of several songs by Gainsbourg, the notion of intertextuality is to be understood in a relatively broad sense (see Kristeva 1969).
2. https://www.ina.fr/ina-eclaire-actu/video/i05063718/serge-gainsbourg-par-denise-glaser [accessed 05-08-2023].
3. https://www.rtlplay.be/gainsbourg-5bis-rue-de-verneuil-p_19465 [accessed 05-11-2023].
4. *"Tu dors au bord du chemin/Une fleur de sang à la main."*
5. This Etude had already given rise to several adaptations, in particular by French crooner Tino Rossi ("Tristesse," 1939). For other examples of recorded instrumental and vocal transcriptions, see Panigel 1949: 52–5.
6. Gainsbourg's lyrics are based on a French language word play on the verb *"bégayer,"* which means "to stutter."

"Les Dessous Chics": Gainsbourg & Musical Analysis

20

Evil Twin? The Poetics of Duality in Serge Gainsbourg

Catherine Rudent

I will highlight here the idea of duality and *écho profanateur* in Serge Gainsbourg's work: an echo which profanes, desecrates, a subversive echo—the echo being the auditory equivalent of the visual reflection. My basis for working will be the songs, the analysis of music and voice, as well as the texts and the way they sound. The analyses will focus on songs that seem to be built on "two levels": diaphonic and dialogic; they also are "dual" songs, organized around one speaker who uses two conflicting voices.

If one considers the song to be a "cultural work" (Prévost-Thomas 2001) comprising a coherence within an artist's repertoire, the peculiar duality at hand appears to be a general marker of Gainsbourg's style, closely related to other dualities for which he was famous, especially regarding the way he presented himself. In France, everyone bears in mind the Gainsbourg-Gainsbarre duet, a striking representation that became a significant element of the artists' image in his later years. There is also a link to be made with the context of his life—a context that was divided into two periods. Indeed, Gainsbourg's active years as a recording artist (1958–91) spanned a transition period in French popular music that started around 1960: at the time, and for the next twenty to thirty years, two trends—*chanson* and "Anglo-Saxon rock music"[1] [*"rock anglo-saxon"*], respectively—appeared to be antagonistic. One of his achievements was to intertwine them.

Levels, Reflections, Zigzags

Dueling Levels

My first example of song is "Les P'tits Papiers," whose melody is built on two levels. More exactly, the melody is split into two separate ensembles, each being transcribed on a different staff in example 20.1. There are differences in the singing (*legato* vs detached pronunciation), the pitch (high vs low), the rhythm (dotted half notes only vs shorter and unequal lengths), and the way time is used (stretched vs tightened). All told, the "phrase" (Chabot-Canet 2008) is contrasted between long legato "discursive"

Example 20.1 "Les P'tits Papiers"'s two melodic levels.

elements, and staccato, "musematic" ones,[2] the latter jostling the continuity of the former. Each of the two ensembles has a perfect internal coherence: the latter consists of the identical reiteration of one element; the former is one long phrase that would form, were it not interrupted every two measures, an autonomous melody.

Based on call and response, these interruptions create a sardonic effect: the dotted rhythm seems to be knocking down the seriousness of the melody with a farce-like, humorous quality. It interferes with its flow and stops it from efficiently seizing the listener. In this regard, it may indeed be characterized as "spoiling" and subversive.

Duality is also present in the text: a long sentence, with full grammatical propositions, is interrupted by listed items, a simple accumulation of noun phrases. This series of paper types is the fruit of an *inventio*, of a peculiar virtuosity of writing style: the difficulty here resides in the number of different papers mentioned. This incongruous list sets a distance with the seriousness of the continuous sentence: it brings irony (Rudent 2012) and tells the listener to not take it too literally. But while it contradicts it, it also pertains to it, through rhymes and subtle meaning connections: it is not a complete stranger to it, but works as an echo, although subversive, of the literal speech held in the first part of the text: "Un peu d'amour—*papier velours*/Et d'esthétique—*papier musique*," etc.

Rhymes—the repetition of the same sounds separated by one or two lines of verse—are themselves "echoes," the reoccurrence of a sound after a brief instant. Here, they link one level to the next, suturing them stitch by stitch: *"amour"* ["love"]/*"papier velours"* ["velvet paper"], *"laissez glisser"* ["let it slide"]/*"papier glacé"* ["shiny paper"], *"les sentiments"* ["feelings"]/*"papier collant"* ["sticky tape"]. In this regard, the second level is indeed an echo of the former. Semantic effects reinforce the connection made by the rhymes. They astutely draw something figurative ("let it slide") and something literal ("glazed paper") closer—glazed paper is slippery. Oftentimes, they also play with a third implicit meaning, as exemplified in the rhyme *"ça impressionne"* ["it's impressive"]/*"papier carbone"* ["carbon paper"], which conveys the supplemental notion of a physical imprint on the mind. This rhyme invites the listener to hear, in the feeling of "strong impression," a "printed" trace on their psyche. The plays on words create unusual associations between words that appear completely unrelated (*"papier carbone"/"impressionne"*), leading the listener to do a double-take and connect the mundane with a more elevated idea, making a delightful whole out of original parts. In sum, the song goes beyond a simple well-chosen metaphor or a sole double entendre. Reinforced by the melodic call and response pattern, this stitching of rhymes and meanings lies in a similarity, that is both symmetrical and antagonistic. It is what I call the "subversive echo" [*"écho profanateur"*].

The Reflection "Ribs" the Original

The system of subversive echo found in "Les P'tits Papiers" calls to mind the "dichotomy" (i.e., the division into two parts) of the famous self-interview broadcast on French television in June 1989, *Gainsbarre interviews Gainsbourg* (Colonna 1989). During this interview, Gainsbarre—on the right side of the screen—mocks in a hostile way his double, Gainsbourg, on the left. And from the very beginning of the sequence, he mentions reflection in the mirror:

— Well, I'm Gainsbarre, and you're Gainsbourg. So? I think you look like shit... right?
— So what do you tell yourself, in the morning, when you emerge from the fog, and you look at yourself in the mirror?

Gainsbarre is indeed presented as a visual reflection of Gainsbourg and his questions as a mocking echo—like the list of *"p'tits papiers."* In this interview, the contrast is also placed between the non-ironic, straightforward Gainsbourg (able to express his feelings) and the sarcastic interrupter, Gainsbarre, each remaining in his own coherence during the whole interview.

It is striking to see how figures such as the antagonistic double, the evil twin or the subversive echo pervade Gainsbourg's work. They are present in the cover of "La Marseillaise," for example, through the interventions of the I Threes, singing *"aux armes, et cætera"* ["to arms, et cætera"]. The chorus, disrespectfully truncated, constitutes a response and an echo which profane the verses of the French national anthem, recited by Gainsbourg.

Zigzags and ... "Bang!"

To further explore the recurring manifestation of duality in Gainsbourg's work, I would like to focus now on a few examples that present a greater singularity, bearing in mind Jean-Marc Chouvel's statement that "style means frequently doing something rare" (1993: 24). "Ford Mustang" is one of these "frequent rarities." Its duality jumps off the song: two voices playing off of each other, finishing each other's sentences. They are both complementary and opposite. Unevenly distributed in the music and time, they are composed of two separate lexical fields, each being coherent—as in "Les P'tits Papiers." Gainsbourg covers everything in standard French, as the woman's voice

Example 20.2 Melodic and harmonic echoes in the first two measures of "Ford Mustang."[3]

Example 20.3 "Ford Mustang": melodic mirror on "Mus—*à gauche*, -tang—*à droite*."

pronounces the Anglicisms, the onomatopoeias, the names of brands, and proper nouns with a British inflexion. This contradiction is amplified by the contrasts between the voices themselves (man vs woman), the intonations (French vs English), and finally the vocal gesture (singing vs talking/singing).

Other echoes may be found in both the harmony and melody of the song. In Example 20.2, the notes circled in a box have an echo in the other box. The second measure is then a literal melodic tracing of the first one, transposed lower by a major third. The chord of the second measure (A♭m9) is also a transposition, by a lower major third, of the Cm9 in the first bar. In other words, the second measure is both a melodic and a harmonic echo of the first one. Then, the melody alternates between two notes, on "Mus—*à gauche*, -tang—*à droite*, et à gauche à droite" ["*Mus*—to the left, -*tang*—to the right, and to the left, to the right"]. If this "shuttle" (Tagg 2014) is an amusing word painting in relation to the lyrics (the car is zigzagging),[4] it is also built as a mirror: this time, the second measure reverses the melody of the first (Example 20.3).

To continue with harmonic symmetries, the chords in the first two bars present a descending halftone (C–C♭) at the heart of the chords (Example 20.2). However, the end of the phrase ("*et à gauche à droite*") contains an ascending halftone (D♭–D♮) because of the unexpected "Neapolitan" degree introducing the dominant (Example 20.4).

Be it in its words, its voices, its melody, or its chords, this song is indeed filled with echo. But are we dealing again with a *subversive* echo, coming to "jostle" the first speech? The effect here has more to do with a distance between the two "levels" than with an actual antagonism. And yet, the Mustang zigzags—to the left, to the right—until it hits the plane trees: it is therefore truly "jostled."

Example 20.4 "Ford Mustang": *"et à gauche à droite."*

Immediate Sound Doublings: Onomatopoeias, Letters, Doubled Syllables

Another figure of echo in Gainsbourg's art is the immediate doubling of sounds that aren't really lexicalized: onomatopoeias or spelled-out letters.[5]

Ironic and Erotic Spelling

Immediate sound doubling occurs in "Chez Max coiffeur pour homme" (from the album *L'Homme à tête de chou*): "She leans in, and there are her bazooms/Like two rose-flavored lokum/Bouncing on the back of my neck, boom boom."[6] The breasts bounce, like a carnal echo, highlighted by the doubling of the onomatopoeia "boom." This singular double onomatopoeia is also an occasion for a brilliant rhyme, since it provides Gainsbourg with a "bouncing effect," in the (difficult) rhyme with the Arabic word "lokum."

This immediate doubling of particular sounds (cf. the specific linguistic status of the onomatopoeia) also appears in "Elaeudanla téïtéïa" ("L, A, *E and A ligature*, T, I, T, I, A"): the spelling of the name Lætitia includes a repetition of the letters "t-i," which is another occasion for Gainsbourg to put a phonemic echo to music—the repetition is actually raised through a rather comical octave leap (Example 20.5):

Here, the octave leap emphasizes the repetition. But this spelling melody also shows other instances of echoes: a musical similarity between the first two "a," another zigzag, this time between low and high-pitched levels. Although the echo isn't truly subversive, there is still an implicit irony in this playful octave leap, quite far from

Example 20.5 "Elaeudanla téïtéïa."

passionate adoration, suggesting a sweet irony on sentimentality that was already present in the "boom boom" from "Chez Max coiffeur pour hommes." Although the echo, in both cases, doesn't entirely profane the feeling of love: it distances itself from it, thus putting it into perspective.

The spelling of the name Lætitia is probably a reminiscence—an "echo"—of Nabokov's *Lolita*: "Lolita, light of my life, fire of my loins. My sin, my soul. Lo-lee-ta: the tip of the tongue taking a trip of three steps down the palate to tap, at three, on the teeth. Lo. Lee. Ta." (1955: 11) The "third meaning" suggested here by Gainsbourg, and his probable allusion to *Lolita*, could be eroticism, a "foretaste" of the name of the desired woman.

As a last and very significant example, "Chez les yé-yé" expresses Gainsbourg's place in the French *chanson* scene, at a time when it was being violently "jostled" by the *yé-yé* movement. Once again, this ingenious text is based on a lexical series: verse line after verse line, words containing a syllable reduplication appear, at the same position in the musical phrase (*"tam-tam"* ["tomtom"], *"grigri"* ["lucky charm"], *"coupe-coupe"* ["machete"], etc.). However, these words aren't more frequently used in French than they are in other languages, and inserting them at the right place requires significant poetic skills.

This trick highlights the central metaphor: *yé-yé*'s are savages from which the narrator, the hero, the savior, will free his young beloved, named precisely Lolita. The sound doubling could imply that the word is "savage," unsophisticated, or even untamed,[7] close to an onomatopoeia. These different analyses tend to show that the reduplication of a tongue shaping—*"boum boum," "téitéï," "tam-tam," "yé-yé," "lolita"*—conveys, in Gainsbourg's work, the idea of an irrational, or even subversive drive: desire.

Vision, Quotations, Allusions

Another instance of echo may be found in "Initials B.B.," a song which, even in its title, plays with the reduplication of sounds/letters, and is again connected with eroticism. Written shortly after Brigitte Bardot and Serge Gainsbourg broke up, it shows numerous forms of "doubles." It includes the romantic theme of the double: reflection, shadow of the hero, or ghost of the lost loved one, coming back to haunt him. Remember that this "backfiring" of unhappy love memory was put to music twice by Gainsbourg through the boomerang metaphor—the echo-object—that comes back and hurts. As he writes in the song, "Comme un boomerang,"

> I feel the booms and the bangs
> Shaking my wounded heart
> Love, like a boomerang
> Returns from days past[8]

In "Initials B.B.," the double is an image of the lost loved one, appearing in a glass of Seltzer water [*"eau de Seltz"*] that the narrator is drinking "one night" [*"une nuit"*] in "some English pub in the heart of London" [*"quelque pub anglais du cœur de Londres"*].

The music itself presents a dual dimension with its use of a famous motive (a rising and descending arpeggio played by brass instruments, on a partially syncopated rhythm) from the first movement of Dvořák's "New World" Symphony. In this respect, it becomes an *écho profanateur* too, by trivializing a canon of classical music. "Initials B.B." also features, in this "minor art form" that is *chanson* (according to Gainsbourg himself), at least two classics of Western poetry: Edgar Allan Poe's "The Raven," and Guillaume Apollinaire's "Chanson du mal-aimé" ("Song of the Poorly Loved"). From "The Raven" comes the love reverie of the loved and lost young lady, the return of this person in an echo ("an echo murmured back the word 'Lenore'"). The raven from the poem only says one word ("nevermore") and, similarly, the song ends on "Almeria," the only word pronounced by the fleeting image of the loved one, a word which is symbolic of their forever broken love.[9] "La chanson du mal-aimé" starts with the vision of deformed doubles of the loved one: "a lout that resembled/My love" [*"un voyou qui ressemblait à/Mon amour"*], then "a woman resembling her" [*"une femme lui ressemblant"*] who "leaves a tavern drunk" [*"sort[it] saoule d'une taverne"*]. The scenery, "an evening of half mist in London" [*"un soir de demi-brume à Londres"*], is close to Gainsbourg's setting.

Conclusion

As I have tried to show, Gainsbourg's work abounds with processes of sound returns using the *écho profanateur*. This form of echo affects musical sounds (repetitions, melodic and harmonic symmetries, voiced dialogues), verbal sounds (duplicated onomatopoeias, a work on rhymes connecting or disjointing the two levels), themes (the image of the loved one, the "boomerang" memory), narrative or creation devices (imitation, dissemination, transformation through repetition), and can go all the way to plagiarism. Ultimately, Gainsbourg's dual style also corresponds to the provocative self-staging (particularly Gainsbourg and Gainsbarre) for which he became famous. In sum, it constitutes a stylistic element that seems to span his entire output.

Notes

1 A more than debatable denomination, which I'm using here only because it was then in use in France to label English-speaking pop music.
2 "Discursive" and "musematic," as understood in Middleton 1983.
3 Descending halftone movement in the harmonic texture (C–C♭).
4 Play on words: we can hear *"tangue à droite,"* the verb *"tanguer"* meaning "to pitch" and suggesting the movement of a boat.
5 As seen earlier, the rhyme is also a phonemic—but more distant—echo.
6 *"Elle se penche, et voilà ses doudounes/Comme deux rahat-loukoums/à la rose qui rebondissent sur ma nuque, boum boum."*
7 In this respect, it probably foreshadows the coarse reduplications in the 1973 album, *Vu de l'extérieur* ("Panpan cucul," "Titicaca," "Pamela Popo").

8 "*Je sens des boums et des bangs/Agiter mon cœur blessé/L'amour, comme un boomerang/Me revient des jours passés.*" See also "Boomerang" in *Anna*'s soundtrack—"She is in my eyes, reversed image … I wipe you from my mind … but … always you come back like a boomerang" [*"Elle est dans mes yeux, image inverse … Je te chasse de mes pensées … mais … toujours tu me reviens comme un boomerang"*].

9 Almeria is the name of the Spanish city where, according to the legend, Bardot—who was there for the shooting of a film in January 1968—ended her relationship with Gainsbourg (Verlant 2000: 358).

21

"Je T'Aime... Moi Non Plus": A *Songscape* Analysis

Thomas MacFarlane

Born Lucien Ginsburg, Serge Gainsbourg always disliked his given name because it sounded like the name of a hairdresser. As he himself confessed to his biographer Gilles Verlant,

> all this "Lucien" business was getting in my head. Everywhere I'd go I would see *Chez Lucien—Men's Hair Stylist*, or *Lucien—Salon for Ladies* ... Some names are lucky and others are curses.
>
> (2000: 127)

In search of an appropriate substitute, he first settled on "Serge" for its Russian overtones and then modified his family name out of admiration for the works of painter, Thomas Gainsborough (Simmons 2001: 25). As the child of Jewish immigrants from Ukraine, his early years were marked by the harsh realities of the Second World War (Verlant 2000: 33–67). His artistic sensibilities evidently sustained him through those challenging times, and also paved the way for a remarkable body of work that would come to encompass both music and film.

As will be argued below, Gainsbourg's trajectory from childhood to his later years invites an intriguing comparison with Antoine Doinel, the main character in a series of films by François Truffaut. The series follows Doinel (played throughout by Jean-Pierre Léaud) as he moves from adolescence into young adulthood, struggling to come to terms with love, desire, and destiny. For Truffaut, the character seems to have functioned as a kind of alter-ego that allowed him to explore some of the difficult elements of his own lived experience (Wiegand 2013: 48). The Gainsbourg-Doinel connection is further emphasized in the final film of the series, *Love on the Run* (1979), in which Doinel writes and publishes a novel (*Les Salades de l'amour*) that recounts his experiences from the previous films—Gainsbourg, in his turn, published a novel in his early fifties. Like Doinel again, Gainsbourg was a rebel who transcended categories, yet perfectly in tune with the eclectic spirit of his times. Rooted in the tradition of *chanson*, he eventually came to be regarded a forward-thinking, pan-cultural artist who started his career recording albums that charted the steady development of his musical artistry before achieving international notoriety with a curious pop song/track called "Je t'aime... moi non plus" in the late 1960s (Hawkins 2000: 159).

Background

Gainsbourg first recorded "Je t'aime... moi non plus" with Brigitte Bardot in 1967. At her request, he eventually pulled that version from general release, but re-recorded the song the following year with Jane Birkin (Clayson 1998: 112, 121). Like the original version, the remake was widely regarded as scandalous and was soon banned in Britain as well as in various European markets (Hawkins 2000: 159). The Vatican condemned it, the Italian police arrested the distributor, and the Catholic Church went so far as to excommunicate the executive of the label (Anderson 2013: 44). Why?

In both versions, the vocal performances are highly suggestive. As a result, a curious legend began to emerge. The general perception was that Birkin and Gainsbourg had released an actual recording of an intimate sexual encounter between the two. This was clearly not the case, but nevertheless, the legend persisted. When asked if it was true, Gainsbourg is reported to have said, "Thank goodness it wasn't, otherwise I hope it would have been a long-playing record" (Simmons 2001: 58).

This writer's first experience with "Je t'aime... moi non plus" came through an instrumental version seemingly free of erotic content. That version was drawn from the soundtrack of Gainsbourg's directorial debut, *Je t'aime... moi non plus* (1976). There, it is first used as the backdrop for a delicate dance between the two main characters. However, it later becomes the underscoring for several scenes that feature explicit sexual encounters. As a result of its strong content, the film received harsh notices and was banned in Britain too.

> In France, with a wider release, [it] did attract a moderate audience, though it failed to have anything like the success of its eponymous single. "François Truffaut and a lot of great, great French names defended it," said Jane [Birkin]. "Truffaut went on live TV saying 'Don't bother going to see my film, see Gainsbourg's. That is a work of art,' so that helped eliminate all the awful things the other people said about it."
>
> (Simmons 2001: 77)

Despite the controversy surrounding the various versions of "Je t'aime... moi non plus," it stands as a testament, not only to the creative genius of its composer, but also to the expressive power of recorded sound. In that spirit, we can now explore the song/track using a *Songscape* approach.

Songscapes

The Jane Birkin/Serge Gainsbourg version of "Je t'aime... moi non plus" will be engaged using an approach that blends descriptions of musical structure and the recording process with interpretations of the virtual space created on the finished track. Following a brief overview of the background information regarding the artist and the work itself (see above), the first level will adopt the composer's stance in order to consider how the basic work materials suggest the musical form that follows. Next will come an exploration of recording techniques that may include the acoustic characteristics of the studio space, issues related to microphone placement, audio production effects, a discussion of multi-tracking strategies, and personal accounts of those who participated in the process. Finally, the analysis will focus on the virtual space of the sound recording in terms of how it might be perceived as a dramatic space for the lyrical text. The intended goal of this approach is to explore the effects generated by the ongoing synthesis of music composition and recorded sound.[1]

Song

One of the first things one notices about "Je t'aime… moi non plus" is the largely stepwise melodic motion that unfolds organically throughout. Played on organ, it is rooted in a rotation of basic chords in the key of C major. The orchestration enhances this motion with a line that often doubles the melody, but periodically drifts away into a curious two-note oscillation that parallels and also expands on the breathy allure of the vocals. In the center of this "diatonic paradise," an electric guitar plays a series of sharp chordal clusters. It is ably supported by electric bass, which, given the idyllic nature of the surroundings, one might expect to be played with fingers. Here, however, a plectrum is used, which effectively separates the instrument from the smooth sounds of the orchestra and also asserts a connection to the earthbound rhythms of the text. Throughout, the organ continues with its steadfast devotion to the melodic line.

The nature of these various musical sounds creates a bed for the expressive performance of the lead vocals. At times, the voices double the main melodic line in a manner that mimes the Greenslade orchestration. Elsewhere, they break free and seem to focus on breath itself as a basic musical element. The variety created by these elements helps to distract listeners from the fact that "Je t'aime… moi non plus" is somewhat repetitious, a quality that will be revisited in the final level of *Songscape*.

Track

Drummer Dougie Wright was among those who played on the session for "Je t'aime… moi non plus." He reports that the track was recorded at the Philips/Fontana studio, 2–4 Stanhope Place, Marble Arch in London. By 1968, Philips had made the full conversion over to eight-track recording (Massey 2015: 73). Thus, it seems reasonable to assume that the 1968 version of "Je t'aime… moi non plus" would have been made using the newly acquired eight-track Ampex machine. Peter Olliff, an engineer on the session and the chief engineer at the Philips Studio at that time, concurs with Wright that this was very likely the case.[2]

According to Wright, the instrumental track was recorded as a live take that involved the rhythm section along with an orchestra conducted by Arthur Greenslade.[3] As for Howard Massey, he describes how "[a] typical session set up would place strings at one end, with the drums and other instruments, including guitars and bass, at the other end; horns and brass would be placed in the middle" (70). In addition to Wright on drums and Dave Richmond on electric bass, the other players in the rhythm section were Roger Coulam on keyboards, Bryan Daly and Vic Flick on guitar, and someone—possibly Jim Lawless or Tristan Fry—on tambourine. Although Jane Birkin and Serge Gainsbourg were present during the recording of the instrumental track, they overdubbed their vocal parts separately (Merlet 2019: 234). Jane Birkin reports that during the recording of the vocals, Gainsbourg "put his hand up—because he was very afraid I was going to go on with the heavy breathing two seconds longer than I should and miss the high note—which was very, very high" (quoted in Simmons 2001: 57).

The fact that the vocals were recorded separately suggests something interesting about the recording process itself. Since the orchestra and the rhythm section were recorded live and the vocals were overdubbed shortly thereafter, the two main elements of the track exist as discrete moments in time that were then stacked vertically and heard simultaneously during playback. Thus, the listener experiences these re-purposed slices of time as a virtual space, which then becomes the dramatic space for the text/lyrics.

Space

The inspiration for the text of "Je t'aime… moi non plus" was reportedly a quote by artist, Salvador Dalí: "Picasso is Spanish, me too. Picasso is a genius, me too. Picasso is a Communist, me neither ['*moi non plus*']" (Clayson 1998: 111; Verlant 2000: 351). The title, which translates as, "I love you… me neither," references the ambiguous nature of love and sex. Gainsbourg seems to build on this by suggesting that the complex nature of any intimate encounter creates a space, or spaces, that each partner can, and perhaps must, actively explore.

The vocal performances of "Je t'aime… moi non plus" suggest close personal contact ("And I am joining you…"); this interaction takes place across and through the spaces previously discussed and seems driven by an implicit need to understand intimacy and its implications for the self. The lyrics also feature several references to the natural world: "Like a vacillating wave I go, I come and I go…" and, "You are the wave, and I am the desert island. You go, you come and you go…" This imagery is accentuated by the ethereal orchestral lines that seem to evoke the tidal forces of nature, as well as the nebulous qualities of romantic love itself. Thus, the sound-space frames the encounter as a part of the natural order.

Earlier, it was asserted that "Je t'aime… moi non plus" was repetitious: we can now revisit this idea from a slightly different angle. In *Over and Over: Exploring Repetition in Popular Music,* Anne Danielsen argues that "every repetition may be experienced as repetition with a difference, because the time is different" (2018: 49). In that sense, although recurring elements of "Je t'aime… moi non plus" may be nearly identical, they are nevertheless experienced by the listener as discrete moments in time. Thus, the recognition of repetition may be properly regarded as an activity of the human mind in which similar instances are grouped together for the sake of efficiency. This may also connect with the way discrete temporal moments serve as the raw material for virtual spaces.

Conclusions

At the outset of this discussion, the sensibility of Serge Gainsbourg was briefly compared with that of Antoine Doinel, the main character in a series of films by François Truffaut. One of these, entitled *Stolen Kisses* (1968), features a remarkable scene in which Doinel stares intently into a mirror while repeatedly saying the name of the beautiful older woman with whom he is infatuated:

DOINEL

Fabienne Tabard, Fabienne Tabard, Fabienne Tabard, Fabienne Tabard, Fabienne Tabard, Fabienne Tabard, Fabienne Tabard, Fabienne Tabard, Fabienne Tabard, Fabienne Tabard, Fabienne Tabard, Fabienne Tabard, Fabienne Tabard, Fabienne Tabard, Fabienne Tabard, Fabienne Tabard, Fabienne Tabard, Fabienne Tabard…

Following a brief pause, Doinel begins to recite the name of his young *fiancée*, Christine Darbon (Claude Jade).

DOINEL

Christine Darbon, Christine Darbon…

He then briefly returns to the name of Fabienne Tabard (Delphine Seyrig), before concluding with a prolonged, increasingly intense recitation of his own name.

DOINEL (continuing)

Fabienne Tabard, Fabienne Tabard, Fabienne Tabard, Fabienne Tabard, Fabienne Tabard, Fabienne Tabard… Antoine Doinel, Antoine Doinel.

Here, the names of those involved in the "Doinel" triangle constitute discrete temporal moments, both as utterances as well as events in the lived experience of the main character. As Doinel recites each name into the mirror in a kind of mantra, one senses that he is using these separate moments to create a space for an extended personal inquiry. The recording of "Je t'aime... moi non plus" seems to function in a similar manner. Using basic musical materials, it creates a space within which one may pose questions regarding the nature of love, desire, and destiny. For Doinel, the mirror is the space in which this inquiry can occur. For Truffaut, it is the feature film in which the scene takes place. For composer Serge Gainsbourg, it is the virtual space created by means of the sound recording. Perhaps this is why artists such as Gainsbourg, Truffaut, and even fictional characters such as Doinel, continue to fascinate and inspire. They create virtual spaces that can function as active fields of inquiry. In the process, they allow us to engage, consider, and explore the full range and potential of human experience.

Notes

1. *Songscape* analysis was first employed in *The Music of George Harrison* (MacFarlane 2019). My thanks to Heidi Bishop for her encouragement in the development of this approach.
2. Dougie Wright, email message to author, April 2, 2018.
3. Peter Olliff, email message to author, March 31, 2018.

"En Relisant Ta Lettre": Gainsbourg & Literature

22

Evguénie Sokolov: Fake Genius, Genial Faker

Christophe Levaux

At the end of March 1980, the French literary season was slowly drawing to a close. The newspaper *Le Monde* had predicted it would be "quite calm" (B.A. 1979), as indeed it had been. After the tidal wave of Georges Perec's *Life: A User's Manual* in 1978–9, the most memorable literary events of 1979–80 were the crowning of the Greek poet Odysseas Elytis with the Nobel Prize for Literature and that of the Acadian author Antonine Maillet with the Prix Goncourt. Meanwhile, Gallimard published a short book with a dark cover and a mysterious title: *Evguénie Sokolov*. Although this novel was the author's first foray into literature, his name was far from unknown to the general public. It appeared in large type: Serge Gainsbourg. The novel, fewer than a hundred pages long, stood out for its irreverence. It retraced the history of a famous painter, leader of the "hyperabstract" trend, who harbors an unspeakable secret regarding his artistic activity. Suffering from an acute form of flatulence, Evguénie Sokolov emits enormous and very frequent farts, directing the wind to orient the movement of his brush and thereby produce a seismographic art the likes of which had never been seen. *Evguénie Sokolov* is the fictional autobiography of this painter, who, from his hospital bed, where he awaits major surgery, tells the story of his unstoppable rise to fame.

The Pinnacle of Modern Art

"The sad truth is, if I can trust my uncertain memory, that from a very early age I must have possessed the inborn gift, nay the iniquitous affliction, of constantly breaking wind," writes Sokolov at the outset (Gainsbourg 1998: 3). "I showed an early and unmistakable aptitude for drawing," he continues, before confessing to being "expelled from school for unruliness," whereupon he went to art school (7, 9).

> I began with charcoal-drawing, and at the crack of dawn would set up my easel near Cellini's *Perseus*, since I was fascinated by the severed throat of the Medusa and, in the often deserted [galleries, where my expulsions,] echoing back to me between the bronzes and the plaster casts, reverberated loudly under the glass roof, I felt to some degree happy.
>
> (10)

From art school, Sokolov leads the reader to his military experience, recounting his stint in the army: "My medical inspection was a noisy affair, during which the army doctors took my disability as a sign of insubordination, and dispatched me at once to a disciplinary camp" (14). In florid style he describes his popularity among his comrades in misfortune:

> Having been declared all-round champion, I was nicknamed the Scent-Bottle, Whizz-Bang, the Gunner, the Artificer, the Artillery-man, Ding-Dong, the Trench-Mortar, the Gas-Bomb, the Bazooka, Big Bertha, Rocket, High Wind, the Blower, the Anesthetist, the Blow-Pipe, the Leak, All-Spice, the Goat, the Skunk, Pit-Gas, Gasogene, Wind in the Willows, Arsenic and Old Lace, Borgia, Zephyr, Sweet Violet, Windy-Windy, Mister Pong, Fart Minor, Stinker, Pipe-Line, Gas Container, Gun-Cotton, Arse Wind, Gas-Oil and the Big One, not to mention other terms I have now forgotten.
>
> (15)

Once out of the army, he returns to drawing and the creation of his comic strip:

> Thus it came about that my pathological disorder gave me the idea of creating a comic strip character who, after being turned down several times by various publishers, became a best seller under the name of Crepitus Ventris, the Jet-Man.
>
> (20)

Finally, Sokolov hits on his great discovery—his seismographic art:

> One day, while I was testing my mastery ... a particularly violent explosion of wind broke a pane in the glass roof, causing my hand to shake like that of an electrolytic child. After contemplating the pieces of broken glass scattered at my feet, I looked up at my drawing and was suddenly transfixed. My arm had functioned like a seismograph.
>
> (21–2)

He then embarks on his artistic ascent, with the help of the Zumsteeg-Hauptmann Gallery, which exhibits his "gasograms." Sokolov conveys the enthusiastic reaction of the critics, who describe his art in terms of "hyper-abstractionism, stylistic emphasis, formalistic mysticism" (27). He then tells of his life as an eccentric and solitary dandy; his fallow periods, marked by melancholy and self-doubt; his first health worries; his various dalliances; his artistic activity; the controversies surrounding him; and his influence on the work of young disciples. Finally, he recounts his meeting with a young deaf woman, Abigail, who happens upon him as he paints with his distinctive technique, and with whom he becomes infatuated. The book closes with Sokolov's last words:

> "Abigail," I immediately cried, as my eyes filled with scalding tears, "would that I could insert between my buttocks, not a shepherd's pipe as shown in that

remarkable detail of the picture of the Garden of Delights in the Prado, but an ultrasonic whistle which, at the first breath, would pierce your deafness, so that you would perhaps come back to me, like a bitch in heat..."

(74–5)

With that, the painter's story ends. A postface follows, with a few sentences recounting the death of the painter after an explosion provoked by his own flatulence during an attempt at electrocoagulation.

One could, of course, find nothing more in *Evguénie Sokolov* than this clinical summary of a half-obscene story by the king of provocation, Serge Gainsbourg. That is what many have done.[1] But that would mean, first of all, overlooking the exquisite writing style, with its nineteenth-century refinement, at times quite poetic. And it would also mean ignoring a crucial aspect of the novel, one that Gainsbourg saw fit to underline on the book's title page: *Evguénie Sokolov* is "a parabolic tale." Viewed through that lens, the novel becomes an allegory of the act of creation, and—more precisely—of that act as imposture, on the one hand, or sublimation, on the other. The present chapter examines this dual allegorical dimension of Gainsbourg's novel as well as the reflection on art and the art world that it implies. To start, however, let's consider the work in terms of the category to which it belongs: namely, scatological literature.

Writing the Obscene

Works devoted entirely or in part to excretion are not uncommon in the history of literature, and particularly French literature. The most frequent occurrences date to the Middle Ages and early Renaissance—François Rabelais is an oft-cited example—but we know of some in the nineteenth and twentieth centuries as well. The axiom, theorized in particular by David Inglis (2001), is simple: the progressive decline of the scatological is intimately linked to the process of modernization in the West, or even to the arrival of the bourgeoisie. Over the centuries filth, associated with danger, came to be identified with the unclean masses, whereas the bourgeoisie embodied hygiene and order; excretion and excrement gradually took on an offensive connotation, and that offense extended to their representation.[2] The scatological in literature thus evolved essentially between two poles: one describing filth, misery, or abandon—with twentieth-century authors such as Henri Calet (*La Belle Lurette*, 1935) and Louis-Ferdinand Céline (*Death on the Installment Plan*, 1936)—and another that treated the subject with colorful Gallic humor. The latter tendency included authors such as Louis Pergaud (*The War of the Buttons*, 1912) and Marcel Aymé (*The Green Mare*, 1933), or even Gabriel Chevalier (*Clochemerle*, 1934). Superficially, *Evguénie Sokolov* can be considered an example of this colorful approach, that of apparently grotesque humor.[3] Indeed, this comical aspect is evident in certain of Gainsbourg's songs: not only the eponymous "Evguénie Sokolov," which appeared on *Mauvaises Nouvelles des étoiles* in 1982, but also "Des vents, des pets, des poums" ["Winds, Farts, Booms"] on *Vu de l'extérieur* (1973), "Eau et gaz à tous les étages" ["Water and Gas on Every Floor"] on *Aux Armes et cætera* (1979), and *Guerre et pets* ["War and Farts"], the album that Gainsbourg wrote for Jacques Dutronc in 1980.[4]

A Parabolic Tale

Evguénie Sokolov was thus seen by some as a vulgar farce. It is indeed a novel that can be read that way—and also as a sort of lexicological variation on the theme of flatulence, with Gainsbourg exhaustively exploring the terminology of farts. This type of face-value treatment, whether bawdy in nature or closer to the Célinian pole of the description of misery, is often encountered in scatological literature. But, as noted earlier, such a reading ignores the parabolic aspect of *Evguénie Sokolov*. Between the lines, or behind the appearances, *Evguénie Sokolov* is above all an allegory of the creative act. More precisely—and this is no doubt what renders the novel so rich—it is an allegory of the creative act as imposture, and at the same time as sublimation.

So who is Evguénie Sokolov? He is an uninspired painter. Having studied at the Academy of Fine Arts, he cannot quite manage to move beyond his training or his teachers:

> I went back to my studio, with its musty smell of linseed oil and turpentine, and at once settled down to work. To begin with, my drawings were reminiscent of Goya and Ingres, then, being subject to depression and self-doubt and unable to break away from the influence of Klee, I found refuge in purely technical problems and undertook to improve and sharpen my visual acuity by working on living models. (Gainsbourg 1998: 17–18)

Sokolov is a mediocre painter who tries his hand at a "minor art," the comic strip, to make a living. There he finds success with the grotesque figure Crepitus Ventris, his fictional double. But then he discovers, completely by accident, a pictorial technique for images that could well be confused with the drawings of a seismograph. Sokolov advances in an art world riddled with other impostors, such as his art dealer. When, during an exhibition, one of his works falls to the ground, its shattered glass piercing the eye of a woman who was admiring it, Sokolov explains:

> The incident was skillfully exploited to the best advantage by my dealer … he saw to it that we figured on the front pages of various mass-circulation papers, which gave a sensational account of the affair, as well as the most flattering photographic representation of Sokolov.
>
> (27)

Ultimately everything in Sokolov's story is imposture: he himself (a mediocre painter held up as a genius), his work (feeble copies of seismographic drawings), and the art market (which doesn't hesitate to join in), as well as the public, the press, and the museums (who follow just as blindly). This allegory portrays contemporary art as a hoax or swindle, a theme that obviously recurs in the history of modern art, and one on which contemporary artists themselves—such as Marcel Duchamp or Andy Warhol—have played. The subject also calls to mind Jean Baudrillard's op-ed in *Libération* in

1996, in which he asserts that "the majority of contemporary art has attempted to ... confiscat[e] banality, waste and mediocrity as values and ideologies" (2005: 27).

This fable on artistic imposture is surely one source of the novel's originality. *Evguénie Sokolov*, however, is a novel with multiple readings, and as in a mirror, this first parabola inverts to form a second: a tale of sublimation through art. Indeed, Sokolov uses that which is most vile, vulgar, intimate, and animal in man in order to elevate it into an art object. He makes this activity his artistic practice, but beyond that, he also writes his own memoirs based on this sublimation. The style of his memoir, as mentioned earlier, is highly refined, occasionally even flirting with poetry. The novel's opening sentence, for example, immediately strikes the reader by virtue of its rhythm, its use of a classic esthetic:

> On this hospital bed, over which dung flies are hovering, images of my life come back to me, sometimes clear, sometimes blurred, out of focus as photographers say, some overexposed and others on the contrary quite dark, and if they were placed end to end they would make up a film at once grotesque and horrific, since it would have the peculiarity that the soundtrack, parallel to the longitudinal perforations along its edge, would emit nothing but explosions of intestinal gas.
> (Gainsbourg 1998: 3)

In terms of style, it evokes an author such as Benjamin Constant, who in fact had deeply impressed Gainsbourg, by the latter's own admission.[5] Thus, recourse to a classical esthetic, refined and sometimes poetic, to address a quintessentially vulgar subject obviously recalls, and indeed realizes, this idea of sublimation through art—the novel's second distinctive feature.[6]

Merda d'artista

Evguénie Sokolov is a milestone in literature for the way it treats (and redirects) the scatological. Nonetheless, the relation it constructs between excretion (in a broad sense) and artistic creation is not entirely trivial. According to Daniel-Philippe de Sudres, art can be a form of psychotherapy that seeks to liberate the artist from inner demons or poorly assimilated memories, sanctifying their excretion on the canvas (2008: 171). In the visual arts, moreover, in a manner reminiscent of *Evguénie Sokolov*, a series of works can be considered at once a critique of artistic imposture and a metaphor of sublimation through art. One example is Piero Manzoni's *Merda d'artista* (1961), influenced by Duchamp's readymades—namely, ninety cylindrical cans hermetically sealed, supposedly containing the artist's excrement. Another is Jacques Lizène's *art nul* ["worthless art"], which he founded in the spirit of Arte Povera: a deliberately mediocre and pathetic art that elicited the creation of several paintings, in the late 1970s, produced with fecal matter. With Manzoni as with Lizène, we can envision, in each work, the idea of sublimation and/or the idea of a critique of art as imposture.[7]

Self-Portrait

But there is still more to *Evguénie Sokolov*: the book can also be understood as an autobiography or a "deformed" self-portrait of Gainsbourg himself, embodied by Sokolov, the impostor painter. Gainsbourg, who shares Russian origins with his anti-hero Sokolov, walked the halls of the Academy of Fine Arts, experienced the army, and was sent to the stockade for insubordination. Gainsbourg, like Sokolov, tried his hand at a "minor art"—popular song—later flirting with far more sophisticated arrangements in albums such as *Histoire de Melody Nelson* (1971). How, indeed, can we fail to see Gainsbourg's features in this figure—marginal and solitary, provocative and controversial? To push the parallel between Sokolov and Gainsbourg a bit further, on the subject of imposture, it is hard not to think of the various borrowings, particularly from the classical tradition, that pervade Gainsbourg's musical work. Dvořák's "New World" Symphony (1893) for "Initials B.B." (1968), Chopin's Prelude for Piano No. 4 in E minor, Op. 28 (1839) for "Jane B." (1969), Beethoven's Piano Sonata No. 23 in F minor, Op. 57 ("Appassionata") for "Ma Lou Marilou" (1976): there is no shortage of examples of classical borrowings in Gainsbourg's discography, to say nothing of his attempts to go beyond pop formulas and tackle a more elaborate instrumentation and narrative outline. It is thus very tempting to link Sokolov's imposture with that of Gainsbourg, that "roguish copier" of the great composers of the classical tradition on whose works he blithely drew. Of course, one could object that the opposite process is at play here—that Gainsbourg tended to transmit a major art through minor ones. Nonetheless, the novel's epigraph seems almost to confirm the idea of Gainsbourg's imposture: "The mask falls, the man remains and the hero fades away," we read. The quotation is from Jean-Baptiste Rousseau's *Ode to fortune* (1721). Gainsbourg, however, does not cite Rousseau. Could this be a clever trick of his? Should the omission of Rousseau's name be a *mise en abyme* of Sokolov's career, or that of Gainsbourg's? Ironically, as if to substantiate Gainsbourg's tale, a quick internet search for the author of these few words points only in the direction of… Gainsbourg.[8]

Notes

1   "Noise for nothing. A fart in the wind" [*"Du bruit pour rien. Un pet de lapin"*] was the verdict of a review of Gainsbourg's novel in the newspaper *Sud Ouest* (P.V. 1980).
2   See Persels & Ganim 2004: xvi. On the scatological in literature, see also Gourfinkel 1936.
3   In the case of *Evguénie Sokolov*, one may be struck by the notion of the carnivalesque, theorized by Mikhail Bakhtin (1984), involving the reversal between power and the dominated, the noble and trivial, and between the refined and the vulgar.
4   The title *Guerre et pets* puns on the French title of Tolstoy's *War and Peace* ["Guerre et paix"].
5   https://www.ina.fr/ina-eclaire-actu/video/i08218014/serge-gainsbourg-se-souvient-de-ses-premieres-lectures [accessed 06-16-2022].

6 Note that Gainsbourg's allegory implies a view of art that is at once conservative and very Romantic: artistic success is, or can only be, a great bluff; or else it can only be achieved by those who suffer disadvantages or handicaps that they manage to sublimate.
7 See especially Delville 2008 on this subject.
8 The following websites (all accessed on February 12, 2019) concur: *Le Figaro* (http://evene.lefigaro.fr/citation/masque-tombe-homme-reste-heros-evanouit-51779.php), *Le Monde* (https://dicocitations.lemonde.fr/citations/citation-45203.php), *Le Parisien* (http://citation-celebre.leparisien.fr/citations/21694).

23

Gainsbourg as a Dandy: Image and Literary Influences

Mickaël Savchenko

Serge Gainsbourg's musical and literary output stands at the crossroads of several art forms: pop music and classical music, painting and visual arts (cinema, comics), but also poetry—and, more generally, literature. Still, one would be hard pressed to label him as a representative of any artistic or literary movement: he was first and foremost a singer-songwriter expressing himself through the medium of *chanson*, a genre that has often been looked down upon. At best, the genre was long deemed a popular art form, at worst, it was described by Gainsbourg himself as a "minor art ... for minors" (Simmons 2001: 82). As he explained on the set of *Apostrophes* (1986), *chanson*, as an art form, does not require any initiation, unlike painting, or architecture. Gainsbourg seemingly despised the genre, claiming to write songs only for the money (Verlant 2000: 448). Yet, at the same time, he also declared that his talent as a lyricist could occasionally "come close" to that of real poets (including Arthur Rimbaud, his idol). In an earlier TV show (*Numéro Un Michel Berger*, 1977), he could even be seen making fun of songwriter Michel Berger's "basic rhymes," as opposed to the "sophisticated rhymes" he used in his *tour de force*, "Comment te dire adieu." In sum, his ambiguous position about pop songs and his own talent as a lyricist might lead to think that his professed contempt for *chanson* was nothing but a cultivated attitude.

That same year, when invited to honor the late musician and writer Boris Vian on French television, Gainsbourg chose to perform "J'suis snob." The song's first-person lyrics make fun of 1950s snobs: caricatural dandies indulging in mundane evenings, delicacies, expensive clothes, sports cars, and rubbing shoulders with baronesses with long aristocratic names. For Vian's character, being a snob is a life of toil ("It's months of hard labor/It's the life of a galley slave"[1]), a life that imposes a set of requirements and constant effort. But such perfectionism is rewarded by being looked at: snobs follow fashion for the sake of external approval, and that is probably where the essential difference between snobbery and dandyism lies. Since the previous decade, Gainsbourg's lyrics had been increasingly influenced by pop culture and consumer society. First cautiously sounding the *yé-yé* era while still clinging to jazzy tunes, he had progressively taken his place in this new musical movement. Echoing Vian's snobs' taste for modern and fashionable objects or gadgets, his lyrics began featuring electric razors, walkie-talkies, or jukeboxes; suddenly, they were full of registered trademarks such as

Remington, Boeing, Kleenex, etc. More generally, abundant proper nouns became characteristic of his lyrics, a tendency that went hand in hand with a marked penchant for "Frenglish" [*"franglais"*]. Indeed, Gainsbourg often used English words in his lyrics, even more so in his song titles, often mingling them with French words—"Qui est 'in' qui est 'out,'" "What tu dis qu'est-ce que tu say," "J'entends des voix off," "Bébé Song," etc. (As is often the case with assimilated loanwords, these borrowings presented prosodic peculiarities when uttered with a French accent or according to French pronunciation rules, which could explain his prominent use of this stylistic feature.)

Another element of Gainsbourg's "dandy" poetics lies in the onomatopoeia found in around twenty songs, mostly written between 1966 and 1975—"Mambo miam miam," "Shu ba du ba loo ba," "Hip Hip Hip Hurrah," "Boum badaboum," "La Fille qui fait tchic ti tchic," "Di Doo Dah," etc. Just as with English words, such sounds generally receive additional emphasis when pronounced by French speakers (Gainsbourg himself or his backing vocalists). But they might also be accentuated by the use of female voices, a gender-based strategy that somehow detached them from the rest of the vocal texture. On the same train of thought, the contribution of Jane Birkin's posh English accent to Gainsbourg's "dandyishness" should not be underestimated. The encounter with Birkin resulted in a more sophisticated appearance and clothing style too: in reference to his poetics and looks, the media began referring to Gainsbourg as a dandy in the 1960s, and continued to do so throughout the 1970s and 1980s (Natta 2022). It was precisely around this time that the singer-songwriter started to develop his own legend, bringing his persona to the forefront and making it an essential component of his songs. While, in common language, a dandy is someone who has style and wears elegant clothes, Gainsbourg's relationship with dandyism extended beyond his dark glasses and white Repetto shoes.

Dandyism appeared in early nineteenth-century England, even though the term itself was already in use in the late-eighteenth century. Its followers distinguished themselves through elegance, but following fashion was not enough: one had to *create* fashion, often by behaving against existing trends. Brilliant wit and irreproachable manners were also prerequisites. In sum, being a dandy was a lifestyle in itself. In his essay *On Dandyism and George Brummell*, Jules Barbey d'Aurevilly argued: "You are not a dandy for the clothes you wear, but rather for the way you wear them! You can wear rags and still be a dandy" (1879: 13).

In France, dandyism influenced several notable writers, such as Honoré de Balzac, Charles Baudelaire, and Théophile Gautier. A theoretician of dandyism, Baudelaire examined the movement in "Le Peintre de la vie moderne." According to him, dandies feel a "burning desire to create a personal form of originality" (1869b: 93). To highlight the "aristocratic superiority of his mind," a dandy is in constant opposition with the outside world, in an act of artistic revolt. One recognizes a dandy by his "cold exterior" (96): coolness, not taking anything too close to heart, and detachment/indifference are attitudes that are not too far apart. Baudelaire stresses that dandyism does not belong to a particular chronological period: it is rather a state of mind that manifests itself every now and then, and is related to societal changes.

Two major nineteenth-century cultural movements were imbued with dandyism: Romanticism and the Decadent movement. Gainsbourg has a strong connection with both. At the beginning of his career, he adapted several Romantic poems into songs, and his own lyrics were hugely influenced by this poetic tradition. The musical inspirations that stem from the Romantic era (Chopin, Brahms, Dvořák) are also patent. The period during which he set poems to music was rather short: it ended in 1962, that is, only four years after his first album was released. And yet, in the late 1980s, he told his biographer Gilles Verlant: "Why did I only sing Romantic poets? Well, because I *am* intrinsically romantic" (2000: 200).

In addition to displaying a taste for French Romantic poets, Gainsbourg's work was also influenced by American writer and poet Edgar Allan Poe. Poe's name is mentioned in no less than seven of the songs he released between 1967 and 1990. Interestingly enough, there is no direct mention of Poe's work (apart from a possible allusion to the very beginning of "The Raven" in "Initials B.B."). It might therefore be assumed that the writer's name was also used for prosodic effect, constituting another "alien" element, along with English words and proper nouns. Nevertheless, Poe was much more than a name to Gainsbourg. The characters in Poe's macabre tales are often endowed with unsettling appearances or corporal deformities: long teeth, big eyes, etc. They differ considerably from those around them. Let us remember that Gainsbourg deemed himself ugly and built his entire personal mythology around his appearance. Poe's characters often suffer from a physical or mental illness, whether apparent or invisible, and are hypersensitive (*The Fall of the House of Usher* is a perfect example of this). This dark and grotesque side of Poe's *œuvre* follows the tradition of Gothic fiction, the situations and settings of which eventually found their way into a more recent and more generalized Gothic/horror tradition perpetuated by fantasy cinema and the French Grand Guignol theater. Gainsbourg's connection with this macabre tradition is apparent in such songs as "Frankenstein," "Mallo Mallory," or "Meurtre à l'extincteur" (in the latter, "l'homme à tête de chou" murders his girlfriend with a fire extinguisher).

In the same vein of what literary theorist Mario Praz calls "Dark Romanticism" (1933), the influence of Baudelaire is one of the most apparent in Gainsbourg's lyrics, as I am about to outline briefly. Quotations from and allusions to this poet (and translator of Poe's short stories) are numerous in Gainsbourg's lyrics. It might be suggested that it was the provocative edge of Baudelaire's poems that appealed to Gainsbourg (in 1857, the publication of *Les Fleurs du mal* led to an unprecedented obscenity trial). Some of Gainsbourg's songs were also attacked, violently criticized, or banned—most notably "Aux Armes et cætera" (the reggae version of "La Marseillaise") and "Je t'aime… moi non plus." The following verses by Baudelaire are an example of his contemplating the vilest aspects of everyday life:

> With heart at rest I climbed the citadel's
> Steep height, and saw the city as from a tower,
> Hospital, brothel, prison, and such hells,
> Where evil comes up softly like a flower.

(1869a)

This "contemplating from high above" stance is reminiscent of Gainsbourg's early caustic songs: in 1958, the year of his discographic debut, a journalist referred to him as "a sort of Daumier of pop song," highlighting the grotesque, caricatural edge of his work (quoted in Verlant 2000: 150).

Thirteen years later, Gainsbourg and Birkin recorded "La Décadanse," whose title made, for the first time, a direct reference to the Decadent movement—albeit in the form of a pun.[2] It must be noted that the spelling difference is indiscernible when spoken. Although the context may not seem grave (the title refers to a new dance Gainsbourg claims to have invented), the lyrics betray despair and a sense of feeling lost: "Decadance/Stronger still/Than our death/Binds our souls and our bodies" [*"La décadanse/Plus encore/Que notre mort/Lie nos âmes et nos corps"*]. Once again, a similar idea may be found in Baudelaire's work when he writes, in "Semper eadem": "For often Death/Still more than Life, binds us in subtle ways" (1861: 51).

As the 1970s progressed, Gainsbourg increasingly turned to decadent esthetics, adopting them completely in the end. This evolution is reflected in the lyrics he wrote in the late 1970s and 1980s. It also shows through his only novel, *Evguénie Sokolov*, which addresses subjects such as death, perversion, and illness. The Decadent movement developed in the last decades of the 1800s. While it lacked a clear-cut manifesto or a leader, a few authors in France were associated with it, including Baudelaire, Verlaine, Barbey d'Aurevilly, Villiers de l'Isle-Adam, Huysmans, Jean Lorrain, Laforgue, and Mallarmé. I purposefully use the term "associated" here, since some of these writers only came to be associated with the movement post mortem (e.g., Baudelaire), while others refused to be affiliated with it—namely Verlaine, despite his contributing in fact to its genesis.

Here is what Verlaine thought about the Decadent movement, as related by fellow writer Ernest Raynaud: "I love the word decadence, resplendent with purple and gold ... This word is associated with ... refined thoughts of an extreme sophistication, a high literary culture, a soul capable of intense voluptuousness" (1920: 64). Further in the text, the poet evokes "the necessity to react against modern-day platitudes with all things delicate, precious and rare" (65). The word "refined" [*"raffiné"*] is central here, considering Baudelaire himself used it as a synonym for dandy (1869b: 91–6). As for Verlaine, his approach puts the emphasis on taste rather than sentiments and sensibility, as was the case with the Romantics. At a time when money became more valued than title, a time when aristocracy was progressively losing ground and mingled with the bourgeoisie to a point where no one could tell who was who anymore, the necessity of an art that distinguished itself from mass culture and proved impenetrable to the common people was deeply felt. Seeking refinement and sophistication, *fin de siècle* decadents attached great importance to dress and fashion in general, as well as to interior design. Collecting objects was also a popular hobby among decadents, and one cannot fail to make a connection here with the interior of Gainsbourg's house in the Rue de Verneuil, its custom decoration and rare trinkets.

Two decadent writers are key in studying Gainsbourg's literary influences. First of all, Joris-Karl Huysmans, the author of the 1884 novel *A Rebours*—translated into English as *Against the Grain*, also known as "the breviary of the decadence" (Velasco 2001). Gainsbourg's biographers have sometimes compared the singer to Des Esseintes, *A Rebours*'s protagonist (Maubert 2005: 31–2, 39–40). The second influential writer is

Jean Lorrain (pen name of Paul Alexandre Martin Duval), a dandy, homosexual, and scandalous author, mostly known for the book, *Monsieur de Phocas* (1900). Gainsbourg knew both novels well. He mentions Huysmans in one of his poems, "Sonnet lolitien," the structure of which betrays familiarity with lesser-known poems by Mallarmé.[3]

Written in a very peculiar style featuring lengthy phrases and whimsical vocabulary, Gainsbourg's one and only novel, *Evguénie Sokolov*, portrays a decadent hero, a century after Huysmans. Both *A Rebours* and *Evguénie Sokolov* are stories of eccentric individuals who are at odds with the outside world (hence the title of Huysmans's work, *Against the Grain*). Both Gainsbourg's and Huysmans's characters suffer from an uncommon illness, which is reminiscent of Romantic characters (François-René de Chateaubriand's René, Benjamin Constant's Adolphe, Alfred de Vigny's Stello). However, the noble psychic disorders of the Romantics are transformed into pedestrian ones: in Huysmans, dyspepsia makes Des Esseintes crave "horrendous" peasant food. The protagonist also suffers from nausea, constipation, neuralgia, etc. As for Evguénie Sokolov, he is the bearer of a ridiculous condition *par excellence*: excessive wind-breaking. He eventually succumbs to the same force he uses to create works of art, hoist with his own petard (pun intended).

In 1981, Gainsbourg composed a song with poignantly personal lyrics, "Ecce homo," using the Latin phrase attributed to Pontius Pilate showing the scourged Christ to the Jews, shortly before his execution. Gainsbourg's lyrics focus on his alter ego's weaknesses and sufferings:

Yeah, Gainsbarre has been nailed
To Mount Golgothar *[sic]*
He's full of reggae and joy
His heart pierced right through[4]

Gainsbarre, a character who appears a number of times in Gainsbourg's songs throughout the 1980s, is the artist's doppelgänger incarnating his vices—alcohol, smoking, misogyny, even narrow-mindedness. In "Ecce Homo," he is paradoxically depicted as crucified, wounded by his own confrontation with the world. Like Christ, he suffers *for* mankind, and *because of* mankind too. From a religious standpoint, this representation desacralizes the image of Christ while profaning it at the same time. Even the spelling of "Golgotha" (Calvary) is deformed so as to make it rhyme with "Gainsbarre." In a different connection, the wounded, pierced stance is evocative of the classical portrayal of St Sebastian by Mantegna—Gainsbourg's favorite painting, so much so that it inspired the cover of Bayon's collection of interviews published in 1992.

As exemplified by "Docteur Jekyll et Monsieur Hyde," doppelgängers appear in Gainsbourg's work as early as 1966. This obsession with doubles may be related to the artist's versatile activity: writing poems and composing music, singing and having others sing his songs, making films and videos, painting, photography—in other words, being ubiquitous. It may also be interpreted as an attempt to hide—after all, creating an alter ego is akin to wearing a mask. The gas mask Evguénie Sokolov wears while working to avoid suffocating on his own emissions also acts as a means to isolate himself from the outer-world. The mask's symbolic value seems corroborated by the unacknowledged quotation from Jean-Baptiste Rousseau which serves as the novel's epigraph: "The mask falls, the man stays, and the hero vanishes" (Gainsbourg 1998: 1). In addition, masks are mentioned in several of Gainsbourg's songs, most notably "I'm the Boy" (1984): "A mask among masks/Tragic or bitter" [*"Masque parmi les masques/ Tragiques ou d'amertume"*]. Similarly, an exaggeratedly ugly, massive-eared Gainsbarre puppet was featured in the *Guignols de l'info* TV show during Gainsbourg's final years. This representation was most likely endorsed by the man himself, considering he appeared on the latter show on a regular basis, conversing with his own effigy.

The eponymous character of Jean Lorrain's novel, *Monsieur de Phocas*, is also obsessed with masks. They alternately fascinate and repel him, and he is also interested in dolls, whose half-human, half-artificial appearance resembles masks in their delusiveness. Not surprisingly, dolls are another powerful symbol in Gainsbourg's work, as he often draws a parallel between desirable women and malleable dolls (see, for example, "Poupée de cire, poupée de son," "La Poupée qui fait," or the photography album *Bambou et les poupées* which was published by Filipacchi in 1981). He strived to make his life a work of art, even a show; in some respects, doubles and masks perfectly match his figure as a trickster and an occasional—seldom-caught—plagiarist.

The starting point for my analysis—equating Gainsbourg to a dandy—may have sounded like a superficial, journalistic *cliché*. Nevertheless, digging up the artist's dandy roots offers a rich perspective on a large part of his literary influences, revealing a coherent dandy-snob-Romantic-Decadent lineage; his take on love and his professed misogyny also align with this philosophy. At the risk of applying a concept of the past to contemporary pop culture, portraying Gainsbourg as a dandy brings to light a correspondence between the artist's public persona and his work. Still, at the end of this chapter, we face a paradox (which I do not aspire to resolve, since dandies are by definition paradoxical): the—often ostentatious—intertextual games, references, and allusions mentioned above are found within the intrinsically light and traditionally oral genre of pop song. Gainsbourg's lyrics seem too complex to fit in with the song genre, and too light for poetry. While other performers crave to be universally liked, he appears to reject any populism and to cultivate sophistication to extremes, almost to the point of martyrdom. In short: Gainsbourg's relationship with highbrow culture is full of contradictions. And yet, for a singer-songwriter, it is exceptionally close.

Notes

1   "Ça demande des mois d'turbin/C'est une vie de galérien."
2   Interestingly, Paul Verlaine had already rhymed *décadence* and *danse* in "Langueur" (1884a: 104).
3   Gainsbourg places Huysmans's initials after his last name at the end of the line, thus making them rhyme with another word, just the way it was facetiously done by Mallarmé in his occasional piece "Rue as-tu peur! de Sèvres onze" (Mallarmé 1945: 84).
4   "Et ouais, cloué le Gainsbarre/Au mont du Golgothar/Il est reggae hilare/Le cœur percé de part en part."

"Des Flashes et des Eclairs": Gainsbourg & The Moving Image

24

L'Eau à la Bouche: Gainsbourg at the Forefront of the "Nouvelle Vague"

Jérôme Rossi

Shot the same year as *Le Beau Serge* (dir. Claude Chabrol, 1958), the film that officially marked the beginning of the "Nouvelle Vague" movement, Jacques Doniol-Valcroze's *L'Eau à la bouche*, was released in France on January 29, 1960. Valcroze, who had co-founded the specialized journal *Les Cahiers du cinema* in 1951, had already shot three short films between 1957 and 1958. *L'Eau à la bouche* was his first feature film, and it was also Serge Gainsbourg's first original film soundtrack. Gainsbourg co-signed it with his working partner, composer and arranger Alain Goraguer. At the time when the film was released, he had already produced two albums, *Du Chant à la une!* and *Serge Gainsbourg No. 2*. The former notably comprised the song "Le Poinçonneur des Lilas," emblematic of the "Rive Gauche" style, inspired by Boris Vian and characterized by its use of puns, its dark topics, and jazz sonorities. Alain Goraguer and his orchestra were entrusted with the arrangements, as was the case for *L'Eau à la bouche*.

Although Gainsbourg's first songs were not very popular, the introduction of his "Rive Gauche" style in film music, along with Goraguer's jazzy sound, represented a truly innovative approach, which placed the two musicians at the forefront of the "Nouvelle Vague." With about 100,000 copies sold (Marchand-Kiss 2015: 91), "L'Eau à la bouche" was Gainsbourg's first commercial success. As such, it launched his career as a singer and film music composer. After briefly presenting some background information to better contextualize the film and its music, this chapter will focus on three main directions: the narrative distance created by the song, the presence of jazz, and the analysis of two instances when the hierarchy between music and image becomes reversed, giving the former a dominant position.

Background Information about the Film

L'Eau à la bouche is a single-location film: it tells the story of four young men and women who gather together in the castle of Aubiry, in Céret (a small town in the Pyrénées-Orientales region). Miguel (Gérard Barray), a young solicitor, summons Lady Henriette's heirs, Myléna, who lives in the castle (Françoise Brion), her cousin

Séraphine (Alexandra Stewart), and Séraphine's brother Jean-Paul (Paul Guers). Jean-Paul is delayed and, following a misunderstanding, Séraphine's ex-lover Robert (Jacques Riberolles), a friend and colleague of Jean-Paul's, impersonates him with the complicity of Séraphine. The truth is not found out until the end of the film upon the arrival of the real Jean-Paul. In the meantime, Robert and Myléna become lovers, as well as Séraphine and Miguel. A third couple, César the butler (Michel Galabru) and Prudence the maid (Bernadette Lafont), adds to this gallery of characters frolicking through the corridors.

Jacques Doniol-Valcroze heard about Serge Gainsbourg through François Truffaut, who had considered hiring him to write a song for the film he was then working on, *Jules et Jim*. Valcroze thus asked Gainsbourg to write one for his own film, "L'Eau à la bouche." Through the image of the saliva (the French idiom *"mettre"* or *"donner l'eau à la bouche"* means "being mouth-watering"), this song bluntly speaks of physical desire, but a desire that must express itself with some caution so as not to provoke rejection. The idiom is used in the film itself by César the butler, who precisely does not use any self-restraint: *"C'est la petite, elle m'a mis l'eau à la bouche, et moi, quand j'ai l'eau à la bouche, il faut que je boive... et elle ne veut pas!"* ["It's this girl, she makes my mouth water, and when my mouth's watering, I must drink... and she won't let me!"] (45:07) Therefore, there is a sharp contrast between Myléna, Robert, Séraphine, and Miguel on the one hand, and the servants on the other hand: the former's love-making only happens after a long and patient seduction game, a staging of desire, while the latter do not beat around the bush—César almost completely strips Prudence of her clothes on the stairs.

From a poetic and musical point of view, the song follows an AABAA structure, every A (verse) standing for one quatrain with the same music and ending with the same two lines (*"Je t'en prie ne sois pas farouche/Quand me vient l'eau à la bouche"* ["Please don't shy away from me/When my mouth is watering"]) that change only in the final verse. The strength of the song is to stage an action: indeed, the narrator's "prayer" (*"écoute ma prière"* ["listen to my prayer"], *"je t'en prie"* ["I'm begging you"]) becomes a beautiful and concrete action in the final verse: *"Vois, je ne prends que ta bouche"* ["See, I only take (kiss) your mouth"]. Although the man's request is courteous, it is none the less adamant, and finally satisfied—as is the case with all three couples in the film.

In the credits, a title card indicates that the music was composed by Serge Gainsbourg "under the direction" of Alain Goraguer. Over sixty years later, we know that Gainsbourg and Goraguer actually composed the score together: "In fact," Goraguer explains,

> we co-composed the music of *L'Eau à la bouche*, including the song. But since Serge was the one who had been asked to do it, we agreed on the following solution: a title card in the credits would read "Music by Serge Gainsbourg," and a second one would read "Arrangements and musical direction by Alain Goraguer." It was so important for him, for his budding career, and Serge was such a close friend, I was happy to help him out.
>
> (Lerouge 2001: 5–6)

00:00 EB	27:25 EB			54:01 EB	01:00:07 EB	01:21:51 EB
		38:54 Judith	41:25 Judith	56:13 Judith	01:01:50 Judith	
08:12 Voiture						01:16:33 Voiture
03:00 Angoisse						01:13:58 Angoisse
09:51 BR	12:07 BR				01:03:22 BR	
		32:41 Jesus	45:33 Jesus		01:04:08 Jesus	

Figure 24.1 Symmetrical effect produced by the musical recurrences in *L'Eau à la bouche*.

The music was recorded in December 1959 by Alain Goraguer and his orchestra, which comprised some of the most talented French jazzmen of the time, such as Roger Guérin (trumpet), Georges Grenu (saxophone), and Pierre Michelot (double bass).

The musical structure of the film is built around the five occurrences of the song "L'Eau à la bouche" (EB), including its instrumental versions. The third occurrence is situated roughly at the golden ratio of the film,[1] establishing a symmetry axis on each side of which the other recurring melodies are distributed. These are either identically repeated (fixed), or varied; we may identify the "Judith" theme (varied), the "cool jazz" themes "Voiture" (fixed) and "Angoisse" (varied, since its first occurrence is shortened), and "Ballade Romantique" (BR—fixed), as well as the theme "Jesus, Joy of Man's Desiring" ("Jesus"—varied), first in its original version played on the organ, then in piano and "third stream" version. The significant quantity of musical occurrences[2]—previously heard melodies as well as new themes—that are distributed after the golden ratio serves at once as a musical recap and as a narrative denouement process leading to the conclusion (Figure 24.1).

Analysis of the Symbolic Role of the Song and the Narrative Distance It Creates in the Film

The song in itself produces a dramatic effect through its five occurrences in the film. It is first sung in its entirety as the opening credits roll. The solo percussions that can be heard in the introduction conveniently create some suspense, as we are presented with a series of portraits of the actors in various poses. Other instruments join in until the arrival of the brass section, as we see the face and understanding smile of the young Florence (Florence Loinod) appear onscreen, thus expressing from the beginning the idea that romance is nothing but a childish game. Jean-Paul will remind us of this at the end of the film: *"Tu sais, quand on joue à un jeu, il y a toujours un perdant ... Mais bon, c'était pour rire, alors faut pas pleurer."* ["You know, when people play a game, there is always a loser ... But, well, it was only for fun, so there's no need to cry."] (01:21:22) The next two shots anticipate the end (and the flash-forward in the opening sequence of the film): we first see Jean-Paul driving his car, then the couple formed by Robert and Myléna. It is on this image (00:48) that the title of the film appears and that Gainsbourg's voice can be heard for the first time, just before a one-minute-long wide shot of the stone rail of the castle as the names of the technicians are listed in the credits. The young Florence then appears on camera, launching the tracking shot that allows us to follow her inside the castle. The yo-yo she's playing with most certainly symbolizes the fickleness of romantic feelings. An effect of perfect symmetry is created when Gainsbourg's rendition of the song returns at the end of the film (01:21:51), along with Florence—still playing with her yo-yo. The girl is again followed by a tracking shot of the camera in the opposite direction from the first one, as she exits the castle and walks back toward the stone rail Myléna and Robert are now leaning on together as a newly formed couple. We can hope that their relationship will last, contrary to the other two.

Present at the beginning and at the end of the film in its vocal version, the song plays a semiotic role: it builds on the film's title and illustrates it with lyrics that sum up what the story is about, while the melody helps convey the meaning of the text throughout the film, including in the instrumental versions of the song. As though directly addressing the viewer and listener, the music of *L'Eau à la bouche* reminds us with each of its occurrences how important it is to control one's urges in the games of love and seduction.

The first purely instrumental occurrence of the song accompanies the opening conversation between Myléna and Robert, which takes place by a nice gazebo surrounded by water. Robert asks Myléna about the nature of her relationship with Miguel—who is shown through the use of parallel editing trying to seduce Séraphine. When Robert asks why Myléna "doesn't get along" with Miguel anymore, the camera zooms in on the young woman's eyes, triggering a flashback of Miguel trying to rape Myléna; only the percussions can be heard as Myléna slaps Miguel across the face (29:00–29:06), then the music stops entirely, silenced by Miguel's brutal desire. It starts again at 29:21, when the same Miguel is on his best behavior with Séraphine, taking her for a stroll on the rooftops of the castle.

The same version of the song is used again later in the film (54:01–55:13), associated with the same place: Séraphine swims naked in the pond surrounding the gazebo, while Miguel is watching her. In this scene, the water (*"l'eau"*) of the film title is real water and arouses Miguel's desire in front of this female body undulating in the moonlight. We will see the two of them embracing each other shortly after that. Here, the song is artificially shortened (the manipulation of the track is rather clearly audible at 55:02) and the original melody is altered, conveying the idea that the characters' desire, too quickly satisfied, cannot end up in a lasting relationship.

A new version of the song, whose melody is this time entrusted to the saxophone instead of the flute, accompanies Robert (01:00:07–01:00:55) when he discovers that Myléna, who had previously rejected him, has left her bedroom door ajar. In front of the mirror, she takes off her necklace before starting to undress. Robert finally joins her. The song serves to remind us of the long and patient approach that has enabled Robert to finally earn Myléna's trust.

Through its various versions (with or without lyrics, played on the flute or the saxophone, in its entirety or shortened), the song illustrates the evolution of the relationships between the four young people as well as the way the director sees his characters, a point of view he shares with the viewer and listener through the prism of Gainsbourg's voice and the melody he is singing.

Jazz and Cinema: Light-Heartedness and Ambivalence

Although the use of jazz as extra-diegetic music became more and more frequent in French thrillers in the late 1950s, it had never been used in a vaudeville comedy film before. In *L'Eau à la bouche*, jazz—mainly in the "cool" style[3]—is used at once for its sophistication, its freedom, and its ambivalence: it is unpredictable, twisty, falsely reassuring, just like the cruel seduction games that Miguel, Myléna, Séraphine, and Robert are indulging in.

The piece entitled "Voiture" is used to characterize the same car ride at the beginning (08:12–08:46: Robert, impersonating Jean-Paul, comes to the castle) and, in a shortened version, at the end of the film (01:16:33–01:16:52: the real Jean-Paul comes to the castle). Its rhythm gives both vehicles a pace at once moderate and determined.

A jazzy ballad ("Angoisse") accompanies the flash-forward at the beginning of the film, when all the characters are looking for Séraphine (03:00–03:35), an event that finally occurs at 01:13:58, when the same ballad can be heard. The music fuels the characters' worry and agitation by alternating a trumpet motif repeated at shorter and shorter intervals—thus creating a feeling of urgency—and oscillation of chords (F♯m and B7) played on the jazz guitar. The mood conveyed by the music is deeply ambivalent: neither sad nor truly merry, its ambiguity echoes Myléna's questioning (01:16:03): *"Fifine a disparu. Peut-être est-elle en train de se tuer pour une amourette? Nous avons joué tous les quatre au jeu stupide de l'amour léger; nous nous sommes pris pour des libertins."* ["Fifine is missing. She may be trying to kill herself over a silly unrequited crush? The four of us have been playing the foolish game of fickle love; we've been acting like libertines."]

The piece entitled "Ballade Romantique" ("Romantic Ballad," BR) is associated with the couple formed by Robert and Myléna. It is more passionately romantic than the song "L'Eau à la bouche." We may also note the way its mixing emphasizes Robert's shock upon seeing Myléna for the first time. Very discreet at first, the music is disproportionately amplified (a kind of "empathetic mixing") as the camera revolves around Robert (09:51–10:01) and stops with a close-up on his eyes. This is undoubtedly an example of the use of film music that Jean-Luc Godard experimented with at length. By drawing attention to the extra-diegetic music through this manipulation, the director encourages viewers to think more deeply about what they are seeing, and puts them in a position of complicity with the character, who they know is lying. When the same music is used again (01:03:22), it is to accompany Myléna and Robert's languorous kiss. It creates continuity with the couple César/Prudence; but when we see Miguel and Séraphine together, the music is brutally interrupted (01:03:57), which cuts short the lyricism of the sequence, once again in a very Godard-like way. Symbolically, this manipulation of the track (like the manipulation of the song at 55:02) underlines the artificiality of this couple that we discover locked in an embrace by the front door of the gazebo. When Séraphine asks him if he loves her (*"Est-ce que tu m'aimes?"*), Miguel sharply replies, *"On a dit pas de sentiments."* ["We had a deal: no feelings involved."]

Inversion of the Hierarchy between Image and Music

In *L'Eau à la bouche*, music takes precedence over the image twice, causing a poetic disturbance in the film. Although this phenomenon constitutes a basic principle in musicals, its occurrence into other cinematic genres for short time intervals only was still very rare in late-1950s French cinema.

I call "Judith" the instrumental theme that can be heard for the first time at 38:54, in reference to the lyrics Gainsbourg added to it shortly after the film was released. Indeed, the track was featured in the EP *Romantique 60*, released in June 1960 (i.e., five months after the film). The EP contained another former instrumental piece with added lyrics, "Cha cha cha du loup," which was originally the theme of the film *Les Loups dans la bergerie*, directed by Hervé Bromberger. With "Judith," Gainsbourg distances himself from his "Rive Gauche" style and openly imitates the *yé-yé* movement[4]: the lyrics are insignificant, and the music is more mainstream and somewhat "tacky," with an ear-catching gimmick played by a flamboyant saxophone on a rumba-rock rhythm. In the film, the commercial nature of the track is materialized upon its first occurrence by a close-up on a disc being placed on a record-player. This piece is in total contrast with the refinement of the previous musical occurrences, and is associated with hedonistic pleasure, as evidenced by Séraphine's casual remark addressed to Myléna: *"De vraies vacances, hein?"* ["Feels like we're on holidays, doesn't it?"] This music is unarguably relaxing, and (almost) makes the characters overcome their initial reserve—Myléna and Séraphine decide to be on first-name terms, Miguel and Robert play billiard together. After another shot of the record player, the music starts again (41:25), and all four characters adopt relaxed postures and start using a more familiar form of address (except between Miguel and Myléna). Having been heard twice already at a substantial volume, the melody is easily recognizable when it is used again as extra-diegetic music in the scene where César chases after Prudence (56:13), gradually stripping her of her clothes until she ends up in only her underwear. The musical whirl ultimately takes over the image itself: the characters seem to dance on the stairs and realism is temporarily forgotten as we are presented with random views of the paintings on the walls—and, above all, a purely abstract vision produced by a speeded-up high angle shot of the central glass roof of the castle, mirroring Robert's point of view (57:46–57:54). This constitutes an example of "supra-diegetic music," a term coined by Rick Altman (1987: 66–71) to refer to the inversion of the traditional link of causality between image and music, where the image traditionally "dominates" the music that accompanies it. Alternatively, when it seems as if the movements that we can see and hear onscreen work as an accompaniment to the musical soundtrack, the music then appears to "dominate" the image to which it imposes its rhythm.

The "third stream" piece ("Jesus, Joy of Man's Desiring") is the opposite of "Judith." The term itself refers to a musical style that intends to combine jazz and classical music. Here, the famous theme from the final chorus of Johann Sebastian Bach's cantata BWV 147, *Herz und Mund und Tat und Leben*, is "jazzified." The original piece is played on the organ by Miguel (32:41), then by Myléna on the piano in a more improvised version (45:33), paving the way for Gainsbourg and Goraguer's "third stream" variation of it (01:04:08), which constitutes the lyrical climax of the film. The theme is first played on the guitar (previously used on the track "Angoisse"), then on the flute (also entrusted with most of the instrumental occurrences of the song "L'Eau à la bouche"). The choral writing of the woodwind section (whose sonorities are close to those of the organ), alternating with the accompanied melody texture of the theme, gives a spiritual quality to this night of lovemaking where all senses are set ablaze. Heard at full volume, the music starts on the distant embrace of Miguel and Séraphine, then lingers on the more passionate one between Robert and Myléna. After revolving around the couple, the camera is taken over by the music and, in a spectacular circular tracking shot, starts to revolve around the castle itself in synchronization with the music. Here again, the link of causality between music and image is reversed as it might be in a video clip: drifting away from the narrative, image is subordinated to music and functions as a vehicle for musical lyricism.

The score of *L'Eau à la bouche* does not revolutionize the codes of film music, but finds subtle and astute ways to refresh them: using a majority of jazz pieces (which was quite innovative back then in the genre of vaudeville comedy film), establishing narrative distance through the various occurrences of the song, occasioning poetic disturbances in the film through the inversion of the hierarchy between image and music, and manipulating the sound volume to promote the viewer's self-reflexive engagement are all choices that contribute to the modernity of Doniol-Valcroze, Goraguer, and Gainsbourg's approach to film music. It is also an opportunity for the latter to tackle his artistic dilemma by attempting to find a balance between his love for the "Rive Gauche" style, represented by the song "L'Eau à la bouche" and associated with a pleasure-seeking, refined elite, and the more commercial style of "Judith"—a track just good enough to accompany the masters' moments of leisure and follow the servants frolicking around. Jazz is still present in the film scores Gainsbourg wrote following *L'Eau à la bouche*, once again with the collaboration of Alain Goraguer: indeed, *Les Loups dans la bergerie* (dir. Hervé Bromberger, 1960) and *Strip-Tease* (dir. Jacques Poitrenaud, 1963) share many similarities with *L'Eau à la bouche* from a musical point of view. After his falling-out with Goraguer, Gainsbourg distanced himself from both the "Rive Gauche" style and jazz, but he never stopped exploring the expressive potential of music in cinema (as exemplified in the music and image dissociations in *La Horse,* 1970), including in his own films.[5]

Notes

1. The film is 5,005 second-long (1h23'25"), which means the golden ratio is situated at 3,093 seconds, or 51:33. The third occurrence of *L'Eau à la bouche* can be heard at 54:01.
2. Two themes are introduced for the first time: a jazzy ballad (01:09:27), and an exuberant march that gives a burlesque tone to the action happening onscreen (01:18:22, then 01:19:58).
3. The storm sequence features a piece of expressionist jazz (14:53–15:58).
4. The record sleeve reads: *Bon pour la danse* ["Good for dancing"].
5. See Rossi & Guilloux 2021.

"Cargo Culte": How Gainsbourg's *Melody* Film Invented a New Long-Form Audiovisual Language

Alex Jeffery

The surprise release of Beyoncé's self-titled "visual album" in 2013 unleashed a wave of media hyperbole, mostly fueled by the novelty of an entire set of videos (seventeen in total) appearing simultaneously and unexpectedly to accompany the tracks. A misleading discourse then spread across online media that *Beyoncé* was somehow a trailblazer for a new audiovisual art form, even though it had, in fact, been around since the 1970s. The year her next visual album, *Lemonade*, came out, *The Independent* assessed the "uneven history of the visual album." Yet the given examples of its precursors (Justin Bieber, Bon Iver, Suede) went no further back than 2009 (Milton 2016). *Lemonade* was even more commented-upon for its artistic ambition, inspiring a wave of scholarship that finally acknowledged the visual album form as significant.[1] Ironically, in 1982, one year after the launch of MTV and following a brief period of video cassette releases by pop and rock artists such as ELO, Soft Cell, and Blondie, former-Monkee Michael Nesmith was already making bold statements around video's potential. These included the claim that "making records with only sound is obsolete," and a comparison of the video album's prospective takeover to stereo's displacement of mono (quoted in Margulies 1982).[2] Within this patchily documented history of the visual/video/audiovisual album,[3] a film was made as early as 1971 that possessed all of the basic form and artistic ambition of today's celebrated visual albums, despite remaining relatively obscure: Serge Gainsbourg's *Melody*.

Melody was screened on December 22, 1971, on French television—at the time the only possible destination for a musical film that was too short and unconventional for theatrical release. As hinted in its title, the film was a visualization of Gainsbourg's album *Histoire de Melody Nelson*, released in June that year, and directed by Jean-Christophe Averty, the *enfant terrible* of French television production with over a decade of visually innovative variety shows, music specials, and drama to his name already. In Averty's film, Gainsbourg stars alongside his then girlfriend, Jane Birkin. They portray two star-crossed lovers—an aging French rock star and an English *ingénue*, characters that in many ways paralleled the age gap and dynamic of their real-life partnership. The fictional couple embark on an affair after he knocks her from her bicycle with his Rolls Royce, but the affair is doomed, and Melody soon dies in a plane crash. This skeleton narrative provides the basic structure around which the audiovisual elements flow over the seven clips. As "narrative form," if that is how we choose to engage with the audiovisual text, *Melody* diverged radically from its main precursor, the pop musical—a genre of films increasingly popular since the mid-1950s, featuring performers such as Elvis Presley and the Beatles with their musical performances set within easy-to-follow stories. Dialogue or scenes that are not already present within the *Histoire de Melody Nelson* album as music and lyrics are completely absent and, for the first time, the audio track in a music film corresponds completely to an album (presented in its original sequence). In doing so, music suddenly assumes a role in the film as primary text. It serves as matrix rather than being relegated to the ancillary role of "soundtrack." By presenting a "story" across several clips (rather than inside a single one), the film invents an almost entirely new narrative language, however ambiguous, that anticipates the long-form music videos that would arrive in the following decades, and that are arguably coming of age now.

Considering how radical a departure it represents, it is surprising that Gainsbourg's work has been the subject of neither Anglo-American histories of music video and the pop audiovisual, nor the French literature on Gainsbourg and Averty. This chapter sets out to explore the film's many trailblazing qualities, and how music, visuals, and basic story elements interacted to produce a new semi-narrated audiovisual language that only recently has come to wider public attention.

Gainsbourg and Averty

In an interview promoting the album for *Pop Music Superhebdo* magazine in May 1971, Gainsbourg was already musing on the artistic possibilities of a film adaptation. He imagined a hand-held camera roaming around a seedy hotel for North African immigrants (Jourd'Hui 1971: 20), although a project with Averty was evidently not yet being planned. More immediately realized were Gainsbourg's ideas for an adaptation of the story into a comic-strip, and a basic two-page strip with visual influence from Art Nouveau was published in the same magazine issue (21–2).

Gainsbourg and Averty had become familiar with one another nearly a decade earlier, the former appearing as a musical guest on Averty's ground-breaking television variety show *Les Raisins verts* (1963–4). The show brought an "avant-garde fantasy" ["*fantaisie d'avant-garde*"] into a primetime family slot on French television that journalist Guillaume Hanoteau felt did not belong there (quoted in Papin 2015: 147). It featured a number of musical guests, including Pierre Louki and Bobby Lapointe, who shared an anti-establishment mentality with the director and were at the time perceived as part of the Left-Bank cabaret scene. Averty continued to work closely with musicians in subsequent shows such as *Au risque de vous plaire* (1966–70) and, in 1968, produced an entire TV special for Gilbert Bécaud titled *Bécaud & Co*. His style was described in a newspaper article almost derisively as "*surréalisme attardé*" ["outmoded surrealism"], meaning lingering or persistent after the fact (Papin 2015: 144). However, the surrealist aspects of Averty's work emerged not through the more established surrealist media of painting and film, but the technological innovation of chromakey, which he helped pioneer in the relatively new televisual medium. Chromakey (variants of which are now used ubiquitously in media from hi-budget Hollywood films to YouTubers in their bedrooms) isolates the performer from the background, with the performer then able to be reinserted into the frame over any moving or still background conceivable, approximating some of the effects previously only possible with full animation. It is used heavily for many of the clips in *Bécaud & Co*, the best known of which, for the song "L'Orange," features minimal and witty organization of its visual elements against a plain black background; the singer's head and body interact with various stop motion animations of oranges, with a basic black, orange, and white color scheme. The clip deploys a playful surrealism, and Averty demonstrates a flair for bringing out musical details in the visuals. To a certain extent, he shared this surrealist esthetic with Gainsbourg, whose second concept album *L'Homme à tête de chou* (1976) was inspired by a surreal bronze sculpture he purchased from sculptor Claude Lalanne.

By the time Averty started working with Gainsbourg on the *Melody* film,[4] his visual style was moving toward an esthetic identifiable more with psychedelia than the simpler graphic clarity of his 1960s work. *Melody* showcases a more multi-layered surface, where captured performances of Gainsbourg and Birkin overlay—or are overlain by—a swirling collage of animated graphics, detailed backgrounds borrowed from surrealist paintings and, in some sequences, highly complex layering of all these elements together. Throughout the film, this layering builds in density, climaxing in the final sequence for "Cargo Culte," with a disorienting mesh of visual information including photographs of tribal people and art. Here, Birkin's dancing figure is superimposed over the photographic background, but her body becomes a canvas in itself, where the dark space of her clothes is filled with the painted elements of the background, even as it shifts and interacts with other layers. As the resulting image becomes more complex, it becomes increasingly difficult to differentiate background and foreground, the manipulation of which has been noted as a key feature of psychedelic music's hallucinogenic experience (Whiteley 2003: 4).

The Audiovisual Context

In the latter half of the 1960s in particular, the budgets for TV specials for major music artists attracted directorial talent, which meant they could be a highly creative platform for promoting these artists nationally. Stars with broad appeal and a range of entertainment skills (the likes of Tom Jones and Cilla Black in the UK) might be awarded series that followed a variety show format—special guests, chat, and sometimes comedy sketches running between musical performances. In contrast, the one-off, often hour-long TV special tended more toward uninterrupted strings of filmed musical performances, which, in their staging and editing, exhibited many of the qualities that we might now identify as music video clips. These provided opportunities for the talent and ingenuity of film or television directors to come to the fore, such as Eddy Matalon and François Reichenbach, responsible for Brigitte Bardot's innovative *Spécial Bardot* in 1968. Averty created three major specials of this kind throughout his career, where his technical skills using chromakey to create novel effects and scenarios came into play: *Bécaud & Co*, *Melody* and *Georges Brassens unique* (1978). These were all crafted in TV studios, where sets could either be imaginatively dressed and filled with props and extras, or the chromakey technique be fully exploited, as with the latter two examples.[5]

As the TV specials began to produce novel audiovisual work in the late 1960s, the pop musical film, particularly from the Beatles' second film *Help!* (1965) onward, began to incorporate more adventurous and surreal sequences—multi camera set-ups, "musical instruments suddenly appearing from nowhere" (Mundy 1999: 171)—that represented a dislocation from the more conventionally staged musical performance, and had their own significant influence on the esthetics of music video (Neaverson 2000: 150). Despite the surrealism in their musical vignettes, the Beatles' films still relied on scenes with dialogue to suture the musical numbers together into a feature-length narrative that could satisfy global audiences. The musical sequences' nonmusical settings (a car) also departed from the "conventional representational regime which privileged performance through the construction of an illusory diegesis" (Mundy 1999: 170), that is, a false authenticity that arose from more naturalistic performance settings—Elvis Presley's performances of "Viva Las Vegas" and "Jailhouse Rock" in the eponymous films were staged within television shows that were part of the diegesis, for example. If the pop musicals were overtly narrative (mostly centered on rise/fall tales of stardom), the TV specials, in contrast, were too magazine-like and heterogeneous to produce any narrative arc across their sequence of clips. *Melody* represents something of an intermediate point, where narrative is *suggested* to the audience through certain frames (lyrical, visual, or musical), yet audience enjoyment and understanding of the film are not necessarily predicated on whether they are making narrative sense of it or not.

Narrativity, Form, and Detail in *Melody*

In *Melody*, formal elements are undeniably present, giving way to point toward narrative construction for those bent on interpretation. The lyrics in the opening and closing tracks ("Melody" and "Cargo Culte") are delivered like a voiceover, providing a degree of exposition to the story. The musical flow and consistent presentation of character also encourage audiences to make connections across the seven musical sequences and twenty-eight minutes of the film. To counterbalance this, disorienting psychedelic tactics (particularly in the visuals) and visual and musical repetition seem to work against a linear narrative experience—to use the parlance of the day, the audience's "trip" doesn't necessarily have to be a storied one. Within the Beatles' animated *Yellow*

Submarine—a 1968 overtly psychedelic film that, like *Melody*, relies on repetition, collage, and surrealism—the journey structure means that clear narrative lines can still be followed. Conversely, much of the material within the inner five tracks of *Melody* falls into static explorations and declarations of love that do not add significant characterization or event (two basic tenets of narrativity). The fifth sequence, "L'Hôtel particulier," is a vignette that places its emphasis on conjuring the decadent, sexual atmosphere of the hotel through which Melody is led, rather than moving story forward by telling us explicitly what occurs there. Story is implied rather than told, and only by repeated listens to the album, viewings of the film or reading interviews with Gainsbourg as paratextual decoding devices is a coherent narrative likely to be pieced together. The sixth sequence, "En Melody," is an instrumental—apart from Birkin's peals of laughter—built on a two-chord funk rock groove, which functions more as a short-energized interlude between the two slower and longer narration-heavy tracks toward the end of the film. The repetition of the music is visually emphasized with Birkin's repeated performance of a bar-length dance pattern, edited like a loop as the camera zooms in and out on her body. Although one might argue that "En Melody" "fits" musically within the overall flow of the album, it is less easy to posit how the visual sequence advances the narrative.

Rather than attempting to sculpt this narrative ambiguity into an easy-to-follow linear storyline (as the comic strip does within its limited two pages), the visuals themselves participate in the ambiguity. This can partly be explained by their role in the evolution of how album and film were devised, which differs significantly from that of assembling a conventional film. According to Jean-Claude Vannier (the arranger on the French recording sessions), the narrative seeds of the album emerged initially from the process of musical composition—Gainsbourg first recorded the basic tracks, and on listening back to them was inspired with both lyrical and visual ideas. When Vannier organized the groove of the opening track in improvisational cells, a prolonged guitar note stood out, which suggested to Gainsbourg the image of the bicycle wheel perpetually spinning after Melody's accident. A single musical note therefore inspired what in the language of screenwriting would be called the "inciting incident"—the event which propels the protagonist(s) into the main action of the story. The fixing of this visual idea then fed back into the ultimate arrangement of the piece, and the spinning bicycle wheel later became a memorable scene within the film's opening sequence (Vannier 2011). Unsurprisingly, circles and spinning motion form a consistent visual motif throughout the film. With the rock star's Rolls Royce, the steering wheel turns, headlights spin around it in an inebriated haze, and the "Spirit of Ecstasy" ornament on its hood slowly rotates (also re-enacted as a mime/dance by a real performer); Birkin's dances tend to be rotations (slower spins in "Valse de Melody," faster ones in "En Melody") and concentric rings of hearts rotate behind the performers in "Ballade de Melody Nelson."[6]

Commenting on the album rather than the film, Darran Anderson's book on *Melody Nelson* picks up on the circularity within the narrative, interpreting it as essentially purgatorial in nature: Gainsbourg is a "god-cursed tragedian of ancient myth," forever re-enacting the cause of his heartbreak, continually finding and losing Melody in a

Möbius time-loop (2013: 118–19). Anderson finds further resonances within the text of the concentric circular constructions of hell in Dante's *Inferno* (74, 118), perhaps represented in a pop-art style by Averty's circles of hearts. Unlike in many song cycles, where at the conclusion the singer simply arrives back to the start point, the implication for the protagonist of *Melody Nelson* is that he is doomed never to escape from the cycle, trapped in endless repetition. This finds further resonances in cinema with Alfred Hitchcock's *Vertigo*, where spirals are used to suggest a *mise en abyme* in which the protagonist is trapped by events, and by his own psychological state.[7] Unsurprisingly, such visual motifs find themselves embedded within the Bernard Herrmann's score as well: in Alex Ross's analysis (1996), the music finds "no acceptable tonal resolution and spirals back on itself." On a musical level, Gainsbourg's "Möbius time-loop" can also be located in the album's two bookends, lengthy tracks of around seven and a half minutes with high musical similarity. Both tracks are built around an elastic bass pattern within a looping two-bar chord sequence, where three of the four chords in the sequence (E, G, D, A) are within an ascending cycle of fifths—a harmonic pattern that can musically repeat forever. As the bass sequence becomes increasingly charismatic in its improvisations around the two-bar pattern, notes bend and slide, frequently landing between tones, as if they are trying, but forever failing to escape from the basic program set for them—stuck in the same loop as Gainsbourg's rock star.

The peculiarities of Gainsbourg's songwriting process, where a simple underlying narrative concept inspires rich textuality, resulted in a complex chain of audio, visual, and audiovisual texts that still prove fascinating to decode. The decision to make a film that corresponded so closely to the album may have been an arbitrary one; however, this decision had hugely important implications for the latter album becoming the primary source for a new audiovisual form that would eventually crystallize into the video/audiovisual album. With the help of Averty, *Melody*'s nascent music video practice helped steer long-form pop audiovisuality away from the conventional narrativity of the pop musical, toward a new narratively ambiguous form that is only decades later becoming widely consumed.

Notes

1   For examples, see Rogers, Vernallis & Perrott 2016; Vernallis 2016; 2017.
2   Nesmith's 1981 "video record" *Michael Nesmith in Elephant Parts* won the inaugural Grammy Award for Video of the Year in 1982, a new category designed to both reflect and promote the growing trend for long-form music videos, which morphed in subsequent years into Best Video Album (1984–5), Best Music Video, Long Form (1986–97), and Best Long Form Music Video (1998–2013). From 2014 it has been termed Best Music Film.
3   A host of other terms have been used over the years, including Nesmith's "video record" and Soft Cell's "video special" *Non-Stop Exotic Video Show*.
4   A similarly styled clip was produced by Averty for Gainsbourg's non-album single "La Décadanse" at around the same time in 1971.

5   More unusually for a pop television special, the American production of Nancy Sinatra's semi-travelogue *Movin' with Nancy* (1967) exploited mostly outdoor locations, such as a theme park and the launch of a hot air balloon.
6   Hearts—a favorite motif of Averty's—feature regularly in his 1960s and 1970s work. They can be found in clips such as "Nathalie" (from *Bécaud & Co*), "Je dors avec l'ordinateur" by Sidonie Sand and "Ce Petit Cœur" by Françoise Hardy, the latter two appearing in another TV series *Si le cœur vous en dit* (1971–2), where hearts formed a persistent theme overall.
7   See Linderman 1991.

26

Gainsbourg for Sale! Serge Gainsbourg and Advertising

Philippe Cathé

To my father (a tireless admirer of the "Requiem pour un con"'s rhythm section), for all the musical enthusiasm he has shared and still shares with me.

Be it for print media, for radio, or television, Serge Gainsbourg both directed and acted in advertisements, lending his voice or his image, writing texts, and composing music. Arguably, one could say that he often, if not always, sold his own name just as much (or even more?) than the product itself. These advertisements prominently featured his attributes, whether extraneous (alcohol or cigarettes, Martini, Gitanes), linked to his public persona—his face (Konika), his beard (Bic), his nightlife (*Sortir*)—or goading the audience to fantasize about his private parts—"Guys who have a pair," as the slogan for *Connexion* read![1] In his perpetual attempt to surprise and provoke, Gainsbourg sometimes irritated the public by associating his image with the suits of Bayard or the high jewelry of Van Cleef & Arpels. After a partly chronological survey of the advertisements with which he was associated, a further exploration will reveal whether a message, a general statement, specific set of values or principles can be found within his advertising choices and connections.

The first ads with which Gainsbourg was involved were made for radio. Apart from its shorter format, this type of ad closely resembles Gainsbourg's songs, sharing the same sound, the same sung/spoken mixture, and the same highly personal way of playing with words and rhymes. The ad for Martini—dubbed "the world-famous aperitif" on many posters—exemplifies many of these song-style characteristics. Dating from the late 1960s, it is also likely to be one of Gainsbourg's very first ads.[2]

Je chante le dernier des tubes
Pour faire de la pub
A mes amours bleues.
Franch'ment, je trouve ce tube
Absolument sub-
lime et merveilleux.

I am grateful to Clare Wilson for her careful rereading of this chapter.

Un Martini et deux cubes
De glace et la sub-
tilité d'un zeste de
Citron et je titube
Ivre de la pub
Ivre de ciel bleu.

The orchestration relies on the typical pop combo of the era. It features a prominent bass guitar, discrete drums, and a piano and a guitar playing chords on each beat and the first backbeat in each measure, respectively. Two instruments complement this rhythm section: a group of violins playing rhythmic ritornellos doubled by the bass, and tubular bells reminiscent of Pierre Henry's "Psyché Rock" from the *Messe pour le temps présent*. The song is akin to a *mise en abyme*, as the lyrics proclaim: "I sing the newest hit/To advertise/My blue loves." The short lines and the rhyming scheme (aabaac aadaab) allow the rare rhyme "-ub" to be heard eight times in less than fifty seconds. To fulfill his duties, Gainsbourg first makes use of the most obvious French words containing the sound—*tube* ["hit"] and *pub* ["ad"], *cube* ["cube"] and *titube* ["stagger"]—then brilliantly, and in his usual offhand manner, he cuts two words in two to achieve the intended rhymes: *sub-lime*, *sub-tilité*.

He recorded more songs for Martini, including one, entirely spoken, that featured Jane Birkin's voice over a rather powerful accompaniment, and another one singing the praises of travel and cocktails made with Martini. In the latter, the sound is different, mainly thanks to the unconventional percussion pattern—a light ostinato of crotales and guiro throughout—in a slow triple time signature, supporting electric piano chords, and a synthesized violin melody. The bass is still prominent, however, and harmonies are largely borrowed from Pachelbel's *Canon,* but also reminiscent of the more recent Aphrodite's Child's song, "Rain and Tears"—a song that was quite popular at the time, having topped the French charts for more than two months in the summer of 1968.

The early 1970s witnessed significant change and considerable self-affirmation, as Gainsbourg was involved in the advertising for Caron's eau de toilette, *Pour un homme*. This ad relied heavily on the characterization of Gainsbourg's persona; this becomes very apparent in the audio through the highlighted and mingled voices of Birkin and Gainsbourg—illustrated in roman and italics typefaces respectively in the transcription below. The first lines presented the self-portrait of Serge Gainsbourg; more exactly, they sketched out an image that matched his general public perception:

Je passe pour un homme *pas très beau garçon*
Pourtant pour un homme *plein d'séduction.*
Ce qui fait mon charme
Et c'est là mon arme
Secrète pour un homme *de Caron.*
C'est que pour un homme *il y a des façons*
Subtiles de mettre une femme à la raison.

> Ce qui fait mon charme
> Et c'est là mon arme
> Secrète pour un homme *de Caron*.
> [End of music. Whispered]
> Pour un homme [Spoken] *de Caron*, [Whispered] une eau de toilette et toute une ligne de charme.

Here, Gainsbourg is bending the French language again with an unconventional, but pleasing turn. The third and fourth lines of each verse present an apparently fine rhyme between *charme* and *arme*: "Ce qui fait mon charme/Et c'est là mon arme/Secrète" ["What makes me so attractive, and this is my secret weapon"]. While the final "e" of *"charme"* is muted, the second, in the stock phrase *"arme secrète"* ["secret weapon"], is not. Gainsbourg easily circumvents the problem by cutting the word in two and postponing the final "e" to the fifth line (*"Et c'est là mon arm/e secrète"*). Showing his awareness of current musical trends, he opts again for harmonies that were in the air at that time: a blend of functional motions (I–vi–IV–ii–V with the cadential I–IV–V–I at the end), and progressions that were reintroduced mainly during the 1960s. These progressions are commonplace to many pop composers of the 1970s as well; for instance, the use of the ♭VII going to I in major or the IV and V mixture on the half-cadence (IV over a V pedal point); combine soft drums, two guitars, an enveloping bass, and a mixdown placing the voices at the forefront—voices were of the utmost importance in ads—and it's a wrap!

In 1976, Serge Gainsbourg was associated with the launch of the third product of the famous brand Bic: the disposable razor. After the ballpoint pen and the lighter, this item was about to become the future market success of the brand. As Jean-Marc Sylvestre explains,

> Jacques Séguéla suggested this incredible advertisement for disposable razors, in which a young Serge Gainsbourg sells his beard to Bic. Judged too provocative, the ad was never broadcast and stayed in Séguéla's drawer. Of all people involved, Gainsbourg was the most disappointed.
>
> (Sylvestre 2017)

After many other features of his persona, Gainsbourg was about to sell his already famous three-day stubble. In this sequence-shot ad, he claims: "I am a consumer product. All my life, I sold myself up. I sold my inspiration to *chanson*, I sold my lungs to cigarette, I sold my brain to alcohol, and I sold my soul to the devil! And today… today I sold my beard." In addition to this, there was an ad for newspapers and magazines, consisting mainly of a cartoonish sketch impersonating a large Bic disposable razor, shouting "Gains-bourg-Cheap-skate!" printed inside a large comic strip bubble. Right below it, a smaller bubble coming from the instantly recognizable Bic Man indicated the very affordable price of the razor. The same year, Gainsbourg was staged again in one of his favorite parts, the role of the night reveler. The only visible character during the sequence, he is first seen from behind, entering the frame. With a cigarette between his lips, sporting an open shirt and a three-day stubble, he performs a funny twirl before facing the camera. Between two puffs—a key element of his behavior—he utters: "*Sortir*, le magazine qui vous donne envie de *sortir*!"

1976 additionally witnessed Gainsbourg's directing debut. Over a two-year period, he shot ads for Woolite—a brand eager to associate its corporate image to female stars—featuring famous French actresses such as Brigitte Fossey, Marlène Jobert and, most obviously, Jane Birkin. Of her, he said: "Jane literally sucked the blood of the product. I directed this film for her greatest glory. All you could see was her, wrapped in a long wool scarf. As a result, the audience forgot it was an ad" (Ciment & Jeancolas 1987: 11). Gainsbourg's statement could hardly be challenged: he did solely film Birkin. During the twenty-second ad, the product is only visible for two seconds near the beginning, and the brand's name doesn't appear on screen until the final two seconds. In the meantime, Jane Birkin fills the screen for no less than eighteen seconds! Additionally, the advertisement puts the famous couple to work as Birkin also sings the lyrics praising the liquid detergent over a basic I–vi–ii–V vamp, followed by Gainsbourg uttering imperishable words such as: "Woolite washes under cold water, safely, without felting or toning down colors," before Birkin's voice returns and urges the viewers to use Woolite.

With regard to advertising, 1980 was a prosperous year for Serge Gainsbourg: he directed two of his most personal and striking commercials. In the first one, he abandoned his usual clothing style, swapping his pair of jeans and his open shirt for a more stylish and elegant suit. He often used the adjective *"classieux,"* a neologism he coined to signify "that which has class."[3] This word stuck and still remains in use today. Over his last decade, Gainsbourg replaced his old wardrobe with this newer dress style, not completely new to him, but surprising for his younger fans, and even more so for the growing number of his despisers. The very short Bayard ad—seven seconds—is hard-hitting. It relies on a strong element of surprise and requires the viewer's participation. The suit is visible during the whole shot; however, but, due to the progressively evolving lighting and the camera movement, Gainsbourg is only recognizable during the last two. *"Un Bayard, ça vous change un homme… N'est-ce pas, monsieur Gainsbourg?"* ["A Bayard [suit] changes a man… Doesn't it, mister Gainsbourg?"], says a soft female voice. Had Gainsbourg not been the recognizable character in the ad and had he not been widely known to favor a completely different dress style, the effect would have been lost. The catch in this clip relies entirely on his persona.

The second spot Gainsbourg directed in 1980 was highly regarded by the people in the profession and earned him a Lion d'argent (Silver Lion) in Cannes, at the prestigious International Advertising Festival (1984). Wearing a white-and-gray-striped polo, a tall, thin teenager resembling the then-famous French singer Michel Berger enters a kitchen snapping his fingers. He catches a package, shakes it like a maraca, bangs on frying pans and even on the lampshade with wooden spoons, continues his frantic drum solo on glass bottles and metal kettles, grabs a pot lid and a large tablespoon and uses them like a pair of orchestral crash cymbals. These "instruments" continue to sound as more and more are added, in the same way a musician would create multiple layers with a looping device. Once the dishwasher is filled with the remaining plates, closed with a kick and switched on—all still perfectly in time—the element of surprise is revealed. The music suddenly stops, but for the finger snaps. Much to their surprise, the viewer then realizes what is being advertised: a Brandt *silent* dishwasher. Were it not for the magical way the successive percussions are looped, the music here would seem diegetic. The clip's direction is also visually interesting, with the camera twirling around the character, but the main idea is fundamentally musical and rhythmical. In the combination of action, music, and sound, the tempo matters above all. This may be Gainsbourg's masterpiece in the genre.

Music was also brought to the fore in the Maggi French onion and cream of tomato soups series. With such a product—a tasteless mix of water and powder—one had to use a bit of cunning to achieve a pleasant result. By choosing a ska beat, Gainsbourg kept with the times. He matched it with doggerel verse. It could be argued that he evolved throughout his career—including in his advertising work—from decidedly literary preoccupations to easy rhymes. Here is the French onion soup rhyme:

Gratinée à l'oignon
Pour estomacs dans les talons
Mais ça m'a l'air très bon
Toutes ces rondelles d'oignon
Serrées en rang d'oignons
—On est bien,
Hein?
—Aux p'tits oignons![4]

The form carries more meaning than the text itself. Gainsbourg gathers two set colloquialisms, using the word "onion": *"[traiter quelqu'un] aux petits oignons"* ["(treating somebody) like a king (or a queen)"], and *"en rang d'oignons"* ["in a row"]. This allows him to use the same word four times for the sake of the rhyme.

During the last decade of his life, Gainsbourg was ubiquitous in advertisements. Epilmatic Babyliss and its synchresis effect, Roudor biscuit and its suave duet of perfect grandfather and grandson, Pepsodent toothpaste, Spring Court, Danone yoghurt, Palmolive soap, Roumillat cheese, Lee Cooper jeans (an excuse to film swaying women sashaying along wearing tight-fitting jeans), Friskies dog food, not to mention half a dozen Saba Continental Edison video cameras, video recorders, and television sets for which he once again wrote doggerel verse—a hallmark of his advertising career.

Amidst this variety of projects, two themes emerge from Gainsbourg's later attempts to give the audience the sales talk. For anyone familiar with him, none of these themes are surprising, but a couple of them had been relatively absent so far: sex—and eroticism—and himself. With Caron, Bic as well as with *Sortir*, or Bayard, Gainsbourg had already featured himself in his ads, but his final attempts went further. In the advertising campaign for RATP (the state-owned public transport operator, responsible for the Paris metro), he included himself with the Beatles—no less—in the list of the personalities present in collective memory. On that occasion, he reminded the public of his gesture from March 11, 1984, something that no one had forgotten in France either that following year or now. On the set of a popular television show, he had burnt a 500 French franc banknote. The fact that this was the largest note in circulation in a country that was then undergoing a recession created an incredibly widespread scandal. Cashing in on that scandal, the clip shot for the Paris metro showed Gainsbourg on a television screen setting fire to a subway ticket.

The same year, he promoted the color film Konica in a highly personal way. The ad is basically Gainsbourg self-staging himself. As the viewer discovers the artist on the screen, with every sentence he pronounces comes a closer shot from medium-long shot to medium shot, to close-up, and eventually tight close-up. The camera then moves from his face to his hand holding a boxed roll of film. The clip ends with a rapid succession of shots punctuated with the sound of a camera shutter, suggesting a photo shoot of the artist's face from different angles. Gainsbourg mainly talks about himself, about his relation to his face, his desire to preserve an image of it, and about the ravages of time: *"La tête que j'ai aujourd'hui, je la regretterai dans dix ans. Alors, pour me tirer le portrait, j'ai choisi la pellicule couleur Konica ... Konica, pour garder une bonne image."* ["Ten years from now, I will miss the face I have now. So, to have my photograph taken, I have chosen the color film Konica ... Konica, to keep a good image."] Were Gainsbourg's reflections only directed at himself? The success of the ad seems to suggest otherwise. As Victor Hugo writes in the preface to *Les Contemplations*,

> None of us has the honor to have a life all his own. My life is yours, your life is mine ... Take this mirror and in it look at yourself. People sometimes complain about writers who say I. Speak to us about us, they cry. Alas! When I speak to you about myself, I am speaking to you about yourself. How is it that you don't see that? Ah, you madman, who think that I am not you!
>
> (1856: 11)

Indeed, Gainsbourg's anxieties are our anxieties.

Does this survey show a certain intellectual coherence or consistency? In a book on television culture, John Fiske held the position that most of the codes of television targeted the widest possible audience with the aim of maintaining a social status quo. Summarizing his views, Ronald Rodman writes that television events "are organized into coherence and social acceptability by the ideological codes, such as those of individualism, patriarchy, race, class, materialism, capitalism, etc." (1997: 21). Taking into account the possible differences between American and French criteria, we may now try to evaluate the principles emerging from Gainsbourg's advertising production. In spite of his rebel image, the values he promotes are predominantly conformist: Consume! Travel round the world, fly in a supersonic aircraft; go to the tropics, to Jamaica, a Martini glass in hand. *Sortir*, going out to nightclubs, to cinemas, to restaurants; buying all the products that are talked up, from toothpaste to household appliances.

As for the gender attitudes, they are never called into question, nor do they raise expectations of a change. The only time a man is shown doing household chores, he is simply adding hot water to an instant soup mix, or—in the case of the ad for the dishwasher—using equipment that allows him to avoid the job entirely. The taboo of the laundry, for instance, is not broken. Washing clothes remains a "women's job." (The worst ad in this respect is that for Woolite with French actress Marlène Jobert, whose black female servant does the laundry for her—gender prejudices are combined with supposedly racial ones.[5])

Gender relations are no more audacious: "Create your own seductiveness!" the advertising slogan for Anny Blatt's wools announces; and, as only women are shown wearing sweaters, it must be understood that it is their job to knit. Generally speaking, beauty is a woman's exclusive preoccupation as ads for Palmolive, Babyliss, and Tutti Free seem to suggest. It is a woman's responsibility to be beautiful! As for masculine products, the implied discrepancy and the humor of the Bayard ad should not mislead us: ultimately, they point to the mere reproduction, and even to the strengthening of the upper classes' dress codes.

In ads, irony is rhetorical rather than liberating. It tries to establish closeness with the television viewer as well as some distance regarding the message. Except that none of this is true. In the Bic ad that was ultimately shelved and remains unaired, Gainsbourg clearly confessed: "I am a consumer product." In this particular case, he tried to sell disposable products that one would have to buy again and again. Irony was just an excuse.

The musical choices could have shown a particular openness, but they did not. In short, music mostly reflected the dominant idiom of its period. This is unsurprising, with the exception of one of the two Maggi ads whose 1950s style was out of step with the times. So, the main and almost unique role of music was to root the spot and the product deeply in its era. There are a few exceptions to this conformism—one regarding the morals, the other regarding music. The musical exception leads us back to the Brandt ad again, obviously an esthetic *unica* in Gainsbourg's mercenary jobs. The series of Gini ads questions one of the key values in society—a couple, with suggested or explicit trios. It is difficult to say how a threesome can be linked to a lemon soft drink, but the association was clearly seen as a success as, after a commission for two advertising spots in 1984, the brand asked Gainsbourg for a third in 1985, going on in the same direction during the following years till the choice of its actual slogan: "the hottest of cold drinks." Nonetheless, this message remains a little bit surprising considering that, in his 1976 concept album *L'Homme à tête de chou*, Marilou was killed with a fire extinguisher precisely because of this moral freedom. In the fifth song, "Flash Forward," the Man with the Cabbage Head—Gainsbourg's alter ego—recounts that, coming back home unexpected, he "listens to the creaking hammock and the springs of the bed" [*"écoute gémir le hamac/Grincer les ressorts du paddock"*]. The effect on him is that of "an electric choc treatment" [*"un électrochoc"*], as he sees Marilou "between two Woodstock festival type macaques, comparable to an electric guitar with two jacks" [*"entre deux macaques/Du genre festival à Woodstock/Semblait une guitare rock/A deux jacks"*]. The narrator's anger is also linked, admittedly, to his exclusion from this intense chamber music session.

The reception of this part of Serge Gainsbourg's creative effort is made difficult by his own ambiguous relationship with brands. If God is a smoker of Havana cigars,[6]

Gainsbourg, for his part, can be seen smoking his Gitanes in any circumstance, be it on a well-paid, sponsored assignment by Seita (the former French state-owned tobacco monopoly) on April 28, 1986, or without compensation on any given day. For that April 28 event, he organized a press conference at the lounge of the select George V Hotel. Three hundred journalists were present, probably waiting for a new provocation. Gainsbourg apparently quoted Scott Fitzgerald and Lichtenberg before declaring in an aristocratic and quasi preacher style: "Today, under my will, Gitanes becomes Blondes!" And so was launched the new light-tobacco cigarette as opposed to the usual dark-tobacco Gitanes. Once again, Gainsbourg had blurred the lines between the artist—who announced the press conference—and the advertising executive who delivered it. The boundary was also unclear between his songs and his ads because his proximity with advertising began many years before his first professional involvement in that business. His entire work is teeming with so many explicit references to brand names that it is not always easy to tell the difference between a genuine song and a product placement. Some titles are brand names—"Harley Davidson," "Ford Mustang"—and many lyrics make specific references to them: in the Ford Mustang, one may find "Un paquet d'Kool," "un Coca-Cola," "Un Browning," etc. In "Marilou Reggae," when the Man with the Cabbage Head has a sexual intercourse with Marilou, Gainsbourg uses a daring image to describe the peak of their intimate moment: *"Au bord climax faire le guet/Changer Vitesse, changer braquet/Et décoller avion Bréguet"* ["On the verge [of the] climax, being on the watch/Changing gear, shifting into high gear/And taking off, Breguet airplane"]. We could reel off a whole string of examples. The distance between potboiler and poetic license is so thin that, after Gainsbourg's death, Guerlain was able to launch an eau de toilette using a part of Gainsbourg's song "Initials B.B." without the slightest change to the lyrics that read: *"Elle ne porte rien d'autre qu'un peu/D'essence de Guerlain dans les cheveux"* ["She doesn't wear anything else/Than a bit of Guerlain eau de toilette in her hair"]. With this final example, the blurring appears full and complete. In the end, maybe one of the only remaining differences between the music and lyrics of his songs and their equivalent in ads is the fact that the former carried his own principles, questioning at times the entire spectrum of society and its moral values, something the latter never did. Cautiously, Gainsbourg never went as far as to bite the hand that fed him.

Notes

1   More precisely, it read: *"Des gars qui en ont"*—a vulgar stock phrase in French, implying the clear and strong sexual reference mentioned above.
2   Wherever possible, I have referred to the radio and television ads available through INA (Institut National de l'Audiovisuel), a specific form of public agency, created and funded by the state and repository of all French radio and television audiovisual archives. This usually precise source has been complemented with less reliable ones as not all ads were preserved.

3   Although the meaning already existed in other expressions, in French, the unusual suffix "-ieux" carried a baroque and permissive connotation.
4   "French onion soup/For starving people/All these onion rings/Standing in rows/Seem very good.
    —We are fine,
    Aren't we?
    —Like kings!"
5   As someone raised and educated in France, I firmly believe that there is only one race—the human race. I do not dispute that racial prejudices exist. My use of the word "supposedly" therefore applies to the concept of race, not to actual manifestations of racial prejudice.
6   Title and main line of a song Gainsbourg wrote and recorded in 1980 with Catherine Deneuve ("Dieu fumeur de havanes"). In the first verse, he sings: *Dieu est un fumeur de havanes* ["God is a smoker of Havana cigars"]; in the second, Deneuve answers: *Tu n'es qu'un fumeur de Gitanes* ["You're just a smoker of Gitanes cigarettes"].

References

Achard, Marcel. 1962. "Alphonse Allais ou le dramaturge malgré lui." *Les Œuvres libres* 192: 3–30.
Aftab, Ali. 2015. "University Challenge, Class of 2015: 8 of the quiz show's best moments this year." *Independent.co.uk*, December 29. https://www.independent.co.uk/student/news/university-challenge-class-of-2015-8-of-the-quiz-show-s-best-moments-this-year-a6788711.html [accessed 06-17-2022].
Albert, Anaïs. 2005. "Serge Gainsbourg ou l'incarnation de la provocation (1969–1991)." Master's thesis, Ecole Normale Supérieure de Lyon.
Allen, Jeremy. 2017. "If Johnny Hallyday was France's Elvis, who is their version of Kanye West?" *The Guardian*, December 6. https://www.theguardian.com/music/shortcuts/2017/dec/06/johnny-hallyday-france-elvis-who-is-their-version-kanye-west [accessed 06-17-2022].
Allen, Jeremy. 2021. *Relax Baby Be Cool: The Artistry and Audacity of Serge Gainsbourg*. London: Jawbone Press.
Altman, Rick. 1987. *The American Film Musical*. Bloomington, IN: Indiana University Press.
Amalvi, Christian. 1998. "L'exemple des grands hommes de l'histoire de France à l'école et au foyer (1814–1914)." *Romantisme. Revue du dix-neuvième siècle* 100 ("Le Grand Homme"): 91–103.
Anderson, Darran. 2013. *Serge Gainsbourg's* Histoire de Melody Nelson. New York: Bloomsbury.
Apollinaire, Guillaume. 1913. *Alcools. Poèmes 1898–1913*. Paris: Gallimard.
Aufray, Hugues. 2007. *Droit dans mes santiags*. Paris: D. Carpentier.
Auslander, Leora. 2005. "Coming Home? Jews in Postwar Paris." *Journal of Contemporary History* 40(2): 237–59.
Auslander, Philip. 2006. "Musical Personae." *The Drama Review* 50(1): 100–19.
Austin, Guy. 2019. "The stink of the sacred: A Batailleanreading of Gainsbourg's film *Je t'aime moi non plus*." *French Cultural Studies* 30(1): 31–43.
Aymé, Marcel. 1958. Liner notes to *Du Chant à la une!* Philips B 76 447 R [33 rpm].
B.A. 1979. "Une rentrée bien tranquille." *Le Monde*, August 31, 10.
Bakhtin, Mikhail. 1941. *Rabelais and His World*. Bloomington, IN: Indiana University Press.
Barbey d'Aurevilly, Jules. 1879 [1845]. *Du Dandysme et de George Brummell*, 3rd edn. Paris: Alphonse Lemerre.
Barzel, Tamar. 2014. *New York Noise: Radical Jewish Music and the Downtown Scene*. Bloomington, IN: Indiana University Press.
Baudelaire, Charles. 1857. *Spleen et idéal*. In *Les Fleurs du mal*, pp. 5–192. Paris: Poulet-Malassis et De Broise.
Baudelaire, Charles. 1861 [1857]. "Semper eadem." In *Les Fleurs du mal*, 2nd edn, pp. 92–3. Paris: Poulet Malassy & De Broise.

Baudelaire, Charles. 1869a. "Epilogue." In *Petits Poèmes en prose*, p. 151. Paris: Michel Lévy Frères.
Baudelaire, Charles. 1869b. "Le Peintre de la vie moderne." In *L'Art romantique*, pp. 51–114. Paris: Michel Lévy Frères.
Baudrillard, Jean. 1996. "Le complot de l'art." *Libération*, May 20, 1. Reprinted in Baudrillard, Jean. 2005. *The Conspiracy of Art*, trans. Ames Hodges, pp. 25–9. New York & Los Angeles: Semiotext[e].
Bayley, Stephen. 2015. "So you think you're ugly? Don't worry—perceptions change." *The Guardian*, November 24. https://www.theguardian.com/commentisfree/2015/nov/23/ugly-perceptions-change-beauty-art [accessed 06-17-2022].
Bayon & Serge Gainsbourg. 1992. *Serge Gainsbourg: Mort ou vices*. Paris: Grasset.
Beddington, Emma. 2016. "I knew what I wanted to be when I grew up: A French woman." *The Telegraph*, April 9. https://www.telegraph.co.uk/women/life/i-always-knew-what-i-wanted-to-be-a-french-woman-then-i-failed-a/ [accessed 06-17-2022].
Beech, Dave & Ilana Kaplan. 2018. "Best of the rest." *The Independent*, June 8. https://advance.lexis.com/api/document?collection=news&id=urn:contentItem:5SH8-7TN1-JCS0-D05T-00000-00&context=1516831 [accessed 10-12-2022].
Bennion, Chris, Joe Clay, Catherine Nixey & Wendy Ide. 2017. "What's on TV and radio this weekend." *thetimes.co.uk*, December 16. https://www.thetimes.co.uk/article/whats-on-tv-and-radio-this-weekend-lj6wfz956 [accessed 06-17-2022].
Bensimon, Doris. 1989. *Les Juifs de France et leurs relations avec Israël (1945–1988)*. Paris: L'Harmattan.
Berkovitz, Jay R. 1989. *The Shaping of Jewish Identity in Nineteenth-Century France*. Detroit: Wayne State University Press.
Bernac, Pierre. 1970. *The Interpretation of French Song*, trans. Winifred Radford. New York: W. W. Norton.
Bingham, Dennis. 2010. *Whose Lives Are They Anyway?: The Biopic as Contemporary Film Genre*. New Brunswick: Rutgers University Press.
Blum, Bruno. 2015. Liner notes for *Gainsbourg & The Revolutionaries*. Mercury/Universal Music France 4731756 [3-CD boxed set].
Bonnafé, Alphonse. 1965. *Georges Brassens*. Paris: Seghers.
Borowice, Yves (ed.). 2010. *Les Femmes dans la chanson. Deux cents portraits (1850–2010)*. Paris: Textuel.
Bossuet, Jacques-Bénigne. 1862. "Premier Sermon pour le IIIe dimanche de carême, sur l'amour et les plaisirs." In *Œuvres complètes*, vol. 9, 2 ("Sermons"), pp. 199–216. Paris: Librairie Louis Vivès.
Boulanger, Alain. 2003. Liner notes to *Cuba in Paris: Rico's Creole Band 1947–1951*. Frémeaux & Associés FA 5055 [CD].
Boulanger, Alain. 2018. *La Havane à Paris. Musiciens Cubains à Paris (1925–1955)*. Saint-Etienne-du-Rouvray: Jazzedit.
Bourderionnet, Olivier. 2011. *Swing troubadours. Brassens, Vian, Gainsbourg: Les Trente Glorieuses en 33 tours*. Birmingham, AL: Summa Publications.
Bourdieu, Pierre. 1996 [1992]. *The Rules of Art: Genesis and Structure of the Literary Field*, trans. Susan Emmanuel. Stanford: Stanford University Press.
Bouvier, Yves-Ferdinand & Serge Vincendet (eds). 2009. *Serge Gainsbourg: L'Intégrale et cætera. Les Paroles 1950–1991*. Paris: Bartillat.

Bowen, Willis H. 1955. "Marcel Aymé. *Les quatre vérités*. Paris. Grasset. 1954. 227 pages. 450 fr." *Books Abroad* 29(3): 313.
Boyle, Jules. 2015. "TEXAS promised to give our charity fans a special show as part of our 7 Nights sessions and they delivered in spades with their best ever show." *Daily Record*, April 17. https://www.dailyrecord.co.uk/entertainment/music/music-news/video-watch-exclusive-interview-texas-5540064 [accessed 06-17-2022].
Brackett, David. 1994. "The Politics of 'Crossover' in American Popular Music, 1963 to 1965." *The Musical Quartely* 78(4): 774–97.
Bray, Elisa. 2018. "The Gruff that keeps on giving." *i-Independent*, June 7. https://advance.lexis.com/api/document?collection=news&id=urn:contentItem:5SH2-B911-JCS0-D436-00000-00&context=1516831 [accessed 10-12-2022].
Bremner, Charles. 2018. "A tear from Brigitte Macron at farewell to Aznavour, master of melancholy." *The Times*, October 6. https://www.thetimes.co.uk/article/a-tear-from-brigitte-macron-at-funeral-of-charles-aznavour-master-of-melancholy-mqq8tsm5f [accessed 06-17-2022].
Brend, Mark. 2012. *The Sound of Tomorrow: How Electronic Music Was Smuggled into the Mainstream*. New York: Bloomsbury.
Brennan, Timothy. 2001. "World Music Does Not Exist." *Discourse* 23(1): 44–62.
Briggs, Jonathyne. 2015. *Sounds French: Globalization, Cultural Communities, and Pop Music in France, 1958–1980*. New York: Oxford University Press.
Brown, Tom & Belén Vidal. 2014. *The Biopic in Contemporary Film Culture*. London & New York: Routledge.
Brunet, Pierre-Julien. 2023. *Serge Gainsbourg. Ecrire, s'écrire*. Rennes: Presses universitaires de Rennes.
Bryan, Kevin. 2018a. "CD reviews: Judith Owen, Matthew Byrne, Arctic Monkeys, Manfred Mann." *Messenger Newspapers*, July 4. https://www.messengernewspapers.co.uk/leisure/16333135.music-reviews/ [accessed 06-17-2022].
Bryan, Kevin. 2018b. "Record Review with Kevin Bryan." *Buxton Advertiser*, July 9; also *Eastwood Advertiser*, July 9; also *Ilkeston Advertiser*, July 9. https://advance.lexis.com/api/document?collection=news&id=urn:contentItem:5SRX-TYC1-F15K-228P-00000-00&context=1516831 [accessed 10-12-2022].
Buckley, Jemma & Sam Creighton. 2015. "Why Je t'aime's ultimate turn-on in the bedroom." *MailOnline*, July 21. https://www.dailymail.co.uk/news/article-3166022/Why-Je-T-aime-s-ultimate-turn-bedroom-Sensual-songs-trick-brain-finding-people-attractive.html [accessed 06-17-2022].
Burgoyne, Robert. 2014. "Gainsbourg: Puppetry in the musical biopic." In Tom Brown & Belén Vidal (eds), *The Biopic in Contemporary Film Culture*, pp. 259–73. New York & London: Routledge.
Burguière, André & Jacques Revel (eds). 1993. *Histoire de la France, 4, Les Formes de la culture*. Paris: Seuil.
Cairns, Dan, Mark Edwards, Lisa Verrico & Clive Davis. 2017. "Pop, rock and jazz." *The Sunday Times*, October 8. https://advance-lexis-com.ezproxy1.hw.ac.uk/api/document?collection=news&id=urn:contentItem:5PNF-G561-JCJY-G3D9-00000-00&context=1516831 [accessed 10-17-2022].
Calvet, Louis-Jean. 2013. *Chansons. La Bande-son de notre histoire*. Paris: L'Archipel.
Canetti, Jacques. 1978. *On cherche jeune homme aimant la musique*. Paris: Calmann-Lévy.

Cantaloube-Ferrieu, Lucienne. 1981. *Chanson et poésie des années 30 aux années 60. Trenet, Brassens, Ferré... ou les "enfants naturels" du surréalisme*. Paris: A.G. Nizet.
Carr, Ian. 2009 [1998]. *Miles Davis: The Definitive Biography*. New York: Da Capo Press.
Cartmell, Deborah & Ashley D. Polasek (eds). 2020. *A Companion to the Biopic*. Hoboken, NJ: John Wiley & Sons.
Castelbajac, Aliénor de. 2019. "Le concept album selon Serge Gainsbourg." Master's thesis, Sorbonne Université.
Cerchiari, Luca. 2012. "The European Songbook: 'Greensleeves' to 'Les Feuilles mortes' ('Autumn Leaves'), 'Gigolo' to "O Sole Mio.'" In Luca Cerchiari, Laurent Cugny & Frantz Kerschbaumer (eds), *Eurojazzland. Jazz and European Sources, Dynamics and Contexts*, pp. 98–122. Boston: Northeastern University Press.
Chabot-Canet, Céline. 2008. *Léo Ferré: une voix et un phrasé emblématiques*. Paris: L'Harmattan.
Chisholm, Kate. 2016. "Radio: Burn Slush! The Shepherd." *The Spectator*, December 10. https://advance.lexis.com/api/document?collection=news&id=urn:contentItem:5MC4-D4T1-JD3P-Y19S-00000-00&context=1516831 [accessed 10-22-2022].
Chouvel, Jean-Marc. 1993. "Matière et manière: le style, une forme pour un fond?" *Analyse musicale* 32: 20–7.
Chrisafis, Angelique. 2015. "Hermès and Jane Birkin resolve spat over crocodile handbags." *The Guardian*, September 12. https://www.theguardian.com/fashion/2015/sep/11/hermes-jane-birkin-crocodile-handbag-peta-luxury [accessed 06-17-2022].
Ciment, Michel & Jean-Pierre Jeancolas. 1987. "Entretien avec Serge Gainsbourg." *Positif* 312 (February): 7–11.
Clay, Joe. 2015. "What to watch on TV tonight." *thetimes.co.uk*, May 15. https://advance.lexis.com/api/document?collection=news&id=urn:contentItem:5G0F-25W1-JCJY-G3PH-00000-00&context=1516831 [accessed 10-12-2022].
Clayson, Alan. 1998. *Serge Gainsbourg: A View from the Exterior*. London: Sanctuary.
Clouzet, Jean. 1974. *Jacques Brel*. Paris: Seghers.
Cochrane, Lauren. 2014. "Prada makes fur harnesses and thin scarves masculine." *The Guardian*, January 13. https://www.theguardian.com/fashion/2014/jan/13/milan-fashion-week-prada-men [accessed 06-17-2022].
Cockroft, Steph. 2015. "University Challenge contestant whose VERY extravagant facial expressions won him a legion of fans and predictions he'll one day be PM admits: 'Yes, I know I'm odd!'" *MailOnline*, December 8. https://www.dailymail.co.uk/news/article-3350722/Yes-know-m-odd-University-Challenge-contestant-extravagant-facial-expressions-won-legion-fans-predictions-ll-one-day-PM.html [accessed 06-17-2022].
Colonna, Dominique (dir.). 1989. "June 24—Spécial Serge Gainsbourg." *Lunettes noires pour nuits blanches*. Antenne 2.
Comoy, Philippe. 2017. Liner notes to *Chansons Exotiques pour Cabarets et Music-Halls, Rythmes Orientaux et Tropicaux—Tropical and Exotic Music from Cabarets and Casinos. Paris–Juan-Les-Pins–St-Tropez–Naples–Oran 1954–1962*. Frémeaux & Associés FA 5658 [3-CD boxed set].
Conway, Kelly. 2004. *Chanteuse in the City: The Realist Singer in French Film*. Berkeley: University of California Press.
Cook, William. 2018. "L'amour de ma vie." *The Independent*, April 20. https://advance.lexis.com/api/document?collection=news&id=urn:contentItem:5S4T-NXD1-JCS0-D4W9-00000-00&context=1516831 [accessed 10-22-2022].

Cordier, Adeline. 2014. *Post-War French Popular Music: Cultural Identity and the Brel-Brassens-Ferré Myth*. Farnham & Burlington, VT: Ashgate.
Corner, Natalie. 2017. "She was gone for years." *MailOnline*, November 12. https://www.dailymail.co.uk/femail/article-5074691/Actress-Charlotte-Gainsbourg-talks-sister-s-death.html [accessed 06-17-2022].
Costaz, Gilles. 1974. *Edith Piaf*. Paris: Seghers.
Cowley, John. 2014. "Mascarade, Biguine and the Bal nègre." In Alain Boulanger, Marc Monneraye & John Cowley (eds), *Creole Music of the West Indies: A Discography, 1900–1959*, pp. 201–358. Holste-Oldendorf: Bear Family Publications.
Cripps, Charlotte. 2015. "Gaz Coombes; Food for Thought." *The Independent*, January 18. https://advance.lexis.com/api/document?collection=news&id=urn:contentItem:5F3G-G8H1-F072-400R-00000-00&context=1516831 [accessed 10-12-2022].
Crocq, Philippe. 1991 "Serge Gainsbourg (1928–1991): Variations on the Theme of Love." *The Billboard: The International Newsweekly of Music and Home Entertainment*, July 27, F-12.
Cusson, Cosima. 1997. "Gainsbourg, des Amours perdues à L'herbe tendre, dix années d'écriture." Master's thesis, Université Jean Moulin Lyon 3.
Custen, Georges F. 1992. *Bio/Pics: How Hollywood Constructed Public History*. New Brunswick: Rutgers University Press.
Dakhlia, Jamil. 2010. *Mythologie de la peopolisation*. Paris: Le Cavalier Bleu.
Dalmace, Patrick. 2017. *La Musique cubaine à Paris entre 1930 et la Seconde Guerre mondiale*. Paris: Edilivre.
Danielsen, Anne. 2018. "Time and Time Again: Repetition and Difference in Repetitive Music." In Olivier Julien & Christophe Levaux (eds), *Over and Over: Exploring Repetition in Popular Music*, pp. 37–50. New York: Bloomsbury.
Davet, Stéphane. 2008. "Le rock français parle en anglais." *Le Monde*, April 12. https://www.lemonde.fr/culture/article/2008/04/12/le-rock-francais-parle-anglais_1033928_3246.html [accessed 04-23-2019].
Davies, Cath. 2012. "No Mere Mortal? Re-materialising Michael Jackson in Death." *Celebrity Studies* 3(2): 183–96.
Davies, Lucy. 2015. "How Breton tops and nautical style sailed into our wardrobes." *telegraph.co.uk*, March 21. http://fashion.telegraph.co.uk/news-features/TMG11474902/How-Breton-tops-and-nautical-style-sailed-into-our-wardrobes.html [accessed 06-17-2022].
Davis, Clive. 2017. "Pop review: Jane Birkin at the Barbican." *thetimes.co.uk*, September 28. https://www.thetimes.co.uk/article/pop-review-jane-birkin-at-the-barbican-ec2-f6zx5vqgw [accessed 06-17-2022].
Davis, Clive. 2018. "Charles Aznavour: one of the most sophisticated songwriters of his era." *thetimes.co.uk*, October 1. https://www.thetimes.co.uk/article/charles-aznavour-one-of-the-most-sophisticated-songwriters-of-his-era-jdknvm7l9 [accessed 06-17-2022].
Davis, Miles with Quincy Troupe. 1990. *Miles: The Autobiography*. New York, London, Toronto & Sydney: Simon and Schuster.
Day, Elizabeth. 2017. "Interview." *The Sunday Times*, November 12. https://advance.lexis.com/api/document?collection=news&id=urn:contentItem:5PXX-M6M1-JCJY-G4Y7-00000-00&context=1516831 [accessed 10-12-2022].
Dejacques, Claude. 1966. Liner notes to *Marilu*. Philips 437 165 BE [45 rpm].

Delville, Michel. 2008. "The Food and Hunger Poet at the Turn of the Century: Anorexia, Anthropoemia, and Abjection." In Michel Delville (ed.), *Food, Poetry, and the Aesthetics of Consumption: Eating the Avant-Garde*, pp. 117–28. New York & Abingdon: Routledge.

Devauchelle, Karine. 1996. "La métrique chez Serge Gainsbourg entre 1954 et 1964." Master's thesis, Université de Nantes.

Dicale, Bertrand. 2009. *Serge Gainsbourg en dix leçons*. Paris: Fayard.

Dicale, Bertrand. 2011. *Les Chansons qui ont tout changé*. Paris: Fayard.

Dicale, Bertrand. 2021 [2016]. *Tout Gainsbourg*, 2nd edn. Paris: Gründ.

Diderot, Denis. 1797. *James the Fatalist and His Master*, vol. I. London: G. G. and Robinson.

Dirvanaudskas, Gabriele. 2016. "Birkin's a babe at 69." *The Sun*, March 30. https://advance.lexis.com/api/document?collection=news&id=urn:contentItem:5JDN-X4W1-DY9P-N228-00000-00&context=1516831 [accessed 10-12-2022].

Doig, Stephen. 2017. "Man Friday Gallic style." *The Daily Telegraph*, January 20. https://advance.lexis.com/api/document?collection=news&id=urn:contentItem:5MNT-F8Y1-DY9P-N23J-00000-00&context=1516831 [accessed 10-12-2022].

Doron, Daniella. 2015. *Jewish Youth and Identity in Postwar France: Rebuilding Family and Nation*. Bloomington, IN: Indiana University Press.

Droit, Michel. 1979. "La 'Marseillaise' de Serge Gainsbourg." *Le Figaro Magazine*, June 1, 18–9.

Ducasse, Isidore (Comte de Lautréamont). 1973 [1870]. "Poésies II." In *Œuvres complètes—Les Chants de Maldoror, Lettres, Poésies I et II*, pp. 279–321. Paris: Gallimard.

Dufour, Valérie. 2015. "Brève introduction à l'étude des principes de la critique musicale. Une axiologie de la critique de la critique aux XIXe et XXe siècles." Paper presented at the International Conference "Theories and Concepts of Music Criticism," Université libre de Bruxelles (Belgium).

Dutheil-Pessin, Catherine. 2004. *La Chanson réaliste. Sociologie d'un genre*. Paris: L'Harmattan.

Dyer, Richard. 1979. *Stars*. London: British Film Institute.

Elan, Priya. 2016a. "Stylewatch: Absolutely fabulous: The movie." *The Guardian*, February 18. https://www.theguardian.com/fashion/2016/feb/18/stylewatch-absolutely-fabulous-the-movie [accessed 06-17-2022].

Elan, Priya. 2016b. "Viva forever: the return of the deep V." *The Guardian*, February 17. https://www.theguardian.com/fashion/2016/feb/17/viva-forever-the-return-of-the-deep-v [accessed 06-17-2022].

Enoch, Nick. 2018. "He was a great man—I was just pretty." *MailOnline*, April 12. https://www.dailymail.co.uk/news/article-5608345/Serge-Gainsbourg-Jane-Birkin-seen-intimate-photos-Calais-museum-exhibition.html [accessed 06-17-2022].

Erlmann, Veit. 1996. "The Aesthetics of the Global Imagination: Reflections on World Music in the 1990s." *Public Culture* 8: 467–87.

Eudeline, Patrick. 2002. *Gonzo: Ecrits rock 1973–2001*. Paris: Denoël.

Fermaglich, Kirsten. 2018. *A Rosenberg by Any Other Name: A History of Jewish Name Changing in America*. New York: New York University Press.

Fogg, Shannon L. 2017. *Stealing Home: Looting, Restitution, and Reconstructing Jewish Lives in France, 1942–1947*. Oxford: Oxford University Press.

Fontana, Cécile. 2007. *La Chanson française. Histoire, interprètes, auteurs, compositeurs*. Paris: Hachette.

Foster, Alistair, Jennifer Ruby & Emma Powell. 2018. "The fans still love it." *The Evening Standard*, June 8. https://advance.lexis.com/api/document?collection=news&id=urn:contentItem:5SHB-69R1-DY9P-N1JG-00000-00&context=1516831 [accessed 10-12-2022].

Fourquet, Jérôme. 2019. *L'Archipel français: naissance d'une nation multiple et divisée*. Paris: Seuil.

Francfort, Didier. 2007. "La Marseillaise de Serge Gainsbourg." *Vingtième Siècle. Revue d'histoire* 93(1): 27–35.

Frantz, Alexis. 2004. Serge Gainsbourg: L'art du double 'je.'" Master's thesis, Université Paris 1 Panthéon-Sorbonne.

Freeth Becky, Caroline McGuire & Charlie Lankston. 2015. "It's in their jeans!" *Mailonline*, January 16. https://www.dailymail.co.uk/tvshowbiz/article-2912594/Alexa-Chung-looks-leggy-tiny-denim-dress-celebrates-AG-Jeans-launch-support-famous-pals.html [accessed 06-17-2022].

Friderichs, Bibiana de Paula. 2015. "Sexo e desejo: o jogo da leitura em *Je t'aime… moi non plus*." *Significação: Revista De Cultura Audiovisual* 43(45): 274–88.

Frith, Simon. 1998. *Performing Rites: On the Value of Popular Music*. Cambridge, MA: Harvard University Press.

Frühauf, Tina & Lily E. Hirsch. 2014. "Introduction." In Tina Frühauf & Lily E. Hirsch (eds), *Dislocated Memories: Jews, Music, and Postwar German Culture*, pp. 1–8. Oxford: Oxford University Press.

Gainsbourg, Serge. 1959. Liner notes to *Serge Gainsbourg No. 2*. Philips B 76 473 R [33 rpm].

Gainsbourg, Serge. 1961. Liner notes to *L'Etonnant Serge Gainsbourg*. Philips B 76 516 R [33 rpm].

Gainsbourg, Serge. 1981. *Bambou et les poupées*. Paris: Filipacchi.

Gainsbourg, Serge. 1991 [1987]. *Mon Propre Rôle*, vols I & II. Paris: Denoël.

Gainsbourg, Serge. 1998 [1980]. *Evguénie Sokolov*, trans. John & Doreen Weightman. Los Angeles: TamTam Books.

Gainsbourg, Serge. 2001. *Gainsbourg: 5 bis, Rue de Verneuil. Interview par Patrick Chompré et Jean-Luc Leray pour France Culture les 15 et 16 novembre 1989*. Editions PC/France Culture/INA [CD].

Gainsbourg, Serge. 2006. *Serge Gainsbourg. Pensées, provocs et autres volutes*. Paris: Le Cherche midi.

Gasquet, Lisou. 1996. "Etude des textes de Serge Gainsbourg, de l'expression vivante et de son évolution dans les trente années de chansons de l'auteur-compositeur-interprète." Master's thesis, Université Paris-Diderot.

Gasquet, Lisou. 2003. *Gainsbourg en vers et contre tout*. Paris: L'Harmattan.

Gassi, Alexia. 2017. "Lolita, leitmotiv de l'œuvre de Serge Gainsbourg." In Yannicke Chupin, Agnès Edel-Roy, Monica Manolescu & Lara Delage-Toriel (eds), *Vladimir Nabokov et la France*, pp. 201–13. Strasbourg: Presses universitaires de Strasbourg.

Gavoty, Bernard. 1974. *Chopin*. Paris: Grasset.

GDB. 2015. "J'ai contribué à un inédit de Gainsbourg… découvrez-le sur gonzomusic!" *Gonzo Music*, June 19. https://gonzomusic.fr/jai-contribue-a-un-inedit-de-gainsbourg-decouvrez-le-sur-gonzomusic.html [accessed 03-21-2019].

Gee, Catherine & Telegraph Writers. 2014. "The 20 best duets." *telegraph.co.uk*, September 20. https://advance.lexis.com/api/document?collection=news&id=urn:contentItem:5D5Y-3TV1-JCJY-G1VT-00000-00&context=1516831 [accessed 10-12-2022].

Genette, Gérard. 1992 [1979]. *The Architext: An Introduction*, trans. Jane E. Lewin. Berkeley, Los Angeles & Oxford: University of California Press.

Genette, Gérard. 1997a [1982]. *Palimpsests: Literature in the Second Degree*, trans. Channa Newman & Claude Doubinsky. Lincoln & London: University of Nebraska Press.
Genette, Gérard. 1997b [1987]. *Paratexts: Thresholds of Interpretation*, trans. Jane E. Lewin. Cambridge, New York & Melbourne: Cambridge University Press.
Gibbons, Katie. 2018. "Lawyers rule out 'write just like a rock star' website." *thetimes.co.uk*, April 14. https://www.thetimes.co.uk/article/lawyers-rule-out-write-just-like-a-rock-star-website-h95jdxpx2 [accessed 06-17-2022].
Gilroy, Paul. 1993. *The Black Atlantic: Modernity and Double Consciousness*. London: Verso.
Gilroy, Paul. 2004. *After Empire: Multiculture or Postcolonial Melancholia*. London: Routledge.
Gourfinkel, Nina. 1936. "Les thèmes scatologiques en littérature." *Le Courrier d'Epidaure: Revue médico-littéraire* 3(9): 26–37; 3(10): 51–9.
Grenaudier-Klijn, France. 2012. "Gainsbourg et ses Gitanes: portrait de l'artiste en fumeur invétéré." In Barbara Lebrun (ed.), *Chanson et performance: mise en scène du corps dans la chanson française et francophone*, pp. 97–107. Paris: L'Harmattan.
Groskop, Viv. 2018. "Spotlight this week: France Gall." *The New European*, January 24. https://advance.lexis.com/api/document?collection=news&id=urn:contentItem:5R XW-6MN1-DYRW-V3PW-00000-00&context=1516831 [accessed 10-12-2022].
Grosse, Fanny. 2011. "Gainsbourg y la reescritura." *El Coloquio de los Perros. Revista de Literatura* 28. http://www.elcoloquiodelosperros.net/numero28/mu28fa.html [accessed 03-31-2019].
Grumbach, Rémy (dir.). 1989. "September 29." *Et si on se disait tout?* TF1.
Guibert, Gérôme. 2018. "Introduction." In Gérôme Guibert & Catherine Rudent (eds), *Made in France. Studies in Popular Music*, pp. 1–16. London & New York: Routledge.
Guilbault, Jocelyne. 2001. "World Music." In Simon Frith, Will Straw & John Street (eds), *The Cambridge Companion to Pop and Rock*, pp. 175–92. Cambridge, New York & Melbourne: Cambridge University Press.
Guillebaud, Christine, Victor A. Stoichita & Julien Mallet. 2010. "La musique n'a pas d'auteur. Ethnographies du copyright." *Gradhiva* 12: 5–19.
Halimi, André. 1959. *On connaît la chanson*. Paris: La Table ronde.
Hall, James. 2018. "An evening of profound tragedy and gentle grace." *The Daily Telegraph*, December 13. https://advance.lexis.com/api/document?collection=news&id=urn:conte ntItem:5TYC-8721-DYTY-C3WX-00000-00&context=1516831 [accessed 10-12-2022].
Halliman, Diane. 2007. *Opera, Liberalism, and Antisemitism in Nineteenth-Century France: The Politics of Halévy's* La Juive. New York: Cambridge University Press.
Hand, Seán. 2015. "Introduction." In Seán Hand & Steven T. Katz (eds), *Post-Holocaust France and the Jews 1945-1955*, pp. 1–25. New York: New York University Press.
Hann, Michael. 2015. "John Whittingdale should realise that there is more to art than profit." *The Guardian*, October 5. https://www.theguardian.com/politics/2015/oct/05/john-whittingdale-conservative-party-conference-british-culture-art [accessed 06-17-2022].
Hardcastle, Ephraim. 2014. "Arabist Tory MP and TV presenter Rory Stewart celebrates birth of first child." *MailOnline*, November 18. https://www.dailymail.co.uk/debate/article-2838711/EPHRAIM-HARDCASTLE-Arabist-Tory-MP-TV-presenter-Rory-Stewart-celebrates-birth-child.html [accessed 06-23-2022].
Hardy, Françoise. 2008. *Le Désespoir des singes et autres bagatelles*. Paris: Laffont.
Harris, Sarah. 2016. "Schools where staff and pupils wear veil could be downgraded." *Daily Mail*, January 27. https://advance.lexis.com/api/document?collection=news&id =urn:contentItem:5HY8-PF61-DYTG-40TV-00000-00&context=1516831 [accessed 10-12-2022].

Harrison, Kim Tracy. 2005. "The Self-Conscious Chanson: Creative Responses to the Art versus Commerce." PhD thesis, University of Leeds.

Hassell, Katherine, 2017. "BBC Radio 1: The station's milestones recalled on its 50th anniversary." *Express Online*, September 24. https://www.express.co.uk/life-style/life/856867/BBC-Radio-1-50th-anniversary-milestones [accessed 10-22-2022].

Hawkins, Peter. 1993. "How Do You Write about *Chanson*?" *French Cultural Studies* 4(10): 69–79.

Hawkins, Peter. 2000. *Chanson. The French Singer-Songwriter from Aristide Bruant to the Present Day*. Aldershot & Burlington, VT: Ashgate.

Helliker, Adam. 2017a. "Queen tickled by her own series…" *Express Online*, May 21. https://advance.lexis.com/api/document?collection=news&id=urn:contentItem:5NKM-WPB1-F021-64R1-00000-00&context=1516831 [accessed 10-12-2022].

Helliker, Adam. 2017b. "Of all the mementos she has." *Scottish Express*, May 21. https://advance.lexis.com/api/document?collection=news&id=urn:contentItem:5NKM-WWB1-DY9P-N1JJ-00000-00&context=1516831 [accessed 10-12-2022].

Herzfeld, Michael. 1992. "La Pratique des stéréotypes." *L'Homme* 121(32): 67–77.

Heuman, Johannes. 2015. *The Holocaust and French Historical Culture, 1945–65*. New York: Palgrave Macmillan.

Hill, Edwin C. 2003. "Aux Armes et cætera! Recovering nation for cultural critique." *Volume! La revue des musiques populaires* 2(2): 115–27.

Hills, Simon. 2015. "In John Lennon's footsteps." *thetimes.co.uk*, August 29. https://www.thetimes.co.uk/article/in-john-lennons-footsteps-20pwz7d8f8b [accessed 06-17-2022].

Hirschi, Stéphane. 2008. *Chanson. L'art de fixer l'air du temps*. Paris: Les Belles Lettres.

Hodgkinson, Will. 2014a. "Beck: Morning Phase." *thetimes.co.uk*, February 21. https://www.thetimes.co.uk/article/beck-morning-phase-shlrwlcd7kj [accessed 06-17-2022].

Hodgkinson, Will. 2014b. "Molly Smitten-Downes: 'It was clock off at Topshop, represent the country at Eurovision.'" *thetimes.co.uk*, May 9. https://www.thetimes.co.uk/article/molly-smitten-downes-it-was-clock-off-at-topshop-represent-the-country-at-eurovision-5s6bptqmrds [accessed 10-24-2022].

Hodgkinson, Will. 2017. "Pop review: Charlotte Gainsbourg; Serge Gainsbourg and Jean-Claude Vannier." *thetimes.co.uk*, November 10. https://www.thetimes.co.uk/article/pop-review-charlotte-gainsbourg-serge-gainsbourg-and-jean-claude-vannier-00xg2s5cm [accessed 06-17-2022].

Hodgkinson, Will. 2018. "Pop review: Arctic Monkeys: Tranquility Base Hotel & Casino." *thetimes.co.uk*, May 11. https://www.thetimes.co.uk/article/pop-review-arctic-monkeys-tranquility-base-hotel-casino-zw660zwwx [accessed 06-17-2022].

Holledge, Richard. 2018. "Family duels." *The New European*, June 13. https://advance.lexis.com/api/document?collection=news&id=urn:contentItem:5SSR-34T1-DYRW-V48C-00000-00&context=1516831 [accessed 10-12-2022].

Holtz, Gérard. 1979. "La Marseillaise version reggae de Serge Gainsbourg." *Journal de 20 heures*, March 17. Antenne 2.

Holtmon, Johannes. 2021. "Sjangerlek og distinksjon i chanson française: En undersøkelse av Serge Gainsbourgs musikk, estetikk og artistpersona." Master's thesis, Norges teknisk-naturvitenskapelige universitet.

Hoskyns, Barney. 2015. "Jane Birkin: 'No, Serge, I won't lick my lips and pout.'" *The Guardian*, April 7. https://www.theguardian.com/music/2015/apr/01/jane-birkin-no-serge-i-wont-lick-my-lips-and-pout [accessed 06-17-2022].

Hubert-Robier, François (dir.). 1990. *Je suis venu vous dire…* CBTV.

Hugo, Victor. 1856. *Les Contemplations*, vol. 1. Paris: Michel Lévy Frères, J. Hetzel, Pagnerre.
Hutson, Darin. 2015. "Chance for music fans to make French connection." *News Post Leader*, October 27. https://advance.lexis.com/api/document?collection=news&id=urn:contentItem:5H7V-C3H1-JDPF-N0Y9-00000-00&context=1516831 [accessed 10-12-2022].
Hyman, Paula. 1998. *The Jews of Modern France*. Berkeley: University of California Press.
Inandiak, Elisabeth D. 1979. "Allons enfants, etc…" *Libération*, March 9, 12.
Inglis, David. 2001. *A Sociological History of Excretory Experience: Defecatory Manners and Toiletry Technologies*. Lewiston, NY: Edwin Mellen Press.
Isaacson, Robert. 2017. "The James Bond of Cherbourg: Imagining Israel in Pompidou's France." *French Historical Studies* 40(4): 675–99.
Isherwood, Christopher. 2010. *The Sixties. Diaries Volume Two: 1960–1969*. London: Chatto & Windus.
Jaminais, Flora. 2019. "De Lucien Ginsburg à Serge Gainsbourg: une passion pour 'l'Art Majeur.'" Master's thesis, Université de Poitiers.
Jan-Muger, Anne-Charlotte. 2016. "L'influence des musiques anglo-américaines sur les musiques populaires françaises du jazz aux yéyés: l'exemple de Serge Gainsbourg." Master's thesis, Université Paris-Sorbonne.
Jarno, Stéphane. 2008. "Gainsbourg et les arrangeurs: lumière sur son armée de l'ombre." *Télérama*, October 17. https://www.telerama.fr/musique/gainsbourg-et-les-arrangeurs-lumiere-sur-son-armee-de-lombre-6822326.php [accessed 04-23-2022].
Jenkins, Henry. 2006. *Convergence Culture: Where Old and New Media Collide*. New York: New York University Press.
Jensen, Joli. 2005. "Introduction: On fandom, celebrity and mediation: Posthumous possibilities." In Steve Jones & Joli Jensen (eds), *Afterlife as Afterimage: Understanding Posthumous Fame*, pp. xv–xxiii. New York: Peter Lang.
Johnson, Helen. 2015. *Painting Is a Critical Form*. Castlemaine, Victoria: 3-ply.
Johnston, Alice. 2016. "University Challenge contestant delights Twitter with his extreme facial expressions as his team win the final." *MailOnline*, April 19. https://www.dailymail.co.uk/femail/article-3547381/University-Challenge-contestant-delights-Twitter-extreme-facial-expressions-team-win-final.html [accessed 06-17-2022].
Johnston, Robert. 2018. "Borrowed from the boys: Why now is the right time for Isabel Marant's 'inevitable' menswear line." *telegraph.co.uk*, February 22. https://www.telegraph.co.uk/luxury/mens-style/isabel-marant-menswear-spring-summer-2018/ [accessed 06-17-2022].
Jourd'hui, Gérard. 1971. "Serge Gainsbourg. 'Melody Nelson, c'est ma vie: la rencontre d'un type de 40 ans avec une jeune fille.'" *Pop Music Superhebdo*, May 6, 19–23.
Joyeux, Louis (dir.). 1967. "April 1." *Central Variétés*. ORTF.
Julien, Olivier. 2018. "'Lost Song': Serge Gainsbourg and the transformation of French popular music." In Gérôme Guibert & Catherine Rudent (eds), *Made in France. Studies in Popular Music*, pp. 47–56. London & New York: Routledge.
Júlíusson, Trausti. 2010. *Le Détournement dans l'œuvre de Serge Gainsbourg*. Bachelor's thesis, University of Iceland.
Kaiser, Marc. 2014. "Pratiques culturelles et politiques publiques: l'approche par le concept de 'scène.'" *Cahiers de recherche sociologique* 57: 133–57.
Kaiser, Marc. 2018. "The record industry in the 1960–1970s: The forgotten story of French popular music." In Gérôme Guibert & Catherine Rudent (eds), *Made in France. Studies in Popular Music*, pp. 57–70. London & New York: Routledge.

Karlin, Daniel. 2005. *Proust's English*. Oxford: Oxford University Press.
Keightley, Keir, 2001. "Reconsidering rock." In Simon Frith, Will Straw & John Street (eds), *The Cambridge Companion to Pop and Rock*, pp. 109–42. Cambridge, New York & Melbourne: Cambridge University Press.
Kennedy, Maev. 2018a. "France Gall: French singer who inspired My Way dies age 70." *The Guardian*, January 7. https://www.theguardian.com/world/2018/jan/07/french-singer-and-eurovision-winner-france-gall-dies-age-70 [accessed 06-17-2022].
Kennedy, Maev. 2018b. "'He was a great man. I was just pretty': Photos tell story of Jane and Serge." *The Guardian*, April 6. https://www.theguardian.com/culture/2018/apr/06/jane-birkin-serge-gainsbourg-great-man-just-pretty-photos-tell-story-exhibition [accessed 06-17-2022].
Khaleeli, Homa. 2015a. "The surgeon's cut: What do doctors listen to in the operating theatre?" *The Guardian*, August 5. https://www.theguardian.com/music/2015/aug/05/surgeons-cut-what-doctors-listen-to-in-the-operating-theatre [accessed 06-17-2022].
Khaleeli, Homa. 2015b. "Where are the breakout stars of University Challenge now?" *The Guardian*, December 10. https://www.theguardian.com/tv-and-radio/shortcuts/2015/dec/09/where-are-the-breakout-stars-of-university-challenge-now [accessed 06-17-2022].
Kidd, Patrick. 2016. "Sex lies and recording tape." *thetimes.co.uk*, August 17. https://www.thetimes.co.uk/article/sex-lies-and-recording-tape-5tb2m3vbh [accessed 06-17-2022].
Kimpton, Peter. 2015. "Feel the beat: how rhythm shapes the way we use and understand language." *The Guardian*, March 6. https://www.theguardian.com/education/2015/mar/06/feel-the-beat-how-rhythm-shapes-the-way-we-use-and-understand-language [accessed 06-17-2022].
Klarsfeld, Serge. 1978. *Le Mémorial de la déportation des Juifs de France*. Paris: Klarsfeld.
Knuutinen, Janiina. 2016. "Tarina legendasta: Elokuvassa *Gainsbourg (vie héroïque)* käytettyjen Serge Gainsbourgin kappaleiden funktioanalyysi." Master's thesis, University of Helsinki.
Koechlin, Stéphane. 2008. "Artiste total: Rencontre avec Frédéric Sanchez, Commissaire de l'exposition *Gainsbourg 2008* au Musée de la Musique." *Cité Musiques: La revue de la Cité de la Musique* 58, 7–8.
Kristeva, Julia. 1969. *Sèméiôtikè*. Paris: Seuil.
Kroubo Dagnigni, Jérémie. 2010. "The Importance of Reggae Music in the Worldwide Cultural Universe." *Études caribéennes* 16. https://journals.openedition.org/etudescaribeennes.4740 [accessed 03-21-2019].
Kyriazis, Stefan. 2015. "Video: One-Hit Wonder Day—Watch our Top 13 (unlucky for them) chart-topping classics." *Express Online*, September 4. https://advance.lexis.com/api/document?collection=news&id=urn:contentItem:5H0P-5V91-JCJY-G46B-00000-00&context=1516831 [accessed 10-12-2022].
L'Estoile, Benoît de. 2007. *Le Goût des autres. De l'Exposition coloniale aux Arts premiers*. Paris: Flammarion.
Lacasse, Serge. 2000. "Intertextuality and Hypertextuality in Recorded Popular Music." In Michael Talbot (ed.), *The Musical Work: Reality or Invention?*, pp. 35–58. Liverpool: Liverpool University Press.
Lacasse, Serge. 2008. "La musique pop incestueuse: une introduction à la transphonographie." *Circuit: musiques contemporaines* 18(20): 11–26.
Lacasse, Serge. 2010. "Une introduction à la transphonographie." *Volume! La revue des musiques populaires* 5(2): 31–57.

Lacasse, Serge. 2018. "Toward a model of transphonography." In Lori Burns & Serge Lacasse (eds), *The Pop Palimpsest: Intertextuality in Recorded Popular Music*, pp. 9–60. Ann Arbor, MI: University of Michigan Press.

Lambrechts, Mehdi. 2006. "Etude de l'exploitation d'expressions onomatopéiques et de référents culturels dans les 'concepts albums' de Serge Gainsbourg." Bachelor's thesis, Université libre de Bruxelles.

Lavige, Laurent & Carine Bernardi. 2003. *Tendance rasta*. Paris: Gallimard.

Leadbeater, Chris. 2017. "The truth behind French stereotypes, from its surly waiters to its lousy music." *The Telegraph*, 6 June; and *telegraph.co.uk*, August 15. https://www.telegraph.co.uk/travel/destinations/europe/france/articles/the-truth-about-french-cliches/ [accessed 06-17-2022].

Lebrun, Barbara. 2014. "Beyond Brassens: Twenty-First Century *Chanson* and the New Generation of Singer-Songwriters." *Modern & Contemporary France* 22(2): 159–75.

Lederer, Robert E. 2001. "Vers une définition du rejet: l'exemple des 'chansons/poèmes' de Gainsbourg." Bachelor's thesis, Université libre de Bruxelles.

Leff, Lisa Moses. 2015. *The Archive Thief: The Man Who Salvaged French Jewish History in the Wake of the Holocaust*. New York: Oxford University Press.

Legge, Charles. 2017. "Was 'Allo 'Allo a hit abroad?" *Scottish Daily Mail*, February 20. https://advance.lexis.com/api/document?collection=news&id=urn:contentItem:5MXD-PD61-DY9P-N2X8-00000-00&context=1516831 [accessed 10-12-2022].

Leibowitch, Ersin & Dominique Loriou. 2011. *Le Paris de Gainsbourg. Itinéraires d'une vie capitale*. Paris: Jacob-Duvernet.

Leigh, Spencer. 2018. "Master of the French chanson who never forgot his Armenian heritage." *The Independent*, October 3. https://advance.lexis.com/api/document?collection=news&id=urn:contentItem:5TD6-V0G1-JCS0-D20J-00000-00&context=1516831 [accessed 10-12-2022].

Lelièvre, Marie-Dominique. 2008. *Gainsbourg sans filtre. Biographie*. Paris: Flammarion.

Leonardi, Susan J. & Rebecca A. Pope. 1996. *The Diva's Mouth: Body, Voice, Prima Donna Politics*. New Brunswick: Rutgers University Press.

Léridon, Jean-Luc (dir.). 1986. "Apostrophes en chanson." *Apostrophes*. Antenne 2.

Lerouge, Stéphane. 2001. "Entretien Alain Goraguer." Liner notes to *Le Cinéma de Serge Gainsbourg: Musiques de Films 1959–1990*, pp. 4–6. Universal 586 818-2 [3-CD boxed set].

Lesprit, Bruno. 2018. "Gainsbourg, je t'aime… eux aussi." *Le Monde*, April 10, 14.

Levy, Andrew & Chris Brooke. 2015. Chris, "It's Bamber Gasgurn!" *Scottish Daily Mail*, December 9. https://advance.lexis.com/api/document?collection=news&id=urn:contentItem:5HJT-H051-DY9P-N31W-00000-00&context=1516831 [accessed 12-10-2022].

Linderman, Deborah. 1991. "The Mise-en-Abîme in Hitchcock's 'Vertigo.'" *Cinema Journal* 30(4): 51–74.

Loeffler, James. 2010. *The Most Musical Nation, Jews and Culture in the Late Russian Empire*. New Haven: Yale University Press.

Looseley, David L. 2003. *Popular Music in Contemporary France: Authenticity, Politics, Debate*. Oxford: Berg.

Looseley, David L. 2015. *Edith Piaf: A cultural History*. Liverpool: Liverpool University Press.

Low, Shari. 2015. "The latest survey." *Daily Record and Sunday Mail*, July 23. https://advance.lexis.com/api/document?collection=news&id=urn:contentItem:5GH5-D7R1-JBVM-Y4DX-00000-00&context=1516831 [accessed 10-12-2022].

Looseley, David L. 2018. "Coda. Rethinking the Popular? Some Reflections on Popular Music in France and Britain." In Gérôme Guibert & Catherine Rudent (eds), *Made in France. Studies in French Popular Music*, pp. 137–49. London & New York: Routledge.

Lucas, John P. 2015. "The Eurovision Song Contest: 10 of the best." *The Guardian*, May 21. https://www.theguardian.com/music/musicblog/2015/may/20/the-eurovision-song-contest-10-of-the-best-abba-conchita-wurst [accessed 06-17-2022].

Luccioni, Cécile. 2011. *Alignement texte-musique dans les chansons de Serge Gainsbourg*. Master's thesis, Université Paris 8.

Macan, Edward. 1997. *Rockin' the Classics: English Progressive Rock and the Counterculture*. Oxford & New York: Oxford University Press.

McColm, Euan. 2016. "Romance of Remain matches bluster of Brexiteers." *The Scotsman*, April 23. https://advance.lexis.com/api/document?collection=news&id=urn:contentItem:5JM1-09C1-JDPF-N0BV-00000-00&context=1516831 [accessed 10-12-2022].

MacFarlane, Thomas. 2019. *The Music of George Harrison*. Oxford & New York: Routledge.

Macksey, Richard. 1997. "Foreword." In Gérard Genette, *Paratexts: Thresholds of interpretation*, trans. Jane E. Lewin., pp. xi–xxii. Cambridge, New York & Melbourne: Cambridge University Press.

McLean, Craig. 2017. "I don't think of Serge whenever I'm singing, otherwise I would cry." *Belfast Telegraph*, September 23. https://www.belfasttelegraph.co.uk/life/features/i-dont-think-of-serge-whenever-im-singing-otherwise-i-would-cry-36159035.html [accessed 06-17-2022].

McLean, Craig. 2018. "Incest? I knew that would cause a stir…" *The Daily Telegraph*, March 26. https://advance.lexis.com/api/document?collection=news&id=urn:contentItem:5RYG-RNH1-JBVM-Y1PD-00000-00&context=1516831 [accessed 10-12-2022].

McLeod, Kembrew & Peter DiCola with Jenny Toomey & Kristin Thomson. 2011. *Creative License: The Law and Culture of Digital Sampling*. Durham & London: Duke University Press.

McMahon, James. 2018. "Charlotte Gainsbourg: 'Art shouldn't be censored.'" *The Observer*, June 9. https://advance.lexis.com/api/document?collection=news&id=urn:contentItem:5SHY-G371-F021-600T-00000-00&context=1516831 [accessed 10-12-2022].

McMullen, Marion. 2016. "Closet confidential." *Birmingham Evening Mail*, January 29. https://advance.lexis.com/api/document?collection=news&id=urn:contentItem:5HYP-1KB1-DY9P-N0BD-00000-00&context=1516831 [accessed 06-23-2022].

Mallarmé, Stéphane. 1887. *Les Poésies de Stéphane Mallarmé*. Paris: La Revue indépendante.

Mallarmé, Stéphane. 1945. *Œuvres complètes*. Paris: Gallimard.

Male, Andrew. 2018. "What's on TV Today." *The Sunday Times*, February 18. https://advance.lexis.com/api/document?collection=news&id=urn:contentItem:5RNT-S931-F021-63MK-00000-00&context=1516831 [accessed 10-12-2022].

Mandel, Maud. 2003. *In the Aftermath of Genocide: Armenians and Jews in Twentieth-Century France*. Durham: Duke University Press.

Manuel, Peter & Wayne Marshall. 2017. "La méthode du riddim: esthétique, pratique et propriété dans le dancehall jamaïcain." *Volume! La revue des musiques populaires* 13(2): 25–59.

Marc, Isabelle. 2014. "Aznavour ou le drame nostalgique populaire." *Volume! La Revue des musiques populaires* 11(1): 55–67.

Marc, Isabelle. 2017. "Plaisirs et fictions dans la chanson française." *Belphégor. Littératures populaires et culture médiatique* 15(2). https://journals.openedition.org/belphegor/997 [accessed 10-20-2022].

Marc, Isabelle & Stuart Green. 2016. "More Than Words: Theorizing the Singer-Songwriter." In Isabelle Marc & Stuart Green (eds), *The Singer-Songwriter in Europe: Paradigms, Politics and Place*, pp. 1–19. London & New York: Routledge.

Marchand-Kiss, Christophe. 2015. *Gainsbourg: Le génie sinon rien*. Paris: Textuel.

Margulies, Lee. 1982. "A Monkee shines anew." *US Magazine*, May 11, 17.

Marshall, Lee & Isabel Kongsgaard. 2012. "Representing popular music stardom on screen: the popular music biopic." *Celebrity Studies* 3(3): 346–61.

Massey, Howard. 2015. *The Great British Recording Studios*. Milwaukee, WI: Hal Leonard Corporation.

Massin, Jean & Brigitte Massin. 1967. *Ludwig van Beethoven*. Paris: Fayard.

Maubert, Frank. 2005. *Gainsbourg for Ever*. Paris: Scali.

Maunsell, Jerome. 2001. "Homage to a Gallic symbol." *The Observer*, Sunday 20 May. https://www.theguardian.com/books/2001/may/20/biography.music [accessed 05-23-2023].

Merlet, Sébastien (ed.). 2019. *Le Gainsbook: En studio avec Serge Gainsbourg*. Paris: Seghers.

Middleton, Richard. 1983. "'Play It Again Sam': Some notes on the productivity of repetition in popular music." *Popular Music* 3: 235–70.

Midgley, Dominic. 2018. "My Way: Who is the girl who inspired Frank Sinatra's classic song?" *Express Online*, January 9. https://advance.lexis.com/api/document?collection=news&id=urn:contentItem:5RCB-3TG1-F021-609W-00000-00&context=1516831 [accessed 10-12-2022].

Mikaïloff, Pierre. 2016. *Gainsbourg confidentiel*. Paris: Prisma.

Miller, Sue. 2014. *Cuban Flute Style: Interpretation and Improvisation*. Lanham, MD: Scarecrow Press.

Miller, Sue. 2021. *Improvising Sabor: Cuban Dance Music in New York*. Jackson: University Press of Mississippi.

Milton, Jamie. 2016. "Beyoncé's 'Lemonade' and the uneven history of the visual album." *Independent*, April 26. https://www.independent.co.uk/arts-entertainment/music/features/beyonces-lemonade-film-and-the-uneven-history-of-the-visual-album-a7001616.html [accessed 03-31-2019].

Mitchell, Eddy. 1979. *Galas galères: souvenirs*. Paris: Jacques Grancher.

Moine, Raphaëlle. 2014. "The Contemporary French Biopic in National and International Contexts." In Tom Brown & Bélen Vidal (eds), *The Biopic in Contemporary Film Culture*, pp. 52–67. London & New York: Routledge.

Moine, Raphaëlle. 2017. *Vies héroïques. Biopics masculins, biopics féminins*. Paris: Vrin.

Mortaigne, Véronique. 2018. *Double je*. Paris: Equateurs.

Mottram, James. 2010. "Gallic symbol." *The Times*, Sunday July 11. https://www.thetimes.co.uk/article/gallic-symbol-g2k95hzqk6f [accessed 06-17-2022].

Mourgues, Elsa & Chloé Leprince. 2018. *Gainsbourg sioniste? L'histoire d'une chanson aux oubliettes*. https://www.franceculture.fr/histoire/gainsbourg-sioniste-lhistoire-dune-chanson-aux-oubliettes [accessed 04-25-2019].

Mugan, Chris. 2016. "Texas." *The Independent*, January 1. https://advance.lexis.com/api/document?collection=news&id=urn:contentItem:5HRP-9RR1-F072-40HM-00000-00&context=1516831 [accessed 10-12-2022].

Mundy, John. 1999. *Popular Music on Screen: From Hollywood Musical to Music Video*. Manchester: Manchester University Press.

Myers, John Paul. 2015. "Standards and Signification between Jazz and Fusion: Miles Davis and 'I Fall in Love Too Easily,' 1963–1970." *Jazz Perspectives* 9(2): 113–36.

Myskow, Nina. 2017. "Jane Birkin at 70." *thetimes.co.uk*, April 8. https://www.thetimes.co.uk/article/jane-birkin-when-my-daughter-died-i-never-thought-id-feel-anything-again-8b2zmdjtr [accessed 06-17-2022].

Nabokov, Vladimir. 1955. *Lolita*. New York: G. P. Putnam's Sons.

Natta, Marie-Christine. 2022. *Gainsbourg*: Making of *d'un dandy*. Paris: Passés composés.

Neaverson, Bob. 2000. "Tell Me What You See: The Influence and Impact of the Beatles' Movies." In Ian Inglis (ed.), *The Beatles, Popular Music and Society*, pp. 150–62. Houndmills & London: Palgrave Macmillan.

Nettelbeck, Colin. 2003. "Music." In Nicholas Hewitt (ed.), *The Cambridge Companion to Modern French Culture*, pp. 272–89. Cambridge, New York & Melbourne: Cambridge University Press.

Niaah, Sonjah Stanley. 2010. *Dancehall. From Slave Ship to Ghetto*. Ottawa: University of Ottawa Press.

Nováková, Soňa. 2017. "Analyses des textes de chansons de Serge Gainsbourg." Bachelor's thesis, Masaryk University.

O'Connor, Roisin. 2017. "More than words." *The Independent*, December 17. https://advance.lexis.com/api/document?collection=news&id=urn:contentItem:5R6C-FKG1-JCS0-D4RD-00000-00&context=1516831 [accessed 10-12-2022].

O'Connor, Roisin, Chris Harvey & Helen Brown. 2018. "The 40 best albums to listen to before you die." *The Independent*, December 4. https://www.independent.co.uk/arts-entertainment/music/features/famous-albums-record-best-all-time-b2132898.html [accessed 10-12-2022].

Oster, Ernst. 1947. "The Fantaisie-Impromptu: A Tribute to Beethoven." *Musicology* 1(4): 407–29.

Ouzan, François S. 2018. *How Young Holocaust Survivors Rebuilt Their Lives: France, the United States, and Israel*. Bloomington, IN: Indiana University Press.

Ozouf, Mona. 1984. "Le Panthéon." In Pierre Nora (ed.), *Les Lieux de mémoire, I, La République*, pp. 155–78. Paris: Gallimard.

P.V. 1980. "Rien." *Sud* Ouest, May 18, 35.

Palmer, Landon. 2013. "Re-collecting David Bowie: The Next Day and late-career stardom." *Celebrity Studies* 4(3): 384–6.

Panigel, Armand. 1949. *L'Œuvre de Frédéric Chopin: Discographie générale*. Paris: Editions de la Revue Disques.

Papanikolaou, Dimitris. 2007. *Singing Poets. Literature and Popular Music in France and Greece (1945–1975)*. Oxford & New York: Oxford University Press.

Papin, Bernard. 2015. "Les Raisins verts: le 'surréalisme attardé' de Jean-Christophe Averty." *Télévision* 1: 143–56.

Paquotte, Anne-Marie & Claire Diterzi. 2007. "Polnareff, le troubadour de l'ère atomique." Audio blog post. *Le Hall de la chanson. iTunes*, March 1. http://www.lehall.com/audio/podcast/hall.xml [accessed 04-23-2019].

Pascuito, Bernard. 2006. *Gainsbourg. Le Livre du souvenir*. Paris: Sand.

Paxton, Robert O. 1973. *La France de Vichy: 1940–1944*. Paris: Editions du Seuil.

Pearson, Allison. 2016. "The idea that Britain's membership of the EU has led to our brilliance in the arts is beyond absurd." *The Daily Telegraph*, May 21. https://advance.lexis.com/api/document?collection=news&id=urn:contentItem:5JTS-GHV1-JBVM-Y4G3-00000-00&context=1516831 [accessed 10-12-2022].

Perrin, Jean-Eric. 1994. Liner notes to *Les Classiques de Gainsbourg*. Decca 448 556–2 [CD].

Perrin, Ludovic. 2013. "Jane Birkin: 'Serge Gainsbourg était un provocateur avec une âme follement romantique.'" *Le Monde* [Online]. https://www.lemonde.fr/culture/article/2013/08/26/jane-birkin-serge-gainsbourg-etait-un-provocateur-avec-une-ame-follement-romantique_3465660_3246.html [accessed 03-21-2019].

Perrone, Pierre. 2015a. "An engaging evening with Spiteri." *The Independent*, April 28. https://advance.lexis.com/api/document?collection=news&id=urn:contentItem:5FVT-CV51-F072-44M3-00000-00&context=1516831 [accessed 10-12-2022].

Perrone, Pierre. 2015b. "Life In Brief; Guy Béart Chansonnier." *i-Independent*, September 23. https://advance.lexis.com/api/document?collection=news&id=urn:contentItem:5H0C-54B1-F072-42D1-00000-00&context=1516831 [accessed 10-12-2022].

Persels, Jeff &Russell Ganim. 2004. "Scatology: The Last Taboo." In Jeff Persels & Russell Ganim (ed.), *Fecal Matters in Early Modern Literature and Art: Studies in Scatology*, pp. xiii–xxi. Aldershot & Burlington, VT: Ashgate.

Petridis, Alexis. 2018. "Arctic Monkeys: Tranquility Base Hotel & Casino review—funny, fresh and a little smug." *The Guardian*, May 10. https://www.theguardian.com/music/2018/may/10/arctic-monkeys-tranquility-hotel-base-casino-review [accessed 06-17-2022].

Picaud, Loïc. 2019. *Gainsbourg, L'Intégrale. L'histoire de tous ses disques*. Vanves: EPA.

Picaud, Loïc & Gilles Verlant. 2011. *L'Intégrale Gainsbourg*. Paris: Fetjaine.

Pigoullié, Jean-François. 2011. "Panthéon spectacle. Le cinéma français et la vogue des films biographiques." *Esprit* 6: 36–43.

Plasketes, George (ed.). 2010. *Play It Again: Cover Songs in Poppular Music*. Farnham & Burlington, VT: Ashgate.

Poe, Edgar A. 1845. *The Raven and Other Poems*. New York: Wiley and Putnam.

Pollard, Alexandra. 2018. "Chris and Tell." *The Independent*, November 17. https://advance.lexis.com/api/document?collection=news&id=urn:contentItem:5TRT-NRR1-JCS0-D1BC-00000-00&context=1516831 [accessed 10-12-2022].

Potton, Ed. 2015. "I never had a chance to give him anything—except being born." *The Times*, March 11. https://www.thetimes.co.uk/article/lulu-gainsbourg-my-dad-serge-wouldnt-have-worn-a-je-suis-charlie-t-shirt-xmkt9cgrz2b [accessed 06-17-2022].

Praz, Mario. 1933. *The Romantic Agony*, trans. Angus Davidson. London: Humphrey Milford.

Prévost-Thomas, Cécile. 2001. "La chanson: une œuvre culturelle au cœur de la dynamique artistique contemporaine. L'exemple de l'œuvre protéiforme et interactive de CharlElie Couture." In Stéphane Hirschi (ed.), *Les Frontières improbables de la chanson*, pp. 351–67. Valenciennes: Presses universitaires de Valenciennes.

Proto, Laura. 2015. "University Challenge contestant delights viewers with amazing array of facial expressions." *standard.co.uk*, December 8. https://www.standard.co.uk/news/uk/university-challenge-contestant-delights-viewers-with-amazing-array-of-facial-expressions-a3132551.html [accessed 06-17-2022].

Pulkrabová, Anna. 2022. *Lolita v životě a díle Serge Gainsbourga*. Bachelor's thesis, Charles University in Prague.

Queneau, Raymond. 1947. *Exercices de style*. Paris: Gallimard.

Queneau, Raymond. 1959. *Zazie dans le métro*. Paris: Gallimard.

Raykoff, Ivan. 2021. *Another Song for Europe: Music, Taste, and Values in the Eurovision Song Contest*. London & New York: Routledge.

Raynaud, Ernest. 1920. *La Mêlée symboliste: portraits et souvenirs. I. 1870–1890*. Paris: La Renaissance du livre.

Rayner, Jay. 2014. "Restaurants: French lessons." *The Observer*, April 20. https://advance.lexis.com/api/document?collection=news&id=urn:contentItem:5C17-RVH1-JCDH-006C-00000-00&context=1516831 [accessed 10-12-2022].

Rees, Caroline. 2017. "Texas singer Sharleen Spiteri: My six best albums." *Express Online*, May 5. https://advance.lexis.com/api/document?collection=news&id=urn:contentItem:5NG6-1HR1-F021-62B1-00000-00&context=1516831 [accessed 10-12-2022].

Reynolds, Simon. 2011. *Retromania. Pop Culture's Addiction to Its Own Past*. London: Faber and Faber.

Ribowski, Nicolas (dir.). 1980. "August 15." *Ah! Vous écrivez?* Antenne 2.

Rice, Carole Ann. 2017. "Jane Birkin opens her heart to me; Happy Mondays." *The Express*, October 2. https://advance.lexis.com/api/document?collection=news&id=urn:contentItem:5PM6-5NT1-DY9P-N31F-00000-00&context=1516831 [accessed 10-14-2022].

Rimbaud, Arthur. 1891. *Reliquaire. Poésies*. Paris: L. Genonceaux.

Rioux, Lucien. 1966. *Vingt ans de chanson en France*. Paris: Arthaud.

Rioux, Lucien. 1969. *Serge Gainsbourg*. Paris: Seghers.

Rioux, Lucien. 1994. *50 ans de chanson française*. Paris: L'Archipel.

Rockwell, John. 1992 [1976]. "The emergence of Art Rock." In Anthony DeCurtis, Holly George-Warren & Jim Miller (eds), *The Rolling Stone Illustrated History of Rock & Roll*, 3rd edn, pp. 492–9. New York: Random House.

Rodger, James. 2016. "The Mustard and Blood Band given licence to thrill Coventry with Belgrade Theatre shows." *Coventry Telegraph*, May 25. https://advance.lexis.com/api/document?collection=news&id=urn:contentItem:5JVM-JT31-F021-603S-00000-00&context=1516831 [accessed 10-14-2022].

Rodman, Ronald. 1997. "And Now an Ideology from Our Sponsor: Musical Style and Semiosis in American Television Commercials." *College Music Symposium* 37: 21–48.

Rogers, Holly, Carol Vernallis & Lisa Perrott. 2016. "Beyoncé's 'Lemonade': She Dreams in Both Worlds." *Film International*, June 2. http://filmint.nu/beyonces-lemonade-lisa-perrott-holly-rogers-carol-vernallis/ [accessed 03-31-19].

Roland, Lise. 2001. "Le personnage lolitesque chez Serge Gainsbourg et Vladimir Nabokov." Bachelor's thesis, Université libre de Bruxelles.

Ross, Alex. 1996. "Vertigo." *New York Times*, October 6. https://www.therestisnoise.com/2006/07/vertigo.html [accessed 03-31-2019].

Rossi, Jérôme & Florian Guilloux (eds). 2021. *Serge Gainsbourg et le cinéma: images, textes et musiques. Revue de l'OICRM* 8(2).

Rudent, Catherine. 2010. "L'Analyse musicale des chansons populaires phonographiques." Mémoire de synthèse pour l'obtention de l'Habilitation à Diriger des Recherches, Paris-Sorbonne University.

Rudent, Catherine. 2011. *L'Album de chansons. Entre processus social et œuvre musicale*. Paris: Honoré Champion.

Rudent, Catherine. 2012. "Ironie corporelle et ambivalences physiques: 'Louxor j'adore' de Katerine, dans la lignée d'une certaine chanson française." In Barbara Lebrun (ed.), *Chanson et performance. Mise en scène du corps dans la chanson française et francophone*, pp. 109–19. Paris: L'Harmattan.

Rudent, Catherine. 2018. "Chanson française: A genre without musical identity." In Gérôme Guibert & Catherine Rudent (eds), *Made in France. Studies in Popular Music*, pp. 137–49. London & New York: Routledge.

s.n. 1970. "Hot 100." *Billboard: The International Music-Record-Tape Weekly*, March 14, 62.

s.n. 2014a. "Pop, rock and jazz." *The Sunday Times*, March 9. https://www.thetimes.co.uk/article/pop-rock-and-jazz-march-9-5lggbnhg2l3 [accessed 06-17-2022].

s.n. 2014b. "Gabrielle brings vocal talent to the jazz club." *North Devon Journal*, June 12. https://advance.lexis.com/api/document?collection=news&id=urn:contentItem:5CD8-5881-JCG2-C3YC-00000-00&context=1516831 [accessed 10-14-2022].

s.n. 2014c. "CHARLI XCX has hinted her upcoming second album will be very erotic" *Metro*, August 27. https://advance.lexis.com/api/document?collection=news&id=urn:contentItem:5D0T-7YD1-DY9P-N39X-00000-00&context=1516831 [accessed 10-14-2022].

s.n. 2014d. "A begging letter by Brigitte Bardot, a plea to the Pope from Catherine of Aragon and Coco Chanel's postcards: Notes penned by famous women up for auction." *MailOnline*, November 12. https://www.dailymail.co.uk/femail/article-2831239/A-begging-letter-Brigitte-Bardot-plea-Pope-Catherine-Aragon-Coco-Chanel-s-postcards-Notes-penned-famous-women-auction.html [accessed 06-17-2022].

s.n. 2014e. "My album of the year." *i-Independent*, December 20. https://advance.lexis.com/api/document?collection=news&id=urn:contentItem:5DW9-CR21-JCS0-D543-00000-00&context=1516831 [accessed 10-14-2022].

s.n. 2015a. "The Disco Smack Festival playlist." *The Sunday Times*, June 28. https://advance.lexis.com/api/document?collection=news&id=urn:contentItem:5G9V-06K1-DY9P-N12Y-00000-00&context=1516831 [accessed 10-14-2022].

s.n. 2015b. "Jane Birkin tells Hermès to change the name of its iconic Birkin bag." *Daily Mail*, July 29. https://www.dailymail.co.uk/femail/article-3177942/Jane-Birkin-tells-Herm-s-change-iconic-Birkin-bag-learning-cruelty-endured-crocodiles-used-make-namesake-accessory.html [accessed 06-17-2022].

s.n. 2015c. "The food of love? I already ate thanks." *Scottish Daily Mail*, July 21. https://www.pressreader.com/uk/scottish-daily-mail/20150721/281844347324946 [accessed 06-23-2022].

s.n. 2016a. "Pocket diva leaves us with no regrets (except failing French)." *The Times*, January 29. https://advance.lexis.com/api/document?collection=news&id=urn:contentItem:5HYN-VWM1-DY9P-N4GP-00000-00&context=1516831 [accessed 10-14-2022].

s.n. 2016b. "Things to do where you live this week." *Surrey Mirror*, July 8. https://advance.lexis.com/api/document?collection=news&id=urn:contentItem:5K5M-P6Y1-JCG2-C477-00000-00&context=1516831 [accessed 10-14-2022].

s.n. 2016c. "What's on TV and radio this weekend." *thetimes.co.uk*, July 9. https://advance.lexis.com/api/document?collection=news&id=urn:contentItem:5K67-2GB1-F021-63BM-00000-00&context=1516831 [accessed 10-14-2022].

s.n. 2016d. "Jane Birkin is interviewed." *The Express*, August 18. https://advance.lexis.com/api/document?collection=news&id=urn:contentItem:5KGS-5F51-JBVM-Y0HK-00000-00&context=1516831 [accessed 10-14-2022].

s.n. 2016e. "British actress and singer Jane Birkin." *The Express*, August 31. https://advance.lexis.com/api/document?collection=news&id=urn:contentItem:5KKH-SG71-JBVM-Y4MX-00000-00&context=1516831 [accessed 10-14-2022].

s.n. 2016f. "Kula Shaker's Crispian Mills Talks 60s Style Closet confidential." *Gloucestershire Echo*, December 10. https://advance.lexis.com/api/document?collection=news&id=urn:contentItem:5MC3-1BC1-DY9P-N2GR-00000-00&context=1516831 [accessed 10-14-2022].

s.n. 2017a. "Festival will have plenty to offer for free." *Western Gazette*, March 9. https://advance.lexis.com/api/document?collection=news&id=urn:contentItem:5N1T-39T1-DYY4-33BW-00000-00&context=1516831 [accessed 10-14-2022].

s.n. 2017b. "Whatever happened to the spirit of '68'?" *The New European*, March 30. https://advance.lexis.com/api/document?collection=news&id=urn:contentItem:5NBK-FG01-JC8V-44CD-00000-00&context=1516831 [accessed 10-14-2022].

s.n. 2017c. "Radio choice." *Scottish Daily Mail*, April 4. https://advance.lexis.com/api/document?collection=news&id=urn:contentItem:5N7K-8XG1-JBVM-Y1WH-00000-00&context=1516831 [accessed 10-14-2022].

s.n. 2017d. "Gunboat navigator defied odds to steer a perilous course." *Nottingham Post*, April 29. https://advance.lexis.com/api/document?collection=news&id=urn:contentItem:5NFC-YFN1-JCG2-C1FN-00000-00&context=1516831 [accessed 10-14-2022].

s.n. 2017e. "7 Worth Staying in for." *The Western Mail*, May 20. https://advance.lexis.com/api/document?collection=news&id=urn:contentItem:5NKC-TKG1-DY9P-N1K1-00000-00&context=1516831 [accessed 10-14-2022].

s.n. 2018a. "France Gall." *The Times*, January 23. https://www.thetimes.co.uk/article/france-gall-obituary-j7dh8nwnt [accessed 06-17-2022].

s.n. 2018b. "Pop." *i-Independent*, February 22. https://advance.lexis.com/api/document?collection=news&id=urn:contentItem:5RPN-JK31-F072-44F6-00000-00&context=1516831 [accessed 10-14-2022].

s.n. 2018c. "Radio Choice" *Scottish Daily Mail*, March 7. https://advance.lexis.com/api/document?collection=news&id=urn:contentItem:5RTF-MH01-DY9P-N0SF-00000-00&context=1516831 [accessed 10-14-2022].

s.n. 2018d. "Jane Birkin remembers larking around in Oxford with Serge Gainsbourg in 1969." *The Daily Telegraph*, April 7. https://www.pressreader.com/uk/the-daily-telegraph-telegraph-magazine/20180407/282372630182917 [accessed 06-23-2022].

s.n. 2018e. "1965. A year in music." *The New European*, May 9. https://advance.lexis.com/api/document?collection=news&id=urn:contentItem:5SHG-2SC1-JC8V-451F-00000-00&context=1516831 [accessed 10-14-2022].

s.n. 2018f. "Radio Choice." *Scottish Daily Mail*, September 13. https://advance.lexis.com/api/document?collection=news&id=urn:contentItem:5T7Y-XK41-DYTY-C0MC-00000-00&context=1516831 [accessed 10-14-2022].

s.n. 2018g. "Charles Aznavour, singer." *Yorkshire Post*, October 2. https://www.yorkshirepost.co.uk/news/charles-aznavour-singer-247519 [accessed 06-17-2022].

s.n. 2018h. "Baxter Dury POP Arts Review." *i-Independent*, November 14. https://advance.lexis.com/api/document?collection=news&id=urn:contentItem:5TR5-VB11-JCS0-D00J-00000-00&context=1516831 [accessed 10-14-2022].

s.n. 2018i. "Farewell Dame June… after an Ab Fab 70-year career." *Scottish Mail on Sunday*, December 30. https://advance.lexis.com/api/document?collection=news&id=urn:contentItem:5V31-XNN1-DYTY-C1RP-00000-00&context=1516831 [accessed 10-14-2022].

s.n. 2018j. "Dame June Whitfield: From carry on to absolutely fabulous." *Irish News*, December 29. https://www.irishnews.com/magazine/entertainment/2018/12/29/news/dame-june-whitfield-from-carry-on-to-absolutely-fabulous-1517501/ [accessed 06-17-2022].

s.n. 2018k. "Dame June Whitfield: From carry on to absolutely fabulous." *The Herald*, December 30. https://www.heraldscotland.com/life_style/arts_ents/17326095.dame-june-whitfield-carry-absolutely-fabulous/ [accessed 06-17-2022].

s.n. 2018l. "June Whitfield's most hilarious roles that changed the face of comedy." *The Mirror*, December 30. https://www.mirror.co.uk/3am/celebrity-news/june-whitfields-most-hilarious-roles-13794980 [accessed 06-17-2022].

s.n. 2018m. "Dame June Whitfield obituary." *The Times*, December 31. https://www.thetimes.co.uk/article/dame-june-whitfield-obituary-xzcbw9lqj [accessed 06-17-2022].

s.n. 2018n. "The first lady of laughter's hits." *Daily Mirror*, December 31. https://www.thefreelibrary.com/The+first+lady+of+laughter%27s+hits.-a0567829261 [accessed 06-23-2022].

s.n. 2018o. "Happy New Year!" *MailOnline*, December 31. https://www.dailymail.co.uk/news/article-6543029/Thousands-pack-banks-Thames-nation-prepares-New-Years-Eve-bang.html [accessed 06-17-2022].

s.n. 2018p. "Remembering June Whitfield, 1925–2018." *Daily Record and Sunday Mail*, December 31. https://advance.lexis.com/api/document?collection=news&id=urn:contentItem:5V36-X4S1-DYTY-C4SY-00000-00&context=1516831 [accessed 10-14-2022].

Sablon, Albéric. 2009. "De Lucien Ginsburg à la création de Serge Gainsbourg: portrait d'un artiste qui ne peut pas se voir en peinture." Master's thesis, Université catholique de Louvain.

Salgues, Yves. 1989. *Gainsbourg ou la provocation permanente*. Paris: Jean-Claude Lattès.

Sandbrook, Dominic. 2015. "World beaters. Britain lost an empire, but has gained a global audience for its popular culture. Why, asks Dominic Sandbrook." *The Sunday Times*, September 27. https://www.thetimes.co.uk/article/world-beaters-pzq0n207trt [accessed 06-17-2022].

Sanderson, David. 2016. "Winning Cambridge student raises Sir Roger's eyebrows." *thetimes.co.uk*, April 19. https://www.thetimes.co.uk/article/victorious-cambridge-student-raises-sir-rogers-eyebrows-8b6h38ktz [accessed 06-17-2022].

Santoro, Gene. 2004. *Highway 61 Revisited. The Tangled Roots of American Jazz, Blues, Rock, & Country Music*. Oxford & New York: Oxford University Press.

Schnapper, Dominique. 1983. *Jewish Identities in France: An Analysis of Contemporary French Jewry*, trans. Arthur Goldhammer. Chicago: University of Chicago Press.

Selway, Jennifer. 2017. "The merry and the melancholy widows." *express.co.uk*, September 30. https://advance.lexis.com/api/document?collection=news&id=urn:contentItem:5PKS-7X81-JBVM-Y4X7-00000-00&context=1516831 [accessed 10-14-2022].

Shepherd, Jack & Matilda Battersby. 2017. "From ABBA to Bucks Fizz: The Eurovision winners that actually became big hits." *The Independent*, May 12. https://www.independent.co.uk/arts-entertainment/music/news/abba-reunite-new-music-eurovision-waterloo-bucks-fizz-sandie-shaw-10250936.html [accessed 06-17-2022].

Simmons, Sylvie. 2001. *Serge Gainsbourg: A Fistful of Gitanes*. New York: Da Capo Press.

Simmons, Sylvie. 2015. "Serge Gainsbourg: The Reggae Years." *Red Bull Music Academy*, October 26. https://daily.redbullmusicacademy.com/2015/10/serge-gainsbourg-the-reggae-years [accessed 03-21-2019].

Simsolo, Noël. 1982. "Episode 1/4. Serge Gainsbourg: 'J'étais amoureux de Charles Trenet, tout gamin j'avais une fixation sur lui.'" *Une journée avec Serge Gainsbourg*. France Culture, November 3. https://www.radiofrance.fr/franceculture/podcasts/les-nuits-de-france-culture/serge-gainsbourg-j-etais-amoureux-de-charles-trenet-tout-gamin-j-avais-une-fixation-sur-lui-5305550 [accessed 05-04-2023].

Simsolo, Noël. 1984. "Serge Gainsbourg: J'ai pris la relève." *L'Arc* 90: 61–3.

Singer, Maya. 2017. "Charlotte Gainsbourg on the secret French beauty tip every woman should know." *The Sunday Telegraph*, April 15. https://www.telegraph.co.uk/beauty/people/iconic-french-actress-model-charlotte-gainsbourg-shares-beauty/ [accessed 06-17-2022].

Sirinelli, Jean-François. 2012. "'Johnny,' un lieu de mémoire?," *Histoire@Politique. Politique, culture, société* 16. https://histoire-politique.fr/index.php?numero=16&rub=autres-articles&item=63 [accessed 10-19-2022].

Skibicki, Marcin. 2010. "Je ne pensais jamais musique. Je pensais mots. Langage (re)inventé de Serge Gainsbourg." *Synergies* 7 (Pologne): 57–65.

Sotonová, Jana. 2015. *Lolita v životě a díle Serge Gainsbourga*. Bachelor's thesis, Charles University in Prague.

Sotonová, Jana. 2019. *Hledání ideálu ženské krásy v Gainsbourgově a Baudelairově díle*. Master's thesis, Charles University in Prague.

Sowray, Bibby. 2015. "Spend Valentine's Day with Jane Birkin and Serge Gainsbourg." *telegraph.co.uk*, February 11. http://fashion.telegraph.co.uk/news-features/TMG11405525/Spend-Valentines-Day-with-Jane-and-Serge-at-Claudie-Pierlot.html [accessed 06-17-2022].

Stanley, Bob. 2014. "Pop School day 1: 20 best bands." *thetimes.co.uk*, February 14. https://www.thetimes.co.uk/article/pop-school-day-1-20-best-bands-d2x25n2sc7z [accessed 06-17-2022].

Stanley, Tim. 2018. "As with the EU, our relationship with Eurovision has been lost in translation." *The Daily Telegraph*, May 12. https://www.telegraph.co.uk/men/thinking-man/eu-relationship-eurovision-has-lost-translation/ [accessed 06-17-2022].

Stendhal. 1822. *De l'amour*. Paris: P. Mongie.

Stolworthy, Jacob. 2018. "Arctic Monkeys frontman Alex Turner lists the songs that inspired new album Tranquility Base Hotel + Casino." *The Independent*, April 26. https://www.independent.co.uk/arts-entertainment/music/news/arctic-monkeys-alex-turner-new-album-songs-inspiration-tranquility-base-hotel-casino-a8323256.html [accessed 06-17-2022].

Stow, Nicola. 2018. "'A Great Woman.' France Gall dead at 70." *The Sun*, January 8. https://advance.lexis.com/api/document?collection=news&id=urn:contentItem:5RC4-Y701-JCJY-G26C-00000-00&context=1516831 [accessed 10-14-2022].

Stuckert, Heather. 2017. s.t. *Evening Times* (Glasgow), October 11. https://advance.lexis.com/api/document?collection=news&id=urn:contentItem:5PP3-WJP1-JD7N-K19F-00000-00&context=1516831 [accessed 10-14-2022].

Sudres, Daniel-Philippe de. 2008. *La Neuroconnectique: Neuroscience de l'éveil*. Paris: L'Originel.

Sylvestre, Jean-Marc. 2017. "Bruno Bich, l'héritier, tout faire pour protéger l'empire BIC des prédateurs." *Atlantico*, August 10 (updated August 16). https://atlantico.fr/article/decryptage/bruno-bich-l-heritier-tout-faire-pour-proteger-l-empire-bic-des-predateurs-jean-marc-sylvestre [accessed 06.09.2022].

Szpirglas, Jérémie. 2011a. Liner notes to *Histoire de Melody Nelson*, 40th Anniversary Edition. Mercury 277824-2 [CD].

Szpirglas, Jérémie. 2011b. "Liner notes to the 2011 compilation." *Intégrale. Edition du 20e anniversaire*. Mercury/Universal Music France 2755441 [20-CD boxed set].

Tagg, Philip. 1989. "Open Letter: 'Black Music,' 'Afro-American Music' and 'European Music.'" *Popular Music* 8: 285–98.

Tagg, Philip. 2014. *Everyday Tonality II: Towards a Tonal Theory of What Most People Hear*. New York & Huddersfield: The Mass Media Music Scholars' Press.

Temkin, Moshik. 2003. "'Avec un certain malaise': The Paxtonian Trauma in France, 1973–74." *Journal of Contemporary History* 38(2): 291–306.

Tinker, Chris. 2002. "Serge Gainsbourg and le *Défi américain*." *Modern & Contemporary France* 10(2): 187–96.

Townsend, Catherine. 2015. "Fashion runs in the family! Jane Birkin's 12-year-old granddaughter makes her modeling debut in new clothing campaign alongside her mother Charlotte Gainsbourg." *MailOnline*, August 26. https://www.dailymail.co.uk/femail/article-3211989/Fashion-runs-family-Jane-Birkin-s-12-year-old-granddaughter-makes-modeling-debut-new-clothing-campaign-alongside-mother-Charlotte-Gainsbourg.html [accessed 06-17-2022].

Trottier, Danick. 2021. *Le Classique fait pop! Pluralité musicale et décloisonnement des genres*. Montréal: XYZ.

Truman, James. 1986. "No. 69 Avec une Balle." *Spin*, October, 98.

Underwood, Nick. 2017. "The Most Beautiful Children: Communist Contests and Poetry for Jewish Youth in Popular Front Paris." *Jewish Social Studies* 23(1): 64–100.

Vaidhyanathan, Siva. 2001. *Copyrights and Copywrongs: The Rise of Intellectual Property and How It Threatens Creativity*. New York: New York University Press.

Valleteau de Moulliac, Marie. 2010. "Serge Gainsbourg: Mémoire sur son œuvre et l'œuvre cinématographique tirée de sa vie." Master's thesis, Université Panthéon-Assas.

Vannier, Jean-Claude. 2011. *Sacem: Paroles de créateurs*. https://www.youtube.com/watch?v=DtTQOAmWD_M [accessed 03-31-2019].

Vannieuwenhuyze, Tessa. 2023. "L'Homme à la Tête de Télé. Serge Gainsbourg's subversive stylization of a television persona." *Image [&] Narrative* 24(1): 138–62.

Velasco, George A. 2001. *The Breviary of the Decadence: J.-K. Huysmans's* A Rebours *and English Literature*. New York: AMS Press.

Verlaine, Paul. 1866. *Poèmes saturniens*. Paris: Lemerre.

Verlaine, Paul. 1874. *Romances sans paroles. Ariettes oubliées. Paysages belges. Birds in the Night. Aquarelles*. Sens: Maurice L'Hermitte.

Verlaine, Paul. 1884a. *Jadis et naguère*. Paris: Léon Vanier.

Verlaine, Paul. 1884b. *Les Poètes maudits*. Paris: Léon Vanier.

Verlaine, Paul. 1888 [1884]. *Les Poètes maudits*, 2nd edn. Paris: Léon Vanier.

Verlant, Gilles (ed.). 1997. *L'Encyclopédie de la chanson française. Des années 40 à nos jours*. Paris: Hors Collection.

Verlant, Gilles. 2000. *Gainsbourg*. Paris: Albin Michel.

Verlant, Gilles (ed.). 2006a. *L'Odyssée de la chanson française*. Paris: Hors Collection.

Verlant, Gilles. 2006b. *Serge Gainsbourg. Pensées, provocs et autres volutes*. Paris: Le Cherche midi.

Verlant, Gilles & Isabelle Salmon. 1994. *Gainsbourg et cætera*. Paris: Vade Retro.

Vernallis, Carol. 2016. "Beyoncé's 'Lemonade,' Avant-Garde Aesthetics, and Music Video: The Past and the Future Merge to Meet Us Here." *Film Criticism* 40(3). https://doi.org/10.3998/fc.13761232.0040.315 [accessed 03-31-2019].

Vernallis, Carol. 2017. "Beyoncé's Overwhelming Opus; or, the Past and Future of Music Video." *Film Criticism* 41(1). https://doi.org/10.3998/fc.13761232.0041.105 [accessed 03-31-2019].

Verrico, Lisa & Clive Davis. 2016. "On Record: Pop, rock and jazz." *The Sunday Times*, February 28. https://www.thetimes.co.uk/article/on-record-7ftwtfglv [accessed 06-17-2022].

Vian, Boris. 1958. "Du chant à la une: Serge Gainsbourg." *Le Canard enchaîné*, November 12, 6.

Vian, Boris. 1966. *En avant la zizique... et par ici les gros sous*. Paris: La Jeune Parque.

Waksman, Steve. 1999. "Black sound, black body: Jimi Hendrix, the electric guitar, and the meanings of blackness." *Popular Music & Society* 23(1): 75–113.

Warburton, Sophie. 2016. "Notebook; This week's style agenda." *The Daily Telegraph*, March 19. https://advance.lexis.com/api/document?collection=news&id=urn:contentItem:5JBB-D591-DY9P-N2PY-00000-00&context=1516831 [accessed 10-14-2022].

Webb, Sam. 2016. "A final smoke: Iconic French cigarette brands Gitanes and Gauloises could be BANNED." *The Mirror*, July 20. https://www.mirror.co.uk/news/world-news/final-smoke-iconic-french-cigarette-8458832 [accessed 06-17-2022].

Weinberg, David. 2015. *Recovering a Voice: West European Jewish Communities after the Holocaust*. Oxford: The Littman Library of Jewish Civilization.

Weiss, Michaela. 2003. "Gainsbourg assassiné par Gainsbarre. Eine Hommage zum 75. Geburtstag von Serge Gainsbourg." *Bulletin des Archivs für Textmusikforschung* 11: 24–9.

Wéry, Hélène. 2002. "Evguénie Sokolov: analyse stylistique, thématique et intertextuelle du conte parabolique de Serge Gainsbourg." Bachelor's thesis, Université libre de Bruxelles.

West Indian. 2008. "Interview Bruno Blum." *Reggae.fr*, February 29. http://www.reggae.fr/lire-article/2480_Interview-Bruno-Blum.html [accessed 03-21-2019].

Whiteley, Sheila. 2003. *The Space Between the Notes: Rock and the Counter-Culture*. London & New York: Routledge.

Wiegand, Chris. 2013. *French New Wave*. Harpenden: Oldcastle Books.

Wieviorka, Michel & Philippe Bataille. 2007. *The Lure of Anti-Semitism: Hatred of Jews in Present-Day France*. Leiden: Brill.

Willsher, Kim. 2015. "Guy Béart obituary." *The Guardian*, September 18. https://www.theguardian.com/music/2015/sep/17/guy-beart [accessed 06-17-2022].

Wolf, Joan B. 2004. *Harnessing the Holocaust: The Politics of Memory in France*. Stanford: Stanford University Press.

Wonfor, Sam. 2015. "It was a big part of my life growing up and studying here." *Evening Chronicle*, May 15. https://advance.lexis.com/api/document?collection=news&id=urn:contentItem:5G0F-FKN1-JBVM-Y3DP-00000-00&context=1516831 [accessed 10-14-2022].

Woodbury, Jason P. 2016. "En Conversation: Mick Harvey of The Bad Seeds Talks Serge Gainsbourg." *Flood Magazine*, July 14. https://floodmagazine.com/38005/en-conversation-mick-harvey-of-the-bad-seeds-talks-serge-gainsbourg/ [accessed 12-06-2022].

Zorn, John. 1997. Liner notes to *Great Jewish Music: Serge Gainsbourg*. Tzadik 7116 [CD].

Index

Adjani, Isabelle 11, 13, 158
   Pull marine 11
      "Beau oui comme Bowie" 11
Air 144
Albinoni, Tomaso 142
   Adagio in G minor 142
Alighieri, Dante 212
Allais, Alphonse 151
Allen, Jeremy 2, 46
Altman, Rick 205
Amalric, Matthieu 17
   Barbara 17
Anderson, Darran 5, 211
Anderson, Kirk 4
Anthony, Richard 130 n.1
Antoine 125, 130
Antwoord, Die 5
Apfelbaum, Grigori Ievseîetch *see* Zinoviev, Grigory
Aphrodite's Child 216
   "Rain and Tears" 216
Apollinaire, Guillaume 18, 44, 114, 129, 173
Archies, The 57
   "Sugar Sugar" 57, 58
Arctic Monkeys, The 45
Arnaud, Michèle 13, 66, 117
   "Recette de l'amour fou, La" 117
   "Ronsard 58" 117, 152
Arpino, André 83, 88, 102
Arvers, Félix 113, 151
Asso, Raymond 22
"At the Gate, the Gate" 141
Aubret, Isabelle 117, 121
   "Arc-en-ciel" 121
   "Chanson de Prévert, La" 117
   "Il n'y a plus d'abonné au numéro que vous avez demandé" 121
   "Pour aimer il faut être trois" 121, 153
Aufray, Hugues 128
   Aufray chante Dylan 128

Averty, Jean-Christophe 6, 207–10, 212, 213 n.6
   Melody 207–12
Aymé, Marcel 70 n.1, 147–8, 185
Azikmen 100
Aznavour, Charles 23, 45, 118
Azuelo, Lisa 17
   Dalida 17
Azzam, Bob 82

Bach, Johann Sebastian 82, 158, 205
   Herz und Mund und Tat und Leben, BWV 147, 205
   Jesus bleibet meine Freude 201, 205
Bacon, Francis 134
Bacsik, Elek 72, 77 n.5
Bad Seeds, The 55
Baker, Josephine 104
Bakhtin, Mikhail 188 n.3
Balavoine, Daniel 98
Balzac, Honoré de 192
Bambou 38
Barbara 12, 13, 17, 18, 34 n.1
   Barbara chante Barbara 77 n.5
Barbey d'Aurevilly, Jules 192, 194
Bardot, Brigitte 1, 4, 11, 13, 14, 23, 24, 46, 117, 118, 119–20, 122, 126, 131, 172, 174 n.9, 176, 210
   "Appareil à sous, L'" 118, 119–20
   "Bonnie and Clyde" 15, 35, 142
   "Bubble gum" 118, 120
   "Contact" 35
   "Harley Davidson" 35, 142, 222
   "Je t'aime … moi non plus" 23, 35, 46, 176
   "Omnibus, Les" 119
Barelli, Minouche 35
   "Boum badaboum" 192
Barray, Gérard 199
Barreto, Don Emilio 81–2, 85
Barretto y su Cuban Boys, Don 82

Barrow, Clyde 142
Barry, John 131
Baudelaire, Charles 18, 24, 44, 113, 114, 151, 152, 154, 157, 192, 193, 194
Baudrillard, Jean 186
Bayley, Stephen 51 n.1
Bayon 195
Béart, Guy 16
Beatles, The 121, 126, 129, 142, 208, 210, 219
   Beatles, The ("White Album") 142
      "Revolution 9" 142
   Help! [film] 210
   Rubber Soul 129
      "Word, The" 129
   Yellow Submarine [film] 210–11
Bécaud, Gilbert 208
   "Nathalie" 213 n.6
   "Orange, L'" 209
Beck 5, 45, 106
Beethoven, Ludwig van 5, 142, 143, 153, 160–1, 188
   Piano Sonata No. 1 in F minor, Op. 2 No. 1 142, 153, 160
   Piano Sonata No. 8 in C minor, Op. 13 ("Pathétique") 153, 161
   Piano Sonata No. 14 in C♯ minor, Op. 27, No. 2 ("Moonlight Sonata") 143
   Piano Sonata No. 23 in F minor, Op. 57 ("Appassionata") 142, 153, 161, 188
Berger, Michel 98, 191, 218
Berry, Chuck 135
   "My Ding-a-Ling" 135
Besman, Michel (Moshe) 37
Beyoncé 207
   Beyoncé 207
   Lemonade 207
Bieber, Justin 207
Biga Ranks 100
Bird, Ronnie 130 n.1
Birkin, Andrew 48, 49
Birkin, Anno 49
Birkin, Jane 3, 5, 12, 13, 14, 16, 23, 24, 43, 46, 48–9, 51, 57, 88, 97, 98, 117–18, 131–2, 134, 135–6, 152, 158, 160, 176, 178, 192, 194, 207, 209, 211, 216, 218

Amours des feintes 135
   "32 Fahrenheit" 135
   "Amours des feintes" 135
   "Love Fifteen" 135
Baby Alone in Babylone 135
   "Baby Alone in Babylone" 135, 153, 157
   "Dessous chics, Les" 135
   "En rire de peur d'être obligée d'en pleurer" 135
   "Fuir le bonheur de peur qu'il ne se sauve" 135
   "Overseas Telegram" 135
   "Rupture au miroir" 135
"Bébé gai" 153
"Bébé Song" 192
Birkin/Gainsbourg: Le Symphonique 135
"Décadanse, La" 194, 212 n.4
"Dépressive" 153, 161, 162
"Di Doo Dah" 192
"Exercice en forme de Z" 152
"Jane B." 15, 132, 143, 150, 152, 150, 162, 188
"Je t'aime … moi non plus" 3, 5, 13, 30, 43, 46–7, 48, 53–5, 57–8, 118, 131, 175–8, 180
Lost Song 135
   "Chose entre autres, Une" 135
   "Lost Song" 135, 153
Bishop, Heidi 180 n.1
Bisson, Louis-Auguste 159
Black, Cilla 209
Blackwell, Chris 96
Blanc-Francard, Dominique 114
Blonde Redhead 106
Blondie 207
Bloy, Léon 147
Blue Star Boys, Les 82
Blum, Bruno 96, 97, 99
Bonnermeier, Andreas 4
Bossuet, Jacques-Bénigne 151
Bouchet, Michel 38
Bouchez, Elodie 13
Bouchitey, Patrick 38
Boulanger, Alain 82
Bourderionnet, Olivier 4, 110, 112, 127
Bourdieu, Pierre 145

Bourgeois, Denis 13, 66
Bowie, David 11
Brackett, David 90
Brahms, Johannes 121, 153, 154, 156 n.12, 157, 193
   Hungarian Dance No. 1 in G minor 153
   Hungarian Dance No. 4 in F minor 153
   Symphony No. 3 in F major, Op. 90 153, 157
Brassens, Georges 17, 18, 30, 72, 74, 77 n.2, 77 n.5, 86, 89, 109, 118, 127, 128, 130
   "Pornographe du phonographe, Le" 74
   "Trompettes de la renommée" 74
Bratschi, Georges 129
Brel, Jacques 13, 17, 18, 30, 45, 86, 89, 109, 118, 130
Breton, André 68
Brialy, Jean-Claude 35, 151
   "G.I. Jo" 35
Briggs, Jonathyne 3
Brion, Françoise 199
Bromberger, Hervé 204, 205
   Loups dans la bergerie, Les 204, 205
Bronstein, Lev Davidovitch *see* Trotsky, Leon
Brown, James 143
   "Funky Drummer" 143
Brubeck, Dave 76
Byrnes, David 143
   My Life in the Bush of Ghosts 143
   "Qu'ran" 143

Cabrel, Francis 128
Calet, Henri 185
Calvet, Louis-Jean 118
Canetti, Jacques 13, 66, 77 n.5
Cantaloube-Ferrieu, Lucienne 111, 114
Capone, Al 121
"Carmagnole, La" 99
Carné, Marcel 85
   Portes de la nuit, Les 85
Cash, Dave 34 n.1
Cathé, Philippe 6
Cave, Nick 55
Cayette, André 44
   Chemins de Katmandou, Les 44

Céline, Louis-Ferdinand 185
Cellini, Benvenuto 183
Cerchiari, Luca 85
Cerdan, Marcel 22, 24
Chabrol, Serge 199
   Beau Serge, Le 199
Chagall, Marc 114
Charles et Johnny 76
Chateaubriand, François-René de 195
Chénier, André 1
Chevalier, Gabriel 185
Chevalier, Maurice 13
Chic 143
   "Good Times" 143
Chopin, Frédéric 5, 15, 33, 46, 82, 132, 142–3, 144, 150, 153, 154, 157, 158, 159–60, 162–3, 188, 193
   Etude for Piano No. 3 in E major, Op. 10 ("Tristesse") 33, 143, 153, 162–3
   Etude for Piano No. 9 in F minor, Op. 10 143, 153, 162
   Fantaisie-Impromptu in C♯ minor, Op. 66 143
   Prelude for Piano No. 4 in E minor, Op. 28 143, 153, 162, 188
   Waltz No. 1 in A♭ major, Op. 69 ("Farewell") 158
Chouvel, Jean-Marc 169
Christine and Redcar 47
Christine and the Queens 47
Chung, Alexa 49
Chung, Michael "Mao" 96
Clair, René 114
   Paris qui dort 114
Clark, Petula 4, 14, 117, 118, 121, 125, 126
   "Gadoue, La" 121
   "Incorruptibles, Les" 121
   "Ô ô Sheriff" 121
   "Vilaine Fille, mauvais garçon" 121
Clark, Shirley 77 n.6
Clerc, Julien 136
Cliff, Jimmy 100 n.1
   "You Can Get It If You Really Want" 100 n.1
Coccinelle 82
Cochran, Eddie 126
   "Somethin' Else" 126

Cocker, Jarvis 45
Cocteau, Jean 114
Cole, Nat "King" 73
Coleman, Gregory C. 143
Colin-Simard, Colette 147
Colombier, Michel 15, 102
Coluche 40
Constant, Benjamin 114, 187, 195
Constantin, Jean 82, 187
Cook, William 48
Coombes, Gaz 45
Corbett, Harry H. 44
Corbière, Tristan 25 n.2
Cortot, Alfred 157, 162
Cotillard, Marion 19, 22
Coulam, Roger 178
Courbet, Gustave 97
Cowley, John 81, 86 n.2
Cusson, Cosima 2

Daddy Nuttea 100
Daddy Yod 100
Daft Punk 45
Dahan, Olivier 3, 17, 19, 22, 23
    Môme, La 3, 17–22, 25, 26 n.4
Daho, Etienne 12
Dalí, Gala 15
Dalí, Salvador 15, 121, 157, 178
Dalida 17, 119, 121
    "Je préfère naturellement" 121
    "Leçon de twist, La" 119
Daly, Bryan 178
Danielsen, Anne 178
Damia 18
Daumier, Honoré 194
Davies, Cath 43
Davis, Clive 44, 48, 49
Davis, Miles 71, 76, 97
    Elevator to the Gallows 97
    You're Under Arrest 76
De Gaulle, Charles 22
De La Soul 5, 106, 144
Deep Purple 149
    Concerto for Group and Orchestra 149
Defoe, Daniel 147
Dejacques, Claude 72, 77 n.5, 84, 88, 127, 129
Delacroix, Eugène 1, 97

Delanoë, Pierre 128
Delaporte, Michel 83
Deneuve, Catherine 11, 13, 160, 223 n.6
    "Dépression au-dessus du jardin" 143, 153, 162
    "Dieu fumeur de havanes" 223 n.6
    "What tu dis qu'est-ce que tu say" 192
Depraz, Xavier 67
Desbordes-Valmore, Marceline 25 n.2
Desmond, Paul 76
Desproges, Pierre 39
Devauchelle, Karine 2
Di Benedetto, Marianne 3
Dicale, Bertrand 98
Diderot, Denis 66
Dietrich, Marlene 13, 26 n.4
Dilla, J 144
Dimitri from Paris 106
Disco Smack 45
Djebbari, Aurélien 4
Djebbari, Elina 4
Doillon, Jacques 97
Doniol-Valcroze, Jacques 6, 199–200
    Eau à la bouche, L' 6, 102, 199–200, 202–5, 206 n.1
Doudou 100 n.1
Dre, Dr 144
Dread, Judge 95
    "Je t'aime … moi non plus" 95
Dreyfus, Alfred 32
Droit, Michel 14, 32, 37, 98
Drouet, Jean-Pierre 83
Drumont, Edouard 38
Duchamp, Marcel 186, 187
Ducomble, Gabrielle 45
Duffin, Stephen 40 n.2
Dufour, Valérie 68
Dufresnoy, Jacques *see* Coccinelle
Dunbar, Lowell "Sly" 31, 95, 96
Dury, Baxter 45
Dutronc, Jacques 15, 125, 130, 185
    Guerre et pets 15, 185, 188 n.4
Dvořák, Antonin 142, 153, 157, 173, 188, 193
    Symphony No. 9, Op. 95 ("From the New World") 142, 153, 157, 173, 188
Dylan, Bob 128

ELO 207
Elytis, Odysseas 183
Eno, Brian 143
   My Life in the Bush of Ghosts 143
   "Qu'ran" 143

Falla, Manuel de 82
   Danse du feu, La 82
Ferré, Léo 17, 30, 86, 89, 109
Ferrer, Nino 130
Fifth Dimension
   "Aquarius"/"Let the Sun Shine In (The Flesh Failures)" 57
Fiske, John 220
Fitzgerald, F. Scott 222
Flick, Vic 178
Foot, Alistair 44
Fossey, Brigitte 218
François, Claude 17, 35, 118, 130 n.1
   "Hip Hip Hip Hurrah" 192
Frank, Tony 38, 49
Fraysse, Claire 4
Fréhel 18, 74, 122
Frères Castellanos, Les 85
Frères Jacques, Les 36
Fry, Tristan 178

Gabriel, Peter 106 n.1, 136
Gainsborough, Thomas 175
Gainsbourg, Charlotte 3, 12, 13, 14, 33, 37, 40 n.5, 48, 49–50, 51, 134, 158, 160, 163
   "Charlotte Forever" 153
   "Lemon Incest" 15, 33, 50, 51, 57, 134, 143, 153, 162–3
Gainsbourg, Lucien ("Lulu") 48, 49–50, 51
Gainsbourg, Serge 1–6, 11–6, 17–25, 29–34, 35–40, 43–51, 53–9, 65–70, 71–6, 81–6, 87–92, 93 n.3, 95–9, 101–6, 109–15, 117–22, 125–30, 131–6, 141–4, 145, 147–55, 157–63, 164 n.1, 164 n.6, 167, 169–73, 174 n.9, 175–6, 178–80, 183, 185, 187–8, 189 n.6, 191–6, 199–200, 202, 204–6, 207–8, 211–2, 215–22
   "69 année érotique" 130, 132
   Anna 35, 151, 174 n.8

"Boomerang" 174 n.8
"C'est la cristallisation comme dit Stendhal" 152
"Poison violent, c'est ça l'amour, Un" 151
Aux Armes et cætera 4, 12, 16, 31–2, 95, 96–100, 185
   "Aux Armes et cætera" 14, 21, 29, 33, 37, 97, 133, 144, 193
   "Des Laids des laids" 14, 16
   "Eau et gaz à tous les étages" 185
   "Nostalgie camarade, La" 38
   "Vieille Canaille" 96
"Bonnie and Clyde" 15, 35, 142
"Cha-cha-cha intellectuel" 82, 86 n.3
"Charlotte Forever" 153
Charlotte for Ever [film] 159
"Chatterton" 132, 151
"Comic Strip" 35, 132
"Comme un boomerang" 172
Couleur Café 45
"Danger" 144
"Décadanse, La" 194
"Dieu fumeur de havanes" 223 n.6
Du Chant à la une! 3, 13, 30, 65, 67, 70 n.1, 71, 76, 112, 199
   "Alcool, L'" 110
   "Charleston des déménageurs de piano" 159
   "Douze Belles dans la peau" 67
   "Femme des uns sous le corps des autres, La" 67, 69, 74, 111, 132
   "Jazz dans le ravin, Du" 74, 76, 110, 112
   "Mortel Ennui, Ce" 110, 112
   "Poinçonneur des Lilas, Le" 13, 30, 36, 44, 67, 69, 75, 110, 112, 119, 129, 199
   "Recette de l'amour fou, La" 68, 160
   "Ronsard 58" 67, 77 n.7
"Eau à la bouche, L'" 81, 84, 199–201, 203, 205
Etonnant Serge Gainsbourg, L' 149
   "Amours perdues, Les" 2, 83
   "Chanson de Maglia" 113, 150
   "Chanson de Prévert, La" 74, 83, 84, 85, 114
   "Rock de Nerval, Le" 113, 132, 133
   "Sonnet d'Arvers, Le" 113, 151

"Evelyne" 144
Gainsbourg Confidentiel 4, 72–6, 77
    n.2, 77 n.5, 101, 127
    "Chez les yé-yé" 73–4, 172
    "Elaeudanla téïtéïa" 111, 171
    "Saison des pluies, La" 72
    "Temps des yoyos, Le" 73–4
Gainsbourg No. 2, Serge 65, 149, 150,
    199
    "Adieu créature" 149
    "Amour à la papa, L'" 149
    "Cha cha cha du loup" 81, 83, 84,
    110, 204
    "Claqueur de doigts, Le" 149
    "Indifférente" 149
    "Mambo miam miam" 81, 83, 110,
    192
    "Nuit d'Octobre, La" 113, 132, 149,
    151
Gainsbourg No. 4, Serge 72
    "Baudelaire" 113, 150
    "Black Trombone" 74
    "Intoxicated Man" 74, 76
Gainsbourg Percussions 4, 71, 72, 75, 77
    n.5, 83, 87–9, 91–2, 101–6, 125,
    127, 133, 143
    "Coco and Co" 75, 76, 77 n.6, 87
    "Couleur café" 81, 83, 88, 91, 92,
    105
    "Joanna" 92, 102, 104
    "Là-bas c'est naturel" 91, 92, 102,
    104
    "Machins choses" 76, 88, 153
    "Marabout" 102, 103, 112
    "New York USA" 87, 88, 92, 102,
    103
    "Pauvre Lola" 102
    "Petits Riens, Ces" 71
    "Quand mon 6.35 me fait les yeux
    doux" 75, 76
    "Sambassadeurs, Les" 92
    "Tatoué Jérémie" 91
"Goering connais pas!" 35
"Herbe tendre, L'" 2
Histoire de Melody Nelson 6, 15, 44, 49,
    53, 89, 130, 132, 152, 158, 188,
    207–8, 212
    "Ballade de Melody Nelson" 211

"Cargo Culte" 152, 209, 210
"En Melody" 211
"Hôtel particulier, L'" 211
"Melody" 210
"Valse de Melody" 211
Homme à tête de chou, L' 15, 89, 133,
    171, 209, 221
    "Chez Max coiffeur pour homme"
    171–2
    "Flash Forward" 221
    "Ma Lou Marilou" 142, 153, 161,
    188
    "Marilou Reggae" 95, 222
    "Meurtre à l'extincteur" 193
"Horse, La" 144
Initials B.B.
    "Black and White" 105
    "Ford Mustang" 142, 169–71, 222
    "Initials B.B." 130, 142, 152, 153,
    157, 172–3, 188, 193, 222
"Je t'aime … moi non plus" 3, 5, 13,
    30, 35, 43, 46–7, 48, 53–5, 57–8,
    89, 96, 118, 130, 131, 134, 136,
    175–8, 180, 193
Je t'aime … moi non plus [film] 176
"Laissez-moi tranquille" 83
Love on the Beat 16, 29, 33, 134, 158
    "I'm the Boy" 196
    "Kiss Me Hardy" 38, 134
    "Lemon Incest" 15, 33, 50, 51, 57,
    89, 134, 143, 153, 162–3
    "Love on the Beat" 47, 134
    "No Comment" 134
    "Sorry Angel" 134, 158
Marilu 127, 129
    "Docteur Jekyll et Monsieur Hyde"
    125, 132, 195
    "Marilu" 128, 130
    "Qui est 'in' qui est 'out'" 125,
    129–30, 132, 142, 192
    "Shu ba du ba loo ba" 128, 129, 192
Mauvaises Nouvelles des étoiles 15, 29,
    32–3, 99, 100 n.3, 134, 185
    "Ecce Homo" 33, 195
    "Evguénie Sokolov" 185
    "Juif et Dieu" 3, 32, 37, 98
Mr Gainsbourg 35
"My Lady Héroïne" 142, 153

"New Delire" 144
"Noyée, La" 152
"Psychasténie" 144
"Requiem pour un con" 144
Rock around the Bunker 3, 31, 38, 39–40, 76, 133
   "J'entends des voix off" 192
   "SS in Uruguay" 31
   "Yellow Star" 31, 39, 133
"Rock de Nerval, Le" 150
Romantique 60 204
"Sable et le soldat, Le" 3, 35, 38, 39–40
"Sois belle et tais toi" 112–13
Sokolov, Evguénie 5, 15, 147, 183, 185–8, 194, 195
"Some Small Chance" 142
Stan the Flasher 13
Vilaine Fille, mauvais garçon
   "Appareil à sous, L'" 126
   "Javanaise, La'" 126, 132
   "Vilaine Fille, mauvais garçon" 126, 127
   "Violon, un jambon, Un" 126
Vu de l'extérieur 15, 133, 173 n.7, 185
   "Je suis venu te dire que je m'en vais" 114, 151
   "Pamela Popo" 173 n.7
   "Panpan cucul" 173 n.7
   "Poupée qui fait, La" 196
   "Sensuelle et sans suite" 15
   "Titicaca" 173 n.7
   "Vents, des pets, des poums, Des" 185
You're Under Arrest 29, 33, 76, 134
   "Aux Enfants de la chance" 16
   "Baille baille Samantha" 134
   "Five Easy Pisseuses" 134
   "Glass Securit" 151
   "Gloomy Sunday" 33, 76
   "Mon Légionnaire" 33, 38
   "Suck Baby Suck" 135
"Zanzibar" 95
Galabru, Michel 200
Gall, France 4, 11, 13, 23, 24, 35, 48, 50, 51, 77 n.3, 117, 118, 120, 121, 122, 125, 126, 127, 133, 134, 160
   "Frankenstein" 193
   "Laisse tomber les filles" 120

   "N'écoute pas les idoles" 120, 126
   "Poupée de cire, poupée de son" 3, 11, 50, 77 n.3, 120, 125, 126, 133, 142, 153, 160, 196
   "Sucettes, Les" 3, 50, 51, 120, 121, 134
Galton, Ray 44
Gamacks, Les 95
Garros, Christian 75, 83, 88, 102
Gasquet, Lisou 2
Gaudry, Michel 72, 88, 102
Gautier, Théophile 192
Gee, Catherine 47
General Murphy 100
Genette, Gérard 5, 145–7, 148–9, 151, 152, 153, 155 n.7
Getz, Stan 105
   Getz-Gilberto 105
   "Desafinado" 75
Gilberto, Astrud 105
   Getz-Gilberto 105
   "Desafinado" 75
Gilberto, João 105
   Getz-Gilberto 105
   "Desafinado" 75
Gilroy, Paul 101
Ginsburg, Joseph 81–2, 83
Giscard-d'Estaing, Valéry 37
Glaser, Denise 75, 88–9, 92, 93 n.2, 103, 129, 157
Godard, Jean-Luc 204
Goldfrapp 106
Goraguer, Alain 66, 67, 71, 72, 75, 76, 83–4, 88, 102, 103, 110, 132, 153, 199–201, 205–6
Gottlieb, Raymond 81–2, 83
Goya, Francisco de 186
Grappelli, Stéphane 73
Gréco, Juliette 13, 77 n.2, 85, 117, 125, 126, 132
   "Accordéon" 117
   "Amour à la papa, L'" 117
   "Amours perdues, Les" 117
   "Javanaise, La" 117, 132
Greenslade, Arthur 127, 130, 131, 177
Grenaudier-Klijn, France 3
Grenu, Georges 102, 201
Grieg, Edvard 153
   Peer Gynt Suite No. 2, Op. 55 153

Grimblat, Pierre 48, 131
    Slogan 48, 131
Gris, Juan 15
Guérin, Roger 201
Guers, Paul 200
Guibert, Yvette 113

Hair 57
Halimi, André 66
Hallyday, Johnny 45, 89, 118, 126, 130 n.1
    "Elle est terrible" 126
Hann, Michael 45
Hanoteau, Guillaume 208
Hardy, Françoise 117, 118, 126, 213 n.6
    "Anamour, L'" 117
    "Comment te dire adieu" 117, 191
    "Petit Cœur, Ce" 213 n.6
Harrison, George 105
Harrison, Kim 56
Harvey, Chris 44
Harvey, Mick 3, 55
Hawkins, Peter 4
Hawkshaw, Alan 15, 133, 135, 136
Hendrix, Jimi 98
Henry, Pierre 216
    Messe pour le temps présent 216
    "Psyché Rock" 216
Heredia, José Maria de 152
Hérold, Nathalie 5
Herrmann, Bernard 212
Hess, Johnny 76
High Fight 100
Hill, Edwin C. 2, 32, 96
Hirschi, Stéphane 68
Hitchcock, Alfred 212
    Vertigo 212
Hitler, Adolf 133
Homer 23
Horizon, L' 35
Horowitz, Vladimir 157
Horse, La 206
Hot Club du Quintette de France, Le 73, 100 n.4
    "Echoes of France" 100 n.4
Houston, Whitney 16
Howerd, Frankie 46
Hubert-Robier, François 1–2
Hugo, Victor 113, 151, 220

HushPuppies 130 n.3
Hutson, Darin 47
Huysmans, Joris-Karl 15, 147, 194, 196 n.3

I Threes, The 96, 169
IAM 106
Inglis, David 185
Ingres, Jean-Auguste-Dominique 186
Isherwood, Christopher 3, 14
Iver, Bon 207

Jacob, Max 114
Jacquinet, Véronique 1
Jade, Claude 179
Jagger, Mick 3, 14
Jah Wisdom 100
Jeffery, Alex 6
Jensen, Joli 43
Jesers 106
    "Javanaise, La" 106
Jimmy Giuffre 3 73
Jobert, Marlène 218, 221
Johnson, Helen 57
Jones, Tom 209
Jourdan, Olivier 130 n.3
Julien, Olivier 5, 39

K2R Riddim 100
Kaiser, Marc 4
Kamenev, Lev 33
Kardashian, Kim 46
Karina, Anna 13, 35
    "G.I. Jo" 35
Katchen, Julius 157
Kaye, Gordon 46
Kennedy, Caroline 3
Kessel, Barney 73
Ketèlbey, Albert W. 142, 153
    In a Persian Market 142
Khachaturian, Aram 142, 153
    Album for Children, Book 1 142, 153
        Andantino ("Ivan Sings") 142, 153
Kidjo, Angélique 106
    "Petits Riens, Ces" 106
Kills, The 106
Klee, Paul 186
Kongsgaard, Isabel 19
Kosma, Joseph 85

"Feuilles mortes, Les" 85
Kristeva, Julia 146
Kroubo Dagnigni, Jérémie 100
Kyriazis, Stefan 47

La Fontaine, Jean de 110
Lacasse, Serge 145
Lafont, Bernadette 200
Laforgue, Jules 194
Laibe, Louis 86
Lalanne, Claude 209
Landru, Henri Désiré 115 n.1
Langolff, Franck 49
Lapointe, Bobby 208
Lautréamont 147, 151
Lavilliers, Bernard 133
Lawless, Jim 178
Leadbeater, Chris 45
Léaud, Jean-Pierre 175
Lebrun, Barbara 56
Led Zeppelin 126
Lee, Bryon 96
Legrand, Michel 45
Lehmann, Beatrix 14
Leibowitch, Ersin 37
Leplée, Louis 22
Lerichomme, Philippe 135
Letissier, Héloïse 47
Levaux, Christophe 5
Levin, Bernard 46
Levitsky, Elisabeth 15, 158
Lichtenberg, Georg Christoph 222
Lichtenstein, Roy 142
Lingendes, Jean de 149
Liszt, Franz 5, 153, 160, 163
    Liebestraum, S. 541 No. 3 153, 163
Lizène, Jacques 187
Loeffler, James 30
Loinod, Florence 202
London, Julie 73
    Her Name Is Julie 73
Looseley, David 25, 26 n.5, 125, 149
Lor, Laura 86 n.3
Lord Kossity 100
Loren, Sophia 82
Loriou, Dominique 37
Lorrain, Jean 194–5, 196
Louiss, Eddy 76, 102

Louki, Pierre 208
Low, Shari 47

McColm, Euan 45
MacFarlane, Thomas 5
McLean, Craig 47
McLean, Jackie 73, 76, 77 n.6
Maillet, Antonine 183
Makeba, Miriam 72, 89–90, 91, 92, 102, 106 n.6
    Many Voices of Miriam Makeba, The 87, 106 n.2
    "Umqokozo" 102
Mallarmé, Stéphane 25 n.2, 151, 194, 195, 196 n.3
Mantegna, Andrea 195
Manzoni, Piero 187
Marc, Isabelle 3
Marini, Marino 82
Markie, Biz 144
Marley, Bob 95, 97, 133
Marriot, Anthony 44
Marshall, Lee 19
Martin, George 142
Massey, Howard 177
Massive Attack 5
Matalon, Eddy 210
MC Solaar 5, 106
Meek, Joe 142
Mehldau, Brad 106
Mercer, Johnny 85
    "Autumn Leaves" 85
Mercier, Michèle 11
    "Fille qui fait tchic ti tchic, La" 192
Michelle, Vicki 46
Michelot, Pierre 88, 102, 201
Milestone 95
Milhaud, Darius 128
Miller, Arthur 14
Miller, Sue 4
Mingus, Charles 76
Minimum Chips 55
Minogue, Kylie 106
Mireille 76
Mitchell, Eddy 89, 126
Mitterrand, François 18, 44
Moine, Raphaëlle 19, 22, 24
Monkees, The 207

Monroe, Marilyn 14
Montand, Yves 23, 67, 85
Moreno, Dario 82
Moustaki, Georges 34 n.1
Musset, Alfred de 113, 114, 132, 149, 151, 157
Mustard and Blood 44, 45

Nabokov, Vladimir 1, 152, 172
Napoleon 141, 144
Nelson, Lord Horatio 134
Nerval, Gérard de 132, 151
Nesmith, Michael 207, 212 n.2, 212 n.3
   Michael Nesmith in Elephant Parts 212 n.2
Niaah, Sonjah Stanley 100
Nicholas, Harold 82
Nicholds, Johnny 44
Nicholson, Jack 134
Nicolas, Pierre 77 n.5

"O Lord, Save Thy People" 141
O'Connor, Roisin 47
O'Sullivan, Gilbert 144
Obélé, Odile 106
   "Javanaise, La" 106
Offenbach, Jacques 142
Olatunji, Babatunde 72, 87, 89–90, 91, 92, 102, 106 n.6, 112, 143
   Drums of Passion 87, 90, 102, 112, 143
   "Akiwowo (Chant to the Trainman)" 87, 102
   "Jin Go Lo Ba" 102
   "Kiyakiya" 102
Olliff, Peter 177, 180 n.3
Ophuls, Marcel 31
   Sorrow and the Pity, The 31
Orbinson, Roy 132
   "Blue Bayou" 136 n.1
Orchestre Typique Castellanos de la Cabane Cubaine 81
Ozouf, Mona 25

Pachelbel, Johann 216
   Canon in D 216
Paget, Jean 40
Paradis, Vanessa 13, 49
   "Vague à lames, La" 49

Parker, Alan 136
Parker, Bonnie 142
Pascuito, Bernard 37
Paxton, Robert 136 n.3
Pearson, Allison 45
Perec, Georges 183
Pereira, Tata 85
Pérez, Michel 73
Pergaud, Louis 185
Perrin, Jean-Eric 148
Petit, Roland 85
   Rendez-vous, Le 85
Piaf, Edith 3, 13, 17–25, 26 n.4, 45, 47, 128
   "Mon Légionnaire" 47
Picasso, Pablo 178
Picaud, Loïc 130
Pierlot, Claudie 49
Pilate, Pontius 195
Pills et Tabet 76
Pivot, Bernard 158
Plante, Jacques 96
Poe, Edgar Allan 68, 114, 152, 173, 193
Poitrenaud, Jacques 205
   Strip-Tease 205
Polnareff, Michel 125, 126, 130
   "Poupée qui fait non, La" 126
Portal, Michel 75, 76, 77 n.5, 88, 102
Porter, Cole 82
Portishead 106
Powell, Oscar 46
Prado, Pérez 83
Praz, Mario 193
Presley, Elvis 208, 210
   "Jailhouse Rock" 210
   "Viva Las Vegas" 210
Prévert, Jacques 85
   "Feuilles mortes, Les" 85
Princess Erika 100
Procol Harum 131
   "Whiter Shade of Pale, A" 131
Proust, Marcel 75
Public Enemy 143
Puente, Tito 83–4

Queneau, Raymond 152, 155 n.5

Rabelais, François 185
Rachmaninoff, Sergeï 157, 158

Rafaelson, Bob 134
   Five Easy Pieces 134
Ragga Dub Band 100
Raggasonic 100
Ras Negus 100
Ravel, Maurice 135, 150
   Pavane pour une infante défunte 135
Raynaud, Ernest 194
Rayner, Jay 45
Reed, Lou 134
   Berlin 134
Régine 35, 117, 118, 122
   "Capone et sa p'tite Philis" 122
   "Il s'appelle reviens" 122
   "Mallo Mallory" 193
   "P'tits Papiers, Les" 118, 122, 167–8, 169
   "Pourquoi un pyjama" 122
   "Si t'attends qu'les diamants t'sautent au cou" 122
Reichenbach, François 210
Reinhardt, Django 73, 100 n.4
"Retour du soldat, Le" 100 n.4
Rhys, Gruff 45
Riberolles, Jacques 200
Richmond, Dave 178
Richter, Anton 157
Rico, Hériberto "Filiberto" 81, 85
Rico's Creole Band 81
Rimbaud, Arthur 1, 25 n.2, 147, 152, 157, 191
Ringer, Catherine 16
Rioux, Lucien 66, 70, 76
Rita Mitsouko 16
Rivet, Sylvie 65
Robinson, Harry 126, 132
Rodman, Ronald 220
Rolling Stones, The 57, 130
   "Honky Tonk Women" 57, 58
   "(I Can't Get No) Satisfaction" 130
Romeo, Max 100 n.1
   "One Step Forward" 100 n.1
Rosenfeld, Lev Borissovitch *see* Kamenev, Lev
Ross, Alex 212
Rossi, Jérôme 5
Rossi, Tino 129, 164 n.5
   "Tristesse" 164 n.5

Rouget de Lisle, Claude Joseph 98, 133, 144
   "Marseillaise, La" 14, 21, 31, 96, 97, 99–100, 100 n.4, 133–4, 141, 144, 169, 193
Rousseau, Jean-Baptiste 188, 196
Rubinstein, Arthur 157
Rudent, Catherine 5, 67
Rush, Billy 99
Ryan, Radcliffe "Dougie" 96

Sabar, Jean-Pierre 102
Sachs, Gunter 46
Sait-on jamais ... 6
Salmon, Kim 3, 54–5, 56, 57, 58
Salvador, Henri 121
Sand, Sidonie 213 n.6
   "Je dors avec l'ordinateur" 213 n.6
Sandbrook, Dominic 45
Sanson, Véronique 18
Sauvage, Catherine 117
   "Goëmons, Les" 117
Savchenko, Mickaël 5
Savile, Jimmy 50
Sawers, Claire 47
Scarlatti, Domenico 82, 157
Schaeffer, Pierre 142
Scherman, Avraham 36, 40
Schumann, Robert 1
Scientists, The 54
   "Swampland" 55
Séguéla, Jacques 217
Selway, Jennifer 49
Seress, Rezső 33
Sex Pistols, The 98, 133
   "God Save the Queen" 133
Seyrig, Delphine 179
Sfar, Johan 3, 17, 23
   Gainsbourg (vie héroïque) 3, 17–25
Shakespeare, Robert "Robbie" 31, 96
Shankar, Ravi 105
Shaw, Bernard 1
Sheila 118
Shepp, Archie 105
Simmons, Sylvie 98
Simone, Nina 46
Simpson, Alan 44
Simsolo, Noël 37, 76

Sinatra, Nancy 213 n.5
Sinclar, Bob 106
Sinsemilia 100
Siri, Florent 17
    Cloclo 17
Sirinelli, Jean François 25
Sitruk, Joseph 37
Sledge, Percy 131
    "When a Man Loves a Woman" 131
"Smoke Gets in Your Eyes" 39, 76
Soft Cell 207, 212 n.3
    Non-Stop Exotic Video Show 212 n.3
Souchon, Alain 109
Spiteri, Sharleen 45
Springsteen, Bruce 134
Stendhal 152
Stereolab 144
Stevenson, Robert Louis 132
Stewart, Alexandra 200
Stone 35
Stravinsky, Igor 150
Stubblefield, Clyde 143
Sudres, Daniel-Philippe de 187
Suede 207
Sugarhill Gang, The 143
    "Rapper's Delight" 143
Surrealists, The 54
    "Anemone" 56
    "Feel" 56
    "I'm Keeping You Alive" 55
Sylvestre, Anne 18
Sylvestre, Jean-Marc 217
Szpirglas, Jérémie 40 n.5

Tatum, Art 73
Tchaikovsky, Pyotr Ilyich 141, 144
    Year 1812, Solemn Overture, The,
        Op. 49 141, 144
Texas 45, 106
Thompson, Uzziah "Sticky" 96
Three Degrees, The 44
    "Dirty Ol' Man" 44
Timbaland 144
Tinker, Chris 2, 3, 53, 56
Tolstoy, Leo 188 n.4
Tonton David 100
Torr, Michèle 120-1, 122
    "C'est dur d'avoir 16 ans" 122 n.1

"Dans tes bras (j'oublie ma peine)" 122 n.1
"Non à tous les garçons" 120
Tortorella's Jazz Band 82
Tosh, Peter 95, 97
Toutes folles de lui 35
Trenet, Charles 4, 13, 17, 45, 73, 76, 109–15
    "Annie, Anna" 111
    "Boum!" 112–13
    "Débit de l'eau, débit de lait" 111
    "Héritage infernal, L'" 111–12
    "Hôtel borgne, L'" 112
    "Il pleut dans ma chambre" 111, 114
    "Je chante" 111
    "Landru" 112, 115 n.1
    "Que reste-t-il de nos amours" 114
    "Soleil et la Lune, Le" 111, 114
    "Verlaine" 113, 114
    "Y'a d'la joie" 110, 114
"Trois Petits Chats" 103, 112
Tropical Islanders, The 95
    "Je t'aime … moi non plus" 95
Trotsky, Leon 33
Trottier, Danick 4
Truffaut, François 175, 176, 179–80, 200
    Jules et Jim 200
    Love on the Run 175
    Stolen Kisses 178
Trump, Donald 46
Tryo 100
Turtles, The 143–4

Underwood, Nick 3
Ursull, Joëlle 106 n.8
    "White and Black Blues" 106 n.8

Valéry, Paul 109
Valvert, Félix 83
Van Gogh, Vincent 1
Vannier, Jean-Claude 15, 44, 102, 211
Vartan, Sylvie 89, 118
"Veillons au salut de l'Empire" 144 n.1
Velvet Underground 134
Verlaine, Paul 25 n.2, 110, 113, 151, 157, 194, 196 n.2
Verlant, Gilles 84, 109, 126, 130, 193
Verrico, Lisa 44

Vian, Boris 3–4, 65–70, 71, 76, 77 n.5, 77 n.7, 109, 110, 111, 127, 147, 191, 199
   "Complainte du progrès ('Les Arts ménagers')" 111
   "J'suis snob" 191
Vidocq 35
Vigny, Alfred de 195
Villiers, Philippe 100 n.1
Villiers de l'Isle-Adam, Auguste de 25 n.2, 194
Vivaldi, Antonio 82
von Paulus, Caroline *see* Bambou
von Paulus, Friedrich 38

Wabotaï, Jean-Paul 106
   AmourS Gainsbourg 106
Wadley, Ian 3, 55
Wailers, The 95
Walter, Dominique 35
Walter, Jimmy 76

Warhol, Andy 142, 186
West, Kanye 46
Whitfield, June 46
Whittingdale, John 45
Wilde, Oscar 1, 11
Winstons, The 143
   "Amen, Brother" 143
Wright, Dougie 177, 180 n.2

XCX, Charli 47

Yardbirds, The 130
   "Heart Full of Soul" 130
"You Rascal You" 96
Youthman Academy 100

Zaoui, David 37
Zinoviev, Grigory 32
Zorn, John 29
Zouk Machine 106 n.8

www.ingramcontent.com/pod-product-compliance
Lightning Source LLC
Chambersburg PA
CBHW050324020526
44117CB00031B/1694